The Complete
ATLAS
of the
WORLD

Written by **Keith Lye**

RSVP
**RAINTREE
STECK-VAUGHN**
P U B L I S H E R S
The Steck-Vaughn Company

Austin, Texas

ABOUT THIS ATLAS

Maps are essential tools for anyone who wants to understand the planet Earth. Their use goes back several thousand years. For example, in ancient Egypt, officials used maps to calculate taxes on property. From the days of the ancient Greeks, maps were a way of summarizing information about the known world.

Topographic and thematic maps
Topographic maps incorporate many features, including the height of the land, political boundaries, and cities and towns. They are a form of abbreviation. One map often contains such a vast amount of information that it would take an entire book to put it in words. Today, maps that portray one particular aspect of the changing world have become increasingly useful aids. These thematic maps help us to compare information about one place with that of another.

Flat maps of a round world
Because most maps depict the earth's curved surface on a flat paper surface, no map can be completely accurate. For this reason cartographers have devised different map projections – mathematical ways of projecting the earth's curvature onto a flat surface. Each projection preserves accurately some of the following features: shape, size, distance, and direction. Only a globe can preserve all of them accurately at the same time. But even the largest globes are far less detailed than most maps – and less convenient to carry about.

World maps
This atlas is a collection of up-to-date thematic maps based on the latest available data. It consists of two main parts: world maps and regional maps. Some world maps present information about the natural world, including physical features, habitats, climate, resources, plants, and soils. Other maps reveal how human activity is increasingly modifying natural environments through the exploitation of the earth's dwindling resources, through farming, the building of cities and roads, and industrialization. The world thematic maps, therefore, give an overview of the extent to which natural and human factors are interrelated around the world. They increase our awareness of the dangers inherent in interfering with nature, pinpointing many dangers that the world faces.

Regional maps
Following the world overview, the atlas then takes an in-depth view of the world, which for this purpose is divided into 23 regions. These regions and the countries included in them are listed below. Each regional section contains topographic and political maps, other thematic maps, and climate data, all of which are interrelated. The maps are supplemented by ready-reference fact panels with data that adds to the information on the maps. Basic data and flags are also provided for every independent country in the world, taking account of the many changes to the world map that have occurred in recent years.

REGIONS OF THE WORLD

Canada and Greenland Canada, Greenland (a province of Denmark)
United States of America United States of America
Mexico, Central America, and the Caribbean Antigua and Barbuda, Bahamas, Barbados, Belize, Costa Rica, Cuba, Dominica, Dominican Republic, El Salvador, Grenada, Guatemala, Haiti, Honduras, Jamaica, Mexico, Nicaragua, Panama, St. Kitts-Nevis, St. Lucia, St. Vincent and the Grenadines, Trinidad and Tobago
South America Argentina, Bolivia, Brazil, Chile, Colombia, Ecuador, Guyana, Paraguay, Peru, Suriname, Uruguay, Venezuela
Nordic Countries Denmark, Finland, Iceland, Norway, Sweden
British Isles Ireland, United Kingdom
France Andorra, France, Monaco
Spain and Portugal Portugal, Spain
Italy and Greece Cyprus, Greece, Italy, Malta, San Marino, Vatican City
Central Europe and the Low Countries Austria, Belgium, Germany, Liechtenstein, Luxembourg, Netherlands, Switzerland
Eastern Europe Albania, Bosnia and Herzegovina, Bulgaria, Croatia, Czech Republic, Hungary, Macedonia, Poland, Romania, Slovakia, Slovenia, Yugoslavia
Russia and Its Neighbors Armenia, Azerbaijan, Belarus, Estonia, Georgia, Kazakhstan, Kyrgyzstan, Latvia, Lithuania, Moldova, Mongolia, Russia, Tajikistan, Turkmenistan, Ukraine, Uzbekistan

Middle East Afghanistan, Bahrain, Iran, Iraq, Israel, Jordan, Kuwait, Lebanon, Oman, Qatar, Saudia Arabia, Syria, Turkey, United Arab Emirates, Yemen
Northern Africa Algeria, Chad, Djibouti, Egypt, Eritrea, Ethiopia, Libya, Mali, Mauritania, Morocco, Niger, Somalia, Sudan, Tunisia
Central Africa Benin, Burkina Faso, Burundi, Cameroon, Cape Verde Islands, Central African Republic, Congo, Equatorial Guinea, Gabon, Gambia, Ghana, Guinea, Guinea-Bissau, Ivory Coast, Kenya, Liberia, Nigeria, Rwanda, São Tomé and Príncipe, Senegal, Seychelles, Sierra Leone, Tanzania, Togo, Uganda, Zaire
Southern Africa Angola, Botswana, Comoros, Lesotho, Madagascar, Malawi, Mauritius, Mozambique, Namibia, South Africa, Swaziland, Zambia, Zimbabwe
Indian Subcontinent Bangladesh, Bhutan, India, Maldives, Nepal, Pakistan, Sri Lanka
China and Taiwan China, Taiwan
Southeast Asia Brunei, Cambodia, Indonesia, Laos, Malaysia, Myanmar, Philippines, Singapore, Thailand, Vietnam
Japan and Korea Japan, North Korea, South Korea
Australia and Its Neighbors Australia, Papua New Guinea
New Zealand and Its Neighbors Fiji, Kiribati, Marshall Islands, Nauru, New Zealand, Solomon Islands, Tonga, Tuvalu, Vanuatu, Western Samoa
Antarctica

AN ANDROMEDA BOOK
Copyright © 1995, text, Steck-Vaughn Company
Copyright ©Andromeda Oxford Limited 1994
Planned and produced by:
Andromeda Oxford Limited

Published in the United States of America by:
Raintree Steck-Vaughn Publishers
8701 North MoPac Expressway, Austin, TX 78755

Flags produced by Lovell Johns, Oxford, U.K. and authenticated by The Flag Research Center, Winchester, Mass.

Library of Congress Cataloging-in-Publication Data

Lye, Keith
        The complete atlas of the world/written by Keith Lye.
                p.   cm.
        Includes index, glossary, and gazetteer.
        ISBN: 0-8114-5804-0
        1. Children's atlases.   [1. Atlases.]   I. Title.   II. Title:
Atlas of the world
G1021.L87   1995   <G&M>
912--dc20   94-19316
                                                                              CIP
                                                                          MAP AC
Printed in the G.C.C.
1 2 3 4 5 6 7 8 9 0 UA 00 99 98 97 96 95 94

CONTENTS

THE WORLD

PHYSICAL

Land covers about 57,259,000 square miles (148,300,000 sq km) of the earth's surface. The land can be divided broadly into physical regions that are distinguished by the topography (surface features) and the climate.

The changing land

Land features such as mountains are constantly changing. While earthquakes and volcanic eruptions cause sudden and catastrophic change, other forces, such as weathering, are slow.

Worn fragments of rock are removed by the forces of erosion. These include running water, particularly in wet regions; glaciers (moving bodies of ice) in cold regions; winds, especially in deserts; and sea waves along coasts. Much of the worn rock is dumped onto sea or lake beds, where it piles up and eventually over many years forms new rock layers. This is part of the rock cycle, which has continued throughout the earth's history.

The changing map

Other forces operate inside the earth. Movements in the partly molten mantle affect parts of the overlying lithosphere, the planet's hard outer shell. As these huge blocks, or tectonic plates, move, they cause volcanic eruptions, earthquakes, and mountain building.

Around 280 million years ago, all the world's land areas were joined together in one supercontinent, which geologists call Pangea. About 200 million years ago, this super-continent started to break up, and the continents we know today gradually drifted to their present positions. These slow but unceasing movements continue today.

Along the ocean ridges on the deep sea floor, plates are moving apart. New rock is formed from molten material from the mantle.

POLITICAL

While natural forces constantly change physical maps, human factors, such as wars, change political maps. For example, the world map in 1946 was substantially different from that of 1939, when World War II began. Another mainly peaceful upheaval occurred in the 1950s and 1960s when many European colonies in Africa and Asia achieved their independence. Many of the independent nations adopted new names for cities and even physical features.

New nations

The latest upheaval occurred in the early 1990s, when the collapse of many communist governments changed the political map of Europe and Asia. For example, when in 1991 the Soviet Union was dissolved, 15 separate nations were born. The former Yugoslavia also has split up into five new nations.

Sovereignty

By 1993 the world contained 188 independent nations. Despite boundary disputes between some neighboring countries, each nation has a defined territory, which is recognized internationally, and a government that is responsible for making and implementing laws. The independent nations are often called sovereign states, because, unlike dependencies or states and provinces within nations, they recognize no authority higher than their own.

Sovereignty has nothing to do with size. The world's five smallest sovereign states have a combined area of about 42 square miles (110 sq km) and a population of about 72,000. Yet they are all sovereign states, unlike Texas, a state within the United States, which covers 267,339 square miles (692,407 sq km) and has 17 million people.

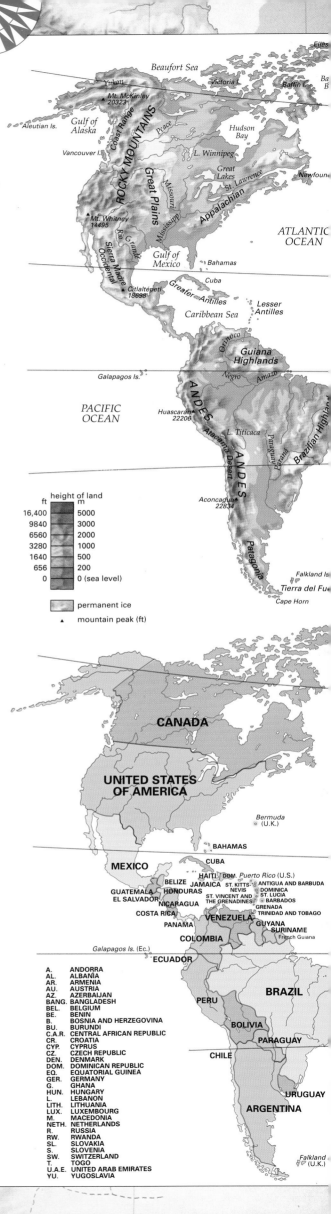

height of land

ft	m
16,400	5000
9840	3000
6560	2000
3280	1000
1640	500
656	200
0	0 (sea level)

permanent ice

▲ mountain peak (ft)

A.	ANDORRA
AL.	ALBANIA
AR.	ARMENIA
AU.	AUSTRIA
AZ.	AZERBAIJAN
BANG.	BANGLADESH
BEL.	BELGIUM
BE.	BENIN
B.	BOSNIA AND HERZEGOVINA
BU.	BURUNDI
C.A.R.	CENTRAL AFRICAN REPUBLIC
CR.	CROATIA
CYP.	CYPRUS
CZ.	CZECH REPUBLIC
DEN.	DENMARK
DOM.	DOMINICAN REPUBLIC
EQ.	EQUATORIAL GUINEA
GER.	GERMANY
G.	GHANA
HUN.	HUNGARY
L.	LEBANON
LITH.	LITHUANIA
LUX.	LUXEMBOURG
M.	MACEDONIA
NETH.	NETHERLANDS
R.	RUSSIA
RW.	RWANDA
SL.	SLOVAKIA
S.	SLOVENIA
SW.	SWITZERLAND
T.	TOGO
U.A.E.	UNITED ARAB EMIRATES
YU.	YUGOSLAVIA

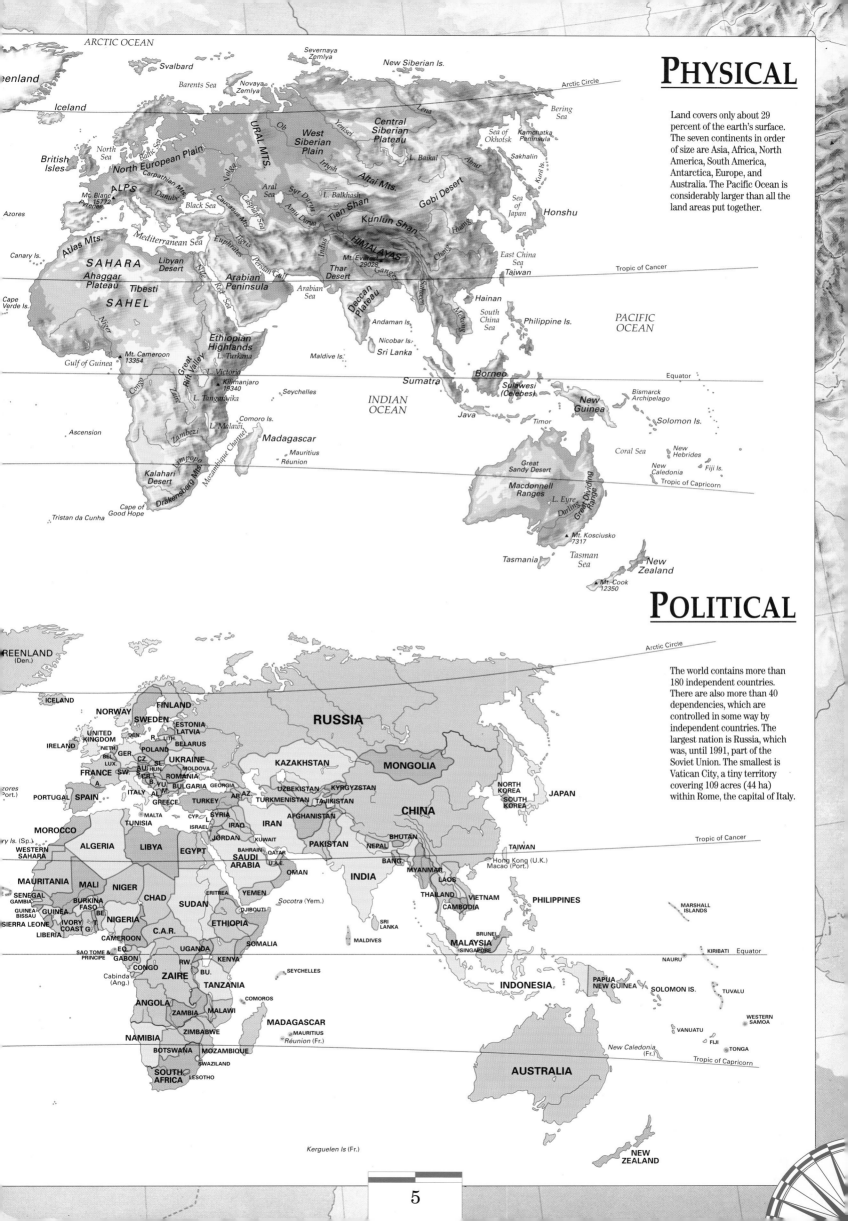

PHYSICAL

Land covers only about 29 percent of the earth's surface. The seven continents in order of size are Asia, Africa, North America, South America, Antarctica, Europe, and Australia. The Pacific Ocean is considerably larger than all the land areas put together.

POLITICAL

The world contains more than 180 independent countries. There are also more than 40 dependencies, which are controlled in some way by independent countries. The largest nation is Russia, which was, until 1991, part of the Soviet Union. The smallest is Vatican City, a tiny territory covering 109 acres (44 ha) within Rome, the capital of Italy.

THE WORLD

CLIMATE

While weather is the day-to-day, or hour-to-hour, condition of the air, climate is the long-term pattern of weather of a place.

Latitude and climate

The earth's atmosphere is always on the move. The reason for the movement of air is the sun, whose rays are most concentrated in tropical zones and least concentrated at the poles. The difference in temperature is mostly responsible for the planetary winds – the trade winds, westerlies, and polar easterlies – which constantly exchange air between hot tropical and cold polar regions.

Terrain and climate

While latitude is a major factor affecting climate, several other factors determine the pattern of world climates. First, winds are affected by the terrain. Warm, moist winds from the ocean pass over a mountain range and are chilled. Because their capacity to retain water vapor is reduced by cooling, the water vapor is turned into tiny droplets, which form rain clouds. It rains on the side of the mountain where the clouds rise. Beyond the mountain peaks, the winds become warmer as they descend, picking up moisture and creating a dry region, called a rain shadow.

The influence of the sea

The sea often has a moderating influence on the climate, and moist winds from the ocean usually bring plenty of rain. These moderating effects are felt less and less the farther one travels inland. Warm ocean currents, such as the Gulf Stream and its extension, the North Atlantic Current, have a warming effect on northwestern Europe. By contrast, eastern Canada in the same latitude is chilled by the cold Labrador Current.

HABITATS

The type of climate a region has determines broadly the kinds of plants and animals that live there. But many factors influence a species' habitat – topographical features, soil, and availability of oxygen, water, and food. A species' total physical, biological, and chemical surroundings make up its habitat. Similar habitats have like temperature and precipitation ranges, and can be classified into zones that follow lines of latitude.

Rain forests and savanna

Tropical rain forests flourish where it is hot and wet all year. They occur around the globe mostly in areas close to the equator. Savannas occur in tropical regions with a dry season.

Arid regions

Deserts are places with an average annual rainfall of less than 10 inches (25 cm). Deserts cover about one-seventh of the earth's land surface and center on a zone between the tropics and middle latitudes.

Forests and grasslands

In the latitudes on either side of the tropics are the temperate zones, or middle latitudes. Deciduous forests of maples, oaks, and beeches give way to grasslands. In North America and Eurasia, coniferous forests grow in the higher latitudes here.

Cold zones

Cold zones include the ice sheets of Antarctica and Greenland and the treeless tundra regions, where plants grow during the short summer.

Mountain habitats

Mountain habitats are determined largely by altitude rather than latitude. The difference in habitats is caused by temperature differences, which decrease by $1°F$ $(0.55°C)$ every 300 feet (100m) in altitude.

CLIMATE

Hot tropical climates are hot and wet all year.	tropical
Tropical monsoon climates have wet and dry seasons.	tropical
Tropical steppe has a short, unreliable rainy season.	tropical
Summers are wet and warm; winters wet and mild.	subtropical
Summers are dry and warm; winters wet and mild.	subtropical
Desert areas have little rain and no cold season.	subtropical
It rains all year with no great temperature variation.	temperate
These climates have warm summers and cold winters.	temperate
It rains all year with no great temperature variation.	temperate
Subarctic winters are very cold; summers are short.	cold
Arctic or ice-cap climates are freezing all year round.	cold

The world's climatic zones are affected by latitude, prevailing winds, terrain (especially high mountain ranges that lie in the path of winds), distance from the sea, and ocean currents.

Surface currents have a marked effect on the climate of coastal regions. Onshore winds passing over cold currents are chilled. Winds passing over warm currents are warmed.

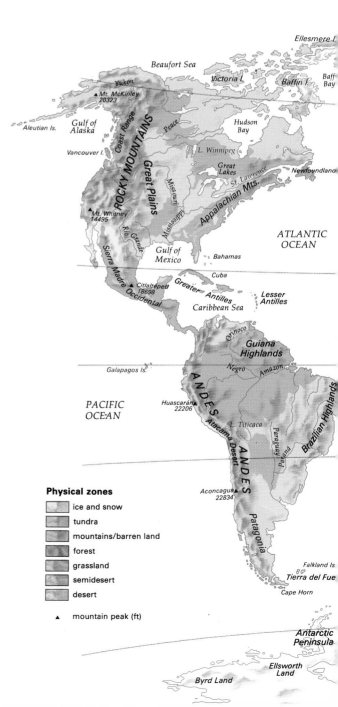

Physical zones

- ice and snow
- tundra
- mountains/barren land
- forest
- grassland
- semidesert
- desert

▲ mountain peak (ft)

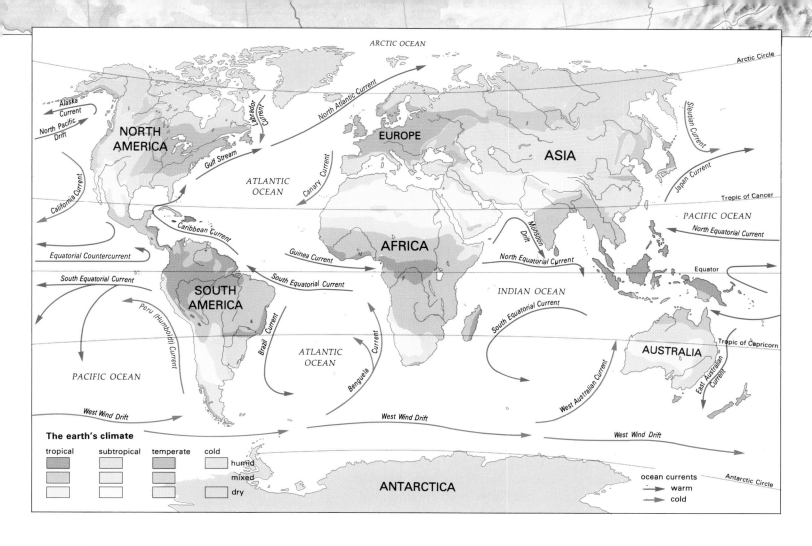

The earth's climate

tropical subtropical temperate cold

humid
mixed
dry

ocean currents
→ warm
→ cold

HABITATS

The different types of habitats
around the world reflect diverse
climates, physical features, rock
types, soils, and plant and
animal life that exist in these
areas. A change in any factor,
such as climate, leads to
changes in the types of living
things that populate an area.

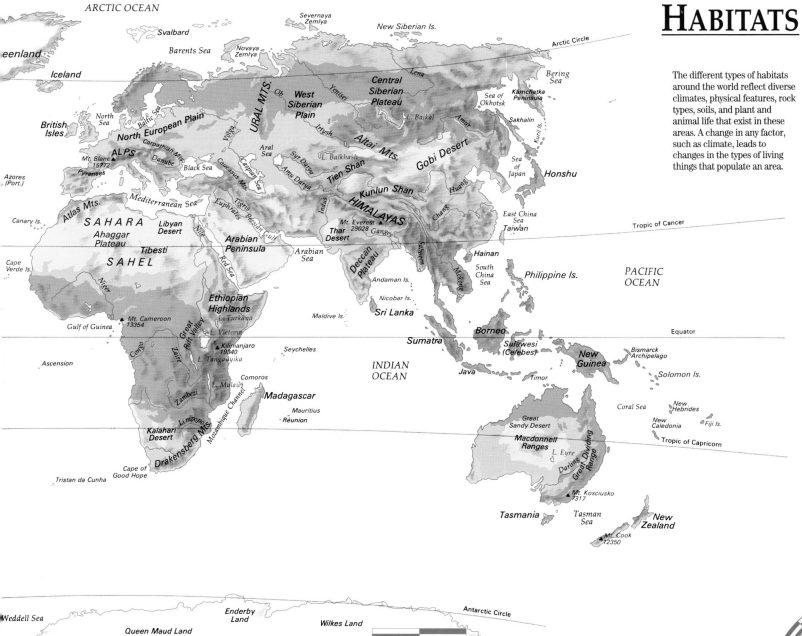

THE WORLD

ENVIRONMENTAL ISSUES

Natural habitats around the world are always undergoing change with variations in climate. These changes occur gradually over hundreds of years. In addition to natural changes, however, many habitats are being greatly modified by increasing human activity.

Deforestation

The temperate middle latitudes were once largely covered by deciduous forests of ash, beech, elm, oak, and maple. However, much of the original deciduous forests have been cut down to provide fuel, timber, and farmland.

Perhaps the most serious environmental issue in the world today is the destruction of the rain forests in South America, Central Africa, and Southeast Asia. These forests contain more than half of the world's species of plants and animals, many of which are rapidly becoming extinct. Rain forest destruction may cause climatic change and contribute to global warming.

Desertification

Soil erosion often occurs when deforestation, overgrazing, and poor farming lays the land bare to wind and rain. In arid regions, soil erosion can turn fertile land into barren desert. The desertification of semiarid grasslands, such as the Sahel region south of the Sahara, is another major environmental issue.

Other problems

In each of the regional sections in this Atlas there is a map showing local environmental problems. Many of them arise from pollution. Major issues include smog, caused by industrial smoke or motor exhaust fumes, acid rain, the pollution of rivers and lakes by industrial wastes or untreated sewage, discharges of nuclear radiation, and the depletion of fresh water resources.

POPULATION

In 1992, the world's population totaled about 5.5 billion. With an annual population growth rate of 1.7 percent in the early 1990s, the world's population will reach almost 6.5 billion by the end of the twentieth century and, experts predict, will double in only 41 years.

The population explosion

Around 10,000 years ago, when people began to grow crops and live in permanent settlements, the world was thinly populated. From around 5 million in 8000 B.C., the population increased steadily to reach 500 million in A.D. 1650. The population then doubled in only 200 years, reaching 1 billion in 1850. The acceleration of population growth continued. By the mid-1920s, world population had reached nearly 2 billion, and it passed the 4 billion mark in the 1970s.

The increases in the last 200 years occurred first in nations that were industrializing. But the rates of population growth in the developed industrial world have recently declined. Today, the highest growth rates are in the developing world.

Where people live

In the early 1990s, about half of the world's people lived on only 5 percent of the world's land area, while about half of the world's land area contained only about 5 percent of the world's population. The population explosion in areas attractive to settlement and the consequent expansion of city populations have all contributed to pollution, while urban living has contributed to many of the environmental problems that exist today.

Population pressure also affects rural areas, where the increasing demand for food has led to the destruction of natural habitats.

The map depicts two regions where natural habitats are at risk. These are the equatorial rain forests, which are being cut down at an alarmingly rapid rate, and semiarid regions, which are being turned into deserts by deforestation and overgrazing.

The world's population is distributed unevenly around the planet. Vast areas, including the Sahara in North Africa, the Australian interior, northern Canada and Siberia, and the Amazon basin in South America are sparsely populated. Other areas in India, Southeast Asia, Western Europe, and the northeastern United States are extremely crowded.

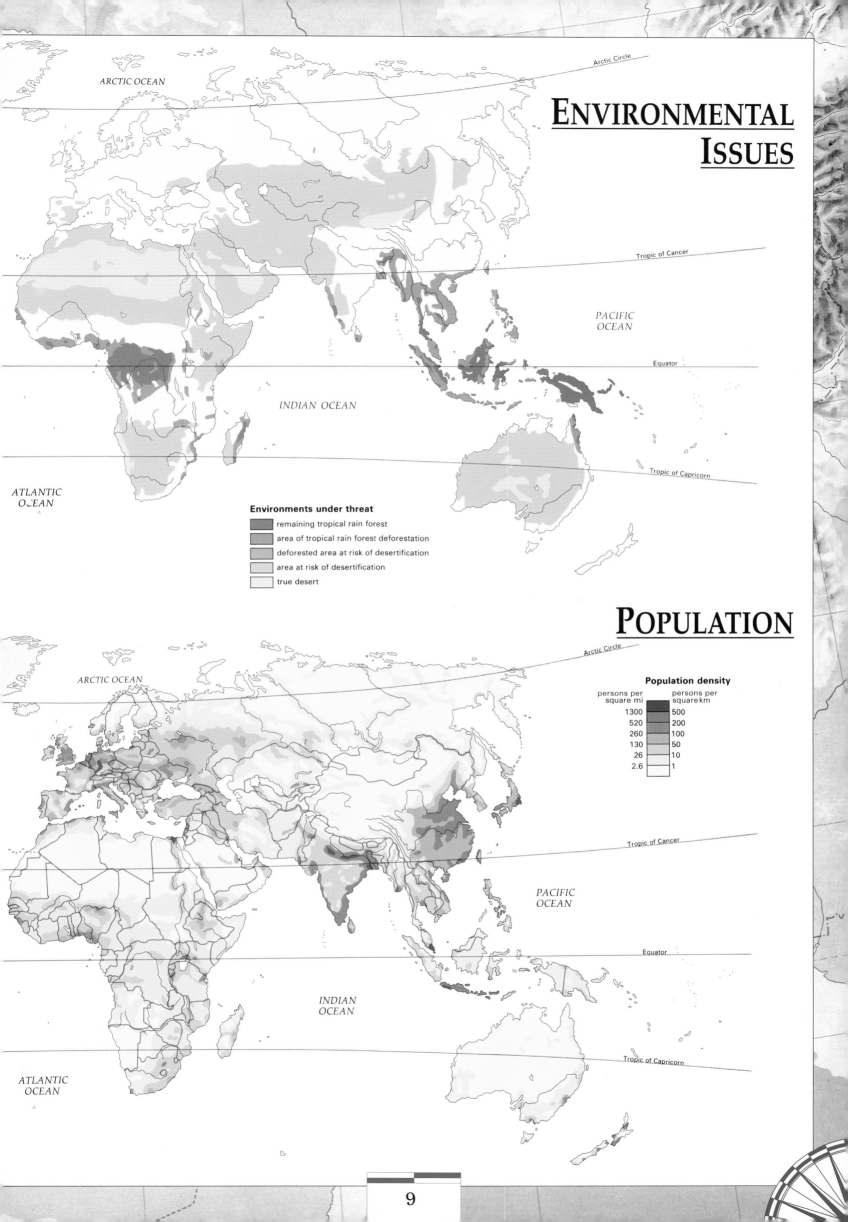

ENVIRONMENTAL ISSUES

ARCTIC OCEAN

Arctic Circle

Tropic of Cancer

PACIFIC OCEAN

Equator

INDIAN OCEAN

Tropic of Capricorn

ATLANTIC OCEAN

Environments under threat

- remaining tropical rain forest
- area of tropical rain forest deforestation
- deforested area at risk of desertification
- area at risk of desertification
- true desert

POPULATION

Arctic Circle

ARCTIC OCEAN

Population density

persons per square mi		persons per square km
1300		500
520		200
260		100
130		50
26		10
2.6		1

Tropic of Cancer

PACIFIC OCEAN

Equator

INDIAN OCEAN

Tropic of Capricorn

ATLANTIC OCEAN

THE WORLD

RESOURCES

The world's leading resources include those that provide fuel, together with metals and nonmetallic minerals used in industry.

Energy resources

Coal, oil, and natural gas are called fossil fuels because they were formed from once-living organisms. Coal was the main fuel during the industrial revolution in the nineteenth century. Today, however, oil and natural gas provide about three-fifths of the world's energy.

Fossil fuels are nonrenewable resources, and some experts estimate that, at present drilling rates, the world's oil reserves will run out by 2035.

Nuclear power continues to be controversial, and so it seems likely that such renewable energy resources as water and solar power will be increasingly used in the future. Also important is the fact that the use of water and solar power, unlike that of fossil fuels, does not cause pollution.

Mineral reserves

Most metals are extracted from ores, which are combinations of minerals. Iron, which is used to make steel, is the most widely used metal. Other major metallic minerals include aluminum, which is obtained from the ore bauxite; copper; lead; tin; and zinc. Uranium is also a metal. It has become important because of its use as a nuclear fuel. Nonmetallic minerals include some building materials, diamonds, phosphates, and sulfur.

Metals are also nonrenewable resources and some are becoming scarce. As a result, recycling is becoming increasingly common: about half of the iron and one-third of the aluminum now used by industry comes from scrap.

AGRICULTURE

Agriculture is the world's leading industry. Not only does it provide food, but it also produces those materials used to make clothing, prepare paints and inks, or make soaps, for example. Forestry and fishing also produce materials used in industry as well as provide food.

The development of agriculture

The deliberate planting and harvesting of crops began around 10,000 years ago, and, soon afterward, farming communities began to displace the traditional hunting and gathering economies. Other early developments were the domestication of animals and irrigation. As of the eighteenth century, farming became increasingly mechanized and scientific. Today, agriculture employs only a small proportion of people in the prosperous developed countries. For example, the United States leads the world in agricultural production, yet agriculture employs only about 3 percent of its work force. By contrast, a high proportion of people in most developing countries work on the land. Much of the agriculture is carried out at subsistence level— that is, farmers produce enough for their families, with comparatively little left over for sale.

Modern transportation methods, especially the use of refrigeration, have made it possible to move perishable goods around the world. Agriculture is big business.

Forestry and fishing

Forests cover about 30 percent of the earth's land area. Forestry is the commercial utilization and management of forests. Wood is a major raw material in industry.

The fishing industry is particularly important in countries such as Japan, where other protein-rich foods are in short supply.

World resources

fossil fuels
- coal
- natural gas
- oil

minerals
- bauxite
- copper
- diamonds
- gold
- iron ore
- potash
- tin

The type of agriculture practiced in any area depends on the climate and soil, though irrigation has made some desert regions highly productive. However, areas with well-drained soils and plenty of rain are normally used for raising crops, with drier areas being used for livestock. Cattle are usually raised on the best pasture, while goats and sheep graze on rough pasture.

RESOURCES

The map shows that fossil fuels, particularly oil and gas, are concentrated in the Northern Hemisphere. North America is especially rich in energy reserves. On the other hand, reserves of metals and other minerals are spread far more evenly around the world.

EUROPE

ASIA

AFRICA

AUSTRALIA

Arctic Circle

Tropic of Cancer

Equator

Tropic of Capricorn

AGRICULTURE

Agricultural zones
- arable
- fruits, vegetables, and tree crops
- pasture
- rough grazing
- woods and forest
- nonagricultural land
- major fishing grounds
- ▲ mountain peak (ft)

ARCTIC OCEAN

Severnaya Zemlya

New Siberian Is.

Arctic Circle

Svalbard

Barents Sea

Novaya Zemlya

Greenland

Iceland

Lena

Bering Sea

Kamchatka Peninsula

Central Siberian Plateau

Yenisei

Sea of Okhotsk

Ob

URAL MTS.

West Siberian Plain

Sakhalin

L. Baikal

North Sea

Baltic Sea

British Isles

North European Plain

Irtysh

Amur

Kuril Is.

Carpathian Mts.

Aral Sea

Altai Mts.

Sea of Japan

Azores (Port.)

Mt. Blanc 15772 ▲

ALPS

Danube

Volga

Syr Darya

L. Balkhash

Tien Shan

Gobi Desert

Honshu

Pyrenees

Black Sea

Caspian Sea

Amu Darya

Huang

Canary Is.

Mediterranean Sea

Caucasus Mts.

Kunlun Shan

Chang

East China Sea

Tropic of Cancer

Atlas Mts.

Euphrates

Tigris

Indus

HIMALAYAS

Taiwan

SAHARA

Libyan Desert

Persian Gulf

Mt. Everest 29028 ▲

Salween

Ahaggar Plateau

Nile

Arabian Peninsula

Thar Desert

Ganges

Hainan

Tibesti

Red Sea

Arabian Sea

Deccan Plateau

South China Sea

Philippine Is.

PACIFIC OCEAN

Cape Verde Is.

SAHEL

Niger

Andaman Is.

Mekong

Ethiopian Highlands

Nicobar Is.

Sri Lanka

Mt. Cameroon 13354 ▲

L. Turkana

Maldive Is.

Gulf of Guinea

Great Rift Valley

L. Victoria

Sumatra

Borneo

Equator

Ascension

Congo

Zaire

▲ Kilimanjaro 19340

Seychelles

Sulawesi (Celebes)

New Guinea

Bismarck Archipelago

L. Tanganyika

INDIAN OCEAN

Java

Timor

Solomon Is.

Comoros

Zambezi

L. Malawi

Madagascar

Mauritius

Réunion

Coral Sea

New Hebrides

New Caledonia

Fiji Is.

Kalahari Desert

Limpopo

Mozambique Channel

Great Sandy Desert

Macdonnell Ranges

L. Eyre

Tropic of Capricorn

Drakensberg Mts.

Great Dividing Range

Cape of Good Hope

Mt. Kosciusko 7317 ▲

Tristan da Cunha

Tasmania

Tasman Sea

New Zealand

Mt. Cook 12350 ▲

11

THE WORLD

SOILS

Soil is one of the earth's vital resources. Most living things on land could not exist without it. Soil is a complex mixture of worn fragments of rock, humus (the decayed remains of plants and animals), water, air, and living organisms. All the living organisms, together with the roots of plants, contribute to breaking down the soil into smaller and smaller pieces.

Soil formation

The character of soil is affected by the parent rock on which it forms. For example, soils that form on shale, a soft rock, usually have a finer texture than those that form on sandstone, which is composed largely of hard grains of quartz.

Soils are usually thin on sloping land, because soil particles tend to move downhill. But they may reach depths of several yards in hollows. In waterlogged areas, dead plants may accumulate to form peat.

Soil types

The most common soil classifications are based on climate. In wet equatorial regions, the heavy rain leaches (dissolves) minerals from the top layers, leaving a red or yellow soil, latosol, which is rich in bauxite.

Brown forest soils are not heavily leached. Their color comes from the large amount of humus in the top layers. Desert soils are often red and sandy, because they are low in humus. Dark-colored chernozems are soils rich in humus, formed from the remains of the plants that grew on temperate grasslands. By contrast, podzols, the grayish soils of the northern coniferous forest zones, are low in humus. They contain a thin acid layer, overlying a heavily leached layer. Tundra soils are often waterlogged and often remain frozen just below the surface. The frozen subsoil is called permafrost.

PLANTS

The vegetation in any area is governed by three main factors: present climate and geographical conditions, past climate conditions (such as those of the ice ages), and geographical changes (such as those caused by plate movements of the continents).

Botanists have divided the world into six floristic kingdoms, where the major plant families have distinct characteristics in common. These kingdoms are divided into regions.

Boreal kingdom

The Boreal ("northern") kingdom includes the cold temperate and subtropical lands of the Northern Hemisphere. One reason for the similarity between the plants in this kingdom is that the land masses were joined together in recent geological times.

Tropical kingdoms

The Paleotropical ("ancient tropical") kingdom includes most of Africa south of the Sahara and tropical southern Asia. The Neotropical ("new tropical") kingdom in Central and tropical South America has distinctive vegetation, which evolved differently from that of Africa after South America began to move away from Africa about 140 million years ago. South America was also isolated from North America until about 2.5 million years ago.

Southern kingdoms

The southern kingdoms include the South African kingdom, with a climate similar to that of the Mediterranean region, and the Australian kingdom, which evolved its unique and diverse species in geographic isolation from the other continents. Finally, there is the Antarctic kingdom, which includes southern South America and also New Zealand.

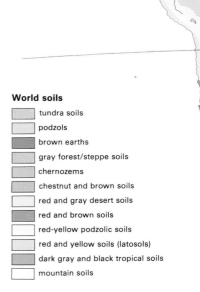

World soils
- tundra soils
- podzols
- brown earths
- gray forest/steppe soils
- chernozems
- chestnut and brown soils
- red and gray desert soils
- red and brown soils
- red-yellow podzolic soils
- red and yellow soils (latosols)
- dark gray and black tropical soils
- mountain soils

PLANTS

Plants are found everywhere on earth, with the greatest number of species in hot and wet tropical regions. The map shows the six main floristic kingdoms, which are further subdivided into regions. These kingdoms and regions reflect both the climate of the areas and the factors that governed the evolution of plant communities over millions of years.

SOILS

The most important factor influencing the development of soils is the climate. Hence, the world distribution of soil types is closely related to the map of climatic zones. Soil types are also influenced by the underlying rocks, terrain, drainage, and vegetation types.

Arctic Circle

Tropic of Cancer

Equator

Tropic of Capricorn

ARCTIC OCEAN

Arctic Circle

CIRCUMBOREAL

CIRCUMBOREAL

ROCKY MOUNTAIN

NORTH AMERICAN ATLANTIC

IRANO-TURANIAN

MADREAN

MACARONESIAN

MEDITERRANEAN

EASTERN ASIATIC

HAWAIIAN

Tropic of Cancer

ATLANTIC OCEAN

CARIBBEAN

SAHARO-ARABIAN

INDIAN

INDOCHINESE

PACIFIC OCEAN

PACIFIC OCEAN

GUIANA HIGHLANDS

SUDANO-ZAMBEZIAN

Equator

AMAZONIAN

GUINEO-CONGOLIAN

MALESIAN

POLYNESIAN

ANDEAN

BRAZILIAN

ST HELENA AND ASCENSION

INDIAN OCEAN

MADAGASCAN

NORTHEAST AUSTRALIAN

FIJIAN

POLYNESIAN

Tropic of Capricorn

KAROO-NAMIB

UZAMBARA-ZULULAND

CENTRAL AUSTRALIAN

NEOCALEDONIAN

FERNANDEZIAN

ATLANTIC OCEAN

SOUTH AFRICAN

SOUTHWEST AUSTRALIAN

CHILE-PATAGONIAN

SOUTH SUBANTARCTIC ISLANDS

NEOZEYLANDIC

Floristic Kingdoms

- Boreal
- Paleotropical
- Neotropical
- South African
- Australian
- Antarctic

— Region boundary

Antarctic Circle

THE WORLD

BIOMES

Wilderness areas around the world are amazingly diverse. However, they can be divided into a few general types, which are characterized by the dominant plant communities, such as grassland, tundra, coniferous forest, or deciduous forest. These broad regions are called biomes.

Major life zones

Biomes are defined as major life zones that are characterized by their vegetation and climate. Biomes can be changed by both natural factors and human activities. Lakes, for example, are silted by rivers flowing into them. Eventually, the lake becomes a marsh, and the marsh in time becomes dry land. Many dry, flat areas in the western United States were once lakes.

Over longer periods the erosion of mountains changes landscapes, and the movements of continents change climates. Species of plants and animals respond to these changes. Some adapt to the new environment, some migrate, and some become extinct.

Biodiversity

There may be as many as 30 million plant and animal species on our planet, even though 98 percent of all the species that have existed are now extinct. Plant and animal species are the basic units of the rich biodiversity on our planet. But human interference is now threatening millions of species, especially in the tropical forests where biodiversity is at its greatest. Experts predict that one-fourth of all the world's plant and animal species face extinction in the next 25 to 50 years, mainly as a result of changes humans cause to biomes. The future well-being of the earth may depend on preserving biodiversity.

CLIMATIC CHANGES

Several ice ages have occurred during the earth's long history. Geologists have found evidence of five major periods of cooling beginning around 2.3 billion years ago, 670 million years ago, 470 million years ago, 300 million years ago, and 2.5 million years ago.

The Pleistocene ice age

The last ice age, in the Pleistocene epoch, was a relatively short one. There were periods of intense cold, called glacial periods, when ice advanced over large parts of the earth, and interglacial periods, when the climate was warmer than it is today. The ice sheets then melted and retreated. The Pleistocene ice age was at its height between 15,000 and 20,000 years ago. At that time, thick ice sheets covered about 30 percent of the earth's land surface, spreading over much of the Northern Hemisphere. In North America, the ice reached a line between the present-day locations of Seattle and New York City. Ice sheets in Europe reached southern England, the Netherlands, and southern Germany.

Ice ages and vegetation

The effects of the last ice age altered all the earth's climatic and vegetation zones. The middle latitudes developed great areas of tundra, while the tropics became much drier. Huge deserts were formed. About 10,000 years ago, the climate became generally warmer, and plants recolonized the barren tundra zones. Since then, there have been minor climatic fluctuations, such as the "Little Ice Age" in Europe between the fifteenth and eighteenth centuries. These natural fluctuations give some idea of what may happen if global warming, caused by human activity, is allowed to continue.

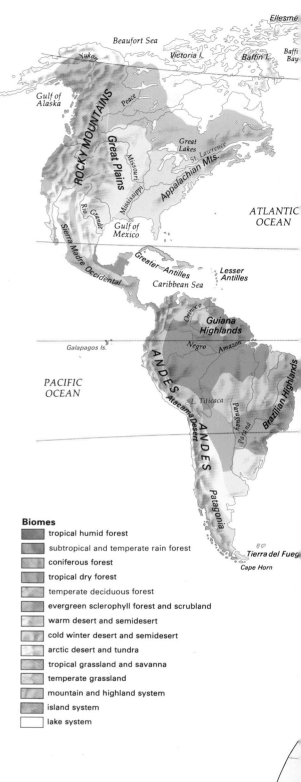

Biomes

- tropical humid forest
- subtropical and temperate rain forest
- coniferous forest
- tropical dry forest
- temperate deciduous forest
- evergreen sclerophyll forest and scrubland
- warm desert and semidesert
- cold winter desert and semidesert
- arctic desert and tundra
- tropical grassland and savanna
- temperate grassland
- mountain and highland system
- island system
- lake system

BIOMES OF THE PAST

The map shows the world's vegetation about 18,000 years ago, when the last ice age was at its peak. The positions of coastlines were different from those of today, because so much water was frozen in the ice sheets, lowering the sea level. This influenced human development. Dry land bridges were created, enabling early people to migrate from one area to another.

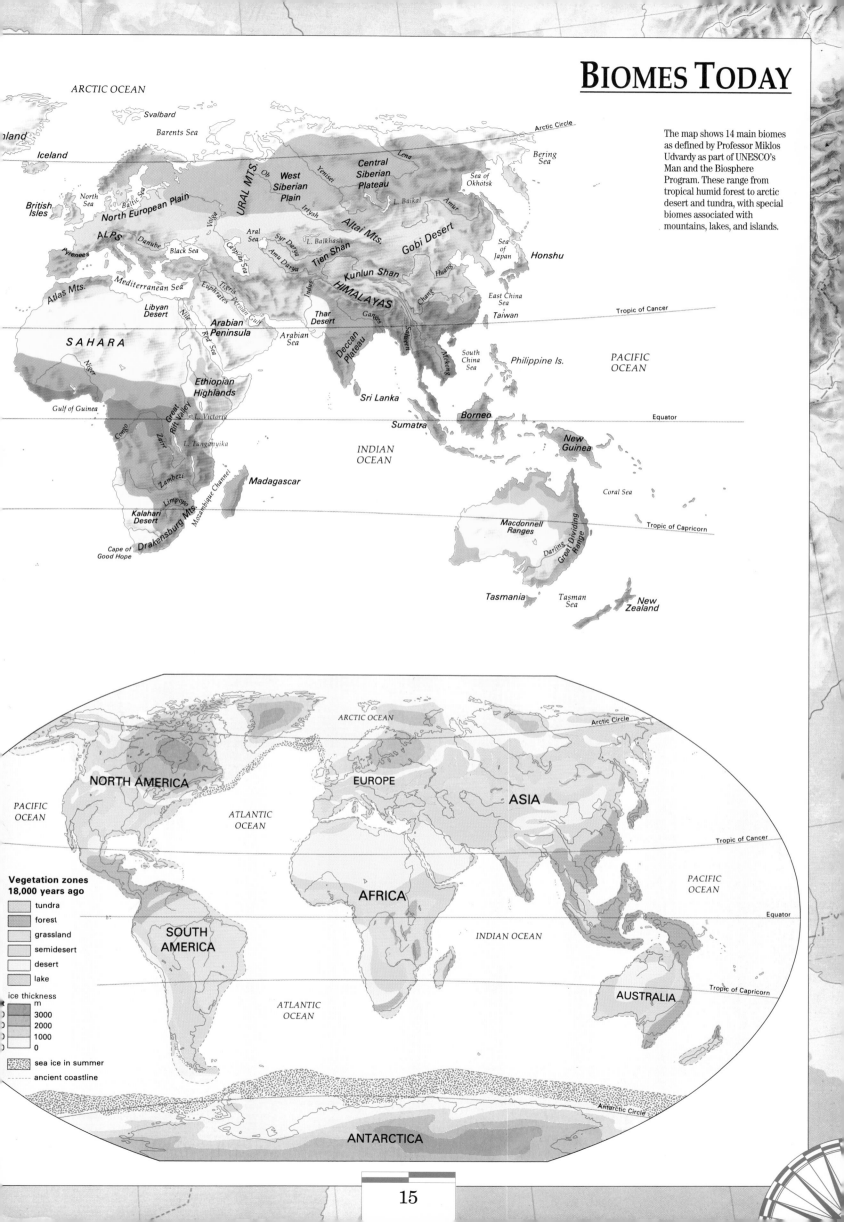

BIOMES TODAY

The map shows 14 main biomes as defined by Professor Miklos Udvardy as part of UNESCO's Man and the Biosphere Program. These range from tropical humid forest to arctic desert and tundra, with special biomes associated with mountains, lakes, and islands.

Vegetation zones 18,000 years ago

- tundra
- forest
- grassland
- semidesert
- desert
- lake

ice thickness

m
3000
2000
1000
0

sea ice in summer

ancient coastline

15

CANADA AND GREENLAND

Northern North America includes Canada, the world's second largest country, and Greenland, the world's largest island. The Arctic islands of Canada are a cold tundra region that contain many glaciers. Two of these islands—Baffin and Ellesmere—are also among the world's ten largest islands. About six-sevenths of Greenland is buried under a thick ice sheet, the world's second largest body of ice after the ice sheet of Antarctica.

Canada's most prominent features include the western mountains, the interior plains, the Canadian Shield, the St. Lawrence lowlands, and, in the southeast, an extension of the Appalachian region. Canada also shares with the United States the world's largest expanse of fresh water—the Great Lakes.

Because of the climate, about 80 percent of Canadians live within 186 miles (300 km) of their southern border. Canada is one of the world's leading mineral exporters and manufacturing nations. Its farming and fishing industries are highly efficient.

Canada has a diverse population. The earliest inhabitants, the Native Americans, entered Canada about 30,000 years ago. They were followed by the Inuits, whose descendants now also live in Greenland. These two peoples make up a small minority of the population. Nearly two-thirds of the people today are English- and French-speaking descendants of European settlers, though Canada also has communities from other parts of Europe, notably Germany, Italy and Ukraine, and from Asia.

Canada and Greenland make up about half of North America. Northern Canada and most of Greenland lie north of the Arctic Circle, while the northern tip of Greenland is about 441 miles (710 km) from the North Pole. Canada's greatest east-west distance is nearly 3,230 miles (5,200 km). This vast distance is reflected by its six time zones. When it is 8:30 A.M. in St. John's, Newfoundland, it is 4.00 A.M. in Vancouver, British Columbia.

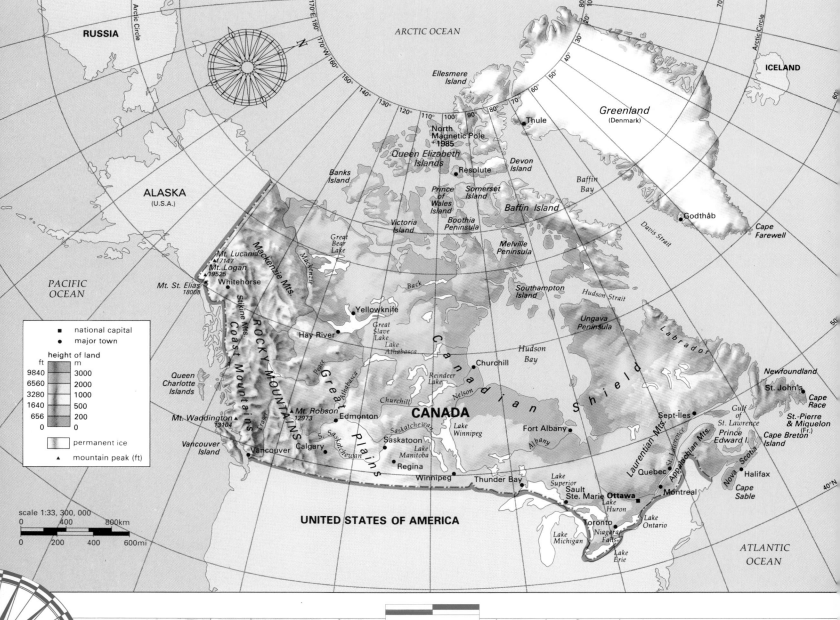

THE POLITICAL AND CULTURAL WORLD

Canada has a federal system of government, but it faces several problems arising from its ethnic diversity. One problem is reconciling the aspirations of the French-speaking people, who form the majority in Quebec, with the different traditions of the English-speaking Canadians. Another problem is how to integrate Native American and Inuit peoples in the modern state.

Greenland is a self-governing province of Denmark, though it is 50 times bigger than the rest of the country. To assert its independence, Greenland left the European Community in 1985, though it continued its relationship with Denmark.

COUNTRIES IN THE REGION

Canada (Greenland, a province of Denmark)

RELIGION

ROMAN CATHOLIC	46.5%
PROTESTANT	41.0%
EASTERN ORTHODOX	1.5%
JEWISH	1.2%
ISLAM	0.4%
HINDU	0.3%
SIKH	0.3%
NONRELIGIOUS	7.4%
OTHERS	1.4%

ETHNIC COMPOSITION

BRITISH	34.4%
FRENCH	25.7%
GERMAN	3.6%
ITALIAN	2.8%
UKRAINIAN	1.7%
AMERINDIAN AND INUIT	1.5%
CHINESE	1.4%
DUTCH	1.4%
MULTIPLE ORIGIN OR OTHERS	27.5%

FORM OF GOVERNMENT

Federal multiparty parliamentary monarchy with two legislative houses

ECONOMIC INDICATORS: 1990

GDP (US$ billions)	570.15
GNP per capita (US$)	20,470
Annual rate of growth of GDP, 1980–1990	3.4%
Manufacturing as % of GDP	13.0%
Central government spending as % of GDP	23.0%
Merchandise exports (US$ billions)	133.5
Merchandise imports (US$ billions)	126.5
% of GNP donated as development aid	0.44%

WELFARE INDICATORS

Infant mortality rate (per 1,000 live births)	
1965	24
1990	7
Daily food supply available (calories per capita, 1989)	3,482
Population per physician (1984)	510
Teacher-pupil ratio (elementary school, 1989)	1 : 16

- ■ national capital
- • provincial capital

Constitutional changes
In the early 1990s, Canadians debated the future of their country. Many French Canadians wanted to create a French Canadian state in Quebec. One proposed change would set up Nunavut, a self-governing territory for the Inuit, to occupy the eastern part of the Northwest Territories. The western part would be a homeland for Native Americans.

Area 3,849,672 sq mi
(9,970,610 sq km)
Population 26,521,000
Capital Ottawa
Chief languages English, French
Currency 1 Canadian dollar (Can $) = 100 cents

Canada

HABITATS

Canada is a land with many varied landforms. Massive mountain ranges, scenic lakes, great evergreen forests, vast prairies, fertile river valleys, and islands covered with snow and ice can all be found in this second largest country in the world.

LAND

Area (incl. Greenland) 4,691,791 sq mi (12,151,739 sq km)
Highest point Mount Logan, 19,525 ft (5,950 m)
Lowest point sea level
Major features Rocky Mountains; Canadian Shield; Arctic islands; Greenland, world's largest island

WATER

Longest river Mackenzie, 2,635 mi (4,240 km)
Largest basin Mackenzie, 681,000 sq mi (1,764,000 sq km)
Highest average flow St. Lawrence, 460,000 cu ft/sec (13,030 cu m/sec)
Largest lake Superior, 32,150 sq mi (83,270 sq km), world's largest freshwater lake

NOTABLE THREATENED SPECIES

Mammals Vancouver Island marmot (*Marmota vancouverensis*)
Other animals Lake lamprey (*Lampetra macrostoma*), Copper redhorse fish (*Moxostoma hubbsi*), Periodical cicada (*Magicicauda septendecim*)
Plants *Armeria maritima* subsp. *interior*; small white lady's slipper (*Cypripedium candidum*); small whorled fogonia (*Isotria medeoloides*); *Limnanthes macounii*; Furbish's lousewort (*Pedicularis furbishiae*); *Phyllitis japonica* subsp. *americana*; *Plantago cordata*; *Salix planifolia* subsp. *tyrrellii*; *Salix silicicola*; *Senecio newcombei*

CLIMATE

The Arctic has frozen seas and ice caps, with temperatures near the freezing point, and tundra regions with brief, chilly summers. Most of Canada has a subarctic climate, with coniferous forests. Only in the south are there climatic regions warm enough for farming.

TEMPERATURE AND PRECIPITATION

	Temperature °F (°C)		Altitude ft (m)	
	January	July		
Resolute	−26 (−32)	39 (4)	200	(64)
Vancouver	36 (2)	63 (17)	45	(14)
Winnipeg	−4 (−20)	68 (20)	787	(240)
Montreal	16 (−9)	72 (22)	98	(30)
Halifax	25 (−4)	64 (18)	98	(30)

	Precipitation in (mm)		
	January	July	Year
Resolute	0.1 (3)	0.8 (21)	5.1 (131)
Vancouver	8.5 (218)	1.2 (31)	42.0 (1,068)
Winnipeg	0.9 (23)	3.1 (79)	21.0 (535)
Montreal	3.3 (83)	3.5 (89)	39.3 (999)
Halifax	5.4 (137)	3.8 (96)	54.4 (1,381)

World's highest recorded snowfall in 24 hours, 46 in (1,180 mm), Lake Lakelse, British Columbia

NATURAL HAZARDS

Cold and snowstorms, drought, gales, avalanches, rockfalls, and landslides

ENVIRONMENTAL ISSUES

Southeastern Canada suffers from acid rain, part of which results from air pollution originating in the northeastern United States. Soil erosion, logging, mining, oil drilling, and water pollution are other hazards.

POPULATION AND WEALTH

Population (in millions)	26.6
Population increase (annual population growth rate, % 1960–1990)	1.3
Energy use (gigajoules/person)	291
Real purchasing power (US$/person)	17,680

ENVIRONMENTAL INDICATORS

CO_2 emissions (mil. m.t. carbon/year)	120
Municipal waste (lbs/person/year)	1,390
Nuclear waste (cumulative m.t. heavy metal)	11,000
Artificial fertilizer use (lbs/acre/year)	43
Automobiles (per 1,000 population)	432
Access to safe drinking water (% population)	100

MAJOR ENVIRONMENTAL PROBLEMS AND SOURCES

Air pollution: urban high; acid rain prevalent; high greenhouse gas emissions
River/lake pollution: medium; *sources:* agricultural, sewage, acid deposition
Land pollution: local; *sources:* industrial, urban/household
Waste disposal problems: domestic; industrial; nuclear
Major events: Mississauga (1979), chlorine gas leak during transportation; Saint Basile le Grand (1988), toxic cloud from waste dump fire

HABITATS

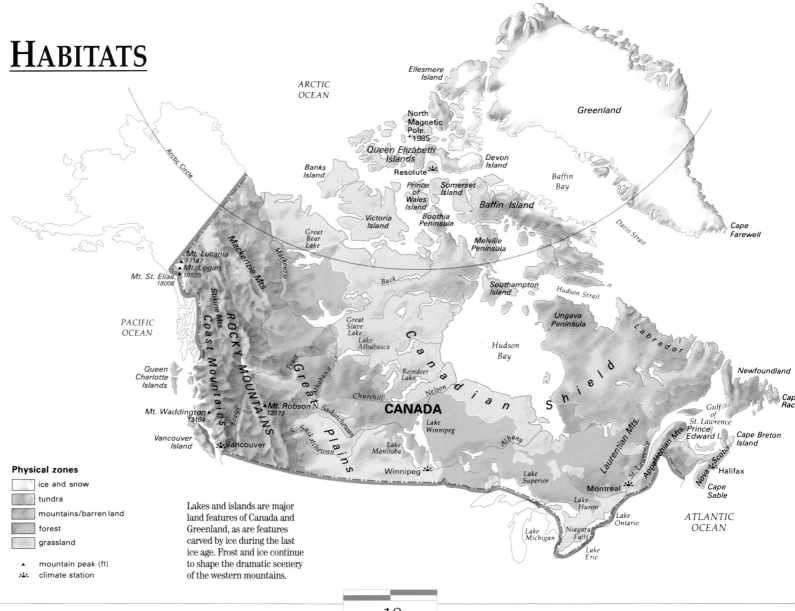

Physical zones

- ice and snow
- tundra
- mountains/barren land
- forest
- grassland

▲ mountain peak (ft)
:•: climate station

Lakes and islands are major land features of Canada and Greenland, as are features carved by ice during the last ice age. Frost and ice continue to shape the dramatic scenery of the western mountains.

ENVIRONMENTAL ISSUES

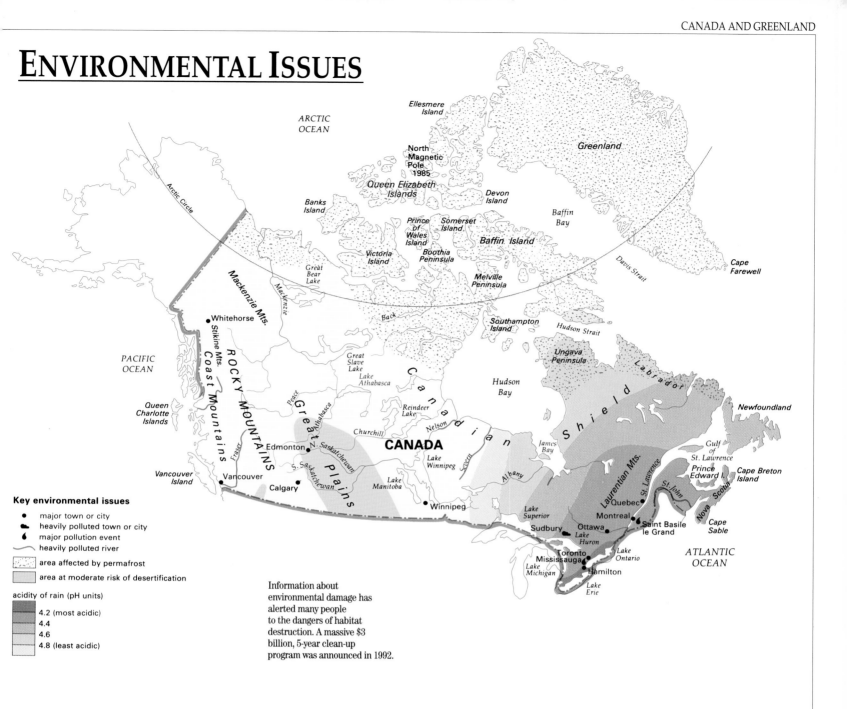

Key environmental issues

- • major town or city
- ◣ heavily polluted town or city
- ◖ major pollution event
- ◠ heavily polluted river
- ⣿ area affected by permafrost
- ▨ area at moderate risk of desertification

acidity of rain (pH units)

- 4.2 (most acidic)
- 4.4
- 4.6
- 4.8 (least acidic)

Information about
environmental damage has
alerted many people
to the dangers of habitat
destruction. A massive $3
billion, 5-year clean-up
program was announced in 1992.

CLIMATE

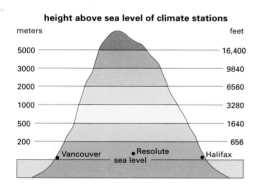

height above sea level of climate stations

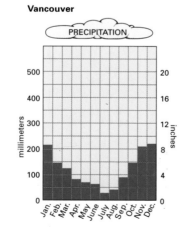

Vancouver

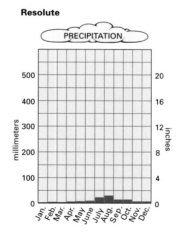

Resolute

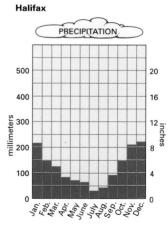

Halifax

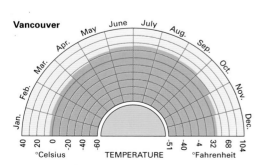

Vancouver

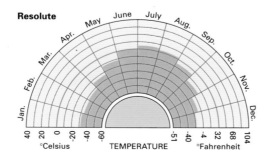

Resolute

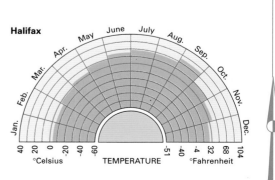

Halifax

POPULATION

Although Canada's population has doubled since 1945—the result of immigration and a high birth rate—Canada has one of the world's lowest average population densities. Most Canadians live near the southern border.

POPULATION

Total population of region (in millions)	26.6
Population density (persons per sq mi)	7.0
Population change (average annual percent 1960–1990)	
Urban	+1.7
Rural	+0.4

URBAN POPULATION

As percentage of total population	
1960	68.9
1990	75.6
Percentage in cities of more than 1 million	29.7

TEN LARGEST CITIES

	Population
Toronto	3,427,000
Montreal	2,921,000
Vancouver	1,381,000
Ottawa †	819,000
Edmonton	785,000
Calgary	671,000
Winnipeg	623,000
Quebec	603,000
Hamilton	557,000
St. Catharines–Niagara	343,000

† *denotes national capital*

INDUSTRY

Canada is rich in minerals and is a major exporter of raw materials. Manufacturing industries belong to two main groups: those that process raw materials and those concerned with making products, such as food and vehicles.

INDUSTRIAL OUTPUT (US$ billion)

Total	Mining	Manufacturing	Average annual change since 1960
171.3	19.7	94.3	+3.5%

MAJOR PRODUCTS (Figures in parentheses are percentages of world production.)

Energy and minerals	Output	Change since 1960
Coal (mil. m.t.)	70.6 (1.5%)	+713%
Oil (mil. barrels)	615.7 (2.8%)	+327%
Natural gas (billion cu meters)	90.8 (4.9%)	+625%
Iron Ore (mil. m.t.)	40.8 (7.2%)	+13.5%
Copper (mil. m.t.)	0.8 (8.8%)	-8.5%
Lead (mil. m.t.)	0.4 (11.5%)	+29%
Zinc (mil. m.t.)	1.5 (20.9%)	+14%
Nickel (mil. m.t.)	0.2 (24.6%)	-18%
Uranium (1,000 m.t.: U content)	12.4 (33.7%)	No data

Manufactures		
Aluminum (mil. m.t.)	1.6 (7.2%)	+72%
Steel (mil. m.t.)	15.1 (2.1%)	+286%
Woodpulp (mil. m.t.)	21.0 (16.5%)	+16%
Newsprint (mil. m.t.)	10.0 (31.5%)	+15%
Sulfuric acid (mil. m.t.)	3.8 (1.4%)	+45%
Automobiles (mil.)	2.0 (4.3%)	+509%

AGRICULTURE

Only 8 percent of the land in Canada is used for farming. The best farmland is in the St. Lawrence lowlands and around the Great Lakes. The other main region is the wheat-growing prairie belt—the northern part of the Great Plains.

LAND (million acres)

Total	Agricultural	Arable	Forest/woodland
2,362 (100%)	192 (8%)	114 (5%)	875 (37%)

FARMERS

472,000 employed in agriculture (4% of workforce)
240 acres of arable land per person employed in agriculture

MAJOR CROPS

	Area mil. acres	Yield 100lbs/acre	Production mil. m.t.	Change since 1960
Wheat	33.3	17.2	26.0 (5)	+69%
Barley	12.3	24.9	14.0 (8)	+262%
Rapeseed	6.6	12.8	3.8 (17)	+1,284%
Oats	3.2	21.1	3.0 (7)	−51%
Corn	2.5	62.6	7.0 (2)	+554%
Linseed	1.5	10.9	0.7 (29)	+42%

MAJOR LIVESTOCK

	Number in mil.	Production mil. m.t.	Change since 1963
Cattle	11.7 (1)	—	+4%
Pigs	10.5 (1)	—	+101%
Milk	—	8.0 (2)	-4%
Fish catch	—	1.6 (2)	–

Numbers in parentheses are percentages of world total.

POPULATION

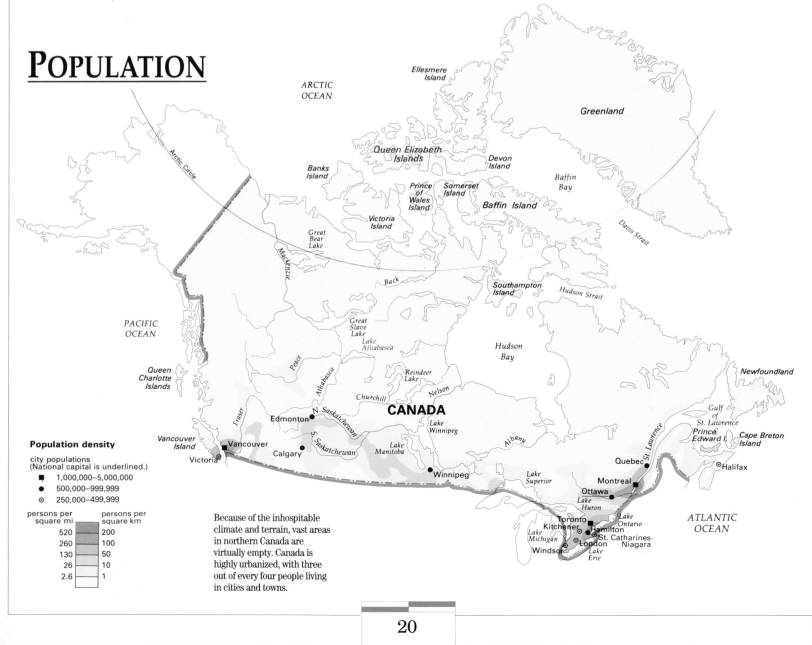

Population density

city populations
(National capital is underlined.)

- ■ 1,000,000–5,000,000
- ● 500,000–999,999
- ◉ 250,000–499,999

persons per square mi	persons per square km
520	200
260	100
130	50
26	10
2.6	1

Because of the inhospitable climate and terrain, vast areas in northern Canada are virtually empty. Canada is highly urbanized, with three out of every four people living in cities and towns.

INDUSTRY

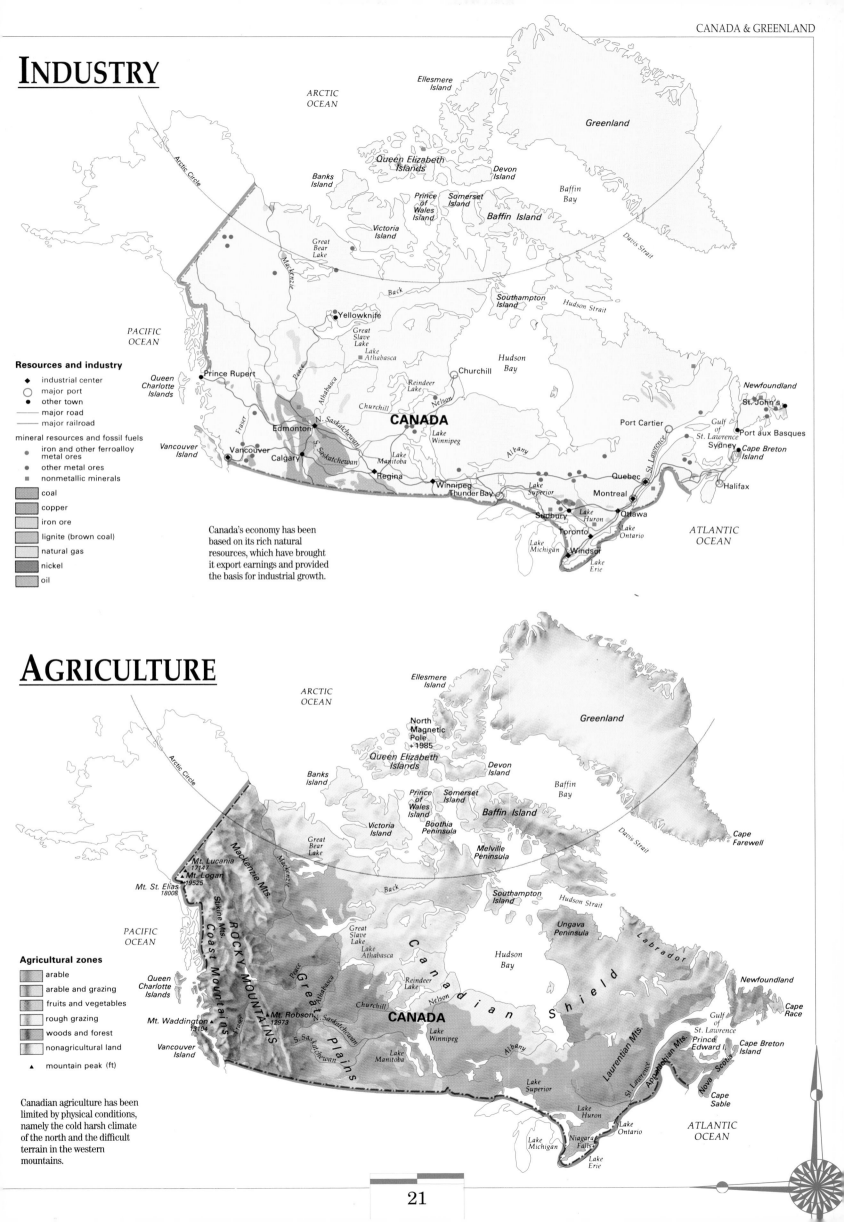

Resources and industry

- ◆ industrial center
- ○ major port
- ● other town
- —— major road
- —— major railroad

mineral resources and fossil fuels

- ● iron and other ferroalloy metal ores
- ● other metal ores
- ■ nonmetallic minerals

- coal
- copper
- iron ore
- lignite (brown coal)
- natural gas
- nickel
- oil

Canada's economy has been based on its rich natural resources, which have brought it export earnings and provided the basis for industrial growth.

AGRICULTURE

Agricultural zones

- arable
- arable and grazing
- fruits and vegetables
- rough grazing
- woods and forest
- nonagricultural land
- ▲ mountain peak (ft)

Canadian agriculture has been limited by physical conditions, namely the cold harsh climate of the north and the difficult terrain in the western mountains.

UNITED STATES OF AMERICA

The United States, the world's fourth largest country, is a land of towering mountain ranges and extensive plains. Prominent land features include the Grand Canyon, great rivers that lead into the interior, deserts, explosive volcanoes in the Cascade Range, and wetlands in the southeast. The climate ranges from the icy shores of the Arctic Ocean to the intense heat of the dry Death Valley in California.

The first inhabitants of the United States, the Native Americans, came from Eurasia about 30,000 years ago across a land bridge over what is now the Bering Strait. They were followed about 6,000 years ago by the ancestors of the Inuit. Since the early sixteenth century, Europeans and, later, people from almost every part of the world, have made their homes in the United States, the richest country in the world.

The bulk of the United States, comprising 48 of the 50 states, lies between Canada to the north and Mexico to the south. The forty-ninth state, Alaska, is in the northwestern corner of North America. The fifti-eth state, Hawaii, is an island chain situated in the North Pacific Ocean.

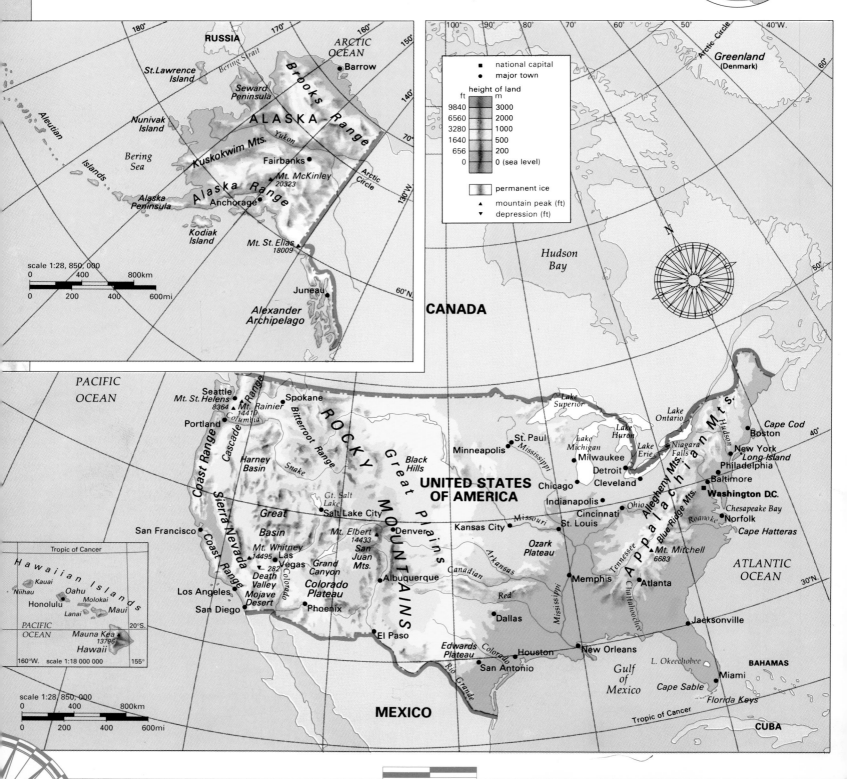

THE POLITICAL AND CULTURAL WORLD

The United States was born during the American Revolution (1775–1783), when the people of the 13 British colonies in the east overthrew British rule. The country expanded westward during the nineteenth century. Alaska was purchased from Russia in 1867, while Hawaii was annexed in 1898. Both territories became states in 1959.

The United States is a federal republic, whose government has three branches. The executive branch is headed by the president, who is also head of state. The legislative branch includes Congress, which consists of the Senate and House of Representatives. The judicial branch is headed by the Supreme Court.

LANGUAGE
Official language English
Percentage of population by first language
English (79%), Spanish (4%), German (3%), Italian (2%), French (1.3%), Polish (1.2%)
Over 90% of the population can speak English.

IMMIGRATION
Percentage of foreign born 6.2
Total immigrants (1990) 1,536,483*
Countries sending most immigrants (1990) Mexico (679,100), El Salvador (80,200), Philippines (63,800), Vietnam (48,800), China and Taiwan (47,000), Dominican Republic (42,200), Korea (32,300), India (30,700)

* Includes persons granted permanent residence under the legalization program of the Immigration Reform and Control Act (IRCA) of 1986.

RELIGION
Protestant (55%), Roman Catholic (29%), nonreligious and atheist (6.8%), Jewish (3.2%), Eastern Orthodox (2.3%), Islam (1.9%), Hindu (0.2%)

MEMBERSHIP OF INTERNATIONAL ORGANIZATIONS
Colombo Plan, North Atlantic Treaty Organization (NATO), Organization of American States (OAS), Organization for Economic Cooperation and Development (OECD)

STYLE OF GOVERNMENT
Multiparty federal republic with two-chamber assembly

ECONOMIC INDICATORS: 1990
GDP (US$ billions)	5,392
GNP per capita (US$)	21,790
Annual rate of growth of GDP, 1980–1990	3.4%
Manufacturing as % of GDP	17.0%
Central government spending as % of GNP	24.0%
Merchandise exports (US$ billions)	495.3
% of GNP donated as development aid	0.21%

WELFARE INDICATORS
Infant mortality rate (per 1,000 live births)
1965	25
1990	9
Daily food supply available (calories per capita, 1989)	3,671
Population per physician (1991)	404
Teacher-pupil ratio elementary and secondary schools, 1990)	1 : 17.2

Area 3,618,770 sq mi
(9,368,900 sq km)
Population (1990) 249,224,000
Armed forces army 760,000;
navy 591,000; air force 572,000;
marines 195,000
Racial composition* White 80.3%
African-American 12.1%
Native American .08%
Asian/Pacific Islander 2.9%
*(Hispanic Americans may fall under
any of these categories.)
Currency 1 United States dollar
(US$) = 100 cents

United States of America

The national flag of the United States is popularly called the Stars and Stripes. The 13 alternating red and white stripes represent the original 13 colonies that declared themselves states in 1776. The 50 white stars on a blue background represent the 50 states of today.

CONN.	CONNECTICUT
D.C.	DISTRICT OF COLUMBIA
DEL.	DELAWARE
MD.	MARYLAND
MASS.	MASSACHUSETTS
MISS.	MISSISSIPPI
N.J.	NEW JERSEY
R.I.	RHODE ISLAND
W. VA.	WEST VIRGINIA

■ national capital
• state capital

HABITATS

The United States is a region of contrasts. In the east, the Appalachian Mountains overlook the eastern Atlantic plains. This range was formed more than 225 million years ago and has been worn down by erosion. West of the Appalachians lie the interior plains, drained by the Mississippi River and its tributaries.

The land rises to the west to form the higher Great Plains, which are bordered by the Rocky Mountains. Formed within the last 65 million years, the Rockies are higher and more rugged than the Appalachians. West of the Rockies lies a region of basins and ranges formed by upward and downward movements of blocks of land along huge faults (cracks) in the earth's crust. In the far west lie the Pacific ranges and lowlands. The country's highest mountain is in Alaska.

LAND

Area 3,618,467 sq mi (9,371,786 sq km)
Highest point Mount McKinley, 20,323 ft (6,194 m)
Lowest point Death Valley, −282 ft (−86 m)
Major features Rocky Mountains, Great Plains and central lowlands, Appalachian Mountains

WATER

Longest river Mississippi–Missouri, 3,740 mi (6,020 km)
Largest basin Mississippi–Missouri, 1,224,000 sq mi (3,222,000 sq km)
Highest average flow Mississippi, 620,000 cu ft/sec (17,500 cu m/sec)
Largest lake Superior, 32,150 sq mi (83,270 sq km)

NOTABLE THREATENED SPECIES

Mammals black-footed ferret (*Mustela nigripes*), gray bat (*Myotis grisescens*), Stephens' kangaroo rat (*Dipodomys stephensi*), red wolf (*Canis rufus*), Hawaiian monk seal (*Monachus schauinslandi*)
Birds California condor (*Gymnogyps californianus*), nene (*Branta sandvicensis*), kamao (*Myadestes myadestinus*), Oahu creeper (*Paroreomyza maculata*), Hawaiian crow (*Corvus hawaiiensis*)
Plants *Agave arizonica*; *Asimina rugelii*; American yellowwood (*Cladrastis lutea*); Cumberland rosemary (*Conradina verticillata*); white fritillary (*Fritillaria liliacea*); mountain golden heather (*Hudsonia montana*); San Clemente Island bush-mallow (*Malacothamnus clementinus*); Knowlton cactus (*Pediocactus knowltonii*); Graves's beach plum (*Prunus gravesii*); needle palm (*Rhapidophyllum hystrix*)
Others San Joaquin leopard lizard (*Gambelia silus*), pallid sturgeon (*Scaphirhynchus albus*), Devil's Hole pupfish (*Cyprinodon diabolis*), acorn pearly mussel (*Epioblasma haysiana*), little agate shells (*Achatinella spp.*), no-eyed and big-eyed wolf spider (*Adelocosa anops*), San Francisco forktail damselfly (*Ischnura gemina*)

HABITATS

Physical zones

- ice and snow
- tundra
- mountains/barren land
- forest
- grassland
- semidesert
- desert

▲ mountain peak (ft)
▼ depression (ft)
☆ climate station

The habitats of the United States range from ice and tundra in Alaska in the far northwest, to forested mountains, flat prairies, hot deserts, and subtropical swamps in the southeast. The Cascade Range contains active volcanoes, such as Mount St. Helens, which erupted in 1980. This range, together with the volcanoes in southern Alaska, form part of a huge zone known as the "Pacific ring of fire."

CLIMATE

The northeastern and midwestern states have hot summers and cold, snowy winters, while the subtropical southeast has mild winters. The eastern coast is sometimes hit by hurricanes, while tornadoes occur in the states north of the Gulf of Mexico.

The Pacific coast as far south as San Francisco has a rainy climate, but winters are mild with temperatures mostly above freezing. This area and the southeastern states both receive over 40 in (1,000 mm) of rain every year. The mountains are cooler and wetter than the dry prairies to the east and desert basins, such as Death Valley, in the Southwest. California has a Mediterranean climate. The Northwest is cooler and wetter. Alaska has polar and subarctic climates, while the tropical climate of Hawaii is moderated by cool trade winds.

TEMPERATURE AND PRECIPITATION

| | Temperature °F (°C) | | Altitude |
	January	July	ft (m)
Barrow	−17 (−27)	39 (4)	13 (7)
Portland	66 (19)	68 (20)	56 (17)
San Francisco	50 (10)	59 (15)	52 (16)
New Orleans	54 (12)	82 (28)	6 (2)
Chicago	25 (−4)	73 (23)	823 (251)

| | Precipitation in (mm) | | |
	January	July	Year
Barrow	0.2 (5)	0.9 (23)	4.3 (110)
Portland	6.1 (155)	0.5 (13)	37.2 (944)
San Francisco	4.7 (119)	0 (0)	18.7 (475)
New Orleans	4,6 (117)	6.5 (168)	53.9 (1,369)
Chicago	2.0 (51)	3.3 (84)	33.2 (843)

NATURAL HAZARDS

Hurricanes and tornadoes in South, earthquakes and volcanic eruptions in West, drought and blizzards in Midwest

CLIMATE

height above sea level of climate stations

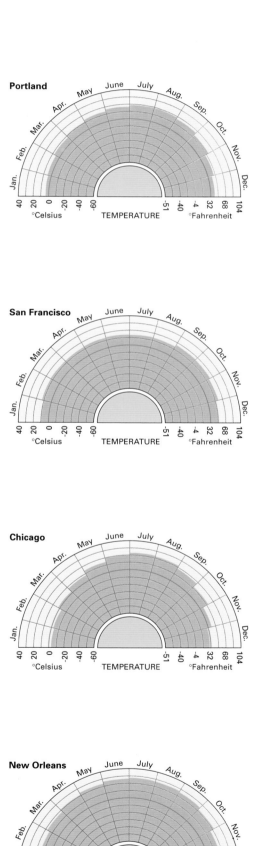

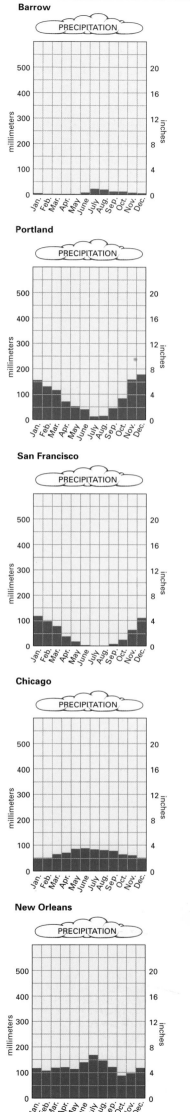

Environmental Issues

Deforestation, large-scale farming, rapid population growth, and the development of industrial cities have all contributed to massive environmental changes in the United States in the last 200 years.

One problem was identified in the 1930s, when farming in the dry prairies turned parts of the midwest into a "dust bowl." New farming methods slowed down desertification and some damaged areas were reclaimed, but soil erosion continues.

Other problems, related to urban growth and rising standards of living, include air pollution, caused by power plants, factories, and car emissions, and water pollution, caused by industrial and domestic waste

disposal. In the 1960s, people became more and more aware of the problems. Policies to protect the environment are now vigorously pursued.

POPULATION AND WEALTH

Population (in millions)	249.2
Population increase (annual population growth rate, % 1960–1990)	1.1
Energy use (gigajoules/person)	280
Real purchasing power (US$/person)	19,850

ENVIRONMENTAL INDICATORS

CO₂ emissions (mil. m.t. carbon/year)	1,000
Municipal waste (lbs/person/year)	1,680
Nuclear waste (cumulative m.t. heavy metal)	17,606
Artificial fertilizer use (lbs/acre/year)	83
Automobiles (per 1,000 population)	550
Access to safe drinking water (% population)	N/A

MAJOR ENVIRONMENTAL PROBLEMS AND SOURCES

Air pollution: locally high, in particular urban; acid rain prevalent; high greenhouse gas emissions
River/lake pollution: medium/high; *sources*: industrial, agricultural, sewage, acid deposition
Marine/coastal pollution: local; *sources*: industrial, agricultural, sewage, oil
Land pollution: locally high; *sources*: industrial, urban/ household, nuclear
Land degradation: *types*: desertification, soil erosion, salinization; *causes*: agriculture, industry
Waste disposal problems: domestic; industrial; nuclear
Resource problems: land use competition
Major events: Love Canal (1978) and Times Beach (1986), evacuated due to chemical pollution; Three Mile Island (1979), nuclear power plant accident; *Exxon Valdez* (1989), major oil spill from tanker in sea off Alaska; Dunsmuir (1991), pesticide spill during transportation

Environmental Issues

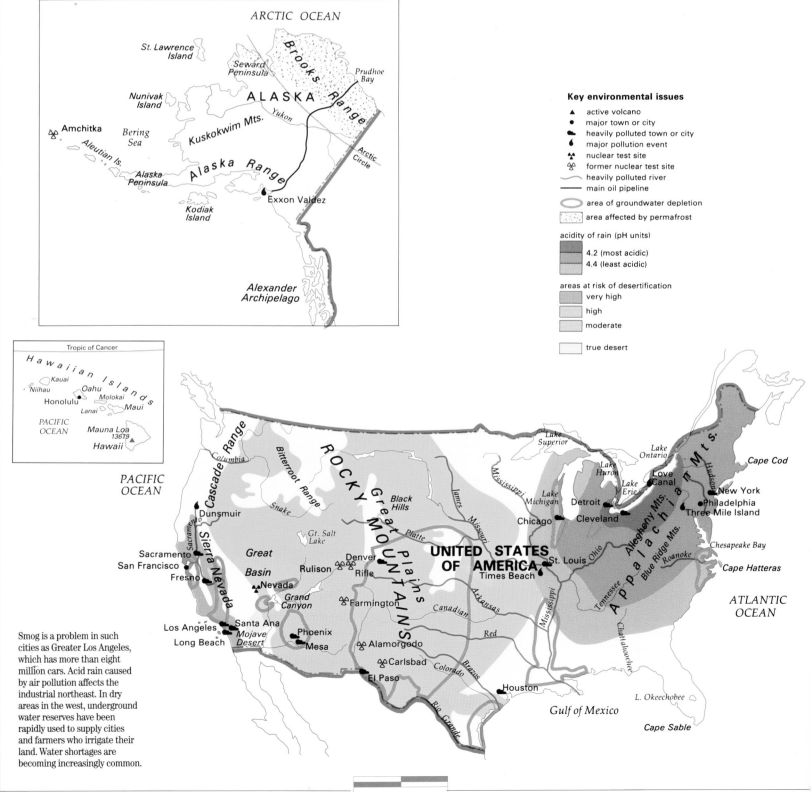

Key environmental issues

- ▲ active volcano
- ● major town or city
- heavily polluted town or city
- major pollution event
- nuclear test site
- former nuclear test site
- heavily polluted river
- main oil pipeline
- area of groundwater depletion
- area affected by permafrost

acidity of rain (pH units)
- 4.2 (most acidic)
- 4.4 (least acidic)

areas at risk of desertification
- very high
- high
- moderate
- true desert

Smog is a problem in such cities as Greater Los Angeles, which has more than eight million cars. Acid rain caused by air pollution affects the industrial northeast. In dry areas in the west, underground water reserves have been rapidly used to supply cities and farmers who irrigate their land. Water shortages are becoming increasingly common.

POPULATION

Between 1890 and 1940, the population of the United States more than doubled from 63 million to 131 million. By 1990, the population had almost doubled again, reaching 249.2 million. This population explosion was caused partly by natural growth, and partly by massive immigration of people from most parts of the world.

The twentieth century also saw another change, from a mainly rural society to an urban one. In 1900, more than 40 percent of the people lived on farms. By 1991, the percentage had fallen to 1.9. Another trend has been the growth of huge city suburbs, occupied by middle-class people who moved out of the decaying city centers, which were often occupied by poorer ethnic minorities. Some inner cities are being restored, and young people, especially, are moving in.

POPULATION

Total population of region (in millions)	249.2
Population density (persons per sq mi)	70
Population change (average annual percent 1960–1990)	
Urban	+1.3
Rural	+0.6

URBAN POPULATION

As percentage of total population	
1960	70.0
1990	74.0
Percentage in cities of more than 1 million	49.5

TEN LARGEST CITIES

	Population
New York	7,323,000
Los Angeles	3,485,000
Chicago	2,784,000
Houston	1,631,000
Philadelphia	1,586,000
San Diego	1,111,000
Detroit	1,028,000
Dallas	1,007,000
Phoenix	983,000
San Antonio	936,000

POPULATION

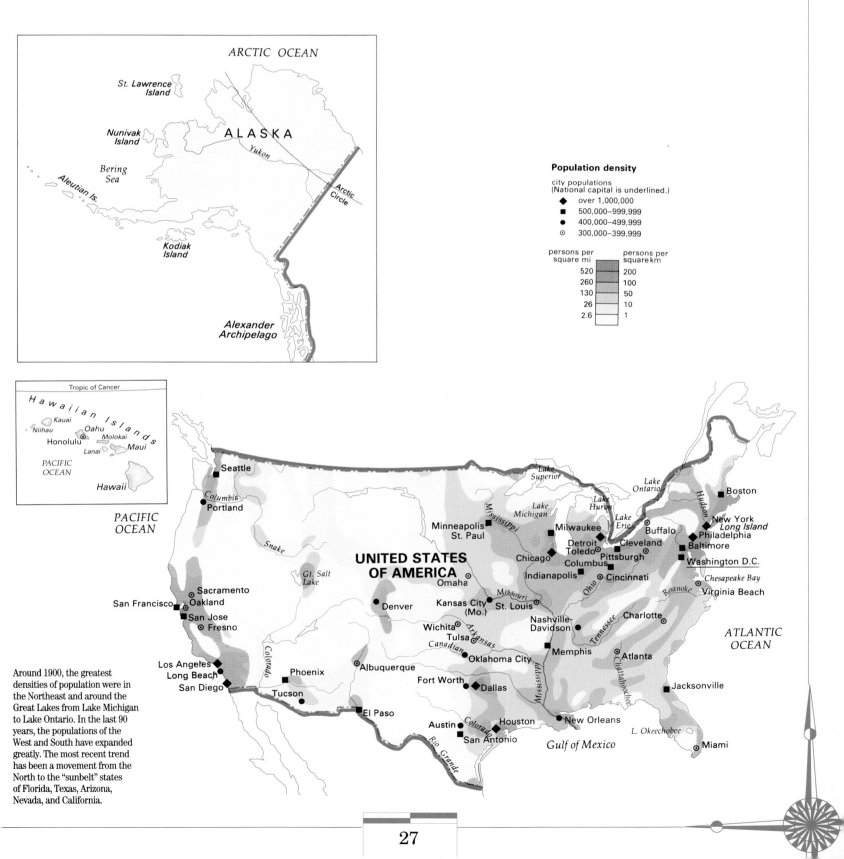

Population density

city populations
(National capital is underlined.)
◆ over 1,000,000
■ 500,000–999,999
● 400,000–499,999
⊙ 300,000–399,999

persons per square mi	persons per square km
520	200
260	100
130	50
26	10
2.6	1

Around 1900, the greatest densities of population were in the Northeast and around the Great Lakes from Lake Michigan to Lake Ontario. In the last 90 years, the populations of the West and South have expanded greatly. The most recent trend has been a movement from the North to the "sunbelt" states of Florida, Texas, Arizona, Nevada, and California.

INDUSTRY

The United States is the world's leading industrial nation. It has huge energy resources, including coal, oil, and natural gas. Its mineral resources include most of the materials needed by modern industry. The United States also has rich human resources: a skilled and mobile workforce.

In the early twentieth century, the country developed heavy industries, such as iron and steel plants. They supplied the materials for car and machinery manufacturers. In the last 40 years, the emphasis has shifted to light and service industries.

Despite increasing competition from Japan and other Pacific nations, the United States remains a leader in high technology, including microelectronics industries. With its highly developed economy, the United States is also the world's leading trading nation.

INDUSTRIAL OUTPUT (US$ billion)

Total	Mining	Manufacturing	Average annual change since 1960
1,249.5	86.4	1,032.9	+2.1%

INDUSTRIAL WORKERS (millions)
(Figures in parentheses are percentages of total labor force.)

Total	Mining	Manufacturing	Construction
32.96	0.85 (0.7%)	23.1 (19%)	8.0 (6.6%)

MAJOR PRODUCTS (Figures in parentheses are percentages of total world production.)

Energy and minerals	Output	Change since 1960
Coal (mil. m.t.)	897.6 (19.2%)	+127%
Oil (mil. barrels)	3,173.9 (14%)	+24%
Natural gas (billion cu meters)	488.5 (25.4%)	+36%
Copper (mil. m.t.)	1.86 (13.7%)	+28%
Lead (mil. m.t.)	1.05 (10.3%)	+72%

Manufactures		
Commercial jet aircraft	2,251 (84.5%)*	No data
Domestic/catering ovens, incl. microwaves (mil.)	20.5 (21.7%)	No data
Cement (mil. m.t.)	67.4 (7%)	+20%
Steel (mil. m.t.)	90.1 (12%)	-1%
Automobiles (mil.)	8.0 (25%)	+20%
Televisions (mil.)	13.6 (16%)	+133%
Synthetic rubber (mil. m.t.)	2.05 (23%)	-19%
Nitrogenous fertilizers (mil. m.t.)	9.5 (13%)	+4%
Semiconductors (US$ billion)	22.3 (40%)	N/A

N/A means production had not begun in 1960.

* Applies only to noncommunist world in 1989

INDUSTRY

Resources and industry

- ◆ industrial center
- ○ major port
- ● other town
- —— major road
- —— major railroad

mineral resources and fossil fuels

- • iron and other ferroalloy metal ores
- ● other metal ores
- ■ nonmetallic minerals
- coal
- copper
- iron ore
- lignite (brown coal)
- natural gas
- oil

Natural resources occur in most parts of the country. For example, major oil-producing states include Texas, Alaska in the North, and Louisiana. California in the West is a major manufacturing state, with high-technology industries in "Silicon Valley," near San Jose. New York, Illinois, Texas, Michigan, Pennsylvania, and New Jersey are other leading manufacturing states.

AGRICULTURE

Although farming accounts for only about 2 percent of the country's gross national product (the value of all goods and services produced), the United States is the world's leading agricultural producer. It not only supplies all its own needs, but it is also the world's leading exporter of agricultural products. For example, it dominates the world's grain markets, especially in wheat.

Farming is highly mechanized, with most farmers using scientific breeding, fertilizers, and pest-control techniques. Yields are generally high. The great variety of land and climatic types means that the country produces a wide range of products. The United States is a world leader in beef, raised largely on western ranches, citrus fruits, corn, and soybeans. It is also a major producer of cotton, dairy and poultry products, pork, tobacco, and vegetables.

LAND (million acres)

Total	Agricultural	Arable	Forest/woodland
2,265 (100%)	1,064 (47%)	464 (20%)	654 (29%)

FARMERS

3.1 million people employed in agriculture (3% of workforce)
150 acres of arable land per person employed in agriculture

MAJOR CROPS

	Area mil. acres	Yield 100lbs/acre	Production mil. m.t.	Change since 1963
Corn	59.3	66.9	179.6 (39)	+88%
Soybeans	57	20.2	52.3 (52)	+168%
Wheat	55.8	22.5	57.4 (11)	+74%
Sorghum	10.6	39	18.8 (30)	+35%
Barley	10.1	25.2	11.5 (6)	+33%
Cotton	10.1	7	3.2 (19)	−1%
Vegetables	—	—	28.0 (7)	+46%
Fruit	—	—	25.7 (8)	+50%

MAJOR LIVESTOCK

	Number in mil.	Production mil. m.t.	Change since 1963
Cattle	102.0 (8)	—	−2%
Pigs	51.2 (6)	—	−11%
Milk	—	64.7 (14)	+13%
Fish catch	—	5.7 (6)	—

FOOD SECURITY (grain exports minus imports)

mil. m.t.	% domestic production	% world trade
+74.2	24	34

Numbers in parentheses are percentages of world total.

AGRICULTURE

Agricultural zones

- arable
- fruits and vegetables
- grazing
- forest with arable and pasture
- nonagricultural land

▲ mountain peak (ft)
▼ depression (ft)

The most extensive arable farming regions are in the interior plains. The main crops are grain, especially corn and wheat. To the west, the plains are drier, and they are used for grazing on ranches. Fruit and vegetable-growing regions are in the Southwest, the Southeast (especially Florida), and small areas in the Northeast.

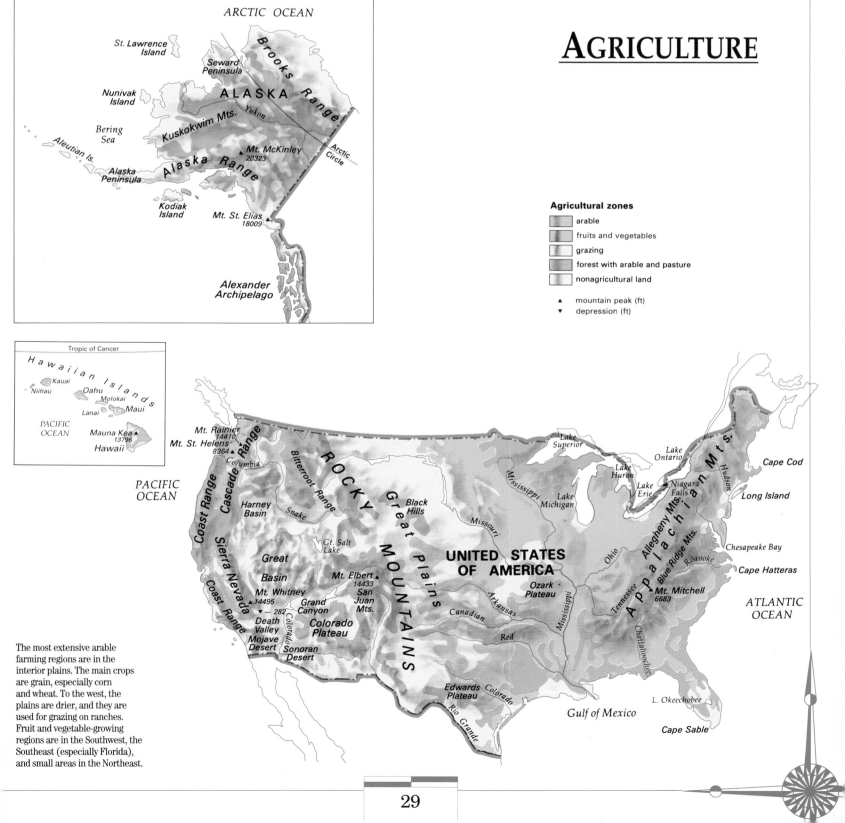

MEXICO, CENTRAL AMERICA, AND THE CARIBBEAN

Mexico and Central America together form a land bridge that extends to the northwest tip of South America. The region also includes 13 independent island nations in the Caribbean, two U.S. territories, and a number of European dependencies. Rugged scenery, active volcanoes, and subtropical and tropical climates are the main characteristics of the region.

The first inhabitants of the region were the Native Americans, who founded such cultures as the Mayan and Aztec empires. Spain conquered the region in the sixteenth century, and Spanish culture dominates to this day. Other elements in this complex cultural mix are African Americans, other Europeans, and some Asians, who were introduced as laborers.

The islands of the Greater Antilles (Cuba, Jamaica, Hispaniola, and Puerto Rico) formed a single landmass about 100 million years ago. Mexico and Central America became joined to South America between 5 million and 2 million years ago. The region was broken up by earth movements.

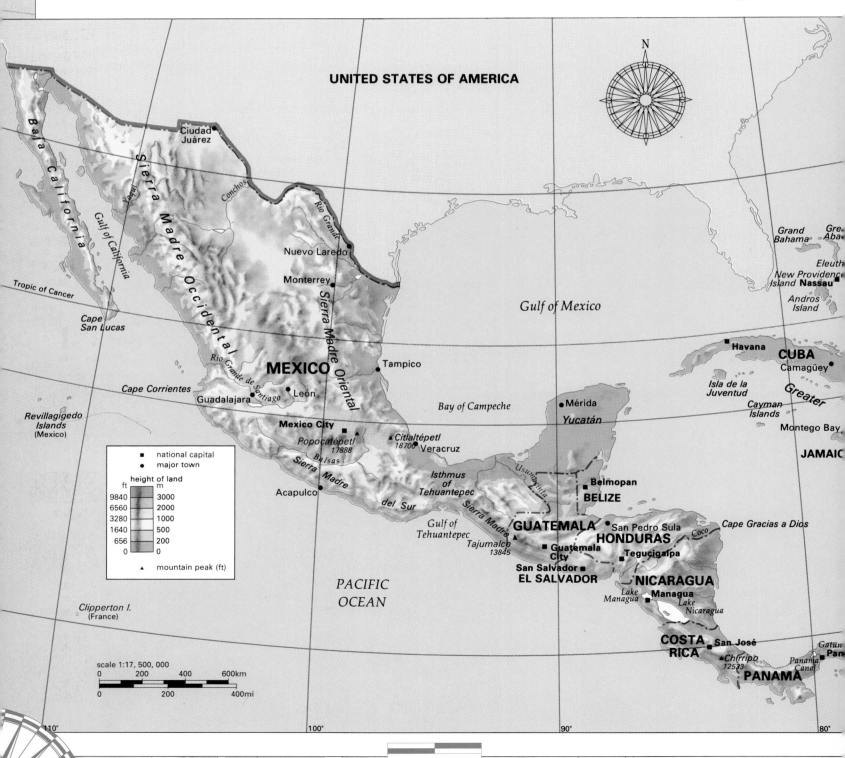

UNITED STATES OF AMERICA

N

Ciudad Juárez

Sierra Madre Occidental

Conchos

Yaqui

Baja California

Gulf of California

Tropic of Cancer

Cape San Lucas

Nuevo Laredo

Monterrey

Sierra Madre Oriental

Rio Grande

Gulf of Mexico

Grand Bahama

Gre Aba

Eleuth New Providence Island Nassau

Andros Island

Rio Grande de Santiago

MEXICO

Tampico

Havana

CUBA
Camagüey

Cape Corrientes

Guadalajara

León

Bay of Campeche

Mérida

Yucatán

Isla de la Juventud

Cayman Islands

Greater

Revillagigedo Islands
(Mexico)

Mexico City

Popocatépetl
17888

Citlaltépetl
18700

Veracruz

Montego Bay

JAMAIC

Sierra Madre

Balsas

Acapulco

Isthmus of Tehuantepec

Usumacinta

Belmopan

BELIZE

national capital
major town

height of land

ft	m
9840	3000
6560	2000
3280	1000
1640	500
656	200
0	0

▲ mountain peak (ft)

Sierra Madre del Sur

Gulf of Tehuantepec

Tajumulco
13845

GUATEMALA

Guatemala City

San Pedro Sula

HONDURAS

Coco

Cape Gracias a Dios

Tegucigalpa

San Salvador

EL SALVADOR

NICARAGUA

Lake Managua

Managua

Lake Nicaragua

PACIFIC OCEAN

Clipperton I.
(France)

COSTA RICA

San José

Chirripó
12533

Gatún

Pan

Panama Canal

PANAMA

scale 1:17, 500, 000

0   200   400   600km

0   200   400mi

110°   100°   90°   80°

30

THE POLITICAL AND CULTURAL WORLD

Although geographically part of North America, most of the region belongs culturally to Latin America. Spanish is the chief language, and Roman Catholicism the main religion, though some Native Americans and African Americans combine the Christian faith with some of their own traditional beliefs.

In the past the region has suffered much instability. Civilian governments have been overthrown by military groups, while brutal dictatorships and civil war have hampered the region's progress. Cuba is the only communist regime. Its policies were unaffected by the changes in its former ally, the Soviet Union.

COUNTRIES IN THE REGION

Antigua and Barbuda, Bahamas, Barbados, Belize, Costa Rica, Cuba, Dominica, Dominican Republic, El Salvador, Grenada, Guatemala, Haiti, Honduras, Jamaica, Mexico, Nicaragua, Panama, St. Kitts-Nevis, St. Lucia, St. Vincent and the Grenadines, Trinidad and Tobago

Dependencies of other states Anguilla, British Virgin Islands, Cayman Islands, Montserrat, Turks and Caicos Islands (U.K.); Aruba, Netherlands Antilles (Netherlands); Guadeloupe, Martinique (France); Puerto Rico, U.S. Virgin Islands (U.S.A.)

LANGUAGE

Countries with one official language
English: Antigua and Barbuda, Bahamas, Barbados, Belize, Dominica, Grenada, Jamaica, St. Kitts-Nevis, St. Lucia, St. Vincent and the Grenadines, Trinidad and Tobago
Spanish: Costa Rica, Cuba, Dominican Republic, El Salvador, Guatemala, Honduras, Mexico, Nicaragua, Panama
Countries with two official languages Creole, French: Haiti

Other languages spoken in the region include Carib, Nahuatl, and other indigenous languages; Creoles and French patois; and Hindi (Trinidad and Tobago).

RELIGION

Countries with one major religion
Antigua and Barbuda (P); Costa Rica, Cuba, Dominica, Dominican Republic, El Salvador, Honduras, Mexico, Nicaragua (RC)
Countries with more than one major religion
Bahamas, Barbados, Belize, Grenada, Jamaica, St. Kitts-Nevis, St. Lucia, St. Vincent and the Grenadines (P, RC); Haiti (P, RC, V); Trinidad and Tobago (H, I, P, RC)

Key: H-Hindu, I-Islam, P-Protestant, RC-Roman Catholic, V-Voodoo

STYLES OF GOVERNMENT

Republics Costa Rica, Cuba, Dominica, Dominican Republic, El Salvador, Guatemala, Haiti, Honduras, Mexico, Nicaragua, Panama, Trinidad and Tobago
Monarchies All other countries of the region
Multiparty states All countries except Cuba, Haiti
One-party states Cuba, Haiti
Military influence Guatemala, Haiti, Honduras

ATLANTIC OCEAN

Bermuda (U.K.)

Tropic of Cancer

20°

BAHAMAS
Long Island
Caicos Islands
lins
nd
Turks Islands
Great Inagua
Hispaniola
Puerto Rico
Virgin Islands
Barbuda
ANTIGUA AND BARBUDA
Antigua
Guantánamo
DOMINICAN REPUBLIC
San Juan
Basseterre
ST. KITTS-NEVIS
St. John's
Guadeloupe
ntiago
HAITI
Santo Domingo
Montserrat
DOMINICA
Cuba
Port-au-Prince
Roseau
Jacmel
Martinique
ton
Antilles
ST. LUCIA
Castries
BARBADOS
Bridgetown
ST. VINCENT AND THE GRENADINES
Kingstown
Caribbean Sea
St. Georges
GRENADA
Lesser Antilles
Tobago
10°N
Aruba
Curaçao
Bonaire
Port of Spain
TRINIDAD AND TOBAGO
Trinidad

VENEZUELA

GUYANA

COLOMBIA

BRAZIL

70°   60°W

Antigua and Barbuda
Area 171 sq mi (442 sq km)

Bahamas
Area 5,382 sq mi (13,939 sq km)

Barbados
Area 166 sq mi (439 sq km)

Belize
Area 8,867 sq mi (22,965 sq km)

Costa Rica
Area 19,730 sq mi (551,100 sq km)

Cuba
Area 42,804 sq mi (110,861 sq km)

Dominica
Area 290 sq mi (750 sq km)

Dominican Republic
Area 18,704 sq mi (48,443 sq km)

El Salvador
Area 8,124 sq mi (21,041 sq km)

Grenada
Area 133 sq mi (345 sq km)

Guatemala
Area 42,042 sq mi (108,889 sq km)

Haiti
Area 10,579 sq mi (27,400 sq km)

Honduras
Area 43,277 sq mi (112,088 sq km)

Jamaica
Area 4,244 sq mi (10,991 sq km)

Mexico
Area 756,066 sq mi (1,958,201 sq km)

Nicaragua
Area 46,467 sq mi (120,349 sq km)

Panama
Area 29,762 sq mi (77,082 sq km)

St. Kitts-Nevis
Area 104 sq mi (269 sq km)

St. Lucia
Area 238 sq mi (617 sq km)

St. Vincent and the Grenadines
Area 150 sq mi (389 sq km)

Trinidad and Tobago
Area 1,980 sq mi (5,128 sq km)

HABITATS

The mainland contains a chain of volcanic highlands that form part of the Pacific "ring of fire." Volcanic eruptions and earthquakes are common. Tropical rain forest and heavy rains occur in the northeast and in the islands, while the northwest is desert or semidesert.

LAND

Area 1,056,183 sq mi (2,735,515 sq km)
Highest point Citlaltépetl, 18,700 ft (5,699 m)
Lowest point Lake Enriquillo, Dominican Republic, −144 ft (−44 m)
Major features volcanic mountain chain and Mexican plateau on isthmus, island chain of the West Indies

WATER

Longest river Conchos–Rio Grande, 1,300 mi (2,100 km)
Largest basin Rio Grande (part), 172,000 sq mi (445,000 sq km)
Highest average flow Colorado, 3,700 cu ft/sec (104 cu m/sec), at head of Gulf of California
Largest lake Nicaragua, 3,100 sq mi (8,029 sq km)

NOTABLE THREATENED SPECIES

Mammals Haitian solenodon (*Solenodon paradoxus*), Central American squirrel monkey (*Saimiri oerstedi*), volcano rabbit (*Romerolagus diazi*), Jamaican hutia (*Geocapromys brownii*), Gulf of California porpoise (*Phocoena sinus*)
Birds St. Vincent amazon (*Amazona guildingii*), highland guan (*Penelopina nigra*), resplendent quetzal (*Pharomachrus mocinno*), ocellated turkey (*Agriocharis ocellata*), cahow (*Procellaria cahow*)
Plants *Ariocarpus agavoides*; *Auerodendron glaucescens*; *Carpodiptera mirabilis*; *Eupatorium chalceorithales*; *Freziera forerorum*; *Guzmania condensata*; *Ipomoea villifera*; *Lincania retifolia*; *Lycaste suaveolens*; *Streblacanthus parviflorus*
Others Kemp's ridley turtle (*Lepidochelys kempii*), Jamaican ground iguana (*Cyclura collei*), golden toad (*Bufo periglenes*)

CLIMATE

The climates of Mexico and Central America vary from hot, humid coastlands to cool, temperate plateaus, to cold mountain areas. Northern Mexico has deserts, but the rainfall increases in the south. The tropical Caribbean islands are warm throughout the year.

TEMPERATURE AND PRECIPITATION

	Temperature °F (°C) January	July	Altitude ft	(m)
Guayamas	64 (18)	88 (31)	19	(6)
Zacatecas	50 (10)	57 (14)	8,567	(2,612)
Mexico City	54 (12)	64 (18)	7,574	(2,309)
Havana	72 (22)	82 (28)	79	(24)
Bluefields	77 (25)	79 (26)	39	(12)
Seawell	77 (25)	81 (27)	184	(56)

	Precipitation in (mm) January	July		Year
Guayamas	0.2 (5)	1.7 (43)		9.9 (252)
Zacatecas	0.3 (7)	2.7 (69)		12.3 (313)
Mexico City	0.5 (13)	6.7 (170)		28.6 (726)
Havana	2.8 (71)	4.9 (125)		45.9 (1,167)
Bluefields	10.4 (264)	29.4 (746)		172.0 (4,370)
Seawell	2.7 (68)	5.6 (141)		59.1 (1,273)

World's greatest recorded rainfall in 5 minutes, 12 in (305 mm) at Portobello in northern Panama

NATURAL HAZARDS

Earthquakes, landslides, volcanic eruptions, hurricanes

Physical zones

- mountains/barren land
- forest
- grassland
- semidesert
- desert

▲ mountain peak (ft)
☀ climate station

THE POLITICAL WORLD

The region contains 21 independent nations and 11 dependencies. They include some of the world's oldest European colonies. Spanish settlement began on Hispaniola as early as 1493. Later colonizers included the British, Dutch, and French. Generally the passage from colonialism to independence has been peaceful.

■ national capital

HABITATS

Northern Mexico is arid. In central Mexico, two ranges enclose a central, well-watered plateau. Central America has high central ranges, bordered in the east by broad coastal plains.

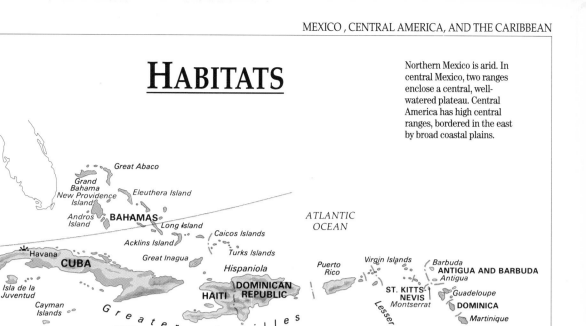

CLIMATE

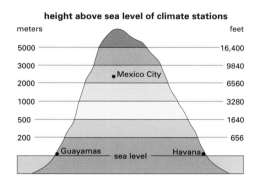

height above sea level of climate stations

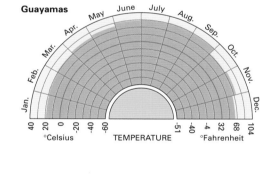

Guayamas

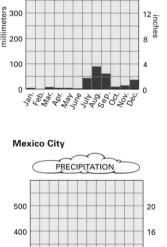

Guayamas

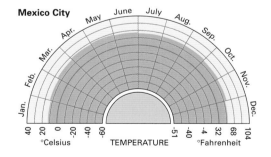

Mexico City

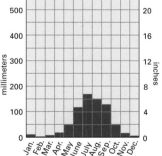

Mexico City

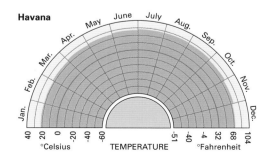

Havana

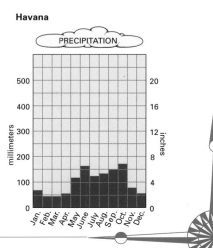

Havana

ENVIRONMENTAL ISSUES

Two key concerns are widespread soil degradation and deforestation in the mountains of mainland Central America and some of the high islands.

Deforestation has in turn caused flooding and the silting of rivers. Other problems include severe air pollution in urban areas, the heavy impact of tourism on coastlines and coral reefs, oil contamination in the Caribbean Sea, and disturbance to the ecology of the seas through overfishing. The main causes are rapid population growth and the poverty of the people, which put excess pressure on resources.

At present rates of loss, only 5 percent of the region's original rain forest will remain by the year 2010. Where forests have been cleared, erosion and desertification are serious problems.

Rapidly growing urban populations put enormous pressure on the environment, both locally and regionally. Mexico City alone has over 18 million inhabitants. As rural migrants flock to the cities, more and more food is demanded from already overused farmland, while pollution problems are becoming worse.

POPULATION AND WEALTH

	Highest	Middle	Lowest
Population (in millions)	88.6 (Mexico)	5.1 (Honduras)	0.3 (Barbados)
Population increase (annual population growth rate, % 1960–1990)	3.3 (Honduras)	2.5 (Panama)	0.3 (Barbados)
Energy use (gigajoules/person)	169 (Trinidad & T)	17 (Panama)	1 (Haiti)
Real purchasing power (US$/person)	6,020 (Barbados)	3,790 (Panama)	970 (Haiti)

ENVIRONMENTAL INDICATORS

	Highest	Middle	Lowest
CO_2 emissions (mil. m.t. carbon/year)	78 (Mexico)	3.3 (Panama)	0.25 (Barbados)
Deforestation ('000s acres/year 1980s)	1,520 (Mexico)	507 (Honduras)	0.2 (Cuba)
Artificial fertilizer use (lbs/acre/year)	159.6 (Costa Rica)	60 (Guatemala)	2.6 (Haiti)
Automobiles (per 1,000 population)	203 (Trinidad & T)	43 (Panama)	5 (Haiti)
Access to safe drinking water (% population)	100 (Barbados)	71 (Mexico)	39 (El Salvador)

MAJOR ENVIRONMENTAL PROBLEMS AND SOURCES

Air pollution: high in urban areas
Land degradation: *types*: soil erosion, deforestation; *causes*: agriculture, population pressure
Resource problems: inadequate drinking water and sanitation; coastal flooding
Population problems: population explosion; inadequate health facilities; tourism
Major event: Ixtoc 1 (1979), oil rig fire and leak; Guadalajara (1992), series of gas explosions

Key environmental issues

- major town or city
- heavily polluted town or city
- major pollution event
- major natural disaster
- active volcano
- heavily polluted river

remaining tropical rain forest
area of deforestation

areas at risk of desertification
- very high
- high
- moderate

POPULATION

Central America and the Caribbean islands were home to people of a wide range of cultures who lived there for at least 12,000 years before Europeans discovered what they called the New World in the late fifteenth century. After this, waves of Europeans invaded the lands, with dreadful results for the native people. The Spanish seized control of Mexico and the Central American neck of land, and their language, religion, and customs prevail there today.

The scattered islands of the Caribbean were colonized by a number of European nations, but the main culture is African, deriving from the millions of slaves shipped there to work in the sugar plantations. People from Asia and Europe also were taken as laborers, making for a great cultural mix.

Until recently the population was mainly rural, but the decline in traditional farming (and the plantation system) has been the cause of massive movement to the cities. The growth of cities has been rapid and unplanned, leaving millions of people without homes or jobs.

POPULATION

Total population of region (in millions)	152.8
Population density (persons per sq mi)	23.6
Population change (average annual percent 1960–1990) Urban	+4.1
Rural	+0.9

URBAN POPULATION

As percentage of total population	
1960	50.1
1990	71.3
Percentage in cities of more than 1 million	25.9

TEN LARGEST CITIES

	Country	Population
Mexico City †	Mexico	18,748,000
Guadalajara	Mexico	2,587,000
Monterrey	Mexico	2,335,000
Havana †	Cuba	2,059,000
Guatemala City †	Guatemala	2,000,000
San Juan †	Puerto Rico	1,816,000
Santo Domingo †	Dominican Republic	1,313,000
Puebla	Mexico	1,218,000
Port-au-Prince †	Haiti	1,144,000
San Salvador †	El Salvador	973,000

† *denotes national capital*

Population density

city populations
(National capital is underlined.)
- ◆ over 5,000,000
- ■ 1,000,000–5,000,000
- ● 500,000–999,999
- ⊙ 250,000–499,999
- × national capital less than 250,000

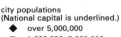

persons per square mi	persons per square km
520	200
260	100
130	50
26	10
2.6	1

ENVIRONMENTAL ISSUES

Earthquakes, such as the one that struck Mexico City in 1985, volcanic eruptions, and hurricanes on the islands and mainland coasts are natural hazards in the region.

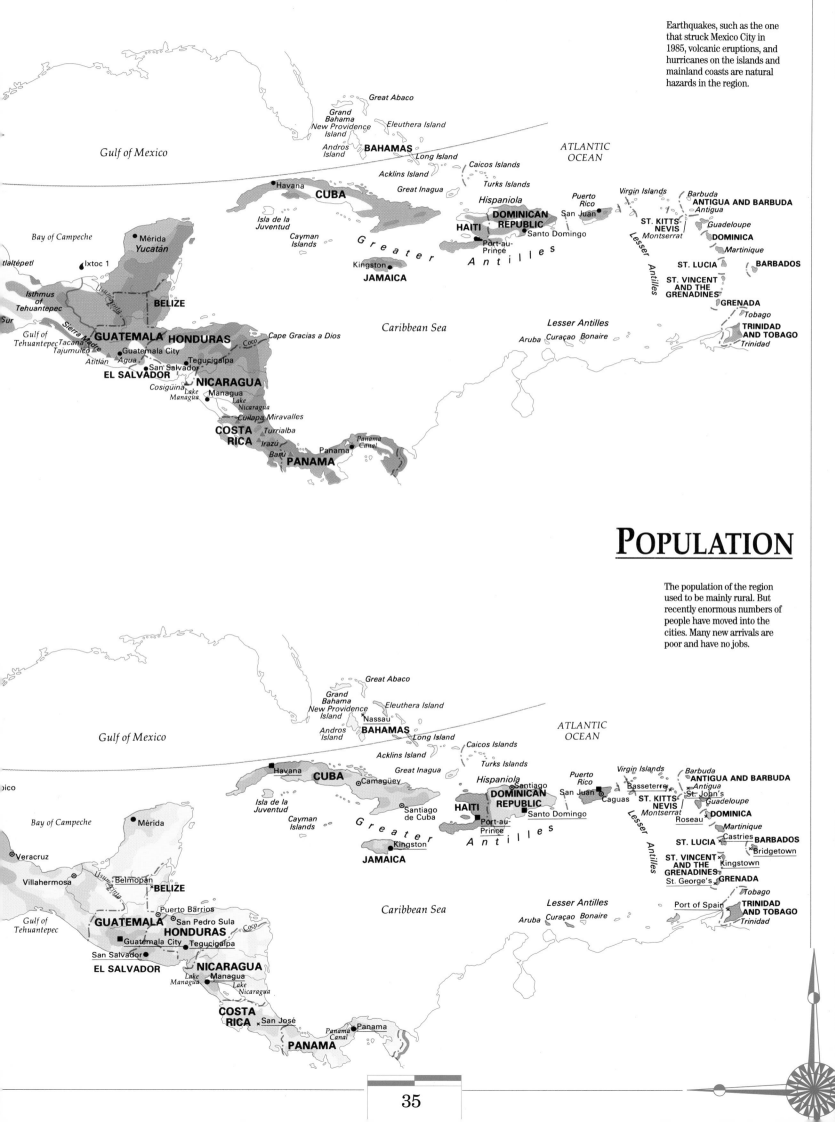

POPULATION

The population of the region used to be mainly rural. But recently enormous numbers of people have moved into the cities. Many new arrivals are poor and have no jobs.

INDUSTRY

The region consists of developing countries that have plenty of resources but lack the money and skilled workers to create truly industrialized economies. Mexico has resources of silver, gold, copper, and oil, and exports crude oil in large quantities. Nicaragua, Guatemala, and Honduras have fewer mineral resources, though Cuba has large nickel reserves and also deposits of limestone, chromium, copper, and iron.

Trinidad and Tobago exports oil and processes chemicals, fertilizers, and machinery. As in many other countries in the Caribbean, a major industry is tourism. On islands where tourism has not developed widely, agriculture is the main industry. Belize and El Salvador, on the mainland, have small-scale industries that produce goods for the local market. Costa Rica's industries are growing, with such products as cement, clothes, cosmetics, fertilizers, foods, textiles, and medicines. Panama, in the far south, has untapped copper reserves and small local industries, but the Panama Canal provides income for the country.

INDUSTRIAL OUTPUT (US$ billion)

Total	Mining	Manufacturing	Average annual change since 1960
101.3	9.9	82.2	+5.3%

INDUSTRIAL WORKERS (millions)
(Figures in parentheses are percentages of total labor force.)

Total	Mining	Manufacturing	Construction
9.4	0.7 (1.4%)	6.06 (12.0%)	2.62 (5.2%)

MAJOR PRODUCTS (Figures in parentheses are percentages of world production.)

Energy and minerals	Output	Change since 1960
Oil (mil. barrels)	1097.2 (4.8%)	+444%
Bauxite (mil. m.t.)	7.5 (7.7%)	-56.3%
Antimony (1,000 m.t.)	3.7 (5.2%)	-18.9%
Silver (1,000 m.t.)	2.4 (12.4%)	+200%
Sulfur (mil. m.t.)	2.1 (14.3%)	+33%
Fluorspar (1,000 m.t.)	756 (16.7%)	No data

Manufactures		
Residual fuel oil (mil. m.t.)	39.7 (5.4%)	No data
Cement (mil. m.t.)	33.7 (3.1%)	+992%
Steel (mil. m.t.)	7.6 (1.1%)	+406%
Fertilizer distributors (1,000)	176 (45.8%)	N/A
Rubber footwear (mil. pairs)	38.8 (4.3%)	N/A
Soft drinks (mil. gallons)	1,482 (9.8%)	N/A

N/A means production had not begun in 1960.

Resources and industry

- ◆ industrial center
- ○ major port
- ● other town
- —— major road
- —— major railroad

mineral resources and fossil fuels
- ● iron and other ferroalloy metal ores
- ● other metal ores
- ■ nonmetallic minerals

- bauxite
- gold
- natural gas
- nickel
- oil
- silver

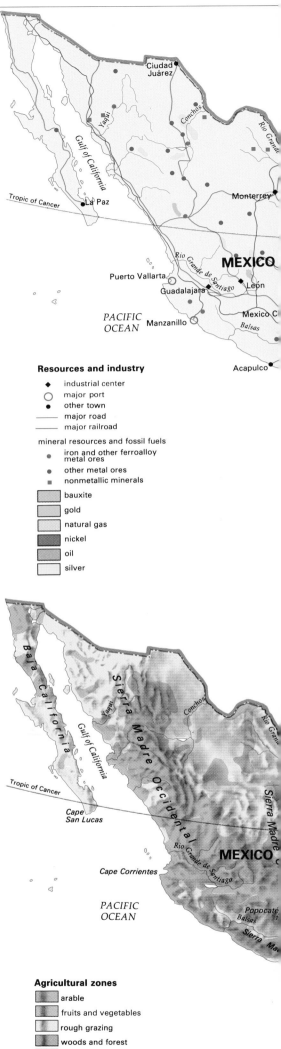

AGRICULTURE

Agriculture plays an important part in the region's economy. Root crops were grown in the region 6,000 years ago. Large-scale commercial farming of crops on plantations and livestock on huge ranches was introduced by the Europeans. There is production of cash crops such as sugar, bananas, and coffee, while the cattle raised on ranches provide meat for consumers in the United States.

Fishing in the Caribbean islands has seen a growth in demand since tourism became a major industry. The wet, warm climate of the region allows a range of tropical crops to be cultivated. Rough pastures in drier areas support cattle ranching. Some groups of people still carry out traditional subsistence farming. Using hand tools, they cultivate corn, beans, and squash as their staple crops and also raise pigs and poultry as livestock. Subsistence farmers may also grow sorghum (a grain), potatoes or other root crops, and tropical fruits. In some parts of Cuba, Mexico, and Panama where there is high rainfall or irrigation, rice is the staple grain.

LAND (million acres)

Total	Agricultural	Arable	Forest/woodland
655 (100%)	328 (50%)	85 (13%)	164 (25%)

FARMERS

16.8 million employed in agriculture (33% of workforce)
5 acres of arable land per person employed in agriculture

MAJOR CROPS

	Area mil. acres	Yield 100lbs/acre	Production mil. m.t.	Change since 1963
Corn	21.7	14.9	14.6 (3)	+59%
Sugarcane	6.2	536	149.9 (16)	+41%
Dry beans	5.9	5.1	1.4 (10)	+33%
Sorghum	5.7	26.3	6.8 (11)	+547%
Bananas	—	—	8.2 (12)	+47%

MAJOR LIVESTOCK

	Number in mil.	Production mil. m.t.	Change since 1963
Cattle	52.5 (4)	—	+45%
Pigs	26.1 (1)	—	+70%
Sheep/goats	20.6 (1)	—	+12%
Milk	—	11.0 (2)	+166%
Fish catch	—	2.0 (2)	—

FOOD SECURITY (grain exports minus imports)

mil. m.t.	% domestic production	% world trade
−8.9	30	4

Numbers in parentheses are percentages of world total.

Agricultural zones

- arable
- fruits and vegetables
- rough grazing
- woods and forest
- nonagricultural land

- ▲ mountain peak (ft)

INDUSTRY

Mexico is a major oil producer and the world's leading silver producer. It also has many other valuable deposits. Several island nations have bauxite deposits.

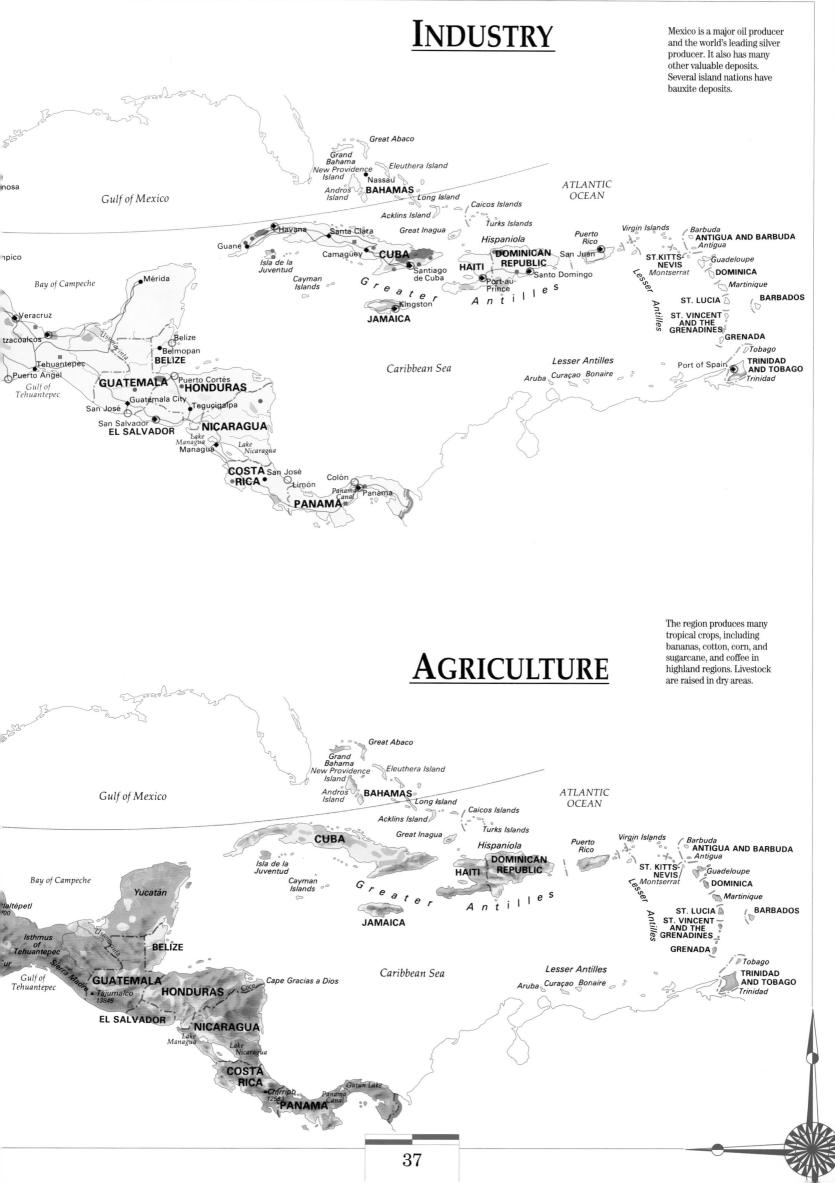

Industry map labels:

Great Abaco
Grand Bahama
New Providence Island
Eleuthera Island
Nassau
Andros Island
BAHAMAS
Long Island
Caicos Islands
Acklins Island
Turks Islands
ATLANTIC OCEAN

Gulf of Mexico

Havana
Santa Clara
Great Inagua
Hispaniola
Puerto Rico
Virgin Islands
Barbuda
ANTIGUA AND BARBUDA
Antigua

Guane
Camagüey
CUBA
DOMINICAN REPUBLIC
San Juan
ST.KITTS-NEVIS
Montserrat
Guadeloupe
DOMINICA

Mérida
Bay of Campeche
Isla de la Juventud
Santiago de Cuba
HAITI
Santo Domingo
Martinique
ST. LUCIA
BARBADOS

Veracruz
Cayman Islands
Port-au-Prince
ST. VINCENT AND THE GRENADINES

tzacoalcos
Greater Antilles
Kingston
GRENADA
Tobago

Usumacinta
Belize
JAMAICA
Lesser Antilles
Port of Spain
TRINIDAD AND TOBAGO
Trinidad

Tehuantepec
Belmopan
BELIZE
Caribbean Sea
Lesser Antilles
Aruba *Curaçao* *Bonaire*

Puerto Ángel
Gulf of Tehuantepec
Puerto Cortés
GUATEMALA
HONDURAS

San José
Guatemala City
Tegucigalpa

San Salvador
NICARAGUA
EL SALVADOR
Lake Managua
Managua
Lake Nicaragua

COSTA RICA
San José
Colón
Limón
Panama Canal
Panama
PANAMA

AGRICULTURE

The region produces many tropical crops, including bananas, cotton, corn, and sugarcane, and coffee in highland regions. Livestock are raised in dry areas.

Agriculture map labels:

Great Abaco
Grand Bahama
New Providence Island
Eleuthera Island
Andros Island
BAHAMAS
Long Island
Caicos Islands
Acklins Island
Turks Islands
ATLANTIC OCEAN

Gulf of Mexico

CUBA
Great Inagua
Hispaniola
Puerto Rico
Virgin Islands
Barbuda
ANTIGUA AND BARBUDA
Antigua

Bay of Campeche
Yucatán
Isla de la Juventud
DOMINICAN REPUBLIC
ST. KITTS-NEVIS
Montserrat
Guadeloupe
DOMINICA

laltépetl
Cayman Islands
HAITI
Martinique

Isthmus of Tehuantepec
Usumacinta
Greater Antilles
ST. LUCIA
BARBADOS

ur
Sierra Madre
BELIZE
JAMAICA
ST. VINCENT AND THE GRENADINES

Gulf of Tehuantepec
GUATEMALA
Tajumulco 13845
HONDURAS
Coco
Cape Gracias a Dios
GRENADA
Tobago

EL SALVADOR
NICARAGUA
Caribbean Sea
Lesser Antilles
TRINIDAD AND TOBAGO
Trinidad

Lake Managua
Lake Nicaragua
Lesser Antilles
Aruba *Curaçao* *Bonaire*

COSTA RICA
Chirripó 12583
Panama Canal
Gatún Lake
PANAMA

SOUTH AMERICA

South America, the fourth largest continent, contains the Andes, the world's longest unbroken mountain range, and the mighty Amazon River, which discharges one-fifth of the world's flow of fresh water into the sea.

Extending from the equatorial lands in the north to Cape Horn, which is just 500 miles (800 km) from Antarctica, the continent has a wide range of climates and habitats.

Native Americans migrating from North America reached the southern tip of South America about 8,000 years ago. One group, the Incas, founded a major civilization in the Andes, but it was crushed by Spanish soldiers in the 1530s. The predominant culture in South America today is Latin American. Roman Catholicism is the main religion, and Spanish and Portuguese are the chief languages.

South America was once joined to Africa, forming part of the supercontinent of Gondwanaland. When the two continents began to move apart about 150 million years ago, the South Atlantic Ocean opened up between them. Plate movements are still going on, further widening the Atlantic.

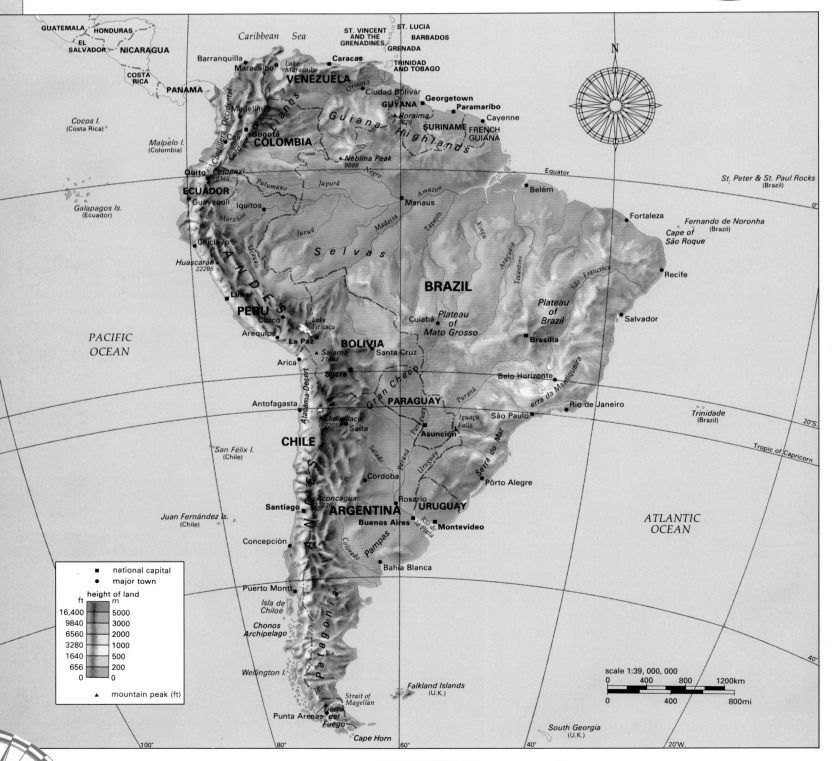

| national capital |
| major town |

height of land

ft	m
16,400	5000
9840	3000
6560	2000
3280	1000
1640	500
656	200
0	0

▲ mountain peak (ft)

scale 1:39, 000, 000

0   400   800   1200km

0   400   800mi

THE POLITICAL AND CULTURAL WORLD

Latin American culture is a complex blend of Native American, European, and African influences. The carnivals held in Rio de Janeiro combine Christian and African traditions, while many Native American Roman Catholics combine Christian dogma with some of the beliefs of their ancestors.

Deep divisions exist between rural people, who are often Native Americans, and urban societies, which are often dominated by people of European or of mixed European and Native American descent. In Peru, for example, such differences have led to civil war. Political instability and the suppression of human rights remain features of South American life.

■ national capital

Like many former European colonies, the countries of South America have made slow progress toward democracy and have seen much political upheaval in recent times. There have been periods of military rule in most countries in the region, with resulting human rights abuses. The governments of both Chile and Paraguay are still under their army's influence.

COUNTRIES IN THE REGION
Argentina, Bolivia, Brazil, Chile, Colombia, Ecuador, Guyana, Paraguay, Peru, Suriname, Uruguay, Venezuela

Island territories Easter Island, Juan Fernández (Chile); Galápagos (Ecuador); Tierra del Fuego (Argentina/Chile); **Dependencies of other states** Falkland Islands and Dependencies (includes South Georgia and South Sandwich Islands) (U.K.); French Guiana (France)

LANGUAGE
Countries with one official language Dutch: Suriname; English: Guyana; Portuguese: Brazil; Spanish: Argentina, Chile, Colombia, Ecuador, Paraguay, Uruguay, Venezuela
Countries with two official languages Quechua and Spanish: Peru
Country with three official languages Aymara, Quechua, Spanish: Bolivia

Other languages spoken in the region include Arawak, Carib, Jivaro, Lengua, Mapuche, Sranang, Tongo, Toba, and numerous other indigenous languages.

RELIGION
Countries with one major religion Argentina, Bolivia, Brazil, Chile, Colombia, Ecuador, Paraguay, Peru, Venezuela (RC)
Countries with more than one major religion Uruguay (P, RC); Guyana, Suriname (H, I, P, RC)

Key: H–Hindu, I–Islam, IR–indigenous religions, P–Protestant, RC–Roman Catholic

STYLES OF GOVERNMENT
Republics All countries of the region
Federal states Argentina, Brazil, Venezuela
Multiparty states All countries of the region except Paraguay
One-party state Paraguay
Military influence Chile, Paraguay

ECONOMIC INDICATORS: 1990

	Brazil	Colombia	Bolivia
GDP (US$ billions)	414.06	41.12	4.48
GNP per capita (US$)	2,680	1,260	630
Annual rate of growth of GDP, 1980–1990	2.7%	3.7%	−0.1%
Manufacturing as % of GDP	26%	21%	13%
Central government spending as % of GNP	36%	15%	19%
Merchandise exports (US$ billions)	31.4	7.1	0.92
Merchandise imports (US$ billions)	20.4	5.6	0.72
% of GNP received as development aid	0.0%	0.2%	10.9%
Total external debt as % of GNP	25.1%	44.5%	100.9%

WELFARE INDICATORS

Infant mortality rate (per 1,000 live births)			
1965	104	86	106
1990	57	37	92
Daily food supply available (calories per capita, 1989)			
	2,751	2,179	1,916
Population per physician (1984)	1,080	2,598	1,530
Teacher-pupil ratio (elementary school, 1989)	1 : 23	1 : 30	1 : 25

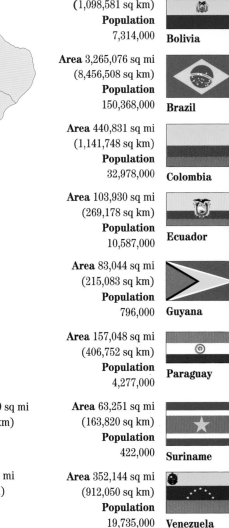

Area 496,225 sq mi (1,285,216 sq km)
Population 22,332,000 **Peru**

Area 292,135 sq mi (756,626 sq km)
Population 13,173,000 **Chile**

Area 1,073,399 sq mi (2,780,092 sq km)
Population 32,322,000 **Argentina**

Area 67,574 sq mi (175,016 sq km)
Population 3,094,000 **Uruguay**

Area 424,164 sq mi (1,098,581 sq km)
Population 7,314,000 **Bolivia**

Area 3,265,076 sq mi (8,456,508 sq km)
Population 150,368,000 **Brazil**

Area 440,831 sq mi (1,141,748 sq km)
Population 32,978,000 **Colombia**

Area 103,930 sq mi (269,178 sq km)
Population 10,587,000 **Ecuador**

Area 83,044 sq mi (215,083 sq km)
Population 796,000 **Guyana**

Area 157,048 sq mi (406,752 sq km)
Population 4,277,000 **Paraguay**

Area 63,251 sq mi (163,820 sq km)
Population 422,000 **Suriname**

Area 352,144 sq mi (912,050 sq km)
Population 19,735,000 **Venezuela**

HABITATS

South America covers almost one-seventh of the world's land surface and contains a wide range of habitats. It stretches from north of the equator almost to Antarctica. The great Amazon River dominates much of the north of the region.

Tropical grasslands, called llanos, are in the north; rain forests, called selvas, cover large areas around the equator; temperate grasslands, or pampas, are in the south; hot deserts border the coasts of Peru and Chile; and arid grasslands cover the cold Patagonian region in the south. The western edge of the continent is divided from the east by the great mountain range of the Andes. Extensive mountain habitats, including snowy peaks and high, wind-swept plateaus, or altiplanos, are found in the Andes ranges.

LAND

Area 6,874,600 sq mi (17,084,526 sq km)
Highest point Aconcagua, 22,834 ft (6,960 m)
Lowest point Salinas Grande, Argentina, −131 ft (−40 m)
Major features Andes, world's longest mountain chain, Guiana Highlands, Plateau of Brazil, Amazon basin

WATER

Longest river Amazon, 4,080 mi (6,570 km)
Largest basin Amazon, 2,375,000 sq mi (6,150,000 sq km)
Highest average flow Amazon, 6,350,000 cu ft/sec (180,000 cu m/sec)
Largest lake Titicaca, 3,220 sq mi (8,340 sq km)
Amazon has world's largest drainage basin and greatest flow.
Angel Falls, Venezuela, at 3,212 ft (979 m) are world's highest, Iguaçu Falls, Brazil–Argentina, one of the widest, 2.5 mi (4 km)

NOTABLE THREATENED SPECIES

Mammals golden lion tamarin (*Leontopithecus rosalia*), emperor tamarin (*Saguinus imperator*), woolly spider monkey (*Brachyteles arachnoides*), maned wolf (*Chrysocyon brachyurus*), giant otter (*Pteronura brasiliensis*), mountain tapir (*Tapirus pinchaque*), marsh deer (*Blastocerus dichotomus*)
Birds Junin grebe (*Podiceps taczanowskii*), white-winged guan (*Penelope albipennis*), little blue macaw (*Cyanopsitta spixii*), Esmereldas woodstar (*Acestrura berlepschi*)
Plants *Aechmea dichlamydea*; *Amaryllis traubii*; *Dalbergia nigra*; *Dicliptera dodsonii*; *Glomeropitcairnia erectiflora*; *Legrandia concinna*; snow mimosa (*Mimosa lanuginosa*); *Mutisia retrorsa*; Rio Palenue mahogany (*Persea theobromifolia*); *Spergularia congestifolia*
Others South American river turtle (*Podocnemis expansa*), Black caiman (*Melanosuchus niger*), ginger pearlfish (*Cynolebias marmoratus*), Galápagos land snails (*Bulimulus*)

HABITATS

The Andes Mountains dominate western South America. The world's largest rain forest covers much of the Amazon basin, while tropical grasslands dominate large parts of the countries in the east. The western coast of Peru is desert.

Physical zones

- mountains/barren land
- forest
- grassland
- semidesert
- desert

▲ mountain peak (ft)
☀ climate station

CLIMATE

The climates of South America vary greatly. The northern regions straddle the equator and are hot and rainy. The south has warm temperate to cool climates. The Andes range contains many climatic zones based on altitude.

Rainfall on the eastern slopes facing the Amazon basin may reach 200 inches (500 cm) a year. The interior basins and gorges have one-tenth of that total rainfall. The western coasts of Peru and northern Chile, though often blanketed in low clouds, have almost no rainfall at all. West of the Andes are some of the world's driest deserts. Central Chile has a Mediterranean climate, with hot, dry summers and warm, moist winters, but the south is rainy with cool summers.

TEMPERATURE AND PRECIPITATION

| | Temperature °F (°C) | | Altitude | |
	January	July	ft	(m)
Maracaibo	66 (19)	69 (21)	19	(6)
Manaus	80 (27)	82 (28)	144	(44)
La Paz	53 (12)	48 (9)	12,000	(3,658)
Buenos Aires	73 (23)	50 (10)	88	(27)
Ushuaia	48 (9)	36 (2)	20	(6)

| | Precipitation in (mm) | | | |
	January	July		Year
Maracaibo	0.9 (23)	4.2 (109)	15.2	(387)
Manaus	9.8 (249)	2.3 (58)	82.7	(2,102)
La Paz	4.4 (114)	0.4 (10)	21.9	(555)
Buenos Aires	3.1 (79)	2.2 (56)	40.4	(1,027)
Ushuaia	2.3 (58)	1.9 (47)	22.6	(574)

Atacama Desert has recorded no rain in 400 years.

NATURAL HAZARDS

Volcanic eruptions, earthquakes, landslides, and mudslides

CLIMATE

height above sea level of climate stations

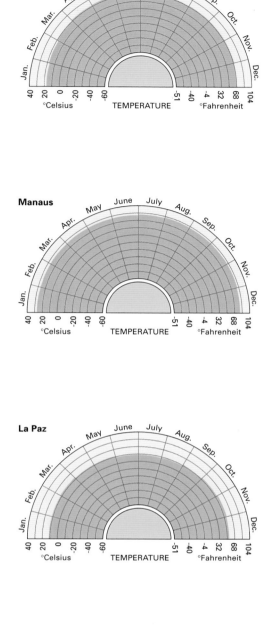

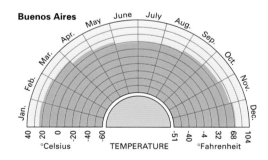

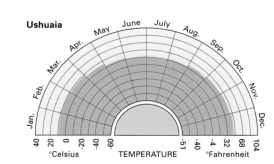

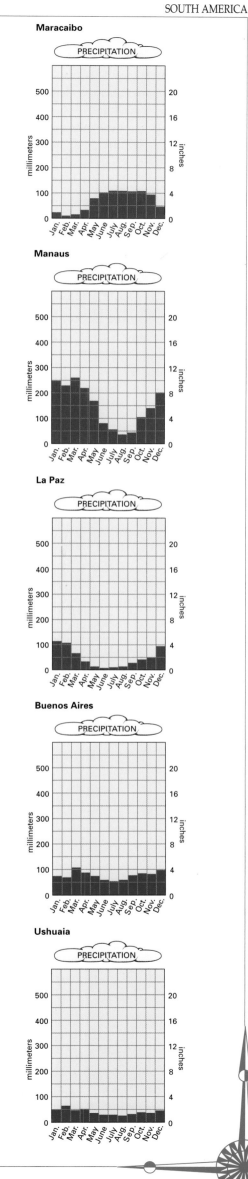

ENVIRONMENTAL ISSUES

The cutting down of the world's largest rain forest in the Amazon basin, together with the disappearance of the world's richest plant and animal life, has become a symbol of human misuse of the planet. In Colombia, for example, half the forest has been destroyed in the last 50 years. Deforestation also threatens the Amerindians who live there. Nearly 100 groups of Amerindians have been wiped out in the last 90 years.

Soil erosion is severe in many areas, especially the Andes, while heavy industrial and urban pollution and poor conditions of sanitation exist in and around the biggest cities. Economic development and improvements to living conditions have been made a high priority, but the impact on the environment has been great.

POPULATION AND WEALTH

	Highest	Middle	Lowest
Population (in millions)	150.4 (Brazil)	13.2 (Chile)	0.4 (Suriname)
Population increase (annual population growth rate, % 1960–1990)	3.3 (Venezuela)	2.5 (Colombia)	0.7 (Uruguay)
Energy use (gigajoules/person)	88 (Venezuela)	22 (Brazil)	8 (Paraguay)
Real purchasing power (US$/person)	5,790 (Uruguay)	3,810 (Colombia)	1,480 (Bolivia)

ENVIRONMENTAL INDICATORS

	Highest	Middle	Lowest
CO$_2$ emissions (mil. m.t. carbon/year)	610 (Brazil)	69 (Colombia)	0.3 (Guyana)
Deforestation (1,000 acres/year)	22,363 (Brazil)	667 (Peru)	7 (Suriname)
Artificial fertilizer use (lbs/acre/year)	143 (Suriname)	38 (Uruguay)	2.6 (Bolivia)
Automobiles (per 1,000 population)	126 (Argentina)	33 (Guyana)	2 (Ecuador)
Access to safe drinking water (% population)	96 (Brazil)	61 (Peru)	35 (Paraguay)

MAJOR ENVIRONMENTAL PROBLEMS AND SOURCES

Air pollution: locally high, in particular urban; high greenhouse gas emissions
River pollution: medium; *sources*: agricultural, sewage
Land degradation: *types*: soil erosion, deforestation, habitat destruction; *causes*: agriculture, industry, population pressure
Resource problems: fuelwood shortage; inadequate drinking water and sanitation; land use competition
Population problems: population explosion; urban overcrowding; inadequate health facilities
Major events: Cubatão, Brazil (1984), accident in natural gas/oil refining facility

ENVIRONMENTAL ISSUES

Besides deforestation, South America also suffers soil erosion in upland areas, desertification, urban and industrial pollution, and land degradation caused by mining and the building of dams.

Key environmental issues

- • major town or city
- ✎ heavily polluted town or city
- ⬧ major pollution event
- ⌇ heavily polluted river
- ▊ remaining tropical rain forest
- ▊ area of deforestation

areas at risk of desertification
- ▊ very high
- ▊ high
- ▊ moderate
- ☐ true desert

POPULATION

South America's population increased by four times between 1930 and 1985. The population explosion is still continuing at about 2 percent a year, making South America's population one of the fastest growing in the world.

In the last 50 years, city populations have also increased rapidly as people have moved away from the countryside. Many cities have elegant districts for the rich elite, and vast shanty towns where the poor live.

For vast numbers of urban dwellers, life is hard. Incomes and standards of living declined throughout the 1980s. The majority now live in overcrowded housing with poor access to services such as water, sanitation, and power. In Venezuela, new city dwellers have built on land they have occupied illegally.

POPULATION

Total population of region (in millions)	296.6
Population density (persons per sq mi)	6.6
Population change (average annual percent 1960–1990)	
Urban	+4.1
Rural	+0.6

URBAN POPULATION

As percentage of total population	
1960	43.2
1990	76.1
Percentage in cities of more than 1 million	12.1

TEN LARGEST CITIES

	Country	Population
São Paulo	Brazil	16,832,000
Rio de Janeiro	Brazil	11,141,000
Buenos Aires †	Argentina	11,126,000
Lima †	Peru	6,234,000
Santiago †	Chile	4,858,000
Bogotá †	Colombia	4,185,000
Belo Horizonte	Brazil	3,446,000
Caracas †	Venezuela	3,247,000
Salvador	Brazil	2,362,000
Fortaleza	Brazil	2,169,000

† denotes national capital

POPULATION

The distribution of South America's population is very uneven. Large areas of forest, mountains, and desert are thinly populated, while some coastal areas are overcrowded.

Population density

city populations
(National capital is underlined.)

◆	over 5,000,000
■	1,000,000–5,000,000
●	500,000–999,999
×	national capital less than 500,000

persons per square mi	persons per square km
520	200
260	100
130	50
26	10
2.6	1

INDUSTRY

Apart from Guyana, the least developed country on the continent, economists classify South American countries as middle-income developing nations. But Argentina and Brazil both have massive industries and are likely to become high-income economies in the twenty-first century. Argentina's factories process food (especially meat), refine oil, produce chemicals, and make electrical equipment and vehicles. Brazil also produces vehicles, as well as aircraft, cement, chemicals, machinery, textiles, foods, and pharmaceuticals. In most other countries, industry is dominated by mining. Chile is the world's leading copper producer. Other minerals include gold and nitrates. Many minerals are exported as raw materials.

INDUSTRIAL OUTPUT (US$ billion)

Total	Mining	Manufacturing	Average annual change since 1960
231.5	22.9	181.7	+6.4%

INDUSTRIAL WORKERS (millions)
(Figures in parentheses are percentages of total labor force.)

Total	Mining	Manufacturing	Construction
23.8	0.56 (0.54%)	16.7 (16.3%)	6.6 (6.4%)

MAJOR PRODUCTS (Figures in parentheses are percentages of world production.)

Energy and minerals	Output	Change since 1960
Oil (mil. barrels)	2674.0 (11.9%)	+109.6%
Iron Ore (mil. m.t.)	119.1 (21.1%)	+91.8%
Bauxite (mil. m.t.)	12.9 (13.2%)	+15%
Copper (mil. m.t.)	1.8 (21.2%)	+89%
Tin (1,000 m.t.)	59.1 (29.4%)	+72%
Silver (1,000 m.t.)	2.5 (12.9%)	+54%

Manufactures		
Tanning extracts (1,000 m.t.)	57.1 (55.3%)	No data
Coffee extracts (1,000 m.t.)	64.5 (11.6%)	No data
Rubber footwear (mil. pairs)	124.7 (13.9%)	No data
Ladies' blouses and underwear (mil.)	891.9 (27.9%)	No data
Cement (mil. m.t.)	51.6 (4.7%)	+406%
Steel (mil. m.t.)	33.9 (4.6%)	+930%
Locks and keys (mil.)	271.7 (69.1%)	No data
Electrical fuses (mil.)	88.8 (12.7%)	No data

INDUSTRY

South America's many rich resources include bauxite in Suriname, copper in Chile, tin in Bolivia, and oil in Venezuela. Argentina was the first country in the region to set up large manufacturing industries.

Resources and industry

- ◆ industrial center
- ○ major port
- ● other town
- —— major road
- —— major railroad

mineral resources and fossil fuels

- • iron and other ferroalloy metal ores
- ● other metal ores
- ■ nonmetallic minerals

- bauxite
- coal
- copper
- gold
- iron ore
- oil
- silver
- tin

AGRICULTURE

Agriculture employs about one-fourth of the workforce, and the region produces a wide range of farm products. Argentina's pampas is one of the world's major cereal-growing zones. The largest cereal crop is that of corn, the only cereal native to the region. It is the staple crop, and contains up to 15 percent protein. Tropical crops, such as bananas and sugarcane, grow in the north, though in some areas farmers find it more profitable to grow plants for the illegal drug trade. Brazil and Colombia are two of the principal producers of coffee beans. Raising cattle is the major activity in Brazil and Argentina, while llamas are raised in the high altitudes of the Peruvian Andes. Fishing and forestry are other major industries.

LAND (million acres)

Total	Agricultural	Arable	Forest/woodland
4,332 (100%)	1,525 (35%)	287 (7%)	2,234 (51%)

FARMERS

24.2 million employed in agriculture (24% of workforce)
12 acres of arable land per person employed in agriculture

MAJOR CROPS

	Area mil. acres	Yield 100lbs/acre	Production mil. m.t.	Change since 1963
Corn	48.6	18.9	41.6 (9)	+133%
Soybeans	33.6	16.9	25.6 (26)	+6,178%
Wheat	23.7	16.6	17.9 (3)	+78%
Rice	18.3	19.1	15.9 (3)	+98%
Sugarcane	13.3	560.2	337.5 (35)	+197%
Coffee	11.6	5.9	3.2 (51)	+26%
Bananas	—	—	15.2 (23)	+38%

MAJOR LIVESTOCK

	Number in mil.	Production mil. m.t.	Change since 1963
Cattle	257.8 (20)	—	+73%
Sheep/goats	129.9 (8)	—	−12%
Pigs	53.9 (6)	—	+37%
Milk	—	29.3 (6)	+93%
Fish catch	—	12.0 (13)	—

FOOD SECURITY (grain exports minus imports)

mil. m.t.	% domestic production	% world trade
+4.2	5	2

Numbers in parentheses are percentages of world total.

AGRICULTURE

Only about one-third of South America is used for agriculture, including simple subsistence farming and high-technology plantations. Large areas are used for grazing.

Agricultural zones

- arable
- fruits, vegetables, and tree crops
- pasture
- rough grazing
- woods and forest
- nonagricultural land

▲ mountain peak (ft)

NORDIC COUNTRIES

T he Nordic countries include Norway, Sweden, Denmark, Finland, and Iceland. Glacial erosion has shaped the land, sculpting rugged mountain scenery, deep fjords, and many ice-scoured basins that now contain lakes.

Iceland has icecaps and volcanoes. Because it straddles the Atlantic ridge, new crustal rock is being formed in Iceland as the plates on either side of the ridge slowly move apart.

Except for Finnish and Lapp, the Nordic peoples speak closely related languages. Their historic Viking traditions have given them a distinctive personality and sense of adventure.

Natural resources, including North Sea oil and hydroelectric power supplies in Norway, iron ore in Sweden, and fisheries and forests, support the economies of the Nordic countries. Farming is important in the south.

The Nordic countries occupy the northwestern corner of Europe. They include various islands. The Faeroe Islands and Greenland are Danish, the Jan Mayen Islands, Bear Island, and Svalbard are Norwegian, and the Ahvenanmaa island group in the Baltic is Finnish.

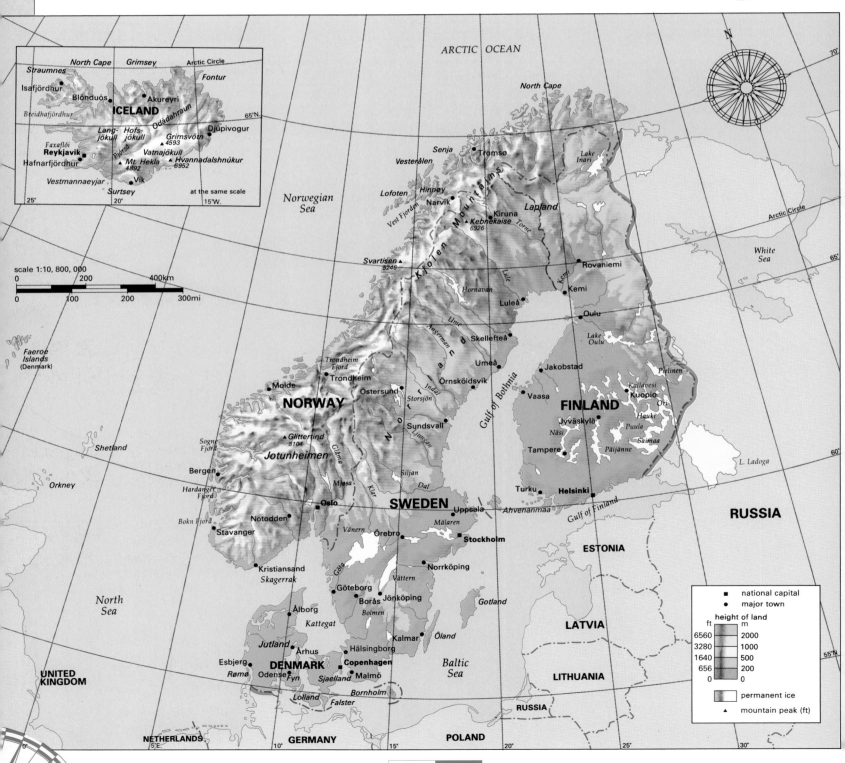

THE POLITICAL AND CULTURAL WORLD

The modern Nordic states began to evolve in the early nineteenth century. Norway became an independent country in 1905, when it broke away from its union with Sweden. In 1944 Iceland broke away from Denmark, which had lost Schleswig and Holstein in a war with Prussia in 1864. Finland declared its independence from Russia in 1917, though it lost land to the Soviet Union in 1944.

Because of their cultural affinity, the Nordic countries collaborate through the Nordic Council of Ministers. Established in 1971, it provides funds for joint institutions. The related Nordic Council is an advisory body.

COUNTRIES IN THE REGION

Denmark, Finland, Iceland, Norway, Sweden

Island territories Ahvenanmaa (Finland); Faeroe Islands (Denmark); Jan Mayen, Svalbard Islands (Norway)
Territories outside region Greenland (Denmark)

LANGUAGE

Countries with one official language Danish: Denmark; Icelandic: Iceland; Norwegian: Norway; Swedish: Sweden
Countries with two official languages Finnish, Swedish: Finland

Faeroese is recognized as an official language in the Faeroe Islands along with Danish.

RELIGION

Denmark Protestant (95%), nonreligious and atheist (3%)
Finland Protestant (92%), nonreligious and atheist (5%)
Iceland Protestant (96%), nonreligious and atheist (2%), Roman Catholic (1%)
Norway Protestant (96%), nonreligious (1%)
Sweden Protestant (68%), nonreligious and atheist (28%), Eastern Orthodox (1%)

STYLES OF GOVERNMENT

Republics Finland, Iceland
Monarchies Denmark, Norway, Sweden
Multiparty states Denmark, Finland, Iceland, Norway, Sweden
One-chamber assembly Denmark, Finland, Norway, Sweden
Two-chamber assembly Iceland

MEMBERSHIP OF INTERNATIONAL ORGANIZATIONS

Council of Europe Denmark, Iceland, Norway, Sweden
European Community (EC) Denmark
European Free Trade Association (EFTA) Finland, Iceland, Norway, Sweden
North Atlantic Treaty Organization (NATO) Denmark, Iceland, Norway
Nordic Council Denmark, Finland, Iceland, Norway, Sweden
Organization for Economic Cooperation and Development (OECD) Denmark, Finland, Iceland, Norway, Sweden

Iceland has no military forces and is not a member of NATO Military Command.

ECONOMIC INDICATORS: 1990

	Denmark	Norway	Sweden
GDP (US$ billions)	130.96	105.83	228.11
GNP per capita (US$)	22,080	23,120	23,660
Annual rate of growth of GDP, 1980–1990	2.4%	2.9%	2.2%
Manufacturing as % of GDP	20%	15%	24%
Central government spending as % of GNP	41%	46%	42%
Merchandise exports (US$ billions)	35.0	33.8	57.5
Merchandise imports (US$ billions)	31.6	27.2	54.7
% of GNP donated as development aid	0.93%	1.17%	0.90%

WELFARE INDICATORS

Infant mortality rate (per 1,000 live births)			
1965	19	17	13
1990	15	8	6
Daily food supply available (calories per capita, 1989)	3,628	3,326	2,960
Population per physician (1984)	400	450	390
Teacher-pupil ratio (elementary school, 1989)	1 : 12	1 : 16	1 : 16

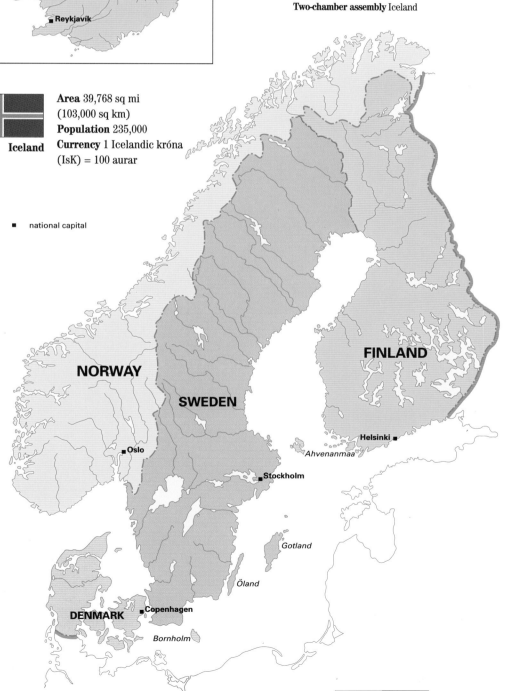

■ national capital

Area 39,768 sq mi (103,000 sq km)
Population 235,000
Currency 1 Icelandic króna (IsK) = 100 aurar
Iceland

Area 125,050 sq mi (323,878 sq km)
Population 4,212,000
Currency 1 Norwegian krone (NKr) = 100 øre **Norway**

Area 173,732 sq mi (449,964 sq km)
Population 8,444,000
Currency 1 Swedish krona (SKr) = 100 öre **Sweden**

Area 130,559 sq mi (338,145 sq km)
Population 4,975,000
Currency 1 markka (Fmk) = 100 pennia **Finland**

Area 16,638 sq mi (43,093 sq km)
Population 5,143,000
Currency 1 Danish krone (DKr) = 100 øre **Denmark**

Denmark, Norway, and Sweden are constitutional monarchies, whose governments are led by elected prime ministers and cabinets. The monarchs have little real power. Finland and Iceland are democratic republics. Finland's president is the country's chief executive. Iceland's president has little real power.

HABITATS

The glaciated mountain core of Norway and Sweden lies between the indented west coast and the hilly Norrland region. There is tundra in Lapland. Fertile lowland plains are situated in southern Finland, Sweden, and Denmark. Iceland is mostly barren.

LAND
Area 484,437 sq mi (1,255,017 sq km)
Highest point Glittertind, 8,104 ft (2,470 m)
Lowest point sea level
Major features islands, fjords, mountains and high plateau in west, lakelands east and west of Gulf of Bothnia, lowlands in south

WATER
Longest river Göta–Klar, 477 mi (720 km)
Largest basin Kemi, 20,000 sq mi (51,000 sq km)
Highest average flow Kemi, 19,000 cu ft/sec (534 cu m/sec)
Largest lake Vänern, 2,080 sq mi (5,390 sq km)

NOTABLE THREATENED SPECIES
Mammals gray wolf (Canis lupus), wolverine (Gulo gulo), polar bear (Ursus maritimus), harbor porpoise (Phocoena phocoena), northern bottlenose whale (Hyperoodon ampullatus), fin whale (Balaenoptera physalus), blue whale (Balaenoptera musculus), bowhead whale (Balaena mysticetus), humpback whale (Megaptera novangliae), narwhal (Monodon monoceros)
Birds lesser white-fronted goose (Anser erythropus), red kite (Milvus migrans), white-tailed sea eagle (Haliaeetus albicilla), corncrake (Crex crex)
Plants Braya linearis; Cephalanthera rubra; Gentianella uliginosa; Liparis loeselii; Najas flexilis; Oxytropis deflexa subsp. norvegica; Papaver lapponicum; Platanthera obtusata subsp. oligantha; Polemonium boreale; Potamogeton rutilus
Others hermit beetle (Osmoderma eremita), tree snail (Balea perversa), large blue butterfly (Maculinea arion), noble crayfish (Astacus astacus)

CLIMATE

The climate of the coasts of Iceland and western Norway are moderated by the North Atlantic Current. The interior of Iceland has icecaps, while northern Sweden and Finland have subarctic climates. Southern Sweden has mild winters, and Norway, the greatest rainfall.

TEMPERATURE AND PRECIPITATION

	Temperature °F (°C) January	July	Altitude ft (m)
Bergen	33 (1)	59 (15)	144 (44)
Oslo	23 (−5)	63 (17)	308 (94)
Stockholm	27 (−3)	64 (18)	144 (44)
Helsinki	21 (−6)	63 (17)	150 (46)
Reykjavik	32 (0)	52 (11)	59 (18)

	Precipitation in (mm) January	July	Year
Bergen	5.6 (142)	5.7 (143)	77.1 (1,958)
Oslo	1.9 (49)	3.2 (82)	29.1 (740)
Stockholm	2.0 (51)	3.3 (86)	21.9 (555)
Helsinki	2.2 (56)	2.7 (68)	25.2 (641)
Reykjavik	3.5 (90)	1.9 (50)	31.7 (805)

NATURAL HAZARDS
Cold, glacier surges, volcanic eruptions in Iceland

ENVIRONMENTAL ISSUES

The main environmental issues in the Nordic countries are pollution of the Baltic Sea and acid rain. Clouds containing acid raindrops drift over from Germany, Poland, and the former Soviet Union. Acid rain has poisoned many lakes, rivers, and forests.

ENVIRONMENTAL INDICATORS

	Highest	Middle	Lowest
CO_2 emissions (mil. m.t. carbon/year)	15 (Denmark)	8.7 (Norway)	0.4 (Iceland)
Municipal waste (lbs/person/year)	1,045 (Norway)	899 (Finland)	699 (Sweden)
Nuclear waste (cumulative m.t. heavy metal)	1,900 (Sweden)	400 (Finland)	0 (Norway)
Artificial fertilizer use (lbs/acre/year)	2,572 (Iceland)	206 (Denmark)	120 (Sweden)
Automobiles (per 1,000 population)	406 (Sweden)	377 (Iceland)	311 (Denmark)
Access to safe drinking water (% population)	100 (Sweden)	100 (Iceland)	97 (Finland)

MAJOR ENVIRONMENTAL PROBLEMS AND SOURCES
Air pollution: acid rain prevalent
River/lake pollution: high; *sources:* acid deposition
Marine/coastal pollution: medium; *sources:* industrial, agricultural
Land pollution: local; *sources:* industrial; acid deposition
Major events: Aker river, Oslo (1980), acid leak from factory; Ålesund (1992), oil spill from tanker Arisan

HABITATS

Physical zones
- ice and snow
- mountains/barren land
- forest
- grassland

▲ mountain peak (ft)
⁘ climate station

During the last ice age, which ended only about 10,000 years ago, ice sheets advanced and retreated over the region. They left their mark in the many glacial features found in the highlands and lowlands.

ENVIRONMENTAL ISSUES

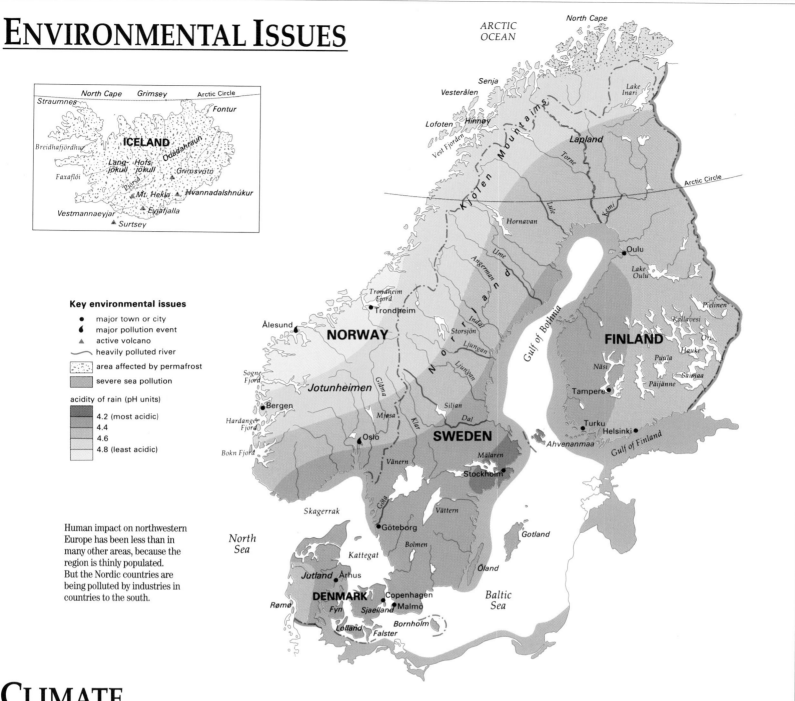

ICELAND

Straumnes · North Cape · Grimsey · Arctic Circle
Fontur
Breidhafjördhur
Lang-jökull · Hofs-jökull · Ódádahraun
Grimsvötn
Faxaflói · Thórsá
Vestmannaeyjar · Mt. Hekla · Hvannadalshnúkur · Eyjafjalla
Surtsey

ARCTIC OCEAN

North Cape
Senja
Vesterålen
Lofoten · Hinnøy
Vest Fjorden
Lapland
Lake Inari
Kjölen Mountains
Torne
Arctic Circle
Hornavan
Ume
Oulu
Lake Oulu
Ångerman
Lule
Kemi
Trondheim Fjord
Trondheim
Ålesund
NORWAY
Storsjön
Indal
Ljungan
FINLAND
Piielinen
Kallavesi
Haukr
Näsi
Puula
Ljusnan
Siemaa
Päijänne
Tampere
Sogne Fjord
Jotunheimen
Gldma
Klar
Siljan
Dal
SWEDEN
Turku
Helsinki
Hardanger Fjord
Mjösa
Ahvenanmaa
Gulf of Finland
Bergen
Oslo
Vänern
Mälaren
Bokn Fjord
Stockholm
Skagerrak
Vättern
Gotland
Göteborg
Bolmen
Öland
Kattegat
Jutland · Århus
DENMARK · Copenhagen
Rømø · Fyn · Sjaelland · Malmö
Lolland · Falster · Bornholm
North Sea
Baltic Sea
Gulf of Bothnia

Key environmental issues

- ● major town or city
- 🌢 major pollution event
- ▲ active volcano
- ∿ heavily polluted river
- ⠶ area affected by permafrost
- ▨ severe sea pollution

acidity of rain (pH units)

- 4.2 (most acidic)
- 4.4
- 4.6
- 4.8 (least acidic)

Human impact on northwestern Europe has been less than in many other areas, because the region is thinly populated. But the Nordic countries are being polluted by industries in countries to the south.

CLIMATE

height above sea level of climate stations

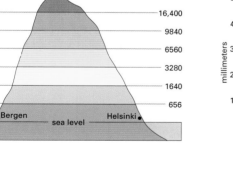

meters		feet
5000		16,400
3000		9840
2000		6560
1000		3280
500		1640
200		656

Reykjavik · Bergen · sea level · Helsinki

Reykjavik

PRECIPITATION

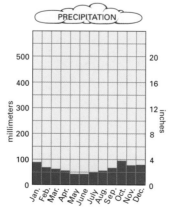

Bergen

PRECIPITATION

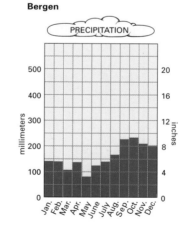

Helsinki

PRECIPITATION

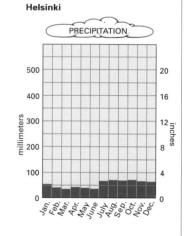

Reykjavik

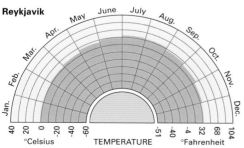

TEMPERATURE

Bergen

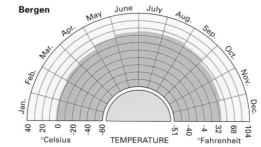

TEMPERATURE

Helsinki

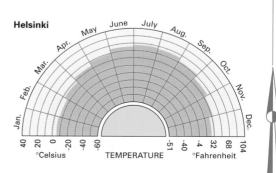

TEMPERATURE

POPULATION

The rugged, mostly forested terrain, combined with the hostile climate, has restricted the population of most Nordic countries to coastal areas except in the far south. Only in Denmark is the population spread evenly, based on a network of farming villages.

POPULATION

Total population of region (in millions)	22.9
Population density (persons per sq mi)	53.8
Population change (average annual percent 1960–1990) Urban	+0.9
Rural	−1.6

URBAN POPULATION

As percentage of total population	
1960	72.3
1990	82.6
Percentage in cities of more than 1 million	12.1

TEN LARGEST CITIES

	Country	Population
Stockholm †	Sweden	1,471,000
Copenhagen †	Denmark	1,339,000
Helsinki †	Finland	994,000
Oslo †	Norway	726,000
Göteborg	Sweden	720,000
Malmö	Sweden	466,000
Turku	Finland	265,000
Tampere	Finland	261,000
Århus	Denmark	258,000
Bergen	Norway	211,000

† denotes national capital

INDUSTRY

The region's natural resources include offshore oil and gas fields belonging to Denmark and Norway, together with metal ores in Norway and Sweden. Sweden has some of the world's richest iron ore deposits in Lapland. The region's leading industry is papermaking.

INDUSTRIAL OUTPUT (US$ billion)

Total	Mining	Manufacturing	Average annual change since 1960
172.1	23.3	95.7	+3.2%

INDUSTRIAL WORKERS (millions)
(Figures in parentheses are percentages of total labor force.)

Total	Mining	Manufacturing	Construction
3.6	0.36 (2.9%)	2.4 (19.8%)	0.8 (6.7%)

MAJOR PRODUCTS (Figures in parentheses are percentages of world production.)

Energy and minerals	Output	Change since 1960
Oil (mil. barrels)	589 (2.6%)	N/A
Natural gas (billion cu meters)	32 (1.7%)	N/A
Iron ore (mil. m.t.)	22.5 (3.9%)	-13.5%
Copper (mil. m.t.)	0.3 (3.7%)	No data
Zinc (mil. m.t.)	0.4 (6.2%)	No data

Manufactures		
Wood pulp (mil. m.t.)	18.9 (15%)	+1%
Newsprint (mil. m.t.)	4.4 (13.8%)	+36%
Steel (mil. m.t.)	7.4 (1.1%)	+86.8%
Ships (mil. gross m.t.)	0.5 (4.5%)	-59.4%
Automobiles (mil.)	0.5 (1.1%)	+397%
Telecommunications equipment (US$ billion)	7.5 (8.1%)	No data

N/A means production had not begun in 1960.

AGRICULTURE

Most of the productive arable land is in Denmark and southern Sweden. Mixed farming is important, especially dairy farming, though livestock are found extensively in the south. To the north, farming is combined with the industries of forestry and fishing.

LAND (million acres)

Total	Agricultural	Arable	Forest/woodland
289 (100%)	29 (10%)	23 (8%)	148 (52%)

MAJOR CROPS

	Area mil. acres	Yield 100lbs/acre	Production mil. m.t.	Change since 1963
Barley	5.4	32.2	8.1 (4)	+46%
Wheat	2.2	42.3	4.4 (1)	+129%
Oats	2.2	27.8	2.8 (7)	−5%
Rapeseed	1.2	16.9	0.9 (4)	+360%

MAJOR LIVESTOCK

	Number in mil.	Production mil. m.t.	Change since 1963
Pigs	13.4 (2)	—	+25%
Cattle	6.5 (1)	—	−29%
Milk	—	13.4 (3)	−8%
Fish catch	—	6.0 (6)	—

Numbers in parentheses are percentages of world total.

POPULATION

Population density

city populations
(National capital is underlined.)

- ■ 1,000,000–5,000,000
- ● 500,000–999,999
- ⊙ 250,000–499,999
- ○ 100,000–249,000
- × national capital less than 100,000

persons per square mi		persons per square km
260		100
130		50
26		10
2.6		1

Most people live in well-planned cities and towns. With green parks, woodlands, and often lakes and waterways, the towns and cities are pleasant places to live.

The exploitation of its forests and mineral resources has enabled the Nordic countries to become a major trading region. It accounts for more than 4.5 percent of world exports.

INDUSTRY

ICELAND

Grimsey · Arctic Circle

Siglufjördhur
Hólmavik · Husavik
Akureyri
Stykkishólmur
Olafsvik · Seydhisfjördhur
Breidhafjördhur · Djúpivogur
Faxaflói
Reykjavik
Keflavik · Hafnarfjördhur
Vestmannaeyjar
Surtsey

Resources and industry

◆ industrial center
○ major port
● other town
— major road
— major railroad

mineral resources and fossil fuels
● iron and other ferroalloy metal ores
● other metal ores
■ nonmetallic minerals

coal
copper
iron ore
nickel

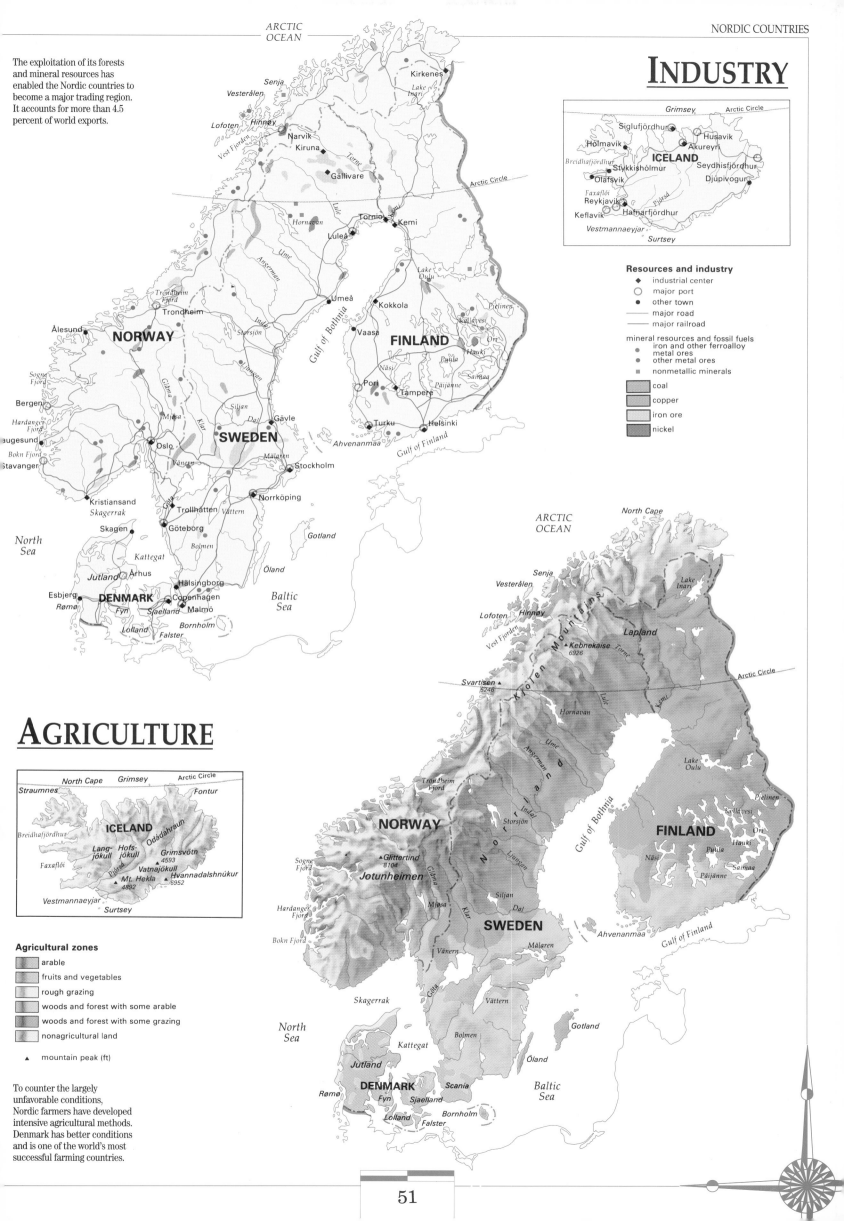

Kirkenes
Senja
Vesterålen
Lake Inari
Lofoten · Hinnøy
Narvik
Kiruna
Vest Fjorden
Gällivare
Torne
Arctic Circle
Hornavan
Lule
Tornio · Kemi
Luleå
Lake Oulu
Umeå
Kokkola
Trondheim Fjord
Trondheim
Vaasa
FINLAND
Ålesund
NORWAY
Storsjön
Indal
Pielinen
Kallavesi
Ori
Hauki
Sogne Fjord
Bergen
Näsi
Puula
Saimaa
Hardanger Fjord
Mjøsa
Siljan
Gävle
Dal
Päijänne
Haugesund
Klar
SWEDEN
Pori
Tampere
Bokn Fjord
Oslo
Vänern
Turku
Helsinki
Stavanger
Stockholm
Ahvenanmaa
Gulf of Finland
Kristiansand
Norrköping
Skagerrak
Trollhättan
Vättern
Gotland
Skagen
Göteborg
Bolmen
Öland
North Sea
Kattegat
Jutland
Århus
Hälsingborg
Baltic Sea
Esbjerg
Rømø
DENMARK
Copenhagen
Fyn · Sjaelland · Malmö
Lolland
Bornholm
Falster

ARCTIC OCEAN

AGRICULTURE

North Cape · Grimsey · Arctic Circle
Straumnes · Fontur
Breidhafjördhur
ICELAND
Lang-jökull · Hofs-jökull · Odádahraun
Grimsvötn
Faxaflói · Vatnajökull
Mt. Hekla · Hvannadalshnúkur
4892 · 6952
Vestmannaeyjar
Surtsey

Agricultural zones

arable
fruits and vegetables
rough grazing
woods and forest with some arable
woods and forest with some grazing
nonagricultural land

▲ mountain peak (ft)

To counter the largely unfavorable conditions, Nordic farmers have developed intensive agricultural methods. Denmark has better conditions and is one of the world's most successful farming countries.

ARCTIC OCEAN · North Cape
Senja
Vesterålen
Lake Inari
Lofoten · Hinnøy
Vest Fjorden
Kebnekaise
6926
Lapland
Svartisen
5246
Torne
Arctic Circle
Kjølen Mountains
Hornavan
Lule
Kemi
Trondheim Fjord
NORWAY
Indal
Storsjön
Lake Oulu
Glittertind
8104
Jotunheimen
Angerman
Ljungan
FINLAND
Pielinen
Sogne Fjord
Glåma
Mjøsa
Siljan
Dal
Kallavesi
Hauki
Hardanger Fjord
Klar
Näsi
Puula
Saimaa
Bokn Fjord
SWEDEN
Päijänne
Vänern
Ahvenanmaa
Gulf of Finland
Göta
Skagerrak
Vättern
Gotland
North Sea
Kattegat
Bolmen
Öland
Jutland
Scania
Baltic Sea
Rømø
DENMARK
Fyn · Sjaelland
Lolland · Bornholm
Falster

BRITISH ISLES

The British Isles contain a great variety of geology and a wide range of highland and lowland scenery that is unusual in such a small area. The climate is mild, mainly because of the influence of the North Atlantic Current, the northern extension of the warm Gulf Stream. The weather is also distinguished by its variability, caused by the depressions that regularly cross the islands from west to east.

Celts settled in the region about 450 B.C. But the population also owes its ancestry to invaders, such as the Romans, Vikings, and Normans. There has recently been further diversification with the arrival of immigrants from Africa, Asia, and the West Indies.

The United Kingdom once ruled the largest empire in history. Though the imperial era has ended, the country remains a world power.

The British Isles consists of two large islands and more than 5,000 smaller ones, rising from the continental shelf off the coast of northwest Europe. It was cut off from the mainland about 7,500 years ago when melting ice sheets filled the North Sea and English Channel.

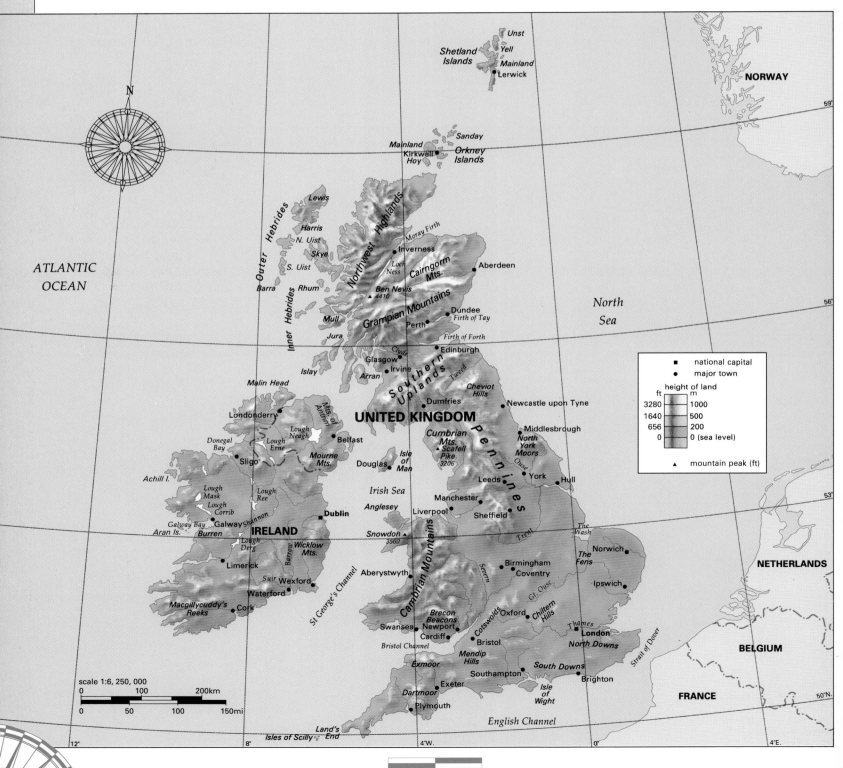

		national capital
		major town
		height of land
ft	m	
3280	1000	
1640	500	
656	200	
0	0 (sea level)	
		▲ mountain peak (ft)

scale 1:6,250,000

THE POLITICAL AND CULTURAL WORLD

The United Kingdom of Great Britain and Northern Ireland is often called Britain. Great Britain consists of England; Wales, which was absorbed by England in 1277; and Scotland, which was formally united with England under the Act of Union of 1707.

Ireland was united with Great Britain from 1801, but it became independent in 1921, with the exception of the six counties of Northern Ireland, which stayed in the United Kingdom.

The rest of Ireland is now a republic, while Britain is a constitutional monarchy. The Channel Islands and the Isle of Man are self-governing territories under the British Crown.

■ national capital

Area 27,137 sq mi (70,285 sq km)
Population 3,720,000
Capital Dublin
Currency 1 Irish pound (Ir£) = 100 new pence

Ireland

Area 94,251 sq mi (244,110 sq km)
Population 57,237,000
Capital London
Currency 1 pound sterling (£) = 100 new pence

United Kingdom

Regional loyalties are strong throughout the British Isles. Both Scotland and Wales have nationalist movements that have demanded a greater degree of home rule and local parliaments.

Habitats

The scenery of the British Isles is varied. There are areas of rocky and barren uplands; low, fertile plains, mostly on coasts; and soft, rolling hills resulting from glaciation, with some forests, moors, and downland reserved from agricultural use.

LAND

Area 121,353 sq mi (314,385 sq km)
Highest point Ben Nevis, 4,408 ft (1,344 m)
Lowest point Holme Fen, Great Ouse, −9 ft (−3 m)
Major features mountains chiefly in northern and western areas, with lower-lying areas in east and south

WATER

Longest river Shannon, 230 mi (370 km)
Largest basin Severn, 8,000 sq mi (21,000 sq km)
Highest average flow Shannon, 7,600 cu ft/sec (198 cu m/sec)
Largest lake Neagh, 150 sq mi (400 sq km)

NOTABLE THREATENED SPECIES

Mammals harbor porpoise *(Phocoena phocoena)*
Birds red kite *(Milvus migrans)*, white-tailed sea eagle *(Haliaeetus albicilla* – reintroduced*)*, corncrake *(Crex crex)*
Others kerry slug *(Geomalachus maculosus)*, checkered skipper butterfly *(Carterocephalus palaemon)*, freshwater pearl mussel *(Margaritifera margaritifera)*, ladybird spider *(Eresus niger)*

BOTANIC GARDENS

National Botanic Gardens, Dublin (25,000 species); Oxford (10,000 species); Royal Botanic Gardens, Edinburgh (12,000 species); Royal Botanic Gardens, Kew (30,000 species)

Climate

The British Isles has a mild, moist climate that is ever-changing because low pressure areas continually arrive from the Atlantic. It is windier in the west. More stable conditions occur when the British Isles comes under the influence of high pressure areas.

TEMPERATURE AND PRECIPITATION

	Temperature °F (°C) January	July	Altitude ft (m)
Aberdeen	36 (2)	57 (14)	194 (59)
Dublin	41 (5)	59 (15)	154 (47)
Valentia	45 (7)	59 (15)	29 (9)
Kew	39 (4)	64 (18)	16 (5)
Plymouth	43 (6)	61 (16)	89 (27)

	Precipitation in (mm) January	July	Year
Aberdeen	3.0 (77)	3.6 (92)	33.0 (837)
Dublin	2.6 (67)	2.8 (70)	29.8 (758)
Valentia	6.5 (164)	4.2 (107)	55.0 (1,398)
Kew	2.1 (53)	2.2 (56)	23.4 (594)
Plymouth	3.9 (99)	2.8 (71)	39.0 (990)

NATURAL HAZARDS

Storms, floods

Environmental Issues

Britain was the first nation to industrialize, and the rapid growth of mining, together with industries burning coal and oil, has caused much environmental damage. New development is currently threatening many habitats even in protected areas.

POPULATION AND WEALTH

	Ireland	U.K.
Population (in millions)	3.7	57.2
Population increase (annual population growth rate, % 1960–1990)	0.9	0.3
Energy use (gigajoules/person)	101	150
Real purchasing power (US$/person)	7,020	13,060

ENVIRONMENTAL INDICATORS

	Ireland	U.K.
CO_2 emissions (mil. m.t. carbon/year)	0.4	150
Municipal waste (lbs/person/year)	681	690
Nuclear waste (cumulative m.t. heavy metal)	0	30,900
Artificial fertilizer use (lbs/acre/year)	601	314
Automobiles (per 1,000 population)	199	353
Access to safe drinking water (% population)	100	100

MAJOR ENVIRONMENTAL PROBLEMS AND SOURCES

Air pollution: locally high, in particular urban; acid rain prevalent; high greenhouse gas emissions
River/lake pollution: local; *sources*: agricultural, sewage, acid deposition
Marine/coastal pollution: medium; *sources*: industrial, agricultural, sewage, oil
Land pollution: local; *sources*: industrial, agricultural, urban/household
Waste disposal problems: domestic, industrial, nuclear
Major events: *Torrey Canyon* (1967), oil tanker accident; Camelford (1989), chemical accident; Mersey River (1989), oil spill

Habitats

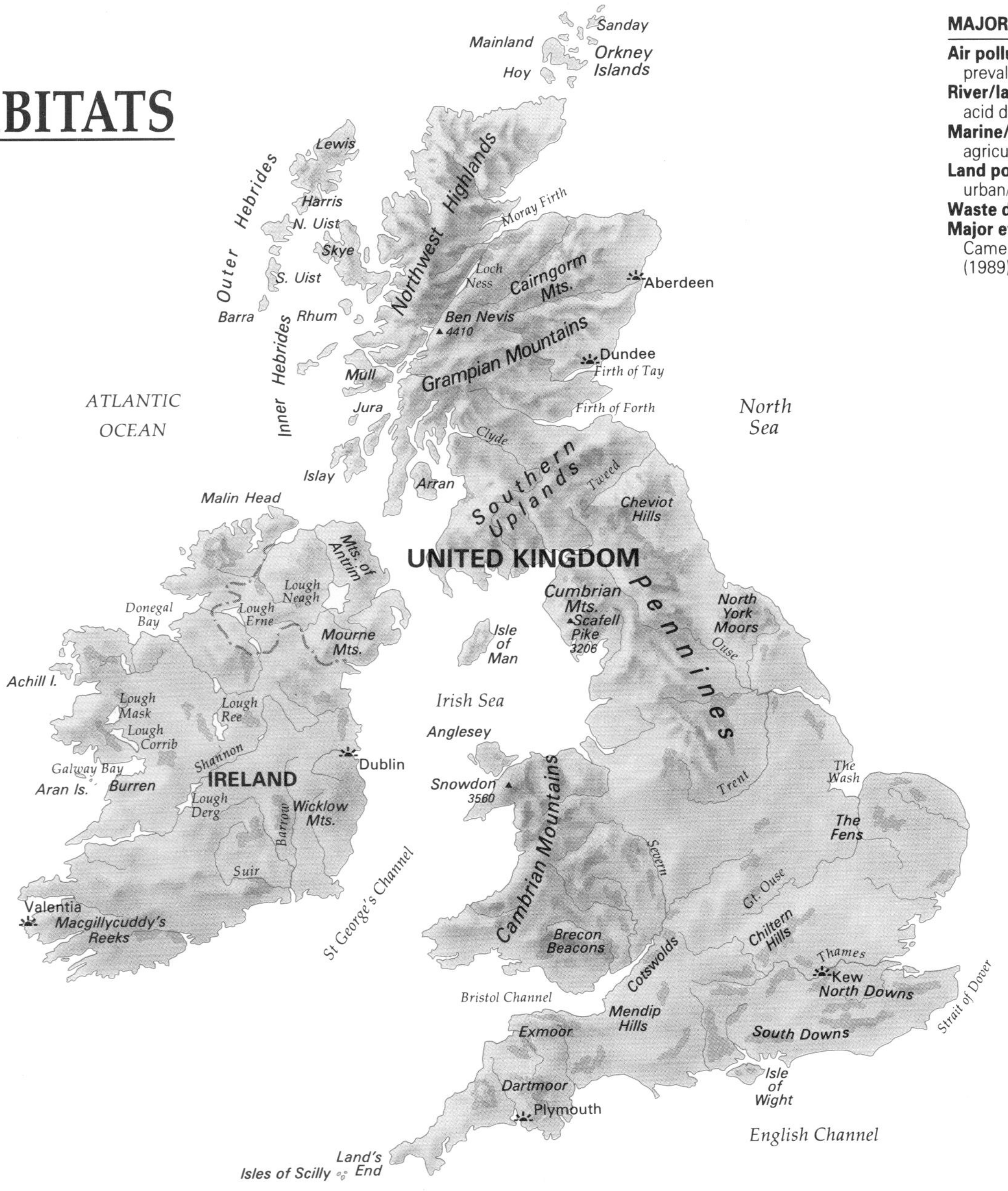

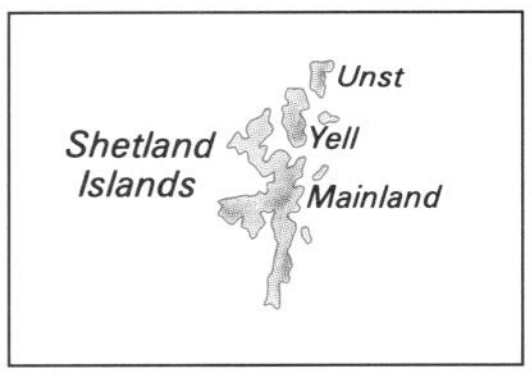

Generally the older highland regions are in the north and west. Younger, lower rocks, which produce more gentle landscapes of limestone and chalk ridges and clay vales, are found in the south and east.

Physical zones

- mountains/barren land
- forest
- grassland

▲ mountain peak (ft)
climate station

ENVIRONMENTAL ISSUES

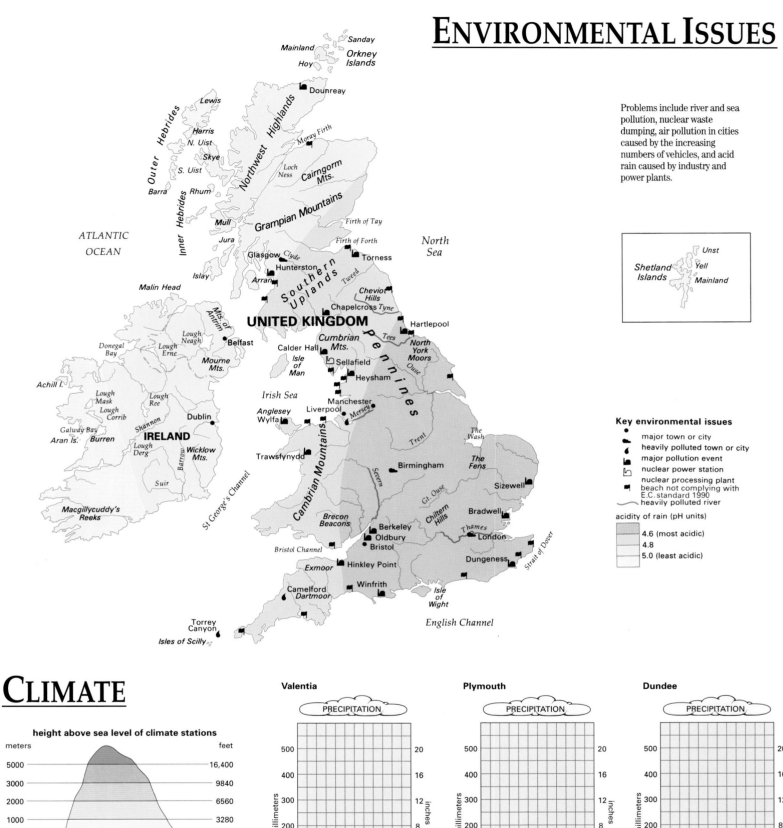

Problems include river and sea pollution, nuclear waste dumping, air pollution in cities caused by the increasing numbers of vehicles, and acid rain caused by industry and power plants.

Key environmental issues

- major town or city
- heavily polluted town or city
- major pollution event
- nuclear power station
- nuclear processing plant
- beach not complying with E.C. standard 1990
- heavily polluted river

acidity of rain (pH units)

- 4.6 (most acidic)
- 4.8
- 5.0 (least acidic)

CLIMATE

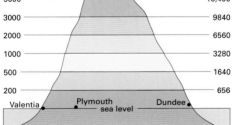

height above sea level of climate stations

meters		feet
5000		16,400
3000		9840
2000		6560
1000		3280
500		1640
200		656

Valentia   Plymouth   Dundee
sea level

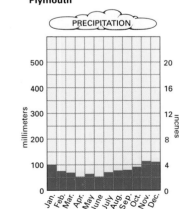

Valentia
PRECIPITATION

Plymouth
PRECIPITATION

Dundee
PRECIPITATION

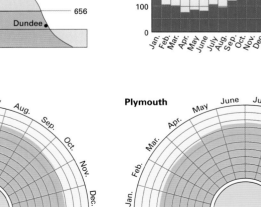

Valentia

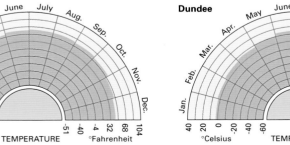

Plymouth

Dundee

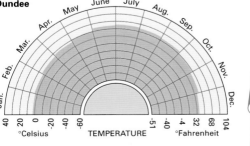

POPULATION

Britain's population density is more than four times greater than the population density in Ireland. The chief centers of population are in England, central Scotland, and south Wales, mainly in the older industrial cities. Fewer people live in rural areas.

POPULATION

Total population of region (in millions)	60.6
Population density (persons per sq mi)	75.1
Population change (average annual percent 1960–1990)	
Urban	+0.7
Rural	-1.6

URBAN POPULATION

As percentage of total population	
1960	84.7
1990	91.8
Percentage in cities of more than 1 million	13.0

TEN LARGEST CITIES

	Country	Population
London †	United Kingdom	6,378,000
Manchester	United Kingdom	1,669,000
Birmingham	United Kingdom	1,400,000
Liverpool	United Kingdom	1,060,000
Dublin †	Ireland	921,000
Glasgow	United Kingdom	730,000
Newcastle upon Tyne	United Kingdom	617,000
Sheffield	United Kingdom	445,000
Leeds	United Kingdom	432,000
Edinburgh	United Kingdom	404,000

† denotes national capital

INDUSTRY

Since the 1960s, the extraction of North Sea natural gas and oil have made Britain the world's fifth largest energy producer. Until recently, Ireland's main source of energy was peat, but offshore gas deposits are now being exploited. Britain has large coal deposits.

MAJOR PRODUCTS (Figures in parentheses are percentages of world production.)

Energy and minerals	Output	Change since 1960
Coal (mil. m.t.)	100.0 (2.1%)	-49.2%
Oil (mil. barrels)	673.6 (3.0%)	N/A
Natural gas (billion cu meters)	43.7 (2.4%)	N/A
Nuclear power (mil. m.t. coal equiv.)	22.2 (3.3%)	No data
Peat (mil. m.t.)	4.4 (21.8%)	+20%
Chalk (mil. m.t.)	14.5 (85.1%)	-10.8%

Manufactures		
Wool yarn (1,000 m.t.)	161.3 (7.2%)	-23%
Synthetic rubber (1,000 m.t.)	312.8 (3.1%)	-4.3%
Steel (mil. m.t.)	18.9 (2.6%)	-23.5%
Automobiles (mil.)	1.9 (2.0%)	+4.0%
Televisions (mil.)	3.1 (2.8%)	+44.8%
Beer (mil. gal.)	1,590.3 (5.8%)	-4.6%
Chocolate (1,000 m.t.)	480.1 (10.1%)	+12%

N/A *means production had not begun in 1960.*

AGRICULTURE

Farming in both Britain and Ireland has become increasingly specialized since the countries joined the European Community. Arable farming is now concentrated in the drier eastern lowlands, with livestock farming in the wetter uplands.

LAND (million acres)

Total	Agricultural	Arable	Forest/woodland
77 (100%)	528 (78%)	19 (25%)	7 (9%)

FARMERS

793,000 employed in agriculture (3% of workforce)
25 acres of arable land per person employed in agriculture

MAJOR CROPS

	Area mil. acres	Yield 100lbs/acre	Production mil. m.t.	Change since 1963
Barley	5.1	45.3	10.8 (6)	+49%
Wheat	4.9	53	12.3 (2)	+220%
Rapeseed	1.0	30.6	1.4 (6)	+45,533%
Sugar beets	0.5	357.3	9.6 (3)	+40%
Potatoes	0.5	317.7	7.5 (3)	-19%
Oats	0.5	41.9	0.6 (1)	-71%
Vegetables	—	—	—	—
Dry peas	—	—	4.3 (1)	+29%

MAJOR LIVESTOCK

	Number in mil.	Production mil. m.t.	Change since 1963
Sheep	29.6 (3)	—	-14%
Cattle	18.1 (1)	—	+8%
Pigs	8.9 (1)	—	+10%
Milk	—	21.5 (5)	+41%
Fish catch	—	1.2 (1)	—

FOOD SECURITY (grain exports minus imports)

mil. m.t.	% domestic production	% world trade
+3.0	12	1

Numbers in parentheses are percentages of world total.

POPULATION

About 200 years ago, most people in the region lived in small rural communities. Today, the United Kingdom is a highly urbanized country, though much of Wales, Scotland, and Northern Ireland remains very rural.

Population density
city populations
(National capital is underlined.)

- ◆ over 5,000,000
- ■ 1,000,000–5,000,000
- ● 500,000–999,999
- ⊙ 250,000–499,999

persons per square mi	persons per square km
520	200
260	100
130	50
26	10

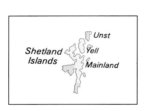

Shetland Islands — Unst, Yell, Mainland

INDUSTRY

Britain has a wide range of mineral resources, though many are expensive to extract. As a result, many raw materials used in industry are imported.

Resources and industry

◆ industrial center
○ major port
● other town
— major road
— major railroad

mineral resources and fossil fuels
◆ iron and other ferroalloy metal ores
● other metal ores
■ nonmetallic minerals

    coal
    iron ore

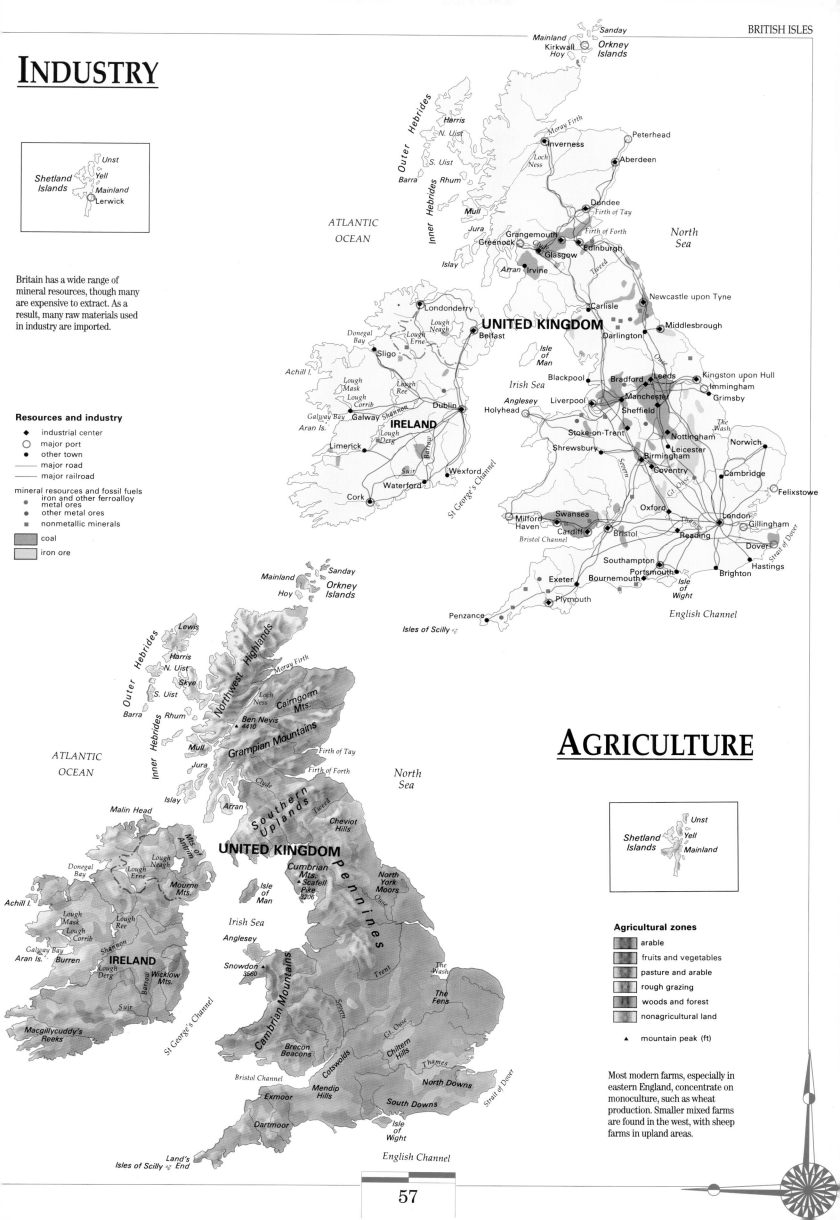

ATLANTIC OCEAN

Sanday
Mainland
Kirkwall
Hoy
Orkney Islands

Outer Hebrides
Harris
N. Uist
S. Uist
Barra
Rhum
Mull
Jura
Islay
Inner Hebrides

Moray Firth
Inverness
Peterhead
Aberdeen
Loch Ness
Dundee
Firth of Tay
Grangemouth
Greenock
Edinburgh
Glasgow
Clyde
Arran Irvine
Tweed

North Sea

Londonderry
Lough Neagh
UNITED KINGDOM
Belfast
Newcastle upon Tyne
Carlisle
Donegal Bay
Lough Erne
Sligo
Isle of Man
Middlesbrough
Darlington

Achill I.
Lough Mask
Lough Corrib
Lough Ree
Lough Shannon
Irish Sea
Blackpool
Bradford Leeds
Kingston upon Hull
Immingham
Anglesey
Liverpool
Manchester
Grimsby
Holyhead
Sheffield
The Wash
Galway
Galway Bay
IRELAND
Dublin
Stoke-on-Trent
Nottingham
Norwich
Aran Is.
Lough Derg
Shrewsbury
Leicester
Birmingham
Limerick
Coventry
Cambridge
Suir
Wexford
Oxford
London
Barrow
Waterford
St George's Channel
Milford Haven
Swansea
Thames
Felixstowe
Cork
Cardiff
Bristol
Reading
Gillingham
Bristol Channel
Dover
Southampton
Portsmouth
Brighton
Hastings
Strait of Dover
Exeter
Bournemouth
Isle of Wight
Plymouth
Penzance
English Channel
Isles of Scilly

AGRICULTURE

Sanday
Mainland
Orkney Islands
Hoy

Lewis
Outer Hebrides
Harris
N. Uist
Skye
S. Uist
Barra
Rhum
Inner Hebrides
Mull
Jura
Islay

Northwest Highlands
Loch Ness
Cairngorm Mts.
Moray Firth
Ben Nevis ▲ 4410
Grampian Mountains
Firth of Tay
Firth of Forth
Arran
Clyde
Tweed
Southern Uplands
Cheviot Hills

ATLANTIC OCEAN

North Sea

Malin Head
Mts. of Antrim
Lough Neagh
Mourne Mts.
Lough Erne
UNITED KINGDOM
Donegal Bay
Lough Mask
Lough Corrib
Lough Ree
Isle of Man
Pennines
Cumbrian Mts.
▲ Scafell Pike 3206
North York Moors
Irish Sea
Anglesey
Ouse
Achill I.
Shannon
IRELAND
Burren
Lough Derg
Snowdon ▲ 3560
Trent
The Wash
Galway Bay
Aran Is.
Barrow
Wicklow Mts.
Cambrian Mountains
The Fens
Suir
Severn
Gt. Ouse
Macgillycuddy's Reeks
St George's Channel
Brecon Beacons
Cotswolds
Chiltern Hills
Thames
Bristol Channel
Mendip Hills
North Downs
Exmoor
South Downs
Strait of Dover
Dartmoor
Isle of Wight
Land's End
Isles of Scilly
English Channel

Agricultural zones

    arable
    fruits and vegetables
    pasture and arable
    rough grazing
    woods and forest
    nonagricultural land

▲ mountain peak (ft)

Most modern farms, especially in eastern England, concentrate on monoculture, such as wheat production. Smaller mixed farms are found in the west, with sheep farms in upland areas.

FRANCE

France is the largest country in Western Europe. Its varied landscapes include rolling plains, hills, beautiful river valleys, the remains of ancient volcanoes, and dramatic mountain scenery in the Alps and Pyrenees.

The north has a cool temperate climate, while the south has the typical hot summers and mild, moist winters of Mediterranean lands. Other variations occur from west to east. While the west comes under the moderating influence of the Atlantic, to the east the climate becomes increasingly continental. Summers are hotter and winters are much colder.

The French have a strong sense of identity, a pride in their culture, and a firm belief in the preeminence of their capital, Paris, as a world center of art and learning. Yet the French owe their origins to many diverse groups, including Celts, Romans, Franks, and Vikings. Recent immigration has been from North Africa, Southeast Asia, and other parts of Europe.

France is a major industrial power, with an increasingly urbanized population. It is also the largest producer of farm products in Western Europe. It is especially famous for its fine wines and wide range of cheeses.

Northern France lies at the western end of the North European Plain – an ancient pathway of human migrations – that extends from the Ural Mountains of Russia to southeastern England. The south and southeast lie in a zone where the African and Eurasian plates have collided, thrusting up young ranges, including the snow-capped Pyrenees and Alps.

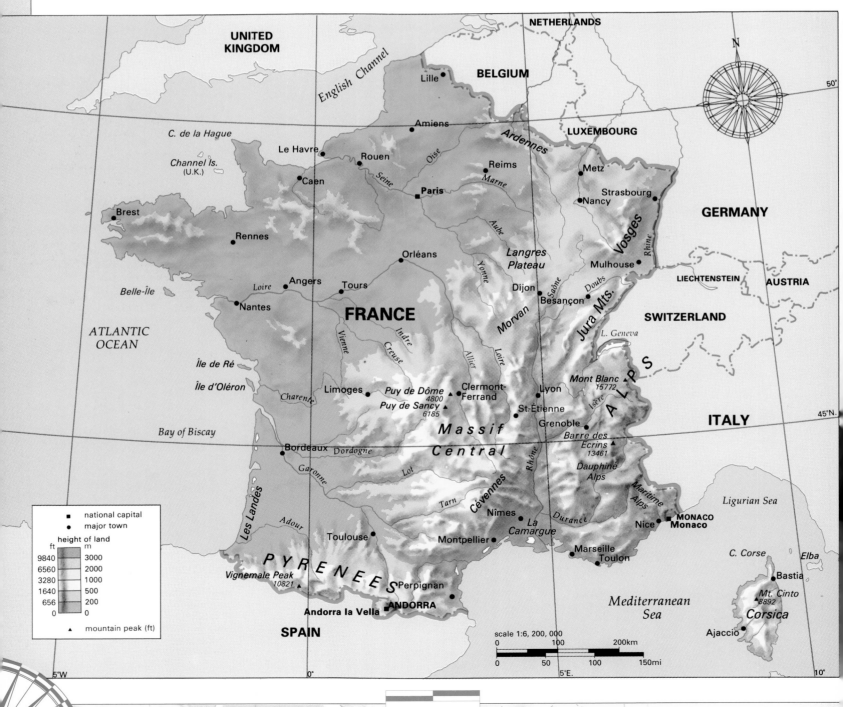

scale 1:6, 200, 000

| national capital |
| major town |

height of land

ft	m
9840	3000
6560	2000
3280	1000
1640	500
656	200
0	0

▲ mountain peak (ft)

THE POLITICAL AND CULTURAL WORLD

Modern France owes its origins to the French Revolution of 1789 and its principles of liberty, equality, and fraternity, which have been incorporated into the constitutions of many other countries. Today France is a parliamentary democracy, whose executive branch is headed by the president and the prime minister.

France has two of Europe's ministates as neighbors. Nestling in the Pyrenees is the tiny state of Andorra, a principality whose heads of state are the president of France and the bishop of Urgel in Spain. The other ministate is Monaco, a principality ruled by the House of Grimaldi since 1308.

COUNTRIES IN THE REGION

Andorra, France, Monaco

Island territories Corsica (France)
Territories outside the region French Guiana, French Polynesia, Guadeloupe, Martinique, Mayotte, New Caledonia, Reunion, St. Pierre and Miquelon, Wallis and Futuna (France)

LANGUAGE

Countries with one official language Catalan: Andorra; French: France, Monaco

Local minority languages in France are Basque, Breton, Catalan, Corsican, German (Alsatian), and Provençal. Significant immigrant languages include Arabic, Italian, Polish, Portuguese, Spanish, and Turkish. English, Italian, and Monégasque are spoken in Monaco; Spanish in Andorra.

RELIGION

Andorra Roman Catholic (99%)
France Roman Catholic (76%), Islam (3%), Protestant (2%), Jewish (1%), non-religious and atheists (3%)
Monaco Roman Catholic (91%), Protestant (2%), Eastern Orthodox (1%)

STYLES OF GOVERNMENT

Republic France
Principalities Andorra, Monaco
Multiparty state France
States without parties Andorra, Monaco
One-chamber assembly Andorra
Two-chamber assembly France, Monaco

MEMBERSHIP OF INTERNATIONAL ORGANIZATIONS

Council of Europe France
European Community (EC) France
North Atlantic Treaty Organization (NATO) France
Organization for Economic Cooperation and Development (OECD) France

France withdrew from NATO Military Command in 1966 but remains a member of the alliance.

ECONOMIC INDICATORS: 1990

	France
GDP (US$ billions)	1,190.78
GNP per capita (US$)	19,490
Annual rate of growth of GDP, 1980–1990	2.2%
Manufacturing as % of GDP	21.0%
Central government spending as % of GNP	43.0%
Merchandise exports (US$ billions)	215.8
Merchandise imports (US$ billions)	233.8
% of GNP donated as development aid	0.79%

WELFARE INDICATORS

Infant mortality rate (per 1,000 live births)
1965	22
1990	7

Daily food supply available (calories per capita, 1989) 3,465
Population per physician (1984) 320
Teacher-pupil ratio elementary school, 1989) 1 : 16

France
Area 210,026 sq mi (543,965 sq km)
Population 56,138,000
Currency 1 franc (f) = 100 centimes

Andorra
Area 181 sq mi (468 sq km)
Population 47,000
Currency 1 French franc (f) = 100 centimes
1 Spanish peseta (Pts) = 100 centimos

Monaco
Area 0.75 sq mi (1.95 sq km)
Population 28,000
Currency 1 French franc (f) = 100 centimes

- national capital
- regional capital

France is divided into 22 metropolitan regions, each governed by an elected council and its own president. The regions are responsible for their own economic planning. The regions are divided into 96 metropolitan departments, each with its own elected council. These councils are responsible for local social services.

HABITATS

Much of northern and western France consists of flat, fertile grassy plains or low, rolling hills. Much of this land is farmed. Wooded mountains rise in the east and south. The southern Massif Central with its spectacular river gorges contains largely poor soils.

LAND

Area 211,272 sq mi (547,492 sq km)
Highest point Mont Blanc, 15,771 ft (4,807 m)
Lowest point sea level
Major features Pyrénées, Alps, and Jura mountains, Massif Central, Paris basin, and basins of Garonne and Rhône rivers

WATER

Longest river Loire, 630 mi (1,020 km)
Largest basin Loire, 44,377 sq mi (115,000 sq km)
Highest average flow Rhône, 53,000 cu ft/sec (1,500 cu m/sec)
Largest lake Geneva, 224 sq mi (580 sq km)

NOTABLE THREATENED SPECIES

Mammals long-fingered bat (*Myotis capaccinii*), pond bat (*Myotis dasycneme*), mouse-eared bat (*Myotis myotis*), Pyrenean desman (*Galemys pyrenaicus*), European mink (*Mustela lutreola*), harbor porpoise (*Phocoena phocoena*), fin whale (*Balaenoptera physalus*)
Birds red kite (*Milvus migrans*), white-tailed sea eagle (*Haliaeetus albicilla*), corncrake (*Crex crex*), little bustard (*Tetrax tetrax*), Audouin's gull (*Larus audouinii*)
Plants *Aldrovanda vesiculosa*; Atlantic angelica (*Angelica heterocarpa*); *Caldensia parnassifolia*; bog orchid (*Hammarbya paludosa*); Pyrenean alyssum (*Hormathophyllum pyrenaica*); *Leucojum nicaeense*; *Lythrum thesioides*; *Primula allionii*; *Saxifraga florulenta*; raven violet (*Viola hispida*)
Others Corsican swallowtail butterfly (*Papilio hospiton*), quimper snail (*Elona quimperiana*), shining macromia dragonfly (*Macromia splendens*), longhorn beetle (*Cerambyx cerdo*)

CLIMATE

Western France is rainy, with cool summers and mild winters. The east is drier, with hotter summers and colder winters. The eastern mountains are snowy. The south has a Mediterranean climate, with hot, dry summers and mild, moist winters.

TEMPERATURE AND PRECIPITATION

	Temperature °F (°C)		Altitude	
	January	July	ft	(m)
Brest	43 (6)	61 (16)	338	(103)
Paris	37 (3)	68 (20)	173	(75)
Strasbourg	32 (0)	66 (19)	505	(154)
Bordeaux	41 (5)	68 (20)	26	(8)
Marseille	43 (6)	73 (23)	13	(4)

	Precipitation in (mm)			
	January	July	Year	
Brest	5.2 (133)	2.4 (62)	44.3	(1,126)
Paris	2.2 (56)	2.3 (59)	23.0	(585)
Strasbourg	1.5 (39)	3.0 (77)	23.9	(607)
Bordeaux	4.3 (109)	2.2 (56)	35.4	(900)
Marseille	1.7 (43)	0.4 (11)	21.5	(546)

NATURAL HAZARDS

Storms and floods, landslides, avalanches

ENVIRONMENTAL ISSUES

By 1992, about 75 percent of France's electricity was produced by the country's 55 nuclear power stations. Hence France is much less affected than most other parts of Europe by the air pollution and acid rain caused by burning fossil fuels.

POPULATION AND WEALTH

Population (in millions)	56.2
Population increase (annual population growth rate, % 1960–1990)	0.7
Energy use (gigajoules/person)	109
Real purchasing power (US$/person)	13,590

ENVIRONMENTAL INDICATORS

CO$_2$ emissions (mil. m.t. carbon/year)	120
Municipal waste (lbs/person/year)	600
Nuclear waste (cumulative m.t. heavy metal)	12,700
Artificial fertilizer use (lbs/acre/year)	264
Automobiles (per 1,000 population)	391
Access to safe drinking water (% population)	100

MAJOR ENVIRONMENTAL PROBLEMS AND SOURCES

Air pollution: locally high, in particular urban
Marine/coastal pollution: medium; *sources*: industrial, sewage, oil
Land pollution: medium; *sources*: industrial, nuclear
Waste disposal problems: domestic; industrial; nuclear
Population problems: tourism
Major events: Val d'Isere (1970), major avalanche; *Amoco Cadiz* (1978), oil tanker accident; Les Arcs (1981), landslide; le Grand Bornand (1987), major flood; Nîmes (1988), major flood; Protex plant, Tours (1988), fire at chemical plant

HABITATS

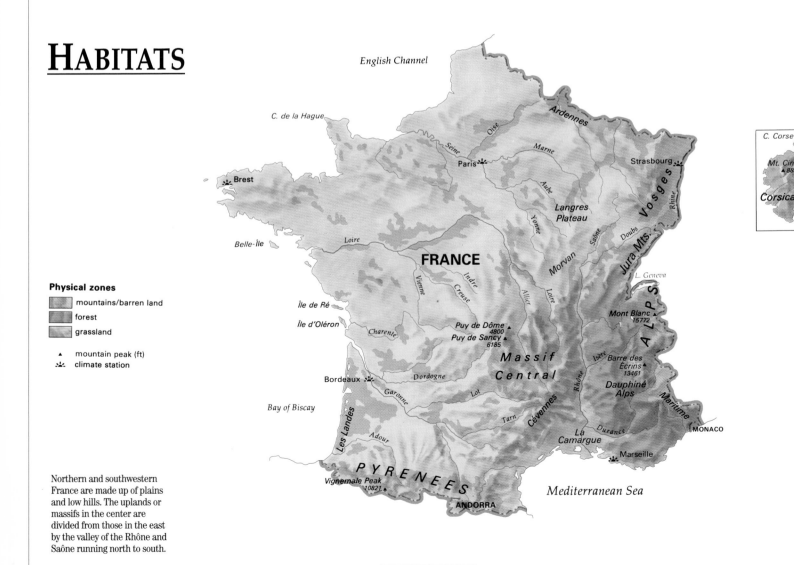

Physical zones

- mountains/barren land
- forest
- grassland

▲ mountain peak (ft)
☀ climate station

Northern and southwestern France are made up of plains and low hills. The uplands or massifs in the center are divided from those in the east by the valley of the Rhône and Saône running north to south.

ENVIRONMENTAL ISSUES

Tourism and industry have polluted coastal areas, while forest fires, avalanches, and soil erosion are common hazards in the south. In recent years, the government has introduced many policies aimed at protecting the environment.

Key environmental issues

- • major town or city
- 🏭 heavily polluted town or city
- 🏭 major pollution event
- + major natural disaster
- 🏭 nuclear power station
- 🏭 nuclear processing plant
- 🏴 beach not complying with E.C. standard 1989
- heavily polluted river
- main area of coastal tourism
- main skiing area
- area of fire risk

remaining forest
- coniferous
- mixed
- deciduous
- scrub

CLIMATE

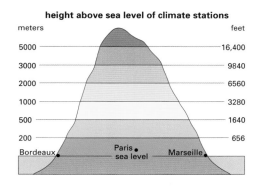

height above sea level of climate stations

meters		feet
5000		16,400
3000		9840
2000		6560
1000		3280
500		1640
200		656

Bordeaux — Paris (sea level) — Marseille

Bordeaux
PRECIPITATION

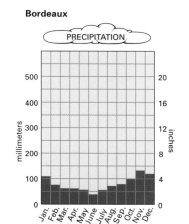

Paris
PRECIPITATION

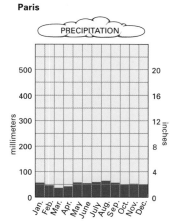

Marseille
PRECIPITATION

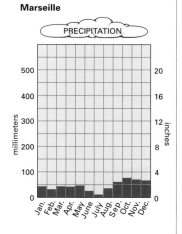

Bordeaux

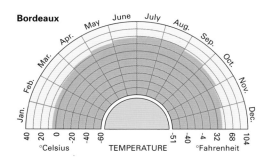

TEMPERATURE
°Celsius / Fahrenheit

Paris

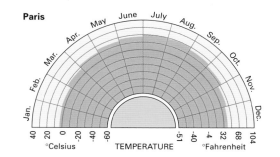

TEMPERATURE
°Celsius / Fahrenheit

Marseille

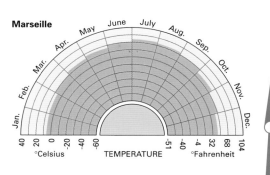

TEMPERATURE
°Celsius / Fahrenheit

POPULATION

Before 1945, the movement of people from the countryside to urban areas was slower in France than in most parts of Europe. But urban areas now house about 75 percent of the people, largely in apartment buildings. Greater Paris is one of the world's largest metropolitian areas.

POPULATION

Total population of region (in millions)	56.2
Population density (persons per sq mi)	263.7
Population change (average annual percent 1960–1990)	
Urban	+1.3
Rural	-0.6

URBAN POPULATION

As percentage of total population	
1960	62.4
1990	74.1
Percentage in cities of more than 1 million	19.7

TEN LARGEST CITIES

	Population
Paris †	8,510,000
Lyon	1,170,000
Marseille	1,080,000
Lille	935,000
Bordeaux	628,000
Toulouse	523,000
Nantes	465,000
Nice	449,000
Toulon	410,000
Grenoble	392,000

† *denotes national capital*

INDUSTRY

France is a major manufacturing nation. Its traditional industries were originally built on local energy and mineral resources, mainly coal and iron. But it now has many dynamic high-tech industries, including aerospace and telecommunications.

INDUSTRIAL OUTPUT (US$ billion)

Total	Mining and Manufacturing	Average annual change since 1960
304.9	191.2	+3.1%

INDUSTRIAL WORKERS (millions)
(Figures in parentheses are percentages of total labor force.)

Total	Mining and Manufacturing	Construction
5.7	4.1 (16.9%)	1.3 (5.3%)

MAJOR PRODUCTS (Figures in parentheses are percentages of world production.)

Energy and minerals	Output	Change since 1960
Coal (mil. m.t.)	13.5 (0.3%)	-76.8%
Oil (mil. barrels)	27.1 (0.1%)	No data
Natural gas (billion cu meters)	2.9 (0.1%)	-62%
Nuclear power (mil. m.t. coal equiv.)	43.1 (13.3%)	N/A
Potash (mil. m.t.)	1.6 (5.5%)	-24%
Bauxite (mil. m.t.)	0.6 (0.7%)	-70.2%

Manufactures		
Cement (mil. m.t.)	30.9 (2.8%)	+115%
Steel (mil. m.t.)	18.9 (2.6%)	+9.4%
Automobiles (mil.)	3.8 (8.0%)	+274.7%
Plastics and resins (mil. m.t.)	3.4 (6.6%)	+57%
Fertilizers (mil. m.t.)	5.8 (3.6%)	+57.6%
Vacuum cleaners (mil.)	2.3 (6.4%)	+51.3%
Telecommunications equipment (US$ billion)	12.0 (12.9%)	No data

N/A *means production had not begun in 1960.*

AGRICULTURE

France is a major producer of farm products. It is the second largest producer of wine and ranks among the world's top ten producers of milk, butter, meat, eggs, wheat, and barley. Only the United States exports more agricultural produce.

LAND (million acres)

Total	Agricultural	Arable	Forest/woodland
136 (100%)	77 (57%)	44 (33%)	37 (27%)

FARMERS

1.4 million people employed in agriculture (6% of workforce)
30 acres of arable land per person employed in agriculture

MAJOR CROPS

	Area mil. acres	Yield 100lbs/acre	Production mil. m.t.	Change since 1963
Wheat	12.1	49.6	27.4 (5)	+119%
Barley	4.9	47	10.5 (6)	+59%
Corn	4.2	63.8	12.5 (3)	+352%
Sunflower seeds	2.5	22.6	2.7 (13)	+10,979%
Grapes	2.5	79.1	9.2 (14)	-4%
Rapeseed	1.7	32.1	2.7 (12)	+1,255%

MAJOR LIVESTOCK

	Number in mil.	Production mil. m.t.	Change since 1963
Cattle	22.8 (2)	—	+13%
Pigs	12.4 (1)	—	+38%
Sheep	10.6 (1)	—	+19%
Milk	—	28.6 (6)	+14%
Fish catch	—	0.8 (1)	—

FOOD SECURITY (grain exports minus imports)

mil. m.t.	% domestic production	% world trade
+26.0	49	12

Numbers in parentheses are percentages of world total.

POPULATION

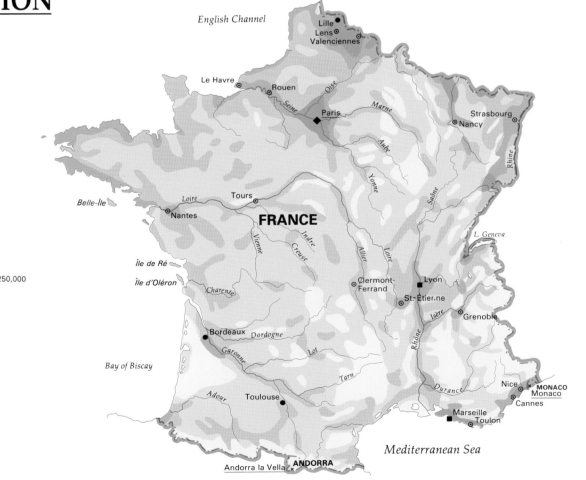

Population density

city populations
(National capital is underlined.)

- ◆ over 5,000,000
- ■ 1,000,000–5,000,000
- ● 500,000–999,999
- ⊙ 250,000–499,999
- × national capital less than 250,000

persons per square mi	persons per square km
520	200
260	100
130	50
65	25

Areas of high population density occur around Paris and in the northern industrial areas. Migration to the south has created some high density areas in the Rhône valley and on the southeast coast.

INDUSTRY

The earliest industrial regions grew up in the northern mining districts. The recent decline in mining has led to the spread of industry to other areas.

Resources and industry

- ◆ industrial center
- ◯ major port
- • other town
- — major road
- — major railroad

mineral resources and fossil fuels
- ● iron and other ferroalloy metal ores
- ● other metal ores
- ■ nonmetallic minerals

- bauxite
- coal
- iron ore
- lignite (brown coal)
- potash

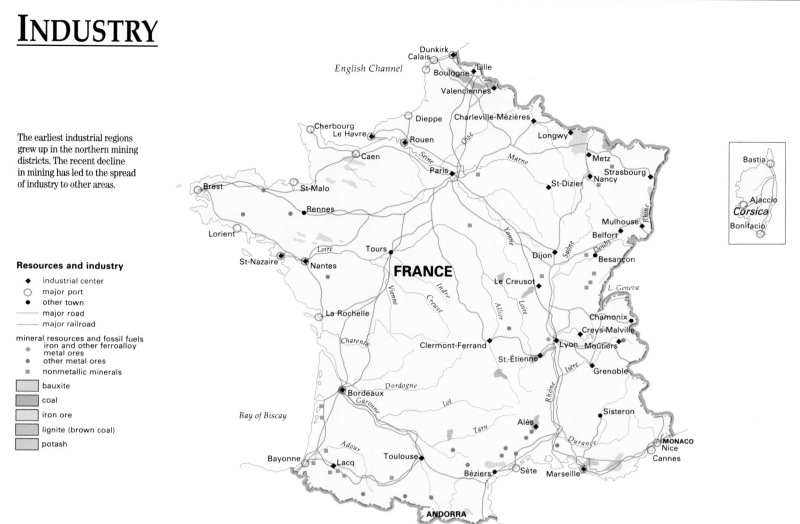

AGRICULTURE

Agricultural zones

- arable
- fruits and vegetables
- pasture
- rough grazing
- woods and forest
- nonagricultural land

- ▲ mountain peak (ft)

The main arable farming zones are in the region around Paris, which is the main grain-producing area, and in major river valleys. Dairy and beef cattle are raised on low-lying pasture, while sheep farms are found in upland areas.

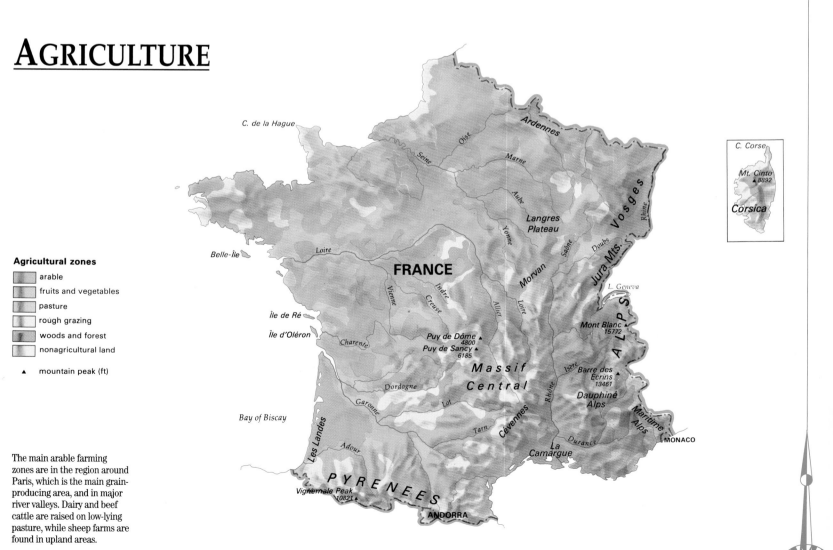

SPAIN AND PORTUGAL

Spain, Portugal, and the tiny British dependency of Gibraltar, which occupies a strategic position near the Strait of Gibraltar, form the Iberian Peninsula, isolated from the rest of Europe by the Pyrenees.

Much of the peninsula is a high plateau, called the Meseta. The Meseta is bordered not only by the Pyrenees, but also by the Cantabrian Mountains in the northwest and the Sierra Nevada in the southeast. Because of its altitude, the Meseta has a severe climate, with hot summers and bitterly cold winters. The Meseta is arid, and parts of the southeast are semidesert. Lowland Portugal's climate is moderated by moist Atlantic winds. Other lowlands include the Ebro and Guadalquivir river valleys in Spain.

From early times, Iberia was invaded by waves of colonizers, including Celts, Phoenicians, Greeks, Carthaginians, Romans, and Visigoths, each of whom left their imprint on Iberian culture. The last invaders were the Moors (Muslim Arabs), who entered the peninsula in the year 711. Their last bastion, the Alhambra palace in Granada, did not fall until 1492, the year Columbus sailed from Spain.

Although Spain and Portugal were both leaders in terms of world exploration, both countries were, by the early twentieth century, among Europe's poorest. Today, as members of the European Community, their economies have been expanding quickly, and Spain is especially growing rapidly. Tourism plays a major part in the economies of both countries.

The Iberian Peninsula occupies the south-western corner of Europe. Separated from North Africa by the Strait of Gibraltar, Iberia often seems to visitors to be almost as much African as European. Spain also includes the Balearic Islands in the Mediterranean and the Canary Islands in the Atlantic. Portugal has two autonomous regions, the Azores in the North Atlantic and the Madeira Islands off the northwest coast of Africa.

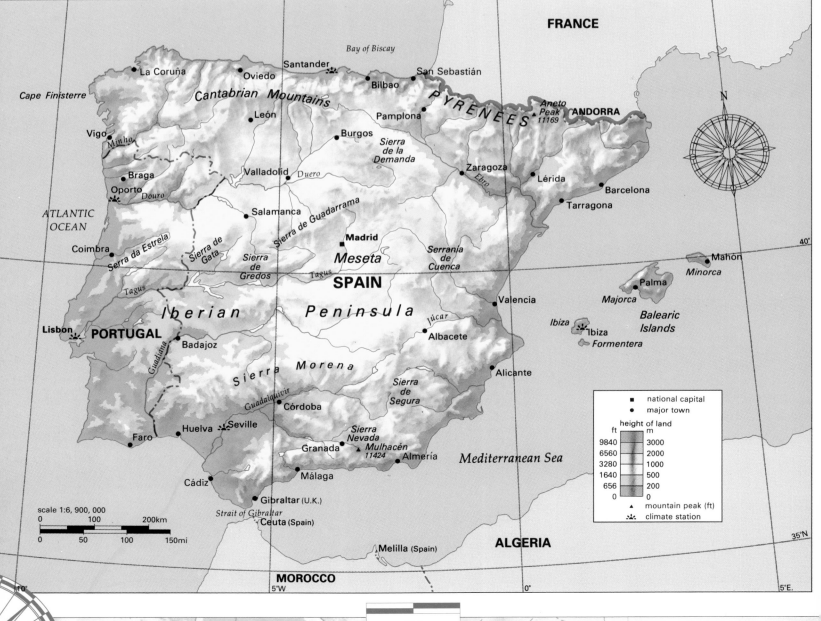

THE POLITICAL AND CULTURAL WORLD

After the Spanish civil war (1936–1939), Spain became a dictatorship under General Franco. When he died in 1975, the monarchy was restored, and Spain became a parliamentary democracy. Between 1928 and 1974, Portugal was also a dictatorship. But after the overthrow of its military leaders, it became a democratic republic.

Spain claims Gibraltar, the world's smallest colony, but Britain justifies its control over the territory by arguing that the majority of Gibraltarians want to remain British. Despite the lack of agreement over sovereignty, cooperation over such matters as the shared use of Gibraltar's airport has increased.

Portugal

Area 35, 672 sq mi (92,389 sq km)
Population 10,285,000
Capital Lisbon
Currency 1 escudo (Esc) = 100 centavos

COUNTRIES IN THE REGION
Portugal, Spain

Integral parts outside the region Azores, Madeira (Portugal); Balearic Islands, Canary Islands, Ceuta, Melilla (Spain)
Territories Macao (Portugal)

LAND
Highest point on mainland, Mulhacén, 11,408 ft (3,482 m); Pico de Teide on Tenerife in the Canary Islands, 12,195 ft (3,718 m)
Lowest point sea level
Major features Meseta plateau in center, Cantabrian Mountains and Pyrenees in north, Sierra Nevada in south

WATER
Longest river Tagus, 630 mi (1,010 km)
Largest basin Douro, 38,000 sq mi (98,000 sq km)
Highest average flow Douro, 11,000 cu ft/sec (312 cu m/sec)

CLIMATE

	Temperature °F (°C)		Altitude
	January	July	ft (m)
Oporto	48 (9)	68 (20)	311 (95)
Lisbon	52 (11)	72 (22)	252 (77)
Santander	48 (9)	66 (19)	216 (66)
Seville	50 (10)	82 (28)	29 (9)
Ibiza	52 (11)	75 (24)	23 (7)

	Precipitation in (mm)		
	January	July	Year
Oporto	6.3 (159)	0.8 (20)	45.3 (1,150)
Lisbon	4.4 (111)	0.1 (3)	27.9 (708)
Santander	4.6 (119)	2.1 (54)	47.6 (1,208)
Seville	2.6 (66)	0.04 (1)	22.0 (559)
Ibiza	1.7 (42)	0.2 (5)	17.5 (444)

LANGUAGE
Countries with one official language Portuguese: Portugal; Spanish: Spain

Local minority languages spoken in Spain are Basque, Catalan, and Galician.

RELIGION
Portugal Roman Catholic (94%), nonreligious (3.8%)
Spain Roman Catholic (97%), nonreligious and atheist (2.6%), Protestant (0.4%)

STYLES OF GOVERNMENT
Republic Portugal
Monarchy Spain
Multiparty states Portugal, Spain
One-chamber assembly Portugal
Two-chamber assembly Spain

ECONOMIC INDICATORS: 1990

	Spain	Portugal
GDP (US$ billions)	421.24	56.82
GNP per capita (US$)	11,020	4,900
Annual rate of growth of GDP, 1980–1990	3.1%	2.7%
Manufacturing as % of GDP	18.0%	9.0%
Central government spending as % of GNP	34.0%	43.0%
Merchandise exports (US$ billions)	56.3	16.3
Merchandise imports (US$ billions)	89.0	23.0
% of GNP donated as development aid	N/A	–

WELFARE INDICATORS

Infant mortality rate (per 1,000 live births)		
1965	38	65
1990	8	12
Daily food supply available (calories per capita, 1989)	3,572	3,495
Population per physician (1984)	320	140
Teacher-pupil ratio (elementary school, 1989)	1 : 25	1 : 17

■ national capital

Spain includes the Balearic Islands of Majorca, Minorca, Ibiza, and Formentera, and several smaller islands; the Canary Islands, and the port cities of Ceuta and Melilla on the north Moroccan coast. Portugal includes the islands of the Azores and Madeira in the Atlantic Ocean. Both Spain and Portugal are now democracies; Spain was governed by General Franco until 1975 and Portugal by the dictator Salazar until 1968. Spain's head of state is King Juan Carlos, who came to the throne in 1975.

Area 194,885 sq mi (504,750 sq km)
Population 39,187,000
Capital Madrid
Currency 1 peseta (Pta) = 100 centimos

Spain

ENVIRONMENTAL ISSUES

The Iberian Peninsula is one of the fastest changing parts of Europe, with new investment paying for rapid development. Tourism has led to the destruction of many coastal wildlife habitats, while the growth of cities has led to serious air and water pollution.

POPULATION AND WEALTH

	Portugal	Spain
Population (in millions)	10.3	39.2
Population increase (annual population growth rate, % 1960–1990)	0.5	0.8
Energy use (gigajoules/person)	39	62
Real purchasing power (US$/person)	4,190	8,250

ENVIRONMENTAL INDICATORS

CO₂ emissions (million m.t. carbon/year)	17	73
Municipal waste (lbs/person/year)	487	606
Nuclear waste (cumulative m.t. heavy metal)	0	2,800
Artificial fertilizer use (lbs/acre/year)	92	88
Automobiles (per 1,000 population)	125	78
Access to safe drinking water (% population)	95	100

MAJOR ENVIRONMENTAL PROBLEMS AND SOURCES

Air pollution: urban high
Marine/coastal pollution: medium; *sources:* industrial, agricultural, sewage, oil
Land degradation: soil erosion; salinization; habitat destruction; *causes:* agriculture, industry, population pressure
Population problems: tourism
Major event: San Carlos de la Rapita (1978), transportation accident

POPULATION

Industrialization occurred later in the Iberian Peninsula than in other parts of Europe. But the industrial cities have grown steadily in the twentieth century. Tourism has led to the development of an urban corridor around the coasts, while the interior is thinly populated.

POPULATION

Total population of region (in millions)	49.5
Population density (persons per sq mi)	253.0
Population change (average annual percent 1960–1990)	
Urban	+1.9
Rural	-1.0

URBAN POPULATION

As percentage of total population	
1960	41.6
1990	59.0
Percentage in cities of more than 1 million	13.1

TEN LARGEST CITIES

	Country	Population
Madrid †	Spain	3,101,000
Barcelona	Spain	1,704,000
Lisbon†	Portugal	1,612,000
Oporto	Portugal	1,315,000
Valencia	Spain	732,000
Seville	Spain	655,000
Zaragoza	Spain	575,000
Málaga	Spain	566,000
Bilbao	Spain	382,000
Las Palmas (Grand Canary I.)	Spain	358,000

† denotes national capital

AGRICULTURE

Despite the growing importance of manufacturing, agriculture remains important in both Spain and Portugal. The main agricultural activities are the cultivation of citrus fruits, olives, grapes, and wheat, and the raising of sheep, pigs, and cattle in the less fertile areas.

LAND (million acres)

Total	Agricultural	Arable	Forest/woodland
146 (100%)	84 (58%)	44 (30%)	47 (33%)

FARMERS

2.5 million employed in agriculture (13% of workforce)
17 acres of arable land per person employed in agriculture

MAJOR CROPS

	Area mil. acres	Yield 100lbs/acre	Production mil. m.t.	Change since 1963
Barley	11.0	19.7	9.9 (5)	+391%
Wheat	6.1	22.0	6.3 (1)	+28%
Corn	1.9	46.7	4.2 (1)	+145%
Grapes	4.4	39.3	7.8 (12)	+29%
Oranges	—	—	2.5 (6)	+46%
Vegetables	—	—	11.4 (3)	+55%
Other fruit	—	—	5.9 (3)	+144%

MAJOR LIVESTOCK

	Number in mil.	Production mil. m.t.	Change since 1963
Sheep/goats	26.4 (2)	—	-10%
Pigs	18.7 (2)	—	+156%
Milk	—	7.0 (2)	+93%
Fish catch	—	1.8 (2)	—

FOOD SECURITY (grain exports minus imports)

mil. m.t.	% domestic production	% world trade
-3.5	17	2

Numbers in parentheses are percentages of world total.

ENVIRONMENTAL ISSUES

Soil erosion caused by farming, combined with drought and deforestation, has affected much of the Iberian Peninsula. Public debate about green issues and conservation is increasing.

Key environmental issues
- major town or city
- heavily polluted town or city
- major pollution event
- heavily polluted river
- main area of coastal tourism

soil degradation
- severe
- high
- moderate
- low

POPULATION

Population density

city populations
(National capital is underlined.)

■ 1,000,000–5,000,000
● 500,000–999,999
◉ 250,000–499,999

persons per square mi	persons per square km
520	200
260	100
130	50
65	25

The areas of high population density in the Iberian Peninsula are mainly situated along the coasts, especially around such industrial cities as Barcelona, Bilbao, Lisbon, Málaga, and Valencia.

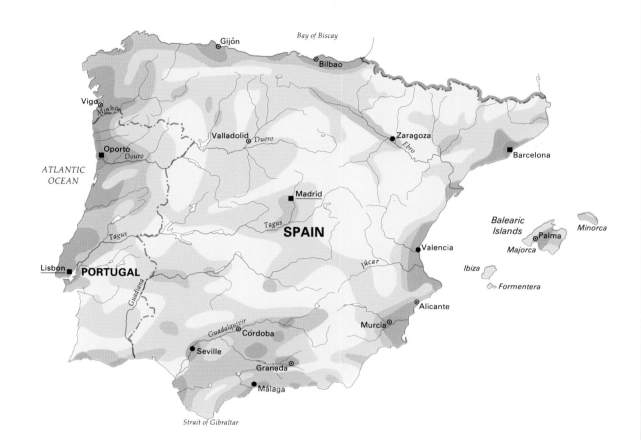

AGRICULTURE

Agricultural zones

arable
fruits and vegetables
rough grazing
woods and forest
nonagricultural land

▲ mountain peak (ft)

Fruits and vegetables are grown on the coasts, while dry parts of the Meseta are used to graze sheep. Many river valleys in the interior are cultivated.

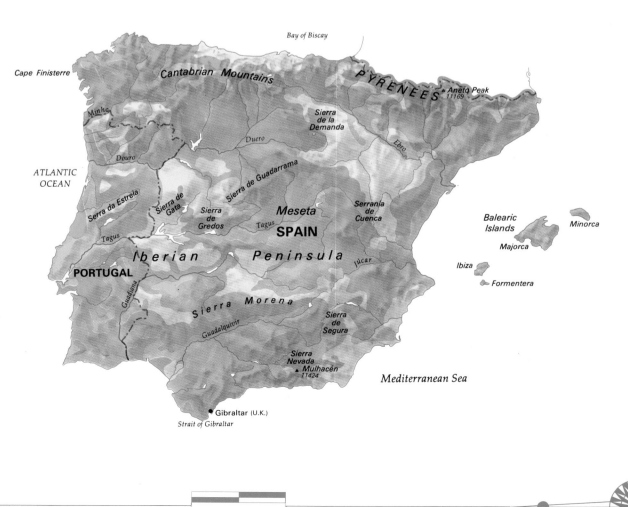

ITALY AND GREECE

Italy and Greece occupy a region where the earth's crust is unstable; there are frequent earthquakes and spectacular volcanic eruptions, especially in southern Italy. The snow-capped Alps in northern Italy were raised up as the result of a collision between the northward-moving African plate and the Eurasian plate.

About 40 percent of the land is mountainous, the Po valley being the most extensive lowland.

The coastlands, with their hot, dry summers and mild, wet winters, are tourist magnets for north Europeans. But the mountains of southern Italy and Greece can be bitterly cold and snowy in the winter months.

The ancient ruins of Greece and Italy are testimony to two major civilizations, whose art, philosophy, and politics lie at the heart of European culture.

Italy and Greece are on two peninsulas that jut into the Mediterranean Sea. Both countries include many islands. Around 440 islands make up about one-fifth of Greece's area.

Malta is an island republic south of Sicily. Cyprus is another island republic in the east.

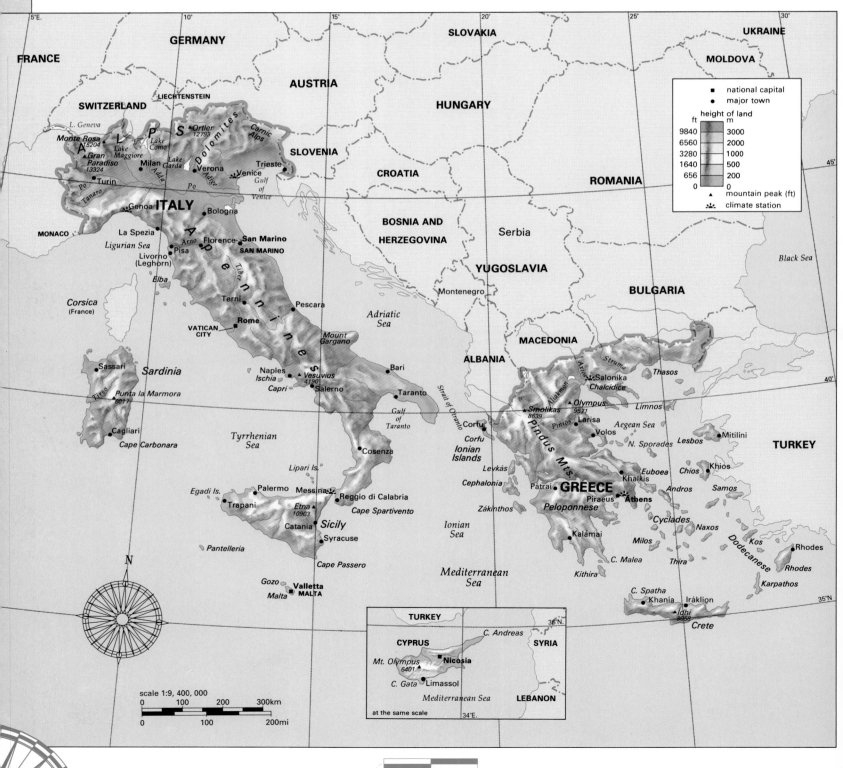

	height of land
■	national capital
●	major town
ft	m
9840	3000
6560	2000
3280	1000
1640	500
656	200
0	0
▲	mountain peak (ft)
⁂	climate station

scale 1:9, 400, 000
0   100   200   300km
0   100   200mi

THE POLITICAL AND CULTURAL WORLD

Italy and Greece have both undergone periods of instability and dictatorship in the twentieth century, though today they are democratic republics.

Greece has a long-standing dispute with Turkey over Cyprus, an island with a Greek majority and a Turkish minority. In 1974 Greece's military regime was implicated in moves to unite Cyprus with Greece. (Cyprus had been independent since 1960.) Turkey invaded northern Cyprus and set up the Turkish Republic of Northern Cyprus, a state that is recognized only by Turkey.

Cyprus
Area 3,572 sq mi
(9,251 sq km)
Population 701,000
Capital Nicosia
Currency 1 Cyprus pound
(C£) = 100 cents
[1 Turkish lira (TL) = 100 kurus]

Greece
Area 50,949 sq mi
(131,957 sq km)
Population 10,047,000
Capital Athens
Currency 1 drachma
(Dr) = 100 lepta

■ national capital

COUNTRIES IN THE REGION
Cyprus, Greece, Italy, Malta, San Marino, Vatican City

Island areas Aegean Islands, Crete, Ionian Islands, (Greece); Elba, Capri, Ischia, Lipari Islands, Sardinia, Sicily (Italy)

LAND
Highest point Monte Rosa, 4,634 m (15,203 ft)
Lowest point sea level
Major features Alps, Apennines, Pindus Mountains, Po valley, islands including Sardinia, Crete, Greek archipelago, and Cyprus

WATER
Longest river Po, 380 mi (620 km)
Largest basin Po, 29,000 sq mi (75,000 sq km)
Highest average flow Po, 54,000 cu ft/sec (1,540 cu m/sec)
Largest lake Garda, 140 sq mi (370 sq km)

CLIMATE

	Temperature °F (°C)		Altitude
	January	July	ft (m)
Genoa	46 (8)	75 (24)	69 (21)
Venice	39 (4)	73 (23)	3 (1)
Messina	52 (11)	79 (26)	117 (54)
Salonika	42 (6)	81 (27)	82 (25)
Athens	48 (9)	82 (28)	351 (107)

	Precipitation in (mm)		
	January	July	Year
Genoa	3.1 (79)	1.6 (40)	50 (1,270)
Venice	1.4 (37)	2.7 (69)	33.6 (854)
Messina	5.7 (146)	0.7 (19)	38.3 (974)
Salonika	1.7 (45)	0.9 (23)	13.3 (339)
Athens	2.4 (63)	0.2 (6)	13.3 (339)

LANGUAGE
Countries with one official language Greek: Greece; Italian: Italy, San Marino
Countries with two official languages English, Maltese: Malta; Greek, Turkish: Cyprus; Italian, Latin: Vatican City

Other languages spoken in the region include Albanian, Macedonian, and Turkish (Greece); Albanian, Catalan, French, German, Greek, Ladin, Sardinian, and Slovenian (Italy).

RELIGION
Cyprus Greek Orthodox (80%), Islam (19%)
Greece Greek Orthodox (97.6%), Islam (1.5%), other Christian (0.5%)
Italy Roman Catholic (83.2%), nonreligious and atheist (16.2%)
Malta Roman Catholic (97.3%), Anglican (1.2%), other (1.5%)
San Marino Roman Catholic (95%), nonreligious (3%)
Vatican City Roman Catholic (100%)

STYLES OF GOVERNMENT
Republics Cyprus, Greece, Italy, Malta, San Marino
City state Vatican City
Multiparty states Cyprus, Greece, Italy, Malta, San Marino
State without parties Vatican City
One-chamber assembly Cyprus, Greece, Malta, San Marino
Two-chamber assembly Italy

ECONOMIC INDICATORS: 1990

	Greece	Italy
GDP (US$ billions)	57.94	1,090.75
GNP per capita (US$)	5,990	16,830
Annual rate of growth of GDP, 1980–1990	1.8%	2.4%
Manufacturing as % of GDP	14.0%	23.0%
Central government spending as % of GNP	36.0%	49.0%
Merchandise exports (US$ billions)	6.4	182.2
Merchandise imports (US$ billions)	18.7	193.6
% of GNP donated as development aid	–	0.32%

WELFARE INDICATORS

		Greece	Italy
Infant mortality rate (per 1,000 live births)			
	1965	34	36
	1990	11	9
Daily food supply available (calories per capita, 1989)		3,825	3,216
Population per physician (1984)		350	230
Teacher-pupil ratio (elementary school, 1989)		1 : 22	1 : 12

Italy
Area 116,324 sq mi
(301,277 sq km)
Population 57,061,000
Capital Rome
Currency 1 lira
(Lit) = 100 centesimi

Malta
Area 122 sq mi
(316 sq km)
Population 353,000
Capital Valletta
Currency 1 Maltese lira
(Lm) = 100 cents = 1,000 mils

San Marino
Area 24 sq mi
(61 sq km)
Population 23,000
Capital San Marino
Currency 1 Italian lira
(Lit) = 100 centesimi

Vatican City
Area 0.17 sq mi
(0.44 sq km)
Population 1,000
Currency 1 Vatican lira
(VL) = 1 Italian lira = 100 centesimi

Both Italy and Greece are republics that once had monarchies and abolished them. Both are highly centralized states. Malta has been a democratic republic within the British Commonwealth since 1964. San Marino claims to be the world's oldest republic.

ENVIRONMENTAL ISSUES

Deforestation in the past has caused extensive soil erosion and has increased the frequency of floods and avalanches. The growth of industrial areas in northern Italy and around Athens in Greece has caused large-scale air, river, and sea pollution.

POPULATION AND WEALTH

	Greece	Italy	Malta
Population (in millions)	10	57.1	0.4
Population increase (annual population growth rate, % 1960–1990)	0.6	0.4	0.2
Energy use (gigajoules/person)	72	105	52
Real purchasing power (US$/person)	6,440	13,000	7,490

ENVIRONMENTAL INDICATORS

	Greece	Italy	Malta
CO₂ emissions (mil. m.t. carbon/year)	20	120	0.2
Municipal waste (lbs/person/year)	570	579	N/A
Nuclear waste (cumulative m.t. heavy metal)	0	1,400	0
Artificial fertilizer use (lbs./acre/year)	152.6	169.5	41
Automobiles (per 1,000 population)	143	398	N/A
Access to safe drinking water (% population)	97	100	100

MAJOR ENVIRONMENTAL PROBLEMS AND SOURCES

Air pollution: locally high, in particular urban; acid rain prevalent; high greenhouse gas emissions
River pollution: medium; *sources:* agricultural, sewage
Marine/coastal pollution: medium/high; *sources:* industrial, agricultural, sewage, oil
Land degradation: *types:* soil erosion; *causes:* agriculture, industry, population pressure

POPULATION

During the Renaissance in the fifteenth to sixteenth centuries, Italy had many wealthy cities that were centers of art and learning. But the population remained largely rural in both Italy and Greece until recent times, when industrial cities began to develop.

POPULATION

Total population of region (in millions)	67.7
Population density (persons per sq mi)	417.3
Population change (average annual percent 1960–1990)	
Urban	+1.1
Rural	-0.5

URBAN POPULATION

As percentage of total population	
1960	55.2
1990	66.3
Percentage in cities of more than 1 million	14.9

TEN LARGEST CITIES

	Country	Population
Athens†	Greece	3,027,000
Rome †	Italy	2,817,000
Milan	Italy	1,464,000
Naples	Italy	1,203,000
Turin	Italy	1,012,000
Salonika	Greece	872,000
Palermo	Italy	731,000
Genoa	Italy	715,000
Bologna	Italy	422,000
Florence	Italy	417,000

† *denotes national capital*

AGRICULTURE

Mountainous terrain, summer droughts, and poor soils have created many problems for farmers. To overcome these difficulties and achieve high agricultural yields, the people have terraced the slopes, drained marshes, and built irrigation systems.

LAND (million acres)

Total	Agricultural	Arable	Forest/woodland
106 (100%)	64 (61%)	29.6 (28%)	22.2 (22%)

FARMERS

2.9 million employed in agriculture (11% of workforce)
10 acres of arable land per person employed in agriculture

MAJOR CROPS

	Area mil. acres	Yield 100lbs/acre	Production mil. m.t.	Change since 1963
Wheat	9.8	26.0	11.6 (2)	+9%
Grapes	3.2	90.3	13.1 (20)	+15%
Barley	1.7	29.1	2.4 (1)	+292%
Sugar beets	0.74	466.4	17.4 (6)	+112%
Vegetables	—	—	18.0 (4)	+58%
Peaches	—	—	2.1 (27)	+62%
Other fruit	—	—	8.2 (3)	+17%

MAJOR LIVESTOCK

	Number in mil.	Production mil. m.t.	Change since 1963
Sheep/goats	27.9 (2)	—	+21%
Pigs	10.8 (1)	—	+101%
Cattle	9.7 (1)	—	-6%
Milk	—	11.6 (3)	+19%
Fish catch	—	0.7 (1)	—

Numbers in parentheses are percentages of world total.

ENVIRONMENTAL ISSUES

Tourism has caused much damage along the coasts and inland at ski resorts. These and other developments, such as the drainage of wetlands, have greatly reduced the area of wilderness in the region.

Key environmental issues

- ● major town or city
- ⬬ heavily polluted town or city
- ◢ major pollution event
- ✛ major natural disaster
- ◢ beach not complying with E C standard 1989
- ⁀ heavily polluted river
- ▬ main area of coastal tourism
- ⬭ main skiing area

remaining forest
- coniferous
- mixed
- deciduous
- scrub

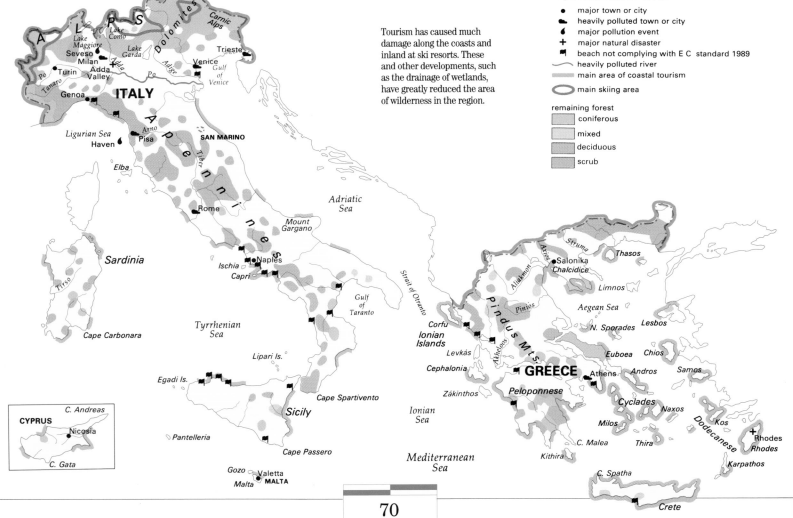

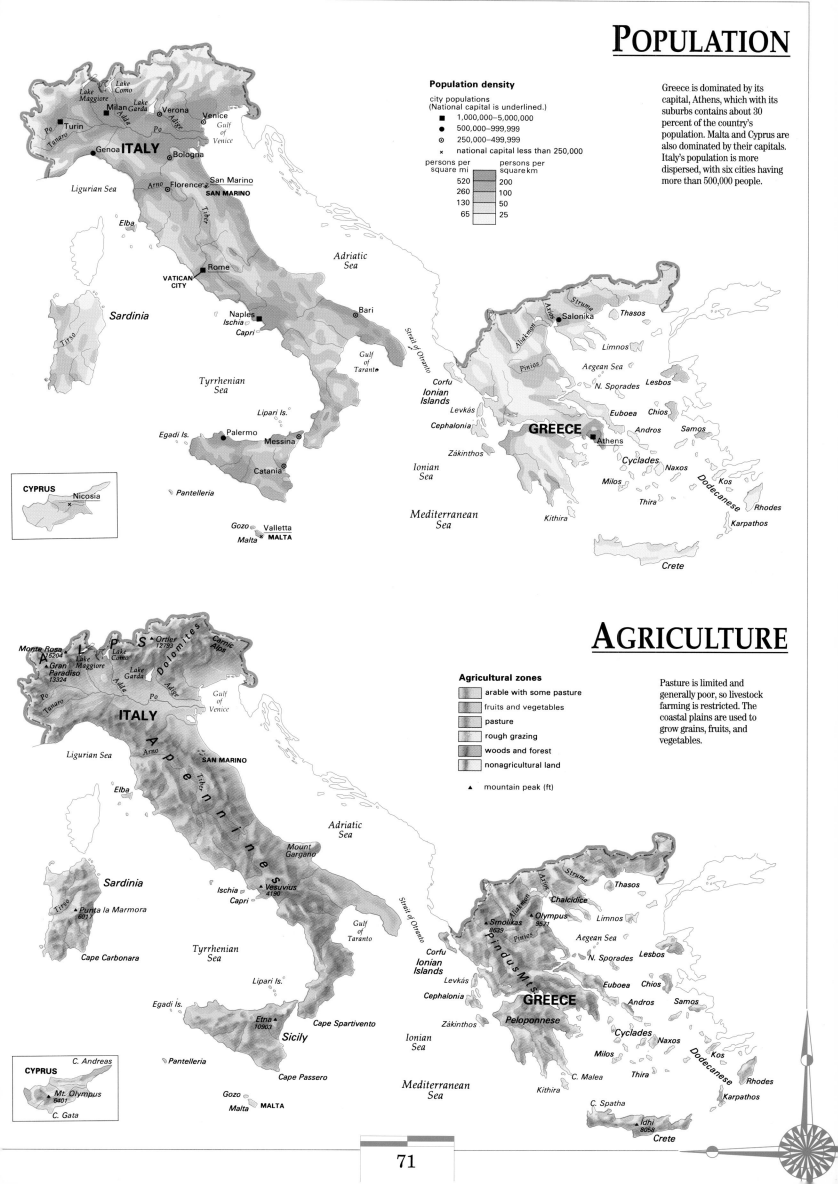

POPULATION

Greece is dominated by its capital, Athens, which with its suburbs contains about 30 percent of the country's population. Malta and Cyprus are also dominated by their capitals. Italy's population is more dispersed, with six cities having more than 500,000 people.

Population density

city populations
(National capital is underlined.)

- ■ 1,000,000–5,000,000
- ● 500,000–999,999
- ◉ 250,000–499,999
- × national capital less than 250,000

persons per square mi	persons per square km
520	200
260	100
130	50
65	25

AGRICULTURE

Pasture is limited and generally poor, so livestock farming is restricted. The coastal plains are used to grow grains, fruits, and vegetables.

Agricultural zones

- arable with some pasture
- fruits and vegetables
- pasture
- rough grazing
- woods and forest
- nonagricultural land

▲ mountain peak (ft)

71

CENTRAL EUROPE AND THE LOW COUNTRIES

The Low Countries—Belgium, Luxembourg, and the Netherlands—together with northern Germany are part of the North European Plain. The flat land of the north contrasts with the spectacular rugged Alpine scenery in the south, which includes Switzerland, Liechtenstein, and Austria.

Most people of the region speak Germanic languages, notably Dutch and German, though French is spoken in Belgium and Switzerland.

Highly efficient farms are found throughout the region. Manufacturing is the main source of wealth, and products include chemicals, electrical and electronic goods, and vehicles.

The Low Countries and their neighbors in Central Europe form part of the world's temperate zone. In the Low Countries, large areas are below sea level—much of the Netherlands has been reclaimed from the sea. The Alps in the south contain majestic peaks and sparkling lakes.

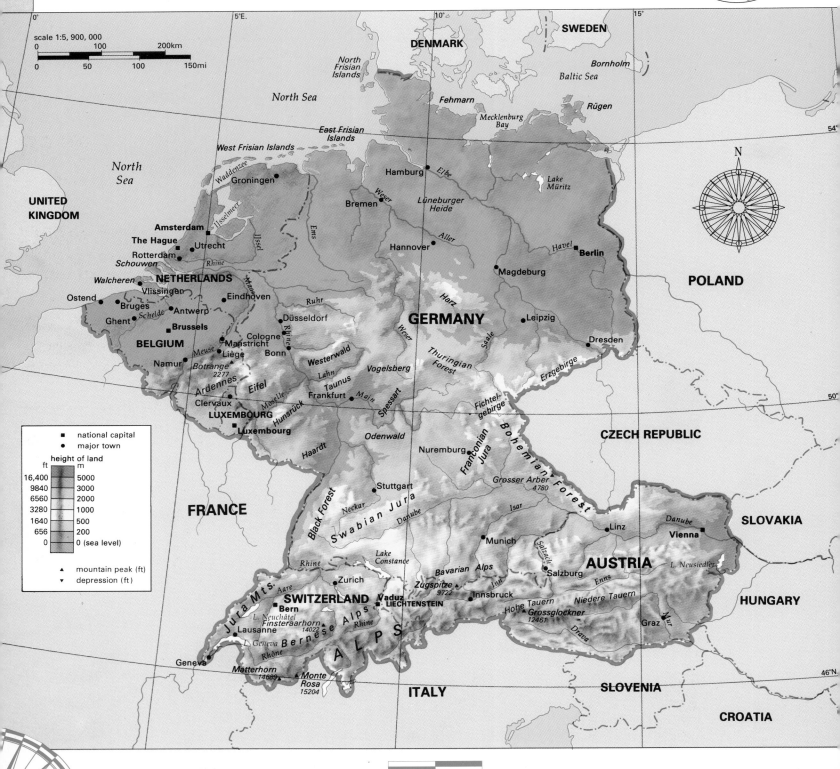

scale 1:5, 900, 000

0	100	200km
0	50 100	150mi

SWEDEN

DENMARK

North Frisian Islands

Baltic Sea

Bornholm

North Sea

Fehmarn

Rügen

Mecklenburg Bay

Lake Müritz

East Frisian Islands

West Frisian Islands

Waddenzee

Groningen

Hamburg

Elbe

Lüneburger Heide

UNITED KINGDOM

North Sea

IJsselmeer

Bremen

Weser

Aller

Hannover

Havel

Berlin

Amsterdam

The Hague

Utrecht

IJssel

Rhine

Ems

Magdeburg

POLAND

Rotterdam

Schouwen

Walcheren

NETHERLANDS

Vlissingen

Eindhoven

Ruhr

Harz

GERMANY

Leipzig

Ostend

Bruges

Antwerp

Düsseldorf

Weser

Saale

Dresden

Ghent

Schelde

Cologne

Rhine

Brussels

Maastricht

BELGIUM

Meuse

Liège

Bonn

Westerwald

Thuringian Forest

Erzgebirge

Namur

Botrange 2277

Lahn

Vogelsberg

Fichtel- gebirge

Ardennes

Eifel

Taunus

Frankfurt

Main

Spessart

CZECH REPUBLIC

Clervaux

Moselle

Hunsrück

Franconian Jura

Bohemian Forest

LUXEMBOURG

Luxembourg

Odenwald

Nuremburg

Grosser Arber 4780

| | national capital |
| | major town |

height of land

ft	m
16,400	5000
9840	3000
6560	2000
3280	1000
1640	500
656	200
0	0 (sea level)

▲ mountain peak (ft)
▼ depression (ft)

FRANCE

Haardt

Black Forest

Neckar

Stuttgart

Swabian Jura

Danube

Isar

SLOVAKIA

Danube

Linz

Vienna

Lake Constance

Rhine

Zurich

Bavarian Alps

Munich

Salzach

AUSTRIA

L. Neusiedler

Zugspitze 9722

Innsbruck

Inn

Salzburg

Enns

SWITZERLAND

Bern

Vaduz

LIECHTENSTEIN

Hohe Tauern

Grossglockner 12461

Niedere Tauern

HUNGARY

Jura Mts.

Aare

L. Neuchâtel

Finsteraarhorn 14022

Lausanne

Bernese Alps

Rhine

ALPS

Drava

Mur

Graz

L. Geneva

Rhône

SLOVENIA

Geneva

Matterhorn 14689

Monte Rosa 15204

ITALY

CROATIA

THE POLITICAL AND CULTURAL WORLD

Of the seven countries in the region, four are parliamentary democracies with monarchs as heads of state. They are the kingdoms of Belgium and the Netherlands, the Grand Duchy of Luxembourg, and the Principality of Liechtenstein. The other three countries—Austria, Germany, and Switzerland—are federal republics.

After World War II, Central Europe played an important part in the Cold War. But after the collapse of communism in Eastern Europe in 1990, West and East Germany, divided since 1945, were reunified politically. The task of economic integration, however, proved to be more costly than many Germans had expected.

COUNTRIES IN THE REGION

Austria, Belgium, Germany, Liechtenstein, Luxembourg, Netherlands, Switzerland

Territories outside the region
Aruba, Netherlands Antilles (Netherlands)

LANGUAGE

Countries with one official language Dutch: Netherlands; German: Austria, Germany, Liechtenstein
Countries with two official languages French, German: Luxembourg
Countries with three official languages Dutch, French, German: Belgium; French, German, Italian: Switzerland

RELIGION

Austria Roman Catholic (85%), Protestant (6%), nonreligious (9%)
Belgium Roman Catholic (90%), nonreligious and atheist (8%), Islam (1.1%), Protestant (0.4%)
Germany Protestant (47%), Roman Catholic (36%), other and nonaffiliated (11.3%), nonreligious (3.6%), Islam (2.1%)
Luxembourg Roman Catholic (93%), nonreligious and atheist (5%), Protestant (1%)
Netherlands Roman Catholic (36.2%), nonreligious (34.7%), Protestant (26.4%), Hindu (1%), Islam (1%)
Switzerland Roman Catholic (49%), Protestant (48%)

STYLES OF GOVERNMENT

Republics Austria, Germany, Switzerland
Monarchies Belgium, Liechtenstein, Luxembourg, Netherlands
Federal states Austria, Germany, Switzerland
Multiparty states Austria, Belgium, Germany, Liechtenstein, Luxembourg, Netherlands, Switzerland
One-chamber assembly Liechtenstein
Two-chamber assembly Austria, Belgium, Germany, Netherlands, Switzerland

ECONOMIC INDICATORS

	Belguim	Netherlands
GDP (US$ billions)	192.39	279.15
GNP per capita (US$)	15,540	17,320
Annual rate of growth of GDP, 1980–1990	2.0%	1.9%
Manufacturing as % of GDP	23.0%	20%
Central government spending as % of GNP	49.0%	53.0%
Merchandise exports (US$ billions)	118.1	131.4
Merchandise imports (US$ billions)	119.8	125.9
% of GNP donated as development aid	0.45%	0.94%

WELFARE INDICATORS

Infant mortality rate (per 1,000 live births)		
1965	24	14
1990	8	7
Daily food supply available (calories per capita, 1989)	3,679	3,151
Population per physician (1984)	330	450
Teacher-pupil ratio (elementary school, 1989)	1 : 10	1 : 17

Area 32,377 sq mi (83,857 sq km)
Population 7,583,000
Currency 1 Schilling (S) = 100 Groschen
Austria

Area 11,783 sq mi (30,518 sq km)
Population 9,845,000
Currency 1 Belgian franc (BF) = 100 centimes
Belgium

■ national capital

Area 137,820 sq mi (356,954 sq km)
Population 77,573,000
Currency 1 Deutsche mark (DM) = 100 Pfennig
Germany
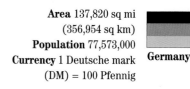

Area 62 sq mi (160 sq km)
Population 28,000
Currency 1 Swiss franc (SF) = 100 centimes
Liechtenstein

Area 999 sq mi (2,586 sq km)
Population 373,000
Currency 1 Luxembourg franc (LuxF) = 100 centimes
Luxembourg

Area 16,163 sq mi (41,863 sq km)
Population 14,951,000
Currency 1 guilder (G) = 100 cents
Netherlands

Area 15,943 sq mi (41,293 sq km)
Population 6,609,000
Currency 1 Swiss franc (SF) = 100 centimes
Switzerland

Belgium, Luxembourg, Netherlands, and former West Germany were founder members in the 1950s of what is now the European Community. Both Switzerland and Liechtenstein were politically neutral during both world wars, while Austria was allied to Germany. After its defeat in 1945, Germany was divided, and its eastern part came under Soviet influence. The two parts of the country were reunited in October 1990.

North Frisian Islands
East Frisian Islands
West Frisian Islands
Fehmarn

■ Amsterdam
The Hague ■
NETHERLANDS

■ Berlin

■ Brussels
BELGIUM

GERMANY

LUXEMBOURG
■ Luxembourg

Vienna ■

LIECHTENSTEIN
■ Vaduz
■ Bern

AUSTRIA

SWITZERLAND

HABITATS

There is a sharp contrast between the Netherlands' flat, cultivated polders, or land reclaimed from the sea, and the rugged Alps, which contain some of Europe's finest scenery. Several rivers, including the Rhine, flow through scenic valleys, with forested mountains on each side.

LAND

Area 172,934 sq mi (448,014 sq km)
Highest point Monte Rosa, 15,203 ft (4,634 m)
Lowest point in west Netherlands, −22 ft (−7 m)
Major features High Alps, Bohemian Forest, Black Forest, very low-lying areas in north Low Countries, Rhine rift valley

WATER

Longest river Rhine 820 mi (1,320 km), Rhine basin 97,000 sq. mi (252,000 sq km), also the upper part of the Danube
Highest average flow Rhine, 88,000 cu ft/sec (2,490 cu m/sec)
Largest lake IJsselmeer, 467 sq mi (1,210 sq km)

NOTABLE THREATENED SPECIES

Mammals pond bat (Myotis dasycneme), mouse-eared bat (Myotis myotis), harbor porpoise (Phocoena phocoena)
Birds red kite (Milvus milvus), white-tailed sea eagle (Haliaeetus albicilla), corncrake (Crex crex), great bustard (Otis tarda), aquatic warbler (Acrocephalus paludicola), lesser kestrel (Falco naumanni)

Plants corncockle (Agrostemma githago); Echinodorus repens; Eriophorum gracile; Halimione pedunculata; bog orchid (Hammarbya paludosa); Luronium natans; Lake Constance forget-me-not (Myosotis rehsteineri); Elb water dropwort (Oenanthe conioides); Petroselinum segetum; pillwort (Pilularia globulifera); Salvinia natans; spiral orchid (Spiranthes spiralis)

CLIMATE

The western part of the region has a temperate, wet climate, with moderately warm summers and cool, mild winters. Eastern Germany has hotter summers and colder winters. Austria and Switzerland have permanently snow-capped mountains.

TEMPERATURE AND PRECIPITATION

	Temperature °F (°C)		Altitude
	January	July	ft (m)
Hamburg	32 (0)	63 (17)	46 (14)
Zurich	30 (−1)	64 (18)	1,886 (569)
Lugano	36 (2)	70 (21)	905 (276)
Munich	28 (−2)	64 (18)	1,732 (528)
Vienna	30 (−1)	68 (20)	695 (212)
Ostend	37 (3)	61 (16)	33 (10)

	Precipitation in (mm)		
	January	July	Year
Hamburg	2.2 (57)	3.3 (84)	28.3 (720)
Zurich	2.9 (75)	5.6 (143)	44.8 (1,137)
Lugano	2.5 (63)	7.3 (185)	68.7 (1,744)
Munich	2.3 (59)	5.5 (140)	38.0 (964)
Vienna	1.6 (40)	3.3 (83)	26.0 (660)
Ostend	1.6 (41)	2.4 (62)	23.5 (598)

NATURAL HAZARDS

Avalanches and landslides in the mountains

ENVIRONMENTAL ISSUES

The Low Countries are among the world's most densely populated areas, and the population has had a great impact on the land. Deforestation and acid rain have damaged the entire region, and industrial pollution has greatly affected eastern Germany.

POPULATION AND WEALTH

	Belgium	Germany	Netherlands
Population (in millions)	9.9	77.7	15
Population increase (annual population growth rate, % 1960–1990)	0.2	0.2	0.9
Energy use (gigajoules/person)	163	396	199
Real purchasing power (US$/person)	13,010	14,620	12,680

ENVIRONMENTAL INDICATORS

CO$_2$ emissions (million m.t. carbon/year)	25	222	43
Municipal waste (lbs/person/year)	279.3	283	400
Nuclear waste (cumulative m.t. heavy metal)	700	3,300	200
Artificial fertilizer use (lbs/acre/year)	455	676.5	614
Automobiles (per 1,000 population)	349	412	346
Access to safe drinking water (% population)	100	100	100

MAJOR ENVIRONMENTAL PROBLEMS AND SOURCES

Air pollution: generally high, urban very high; acid rain prevalent
River/lake pollution: high; sources: agricultural, industrial, sewage
Marine/coastal pollution: high; sources: industrial, agricultural, sewage, oil
Land pollution: high; sources: industrial, agricultural, urban/household, nuclear
Waste disposal problems: domestic, industrial, nuclear
Resource problems: land use competition, coastal flooding, water level control and flooding
Major event: Lekkerkerk (1980), toxic waste dump discovered, Sandoz near Basel (1987), chemical spill

Glaciation has left its mark on the land. Northern Germany is covered by moraine left behind by the Scandinavian glaciers. Glaciers continue to shape the land in the Alps.

HABITATS

North Frisian Islands
North Sea
Fehmarn
Baltic Sea
Mecklenburg Bay
Rügen
East Frisian Islands
West Frisian Islands
Eelde
Hamburg
Elbe
Lake Müritz
Lüneburger Heide
Weser
IJsselmeer
IJssel
Ems
Aller
Havel
Veluwe
Rhine
NETHERLANDS
Ostend
Ruhr
Harz
GERMANY
Dresden
Schelde
Kempenland
Rhine
Weser
Saale
Brussels
BELGIUM Geulle
Thuringian Forest
Erzgebirge
Meuse
Botrange 2277
Westerwald
Vogelsberg
Fichtel-gebirge
Bohemian Forest
Ardennes
Eifel
Taunus
Main
LUXEMBOURG
Luxembourg
Hunsrück
Moselle
Lahn
Spessart
Franconian Jura
Odenwald
Grosser Arber 4780
Haardt
Black Forest
Neckar
Swabian Jura
Danube
Isar
Danube
Vienna
Munich
AUSTRIA
L. Neusiedler
Rhine
Lake Constance
Bavarian Alps
Salzach
Jura Mts.
Aare
Zurich
SWITZERLAND
LIECHTENSTEIN
Zugspitze 9722
Inn
Enns
Hohe Tauern
Niedere Tauern
Mur
Finsteraarhorn 14022
Bernese Alps
Rhine
ALPS
Grossglockner 12461
Drava
L. Neuchâtel
L. Geneva
Rhône
Matterhorn 14689
Monte Rosa 15204
Lugano

Physical zones

mountains/barren land
forest
grassland

▲ mountain peak (ft)
☼ climate station

ENVIRONMENTAL ISSUES

Farming and industrialization have badly damaged many natural habitats in the region. Much of the air pollution originates in Germany. Tourism has badly affected some popular areas.

Key environmental issues

- major town or city
- heavily polluted town or city
- major pollution event
- beach not complying with E C standard 1989
- heavily polluted river
- main skiing area

remaining forest
- coniferous
- mixed
- deciduous

CLIMATE

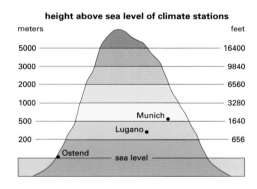

height above sea level of climate stations

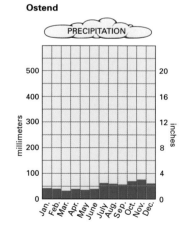

Ostend

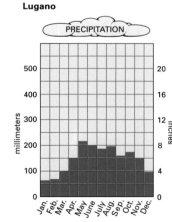

Lugano

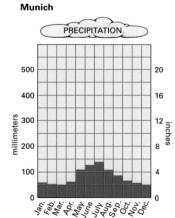

Munich

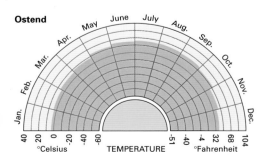

Ostend

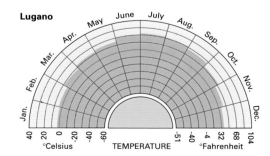

Lugano

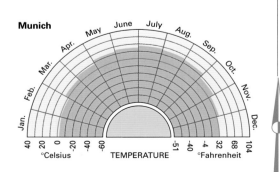

Munich

POPULATION

Industrialization led to a rapid increase in the region's population from the late 1800s. New cities grew up near coal or iron fields. Older cities, such as Berlin and Vienna, have also grown in the last 50 years. The Netherlands has towns on land reclaimed from the sea.

POPULATION

Total population of region (in millions)	116.2
Population density (persons per sq mi)	715.2
Population change (average annual percent 1960–1990)	
Urban	+0.8
Rural	-1.2

URBAN POPULATION

As percentage of total population	
1960	81.8
1990	88.4
Percentage in cities of more than 1 million	4.1

TEN LARGEST CITIES

	Country	Population
Berlin †	Germany	3,301,000
Vienna †	Austria	2,044,000
Hamburg	Germany	1,594,000
Munich	Germany	1,189,000
Rotterdam	Netherlands	1,040,000
Amsterdam †	Netherlands	1,038,000
Brussels †	Belgium	976,000
Cologne	Germany	928,000
Zurich	Switzerland	839,000
The Hague †	Netherlands	684,000

† denotes national capital (Netherlands has two capitals – The Hague is the government seat; Amsterdam is a nominal capital.)

INDUSTRY

Germany is Europe's top industrial power. Its industries were based on local supplies of fuels and metals, but many raw materials are now imported. In some countries, such as Switzerland, much industry has been based on crafts, such as clock-making.

INDUSTRIAL OUTPUT (US$ billion)

Total	Mining	Manufacturing	Average annual change since 1960
882.0	56.9*	652.5**	+2.9%

* Figure relates to West Germany (preunification in 1990).
** Figure includes mining in Austria, East Germany (preunification in 1990), and Switzerland.

MAJOR PRODUCTS (Figures in parentheses are percentages of world production.)

Energy and minerals	Output	Change since 1960
Coal (mil. m.t.)	498.0 (5.23%)	-83%
Natural gas (billion cu meters)	76.2 (1.95%)	N/A
Nuclear power (mil. m.t. coal equiv.)	15.2 (2.2%)	N/A

Manufactures		
Steel (mil. m.t.)	58.0 (3.95%)	+9.7%
Automobiles (mil.)	4.85 (10.2%)	+221%
Papermaking/printing machines (thousands)	299.7 (86.8%)	No data
Petroleum (mil. m.t.)	78.5 (2.8%)	+95.9%
Plastics and resins (mil. m.t.)	5.2 (10.3%)	+340%

N/A means production had not begun in 1960.

AGRICULTURE

The farmers of the Low Countries produce some of the world's highest yields. Arable farming is important in northern and central Germany, but more than 50 percent of the land in Austria and 75 percent in Switzerland is too mountainous to be farmed.

LAND (million acres)

Total	Agricultural	Arable	Forest/woodland
133 (100%)	69.1 (51.5%)	39.5 (29%)	39.5 (29%)

FARMERS

2.7 million people employed in agriculture (4% of workforce)
15 acres of arable land per person employed in agriculture

MAJOR CROPS

Numbers in parentheses are percentages of world average yield and total world production.

	Area mil. acres	Yield 100lbs/acre	Production mil. m.t.	Change since 1963
Barley	7.6	41.0	14.2 (8)	+162%
Wheat	7.6	51.6	17.7 (3)	+75%
Rye	2.9	32.6	42.1 (12)	-19%
Potatoes	2.2	329	30.5 (10)	+25%
Oats	1.7	38.2	2.9 (7)	-14%
Sugar beets	1.9	440.7	42.2 (14)	+82%
Rapeseed	1.5	25.0	1.7 (8)	+508%
Grapes	0.5	97.1	1.8 (3)	+74%
Other fruit	—	—	4.8 (1)	-10%
Vegetables	—	—	8.8 (10)	-56%

MAJOR LIVESTOCK

	Number in mil.	Production mil. m.t.	Change since 1963
Cattle	16.8 (2)	—	+19%
Pigs	63.1 (3)	—	+174%
Milk	—	28.4 (6)	+34%
Fish catch	—	0.9 (1)	

FOOD SECURITY (grain exports minus imports)

mil. m.t.	% domestic production	% world trade
-4.7	92	5

The Netherlands and Belgium, together with the Ruhr and Rhine valleys in Germany, have population densities of more than 500 per sq mi (200 per sq km). Parts of Switzerland and Austria are thinly populated.

POPULATION

Population density

city populations
(National capital is underlined.)

■ 1,000,000–500,000
● 500,000–999,999
◉ 250,000–499,999
× national capital less than 250,000

persons per square mi		persons per square km
520		200
260		100
130		50
65		25

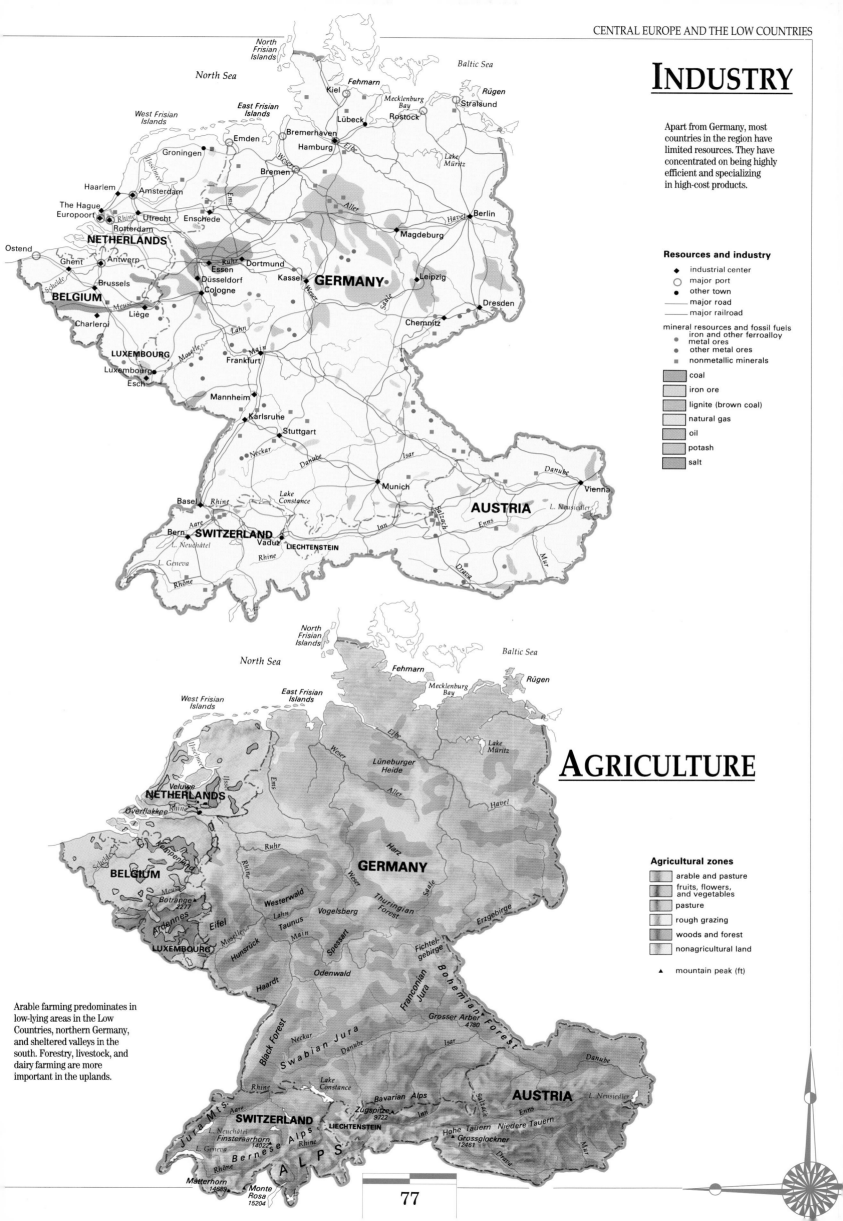

INDUSTRY

Apart from Germany, most countries in the region have limited resources. They have concentrated on being highly efficient and specializing in high-cost products.

Resources and industry

♦ industrial center
○ major port
● other town
— major road
— major railroad

mineral resources and fossil fuels
● iron and other ferroalloy metal ores
● other metal ores
■ nonmetallic minerals

coal
iron ore
lignite (brown coal)
natural gas
oil
potash
salt

AGRICULTURE

Arable farming predominates in low-lying areas in the Low Countries, northern Germany, and sheltered valleys in the south. Forestry, livestock, and dairy farming are more important in the uplands.

Agricultural zones

arable and pasture
fruits, flowers, and vegetables
pasture
rough grazing
woods and forest
nonagricultural land

▲ mountain peak (ft)

77

EASTERN EUROPE

Eastern Europe extends from the cool Baltic Sea region in the north to the Mediterranean lands in the south. Until 1989, Eastern Europe formed a buffer zone of communist states between Western Europe and the Soviet Union.

Eastern Europe extends from the dune-lined Baltic coast in the north, through part of the North European Plain in Poland and a series of uplands in the south, to the Adriatic Sea in the southwest, and the Black Sea, outlet of the Danube River, in the southeast. The plains in the region include the Great Alföld in Hungary. The north is cold and dry, but the south has a subtropical climate.

The region is culturally complex. It contains several language groups, including Slavic, Germanic, Finno-Ugric, and Romance languages. Religions, mainly Roman Catholicism, Orthodox Christianity, and Islam, also divide the people.

Agriculture was the chief activity in the past. Under communism, however, great efforts were made to industrialize the region. This has caused extensive damage to the environment.

KEY
- ■ national capital
- ● major town

height of land

ft	m
6560	2000
3280	1000
1640	500
656	200
0	0

▲ mountain peak (ft)

scale 1:8,800,000

0   100   200   300km
0   100   200mi

THE POLITICAL AND CULTURAL WORLD

Eastern Europe contains 12 countries. Of these, Bosnia and Herzegovina, Croatia, Macedonia, Slovenia, and Yugoslavia (now consisting only of Serbia and Montenegro) made up Yugoslavia between 1918 and 1991. The Czech Republic and Slovakia came into being on January 1, 1993, when Czechoslovakia was divided into two parts.

This group of formerly communist countries has faced many problems since the collapse of their ideology in the late 1980s and early 1990s. Rivalries between ethnic groups have resurfaced, causing civil war in Yugoslavia. The countries have also faced many problems as they seek to reestablish free-enterprise economies.

COUNTRIES IN THE REGION

Albania, Bosnia and Herzegovina, Bulgaria, Croatia, Czech Republic, Hungary, Macedonia, Poland, Romania, Slovakia, Slovenia, Yugoslavia

LANGUAGE

Countries with one official language Albanian: Albania; Bulgarian: Bulgaria; Czech: Czech Republic; Hungarian: Hungary; Macedonian: Macedonia; Polish: Poland; Romanian: Romania; Serbo-Croat: Bosnia and Herzegovina, Croatia, Yugoslavia; Slovak: Slovakia; Slovene: Slovenia

Other languages spoken in the region include German (Czech Republic, Hungary), Greek (Albania), Romany (Bulgaria, Romania, Yugoslavia), Tatar (Romania), Turkish (Bulgaria), and Ukrainian (Czech Republic, Poland, Romania).

RELIGION

Countries with one major religion Bulgaria (BO); Czech Republic, Hungary, Poland (RC); Romania (RO)
Countries with more than one major religion Albania (A,AO,I); Yugoslavia (EO,I,O,RC)

Key: A-Atheist, AO-Albanian Orthodox, BO-Bulgarian Orthodox, EO-Eastern Orthodox, I-Islam, O-other, RC-Roman Catholic, RO-Romanian Orthodox

STYLES OF GOVERNMENT

Republics All countries in the region
Multiparty states All countries in the region
One-chamber assembly Albania, Bulgaria, Hungary, Macedonia, Yugoslavia
Two-chamber assembly Bosnia, Czech Republic, Poland, Romania, Slovakia, Slovenia
Three-chamber assembly Croatia

ECONOMIC INDICATORS: 1990

	Hungary	Poland	Romania
GDP(US$ billions)	32.92	63.59	34.73
GNP per capita (US$)	2,780	1,690	1,640
Annual rate of growth of GDP, 1980–1990	1.3%	1.8%	2.1%
Manufacturing as % of GDP	27%	20%	N/A
Central government spending as % of GNP	55%	40%	34%
Merchandise exports (US$ billions)	7.14	8.9	N/A
Merchandise imports (US$ billions)	6.1	7.4	N/A

WELFARE INDICATORS

Infant mortality rate (per 1,000 live births)

1965	39	42	44
1990	15	16	27

Daily food supply available (calories per capita, 1989)

	3,644	3,505	3,155
Population per physician (1984)	3,100	490	570
Teacher-pupil ratio (elementary school, 1989)	1 : 13	1 : 16	1 : 21

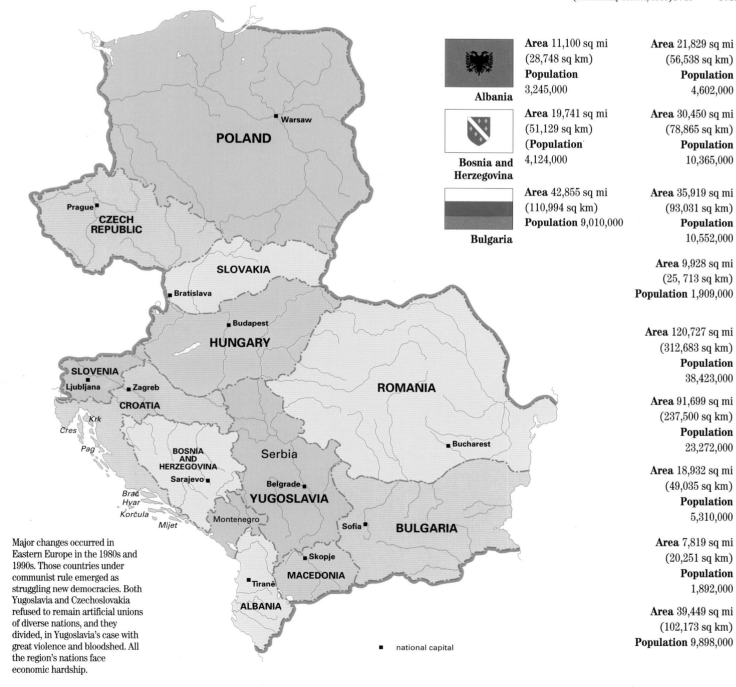

Major changes occurred in Eastern Europe in the 1980s and 1990s. Those countries under communist rule emerged as struggling new democracies. Both Yugoslavia and Czechoslovakia refused to remain artificial unions of diverse nations, and they divided, in Yugoslavia's case with great violence and bloodshed. All the region's nations face economic hardship.

■ national capital

Albania Area 11,100 sq mi (28,748 sq km) Population 3,245,000

Bosnia and Herzegovina Area 19,741 sq mi (51,129 sq km) (Population 4,124,000

Bulgaria Area 42,855 sq mi (110,994 sq km) Population 9,010,000

Croatia Area 21,829 sq mi (56,538 sq km) Population 4,602,000

Czech Republic Area 30,450 sq mi (78,865 sq km) Population 10,365,000

Hungary Area 35,919 sq mi (93,031 sq km) Population 10,552,000

Macedonia Area 9,928 sq mi (25, 713 sq km) Population 1,909,000

Poland Area 120,727 sq mi (312,683 sq km) Population 38,423,000

Romania Area 91,699 sq mi (237,500 sq km) Population 23,272,000

Slovakia Area 18,932 sq mi (49,035 sq km) Population 5,310,000

Slovenia Area 7,819 sq mi (20,251 sq km) Population 1,892,000

Yugoslavia Area 39,449 sq mi (102,173 sq km) Population 9,898,000

HABITATS

The region contains large farming areas, grasslands, and wooded mountain ranges. The cool northern plains are drained by rivers that rise in the Sudetic and Carpathian mountains. The warmer southern plains are drained by the Danube River.

LAND

Area 492,224 sq mi (1,275,191 sq km)
Highest point Musala, 9,594 ft (2,925 m)
Lowest point near Gulf of Gdańsk, −33 ft (−10 m)
Major features northern lowlands, Carpathian Mountains, Balkan Mountains, Dinaric Alps, Great Alföld, Danube valley

WATER

Longest river Danube, 1,770 mi (2,850 km)
Largest basin Danube, 298,000 sq mi (773,000 sq km)
Highest average flow Danube, 227,000 cu ft/sec (6,430 cu m/sec)
Largest lake Balaton, 230 sq mi (590 sq km)

NOTABLE THREATENED SPECIES

Mammals European bison (Bison bonasus), gray wolf (Canis lupus), European mink (Mustela lutreola), long-fingered bat (Myotis capaccinii), mouse-eared bat (Myotis myotis)
Birds Dalmatian pelican (Pelecanus crispus), white-headed duck (Oxyura leucocephala), lesser kestrel (Falco naumanni), great bustard (Otis tarda), aquatic warbler (Acrocephalus paludicola)
Plants Astragalus ornacantha; Cochlearia polonica; Daphne arbuscula; Degenia velebitica; Dianthus uromoffii; Forsythia europaea; Lilium rhodopaeum
Others olm (Proteus anguinus), Danube salmon (Hucho hucho), scarce fritillary butterfly (Euphydryas maturna)

HABITATS

CLIMATE

The northern parts of Eastern Europe have a continental climate, with rain throughout the year. The southern part of the region has warmer summers. Winters are cool, and occasionally a strong, cold wind, called the bora, blows down from the north.

TEMPERATURE AND PRECIPITATION

	Temperature °F (°C) January	July	Altitude ft (m)
Gdańsk	30 (−1)	64 (18)	39 (12)
Prague	27 (−3)	64 (18)	861 (262)
Tiranë	45 (7)	75 (24)	292 (89)
Bucharest	27 (−3)	73 (23)	301 (92)

	Precipitation in (mm) January	July	Year
Gdańsk	1.2 (31)	2.9 (73)	19.6 (499)
Prague	0.7 (18)	2.6 (68)	20.0 (508)
Tiranë	5.3 (135)	1.2 (32)	46.8 (1,189)
Bucharest	1.8 (46)	2.1 (53)	22.8 (578)

NATURAL HAZARDS

Earthquakes, landslides, and floods

ENVIRONMENTAL ISSUES

Deforestation, intensive farming, and industrialization have caused much environmental damage in Eastern Europe in the last 40 years. Coal-burning power plants have caused air pollution and acid rain, especially in Poland and the Czech Republic.

POPULATION AND WEALTH

	Highest	Middle	Lowest
Population (in millions)	38.4 (Poland)	15.7 (Czech.)	3.3 (Albania)
Population increase (annual population growth rate, % 1960–1990)	2.4 (Albania)	0.8 (Romania)	0.2 (Hungary)
Energy use (gigajoules/person)	185 (Czech.)	136 (Romania)	38 (Albania)
Real purchasing power (US$/person)	5,920 (Hungary)	4,860 (Yugoslavia)	4,190 (Poland)

ENVIRONMENTAL INDICATORS

CO$_2$ emissions (million m.t. carbon/year)	56 (Poland)	25 (Romania)	1.2 (Albania)
Municipal waste (lbs/person/year)	1,666 (Bulgaria)	1,448 (Hungary)	467 (Poland)
Nuclear waste (cumulative m.t. heavy metal)	100 (Yugoslavia)	N/A	0 (Albania)
Artificial fertilizer use (lbs/acre/year)	270 (Czech.)	160 (Bulgaria)	116 (Romania)
Automobiles (per 1,000 population)	174 (Czech.)	122 (Bulgaria)	11 (Romania)
Access to safe drinking water (% population)	100 (Czech.)	97 (Hungary)	73 (Yugoslavia)

MAJOR ENVIRONMENTAL PROBLEMS AND SOURCES

Air pollution: generally high, urban very high; acid rain prevalent; high greenhouse gas emissions
River/lake pollution: high; sources: industrial, agricultural, sewage, acid deposition
Land pollution: high; sources: industrial, agricultural, urban/household, nuclear

Figures for Yugoslavia relate to the former Yugoslav Republic now divided into individual states.
Figures for Czechoslovakia are pre-partition in 1993.

Physical zones
mountains/barren land
forest
grassland
▲ mountain peak (ft)
☀ climate station

The mountains include the young Carpathians and the old Sudetic Mountains. Some old ranges have been worn down to form plateaus. Lowlands occur in the north and center.

ENVIRONMENTAL ISSUES

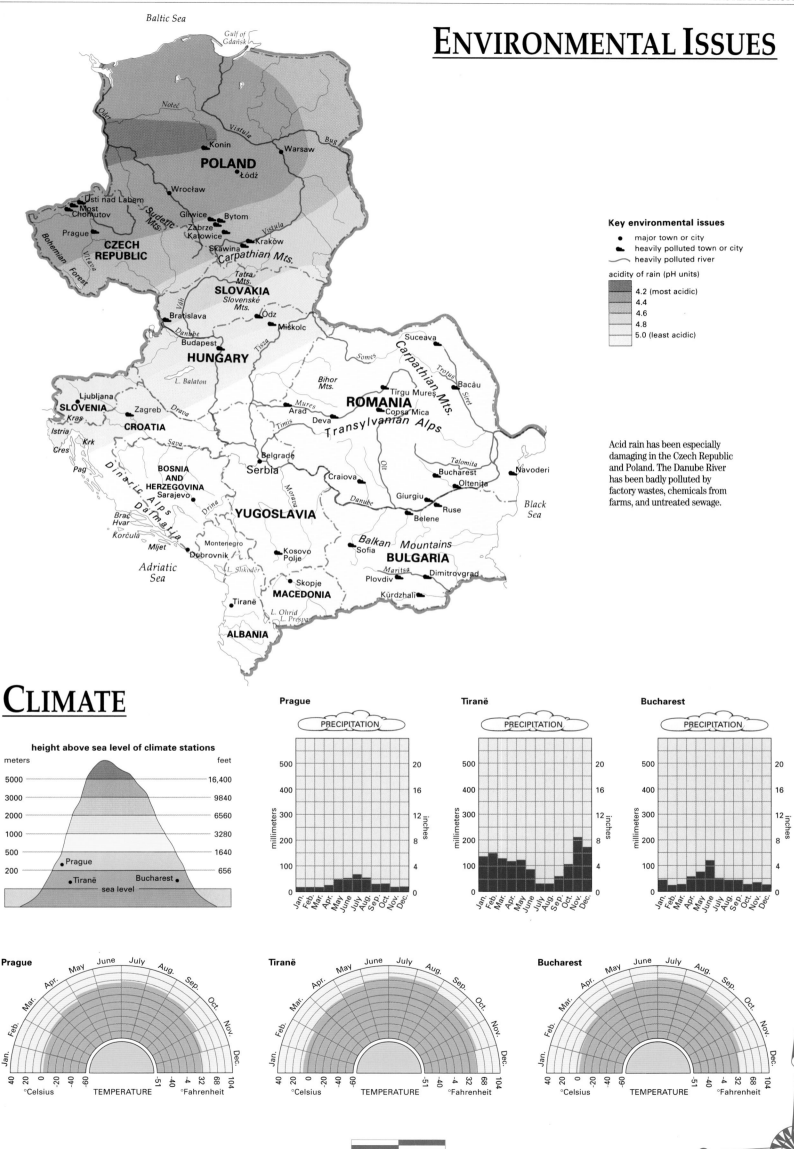

Key environmental issues

- ● major town or city
- ◖ heavily polluted town or city
- ◡ heavily polluted river

acidity of rain (pH units)

- 4.2 (most acidic)
- 4.4
- 4.6
- 4.8
- 5.0 (least acidic)

Acid rain has been especially damaging in the Czech Republic and Poland. The Danube River has been badly polluted by factory wastes, chemicals from farms, and untreated sewage.

Map labels:

Baltic Sea • Gulf of Gdańsk • Oder • Noteć • Vistula • Bug • Konin • Warsaw • POLAND • Łódź • Wrocław • Ustí nad Labem • Most • Chomutov • Sudetic Mts. • Gliwice • Bytom • Zabrze • Katowice • Kraków • Prague • Skawina • Vltava • CZECH REPUBLIC • Bohemian Forest • Carpathian Mts. • Tatra Mts. • SLOVAKIA • Slovenské Mts. • Váh • Bratislava • Ódz • Miskolc • Danube • Budapest • Tisza • HUNGARY • Suceava • Carpathian Mts. • Somes • Bihor Mts. • Tirgu Mures • Bacău • Trotus • Siret • L. Balaton • ROMANIA • Ljubljana • Mures • Copsa Mica • SLOVENIA • Zagreb • Arad • Deva • Transylvanian Alps • Kras • Drava • Timis • CROATIA • Istria • Krk • Cres • Sava • Belgrade • Oit • Ialomita • Bucharest • Navoderi • Pag • Serbia • Craiova • Olteniţa • Black Sea • BOSNIA AND HERZEGOVINA • Sarajevo • Morava • Danube • Giurgiu • Dinaric Alps • Drina • Dalmatia • Ruse • Brač • Hvar • YUGOSLAVIA • Belene • Korčula • Mljet • Montenegro • Balkan Mountains • Dubrovnik • Kosovo Polje • Sofia • BULGARIA • L. Shkodër • Adriatic Sea • Maritsa • Dimitrovgrad • Skopje • Plovdiv • Tiranë • MACEDONIA • Kürdzhali • L. Ohrid • L. Prespa • ALBANIA

CLIMATE

height above sea level of climate stations

meters		feet
5000		16,400
3000		9840
2000		6560
1000		3280
500		1640
200	● Prague	656
	● Tiranë Bucharest ●	
	sea level	

Prague
PRECIPITATION
(millimeters: 500, 400, 300, 200, 100; inches: 20, 16, 12, 8, 4, 0)
Jan. Feb. Mar. Apr. May June July Aug. Sep. Oct. Nov. Dec.

Tiranë
PRECIPITATION
(millimeters: 500, 400, 300, 200, 100; inches: 20, 16, 12, 8, 4, 0)
Jan. Feb. Mar. Apr. May June July Aug. Sep. Oct. Nov. Dec.

Bucharest
PRECIPITATION
(millimeters: 500, 400, 300, 200, 100; inches: 20, 16, 12, 8, 4, 0)
Jan. Feb. Mar. Apr. May June July Aug. Sep. Oct. Nov. Dec.

Prague
TEMPERATURE
°Celsius °Fahrenheit
Jan. Feb. Mar. Apr. May June July Aug. Sep. Oct. Nov. Dec.

Tiranë
TEMPERATURE
°Celsius °Fahrenheit
Jan. Feb. Mar. Apr. May June July Aug. Sep. Oct. Nov. Dec.

Bucharest
TEMPERATURE
°Celsius °Fahrenheit
Jan. Feb. Mar. Apr. May June July Aug. Sep. Oct. Nov. Dec.

POPULATION

Industrialization came later to Eastern Europe than it did to most other parts of the continent. Even today the proportion of people in rural areas is comparatively high, though urban areas now contain about 65 percent of the population.

POPULATION

Total population of region (in millions)	124
Population density (persons per sq mi)	112.5
Population change (average annual percent 1960–1990)	
Urban	+1.7
Rural	−0.7

URBAN POPULATION

As percentage of total population	
1960	47.0
1990	64.3
Percentage in cities of more than 1 million	5.7

TEN LARGEST CITIES

	Country	Population
Budapest †	Hungary	2,115,000
Bucharest †	Romania	2,014,000
Warsaw †	Poland	1,674,000
Belgrade †	Serbia	1,470,000
Prague †	Czech Republic	1,209,000
Zagreb †	Croatia	1,175,000
Sofia †	Bulgaria	1,129,000
Lódź	Poland	852,000
Kraków	Poland	744,000
Wroclaw	Poland	640,000

† denotes national capital

POPULATION

Population density

city populations
(National capital is underlined.)

- ■ 1,000,000–5,000,000
- ● 500,000–999,999
- ⊙ 250,000–499,999
- × national capital less than 250,000

persons per square mi	persons per square km
520	200
260	100
130	50
26	10

The main concentrations of population are in the industrial regions of the Czech Republic and Poland, and also around the regions' national capitals.

INDUSTRY

Apart from Poland's rich coal deposits and some other minerals, the region lacks natural resources. Many industries were set up under communist rule, and their managers are now having great difficulties in converting to private enterprise.

MAJOR PRODUCTS (Figures in parentheses are percentages of world production.)

Energy and minerals	Output	Change since 1960
Coal (mil. m.t.)	559.2 (11.9%)	+165%
Copper (mil. m.t.)	0.65 (7.6%)	+116.5%
Lead (mil. m.t.)	0.28 (8.3%)	−16.4%
Sulfur (mil. m.t.)	5.05 (33.7%)	N/A

Manufactures		
Linen fabrics (mil. yd)	220 (19.7%)	No data
Knitted sweaters (mil.)	416.7 (35.7%)	No data
Men's and boys' suits (mil.)	7.75 (11.7%)	No data
Footwear (mil. pairs)	571.7 (12.9%)	No data
Nitric acid (mil. m.t.)	4.95 (18.2%)	+149%
Cement (mil. m.t.)	60.9 (5.5%)	+196.5%
Steel (mil. m.t.)	52.6 (7.2%)	+132.5%
Buses (1,000s)	39.3 (11.9%)	No data
Railroad locomotives and rolling stock (1,000s)	30.3 (16.5%)	No data

N/A means production had not begun in 1960.

AGRICULTURE

While large tracts of Eastern Europe can be used for arable farming, irrigation is essential in the south because of the hot, dry summers. One-fifth of the land in this region is mountainous and is only used for rough grazing.

LAND (million acres)

Total	Agricultural	Arable	Forest/woodland
284 (100%)	170 (60%)	113 (40%)	89 (31%)

FARMERS

12.2 million people employed in agriculture (20% of workforce)
10 acres of arable land per person employed in agriculture

MAJOR CROPS

	Area mil. acres	Yield 100lbs/acre	Production mil. m.t.	Change since 1963
Wheat	24	35.9	39.6 (8)	+132%
Corn	17.5	47.7	38.0 (8)	+122%
Barley	8.4	35.4	13.5 (7)	+143%
Rye	7.4	22.8	7.7 (22)	−14%
Potatoes	6.9	158.7	50.6 (18)	−11%
Sunflower seed	3.4	17.9	2.9 (14)	+147%
Sugar beets	2.9	291	39.4 (13)	+39%

MAJOR LIVESTOCK

	Number in mil.	Production mil. m.t.	Change since 1963
Pigs	61.5 (7)	—	+60%
Sheep	45.7 (4)	—	+12%
Cattle	31.7 (2)	—	+13%
Milk	—	36.7 (8)	+50%
Fish catch	—	1.2 (1)	—

FOOD SECURITY (grain exports minus imports)

mil. m.t.	% domestic production	% world trade
−1.3	1	1

Numbers in parentheses are percentages of world average yield and total world production.

INDUSTRY

Baltic Sea

Resources and industry

◆ industrial center
○ major port
● other town
— major road
— major railroad

mineral resources and fossil fuels
● iron and other ferroalloy metal ores
● other metal ores
■ nonmetallic minerals

coal
iron ore
lignite (brown coal)

Before 1945, industry was confined mainly to Poland and what is now the Czech Republic. Under communist rule, many natural resources were exploited, and industries were set up throughout the region.

Gulf of Gdańsk
Gdynia
Gdańsk
Szczecin
Stargard
Bydgoszcz
Notec
Oder
Poznań
Vistula
Warsaw
Bug
POLAND
Łódź
Wrocław
Prague
Katowice
Kraków
Vistula
Plzen
CZECH REPUBLIC
Ostrava
Brno
Žilina
Ružomberok
Vltava
SLOVAKIA
Miskolc
Danube
Tisza
Debrecen
Budapest
Somes
HUNGARY
L. Balaton
Ljubljana
Drava
ROMANIA
SLOVENIA
Zagreb
Mures
Arad
Sibiu
Braşov
CROATIA
Rijeka
Sava
Draba
Ploiesti
Cres
Olt
Sulina
Pag
BOSNIA AND HERZEGOVINA
Belgrade
Bucharest
Sarajevo
Serbia
Danube
Constanţa
Split
Drina
Ruse
Black Sea
Brač
Hvar
Morava
Varna
Korčula
Niš
Mljet
YUGOSLAVIA
Montenegro
Adriatic Sea
Sofia
BULGARIA
Bar
L. Shkodër
Burgas
Shkodër
Skopje
Maritsa
Plovdiv
Durrës
MACEDONIA
Tiranë
L. Ohrid
L. Prespa
ALBANIA

Baltic Sea
Gulf of Gdańsk

Oder
Notec
Vistula
POLAND
Bug
Erzgebirge
Sněžka 5259
Sudetic Mts.
Silesian Plain
Vistula
CZECH REPUBLIC
Bohemian Forest
Vltava
Carpathian Mts.
Tatra Mts.
Gerlachovka 8711
SLOVAKIA
Slovenské Mts.
Váh
Danube
Kékes 3330
HUNGARY
Great Alföld
Tisza
Somes
Carpathian Mts.
Triglav 9393
Balaton
SLOVENIA
Bihor Mts.
Kras
Drava
ROMANIA
Istria
CROATIA
Mures
Krk
Sava
Transylvanian Alps
Cres
Moldoveanu 8343
Pag
BOSNIA AND HERZEGOVINA
Dinaric Alps
Dalmatia
Olt
Brač
Hvar
Serbia
Korčula
Durmitor 8295
Montenegro
Mljet
Morava
Danube
Drina
YUGOSLAVIA
Black Sea
Daravica 8714
Balkan Mountains
Adriatic Sea
Musala 9597
BULGARIA
L. Shkodër
Maritsa
Rhodope Mts.
MACEDONIA
Pirin
L. Ohrid
L. Prespa
ALBANIA

AGRICULTURE

Agricultural zones

arable and pasture
fruits and vegetables
pasture
rough grazing
woods and forest
nonagricultural land

▲ mountain peak (ft)

The most fertile regions are the North European Plain in Poland and the lowlands of Hungary, Romania, Croatia, and northern Serbia. Livestock are raised in upland areas.

RUSSIA AND ITS NEIGHBORS

The region consists of the 15 republics that made up the Soviet Union, together with land-locked Mongolia. In the west is part of the North European Plain, which extends from northern France to the Ural Mountains. East of the Urals is Siberia, a monotonous landscape of plains and plateaus, with uplands in the east. The far east contains the Kamchatka Peninsula, which has active volcanoes and forms part of the Pacific "ring of fire." The region also contains the Caucasus Mountain range between the Black and Caspian seas, and two bleak deserts, the Kara Kum and the Kyzyl Kum. On the region's southern flanks are the Pamirs and the Altai Mountains, which extend into Mongolia. Mongolia contains part of the cold Gobi Desert.

The former Soviet government recognized the existence of almost 100 nationalities within its borders. Slavs, including Belorussians, Russians, and Ukrainians, form the largest group. Like most people in the western part of the region, including Latvians and Lithuanians, their languages belong to the Indo-European family.

During the Cold War, the threat of the military strength of the Soviet Union was pitted against that of the West. But economic crises in the late 1980s, caused partly by the high expenditure on defense, led to the collapse of communism and the breakup of the country into 15 separate republics. The newly independent Baltic states restored cultural links with the neighboring Nordic countries.

The region covers about one-sixth of the world's land area. It straddles two continents, including the eastern parts of Europe and the northern part of Asia. It contains Russia, which stretches from the Baltic Sea to the Bering Sea, a distance of about 6,000 miles (9,650 km). Russia is also divided between Europe and Asia. The boundary runs down the Ural Mountains, through the Caspian Sea, and along the crest of the Caucasus Mountains.

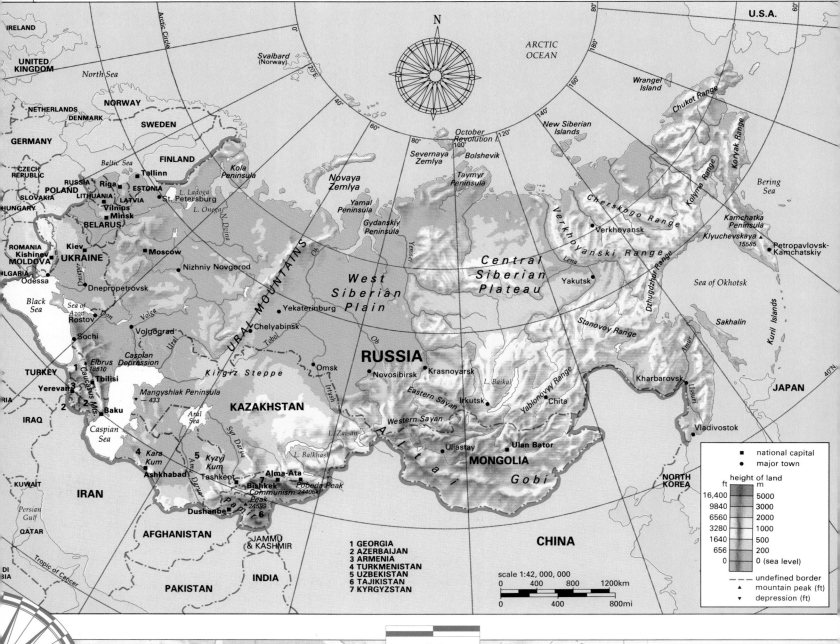

1 GEORGIA
2 AZERBAIJAN
3 ARMENIA
4 TURKMENISTAN
5 UZBEKISTAN
6 TAJIKISTAN
7 KYRGYZSTAN

scale 1:42, 000, 000

0   400   800   1200km
0   400   800mi

- national capital
- major town

height of land

ft	m
16,400	5000
9840	3000
6560	2000
3280	1000
1640	500
656	200
0	0 (sea level)

--- undefined border
▲ mountain peak (ft)
▼ depression (ft)

THE POLITICAL AND CULTURAL WORLD

Dramatic changes occurred in the late 1980s, when the leaders of the Soviet Union introduced new policies that involved radical political changes and the introduction of free market trading and private ownership. Estonia, Latvia, and Lithuania, former republics of the Soviet Union, became independent nations in 1991, and at the end of that year, the Soviet Union was formally abolished. The remaining 12 republics became independent states, though all except Georgia joined a loose structure called the Commonwealth of Independent States. Mongolia followed the Soviet Union in abandoning communism in 1992.

LANGUAGE

Countries with one official language Armenian: Armenia; Azeri: Azerbaijan; Belorussian: Belarus; Estonian: Estonia; Georgian: Georgia; Kasakh: Kazakhstan; Kyrgyz: Kyrgyzstan; Latvian: Latvia; Lithuanian: Lithuania; Romanian: Moldova; Khalka Mongolian: Mongolia; Russian: Russia; Tajik: Tajikistan; Turkmen: Turkmenistan; Ukrainian: Ukraine; Uzbec: Uzbekistan

Over 200 languages are spoken in the republics of the former Soviet Union. Russian is the second language in all the non-Russian republics. Other languages include Bashkir, Chuvash, German, Mordvian, Polish, and Tatar.

RELIGION

Countries with one major religion Armenia (AAC) ; Georgia (GO); Azerbaijan, Kazakhstan, Kyrgyzstan, Tajikistan, Turkmenistan, Uzbekistan (I); Moldova (EO) ; Mongolia (B)
Countries with more than one major religion Belarus, Ukraine (EO,RC); Estonia, Latvia (L,RO,P); Lithuania (RC,L,RO); Russia (RO,RC,P,I,J,B)

Key: AAC-Armenian Apostolic Church, B-Buddhism, EO-Eastern Orthodox, GO-Georgian Orthodox, I- Islam, J-Jewish, L-Lutheran, P-other Protestant, RC-Roman Catholic, RO-Russian Orthodox

STYLES OF GOVERNMENT

Republics All the countries in the region
Multiparty states All the countries in the region
One-chamber assembly Mongolia
Two-chamber assembly (in 1990) all the former Soviet republics

1 GEORGIA
2 AZERBAIJAN
3 ARMENIA
4 TURKMENISTAN
5 UZBEKISTAN
6 TAJIKISTAN
7 KYRGYZSTAN

■ national capital

The newly independent countries in the region include Estonia, Latvia, and Lithuania in the northeast, and Belarus and Ukraine in the west. Moldova lies south of Ukraine. Between the Black Sea and the Caspian Sea lie Georgia, Azerbaijan, and Armenia.

Armenia
Area 11,500 sq mi (29,800 sq km)
Population 3,376,000
Capital Yerevan

Azerbaijan
Area 33,400 sq mi (86,600 sq km)
Population 7,137,000
Capital Baku

Belarus
Area 80,200 sq mi (207,600 sq km)
Population 10,260,000
Capital Minsk

Estonia
Area 17,400 sq mi (45,100 sq km)
Population 1,582,000
Capital Tallinn

Georgia
Area 26,900 sq mi (69,700 sq km)
Population 5,464,000
Capital Tbilisi

Kazakhstan
Area 1,049,200 sq mi (2,717,300 sq km)
Population 16,793,000
Capital Alma-Ata

Kyrgyzstan
Area 76,600 sq mi (198,500 sq km)
Population 4,422,000
Capital Bishkek

Latvia
Area 24,900 sq mi (64,500 sq km)
Population 2,681,000
Capital Riga

Lithuania
Area 25,200 sq mi (65,200 sq km)
Population 3,728,000
Capital Vilnius

Moldova
Area 13,000 sq mi (33,700 sq km)
Population 4,367,000
Capital Chisinău

Mongolia
Area 604,800 sq mi (1,566,500 sq km)
Population 2,190,000
Capital Ulan Bator

Russia
Area 6,592,800 sq mi (17,075,400 sq km)
Population 148,543,000
Capital Moscow

Tajikistan
Area 55,300 sq mi (143,100 sq km)
Population 5,358,000
Capital Dushanbe

Turkmenistan
Area 188,500 sq mi (488,100 sq km)
Population 3,714,000
Capital Ashkhabad

Ukraine
Area 233,100 sq mi (603,700 sq km)
Population 51,944,000
Capital Kiev

Uzbekistan
Area 172,700 sq mi (447,400 sq km)
Population 20,708,000
Capital Tashkent

HABITATS

The northern part of Russia is tundra, which merges into a vast belt of coniferous forest. Steppes occur in the southeastern parts of Russia and Kazakhstan, with desert in the Aral-Caspian lowland and Mongolia. There are mountains in much of the south.

LAND

Area 9,251,339 sq mi (23,967,200 sq km), including largest country on earth
Highest point Communism Peak, 24,590 ft (7,495 m)
Lowest point Mangyshlak Peninsula, −433 ft (−132 m)
Major features plains and plateaus of north, Ural Mountains, Caucasus Mountains, Pamirs and Altai ranges, Kara Kum, Kyzyl Kum, and Gobi deserts, Arctic islands

WATER

Longest river Yenisei, 3,650 mi (5,870 km)
Largest lake Caspian Sea, 143,240 sq mi (371,000 sq km), largest area of inland water in world; Lake Baikal is world's greatest in volume, at 5,500 cu mi (22,000 cu km) and depth, at 6,365 ft (1,940 m)

NOTABLE THREATENED SPECIES

Mammals Manzbier's marmot *(Marmota menzbieri)*, Russian desman *(Desmana moschata)*
Plants *Astragalus tanaiticus, Elytrigia stipifolia, Eremurus korovinii, Fritillaria eduardii, Iris paradoxa, Lilium caucasicum, Potentilla volgarica, Rhododendron fauriei, Scrophularia cretacea, Tulipa kaufmanniana*
Others Amur sturgeon *(Acipenser schrencki)*, Balkhash perch *(Perca schrenki)*, Caucasian relict ant *(Aulacopone relicta)*

CLIMATE

A subarctic zone called the taiga stretches from northwest Russia to the Pacific Ocean. Summers are short but warm. Winters are long and cold. The west-central areas have a continental climate, while in the far south are deserts and semidesert areas.

TEMPERATURE AND PRECIPITATION

| | Temperature °F (°C) | | Altitude | |
	January	July	ft	(m)
Moscow	8.6 (−13)	64 (18)	512	(156)
Sochi	45 (7)	73 (23)	102	(31)
Krasnovodsk	36 (2)	82 (28)	68	(21)
Ulan Bator	−15 (−26)	61 (16)	4,345	(1,325)
Verkhoyansk	−60 (−51)	57 (14)	328	(100)
Vladivostok	7 (−14)	66 (19)	95	(29)

| | Precipitation in (mm) | | | |
	January		July		Year
Moscow	1.2 (31)	3.5 (88)	22.6 (575)
Sochi	7.9 (201)	2.4 (60)	57.1 (1,451)
Krasnovodsk	0.5 (13)	0.2 (5)	3.6 (92)
Ulan Bator	0.04 (1)	3.0 (76)	8.2 (209)
Verkhoyansk	0.2 (5)	1.1 (28)	6.1 (155)
Vladivostok	0.3 (8)	3.3 (84)	32.4 (824)

ENVIRONMENTAL ISSUES

Rapid industrialization that began after the Russian Revolution of 1917 caused great ecological destruction. Russia's Lake Baikal has been polluted by industrial wastes, and the Aral Sea is shrinking because its water has been used for irrigation.

POPULATION AND WEALTH

	*Former U.S.S.R.	Mongolia
Population (in millions)	288.6	2.2
Population increase (annual population growth rate, % 1960–1990)	1.0	2.8
Energy use (gigajoules/person)	194	53
Real purchasing power (US$/person)	N/A	N/A

ENVIRONMENTAL INDICATORS

CO$_2$ emissions (mil. m.t. carbon/year)	690	1.9
Municipal waste (lbs/person/year)	N/A	N/A
Nuclear waste (cumulative m.t. heavy metal)	N/A	0
Artificial fertilizer use (lbs/acre/year)	105	16
Automobiles (per 1,000 population)	55	N/A
Access to safe drinking water (% population)	100	65

MAJOR ENVIRONMENTAL PROBLEMS AND SOURCES

Air pollution: generally high, urban very high; acid rain prevalent; high greenhouse gas emissions
River/lake pollution: high; *sources:* industrial, agricultural, sewage, acid deposition, nuclear
Land pollution: high; *sources:* industrial, agricultural, urban/household, nuclear
Land degradation: *types:* desertification, soil erosion, salinization, deforestation; *causes:* agriculture, industry
Waste disposal problems: domestic; industrial; nuclear
Major events: Chernobyl (1986) and Sosnovyy Bor (1992), nuclear accidents; Kyshtym (1957) hazardous waste spill; Novosibirsk (1979) catastrophic industrial accident

* All figures relate to the former Soviet Union.

HABITATS

A band of subarctic tundra lies across the north, and huge forested taiga plains lie farther south. In the west are broad regions of dry grasslands called steppes, while semideserts and deserts cover much of the south.

Physical zones
- tundra
- mountains/barren land
- forest
- grassland
- semidesert
- desert

▲ mountain peak (ft)
▼ depression (ft)
⁎ climate station

1 GEORGIA
2 AZERBAIJAN
3 ARMENIA
4 TURKMENISTAN
5 UZBEKISTAN
6 TAJIKISTAN
7 KYRGYZSTAN

ENVIRONMENTAL ISSUES

Key environmental issues

- major town or city
- heavily polluted town or city
- major pollution event
- heavily polluted river
- area affected by permafrost
- dead lake

annual air pollution (tons per square mi)

- 8
- 4
- 2
- 0.8

Air and water pollution are greatest in the industrialized west. The 1986 explosion at Chernobyl's nuclear power plant was a disaster that polluted land over much of Europe.

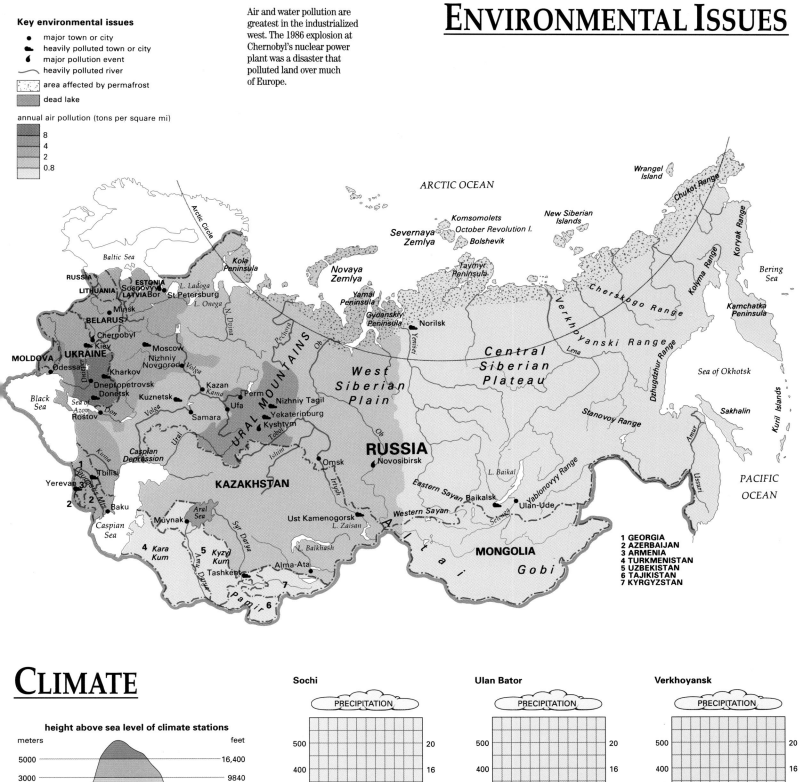

1 GEORGIA
2 AZERBAIJAN
3 ARMENIA
4 TURKMENISTAN
5 UZBEKISTAN
6 TAJIKISTAN
7 KYRGYZSTAN

CLIMATE

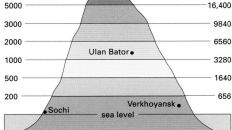

height above sea level of climate stations

meters		feet
5000		16,400
3000		9840
2000	Ulan Bator	6560
1000		3280
500		1640
200	Verkhoyansk	656
Sochi	sea level	

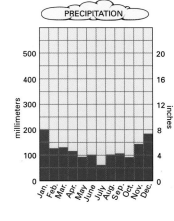

Sochi
PRECIPITATION

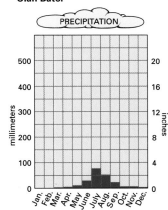

Ulan Bator
PRECIPITATION

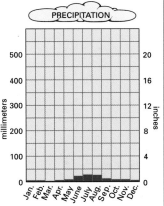

Verkhoyansk
PRECIPITATION

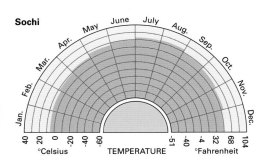

Sochi
TEMPERATURE

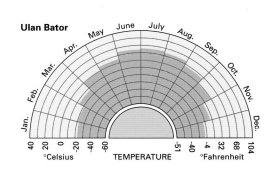

Ulan Bator
TEMPERATURE

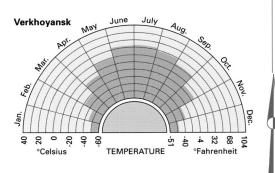

Verkhoyansk
TEMPERATURE

POPULATION

About two-thirds of the population of the region live in the European, western part rather than in the eastern, Asian part. However, under communist rule, the government encouraged the growth of industrial cities in the east, with some success.

POPULATION

Total population of region (in millions)	290.7
Population density (persons per sq mi)	33
Population change (average annual percent 1960–1990) Urban	+2.1
Rural	−0.5

URBAN POPULATION

As percentage of total population	
1960	48.8
1990	67.5
Percentage in cities of more than 1 million	14.6

TEN LARGEST CITIES

	Country	Population
Moscow †	Russia	8,967,000
St. Petersburg (Leningrad)	Russia	5,020,000
Kiev †	Ukraine	2,587,000
Tashkent †	Uzbekistan	2,073,000
Baku †	Azerbaijan	1,757,000
Kharkov	Ukraine	1,611,000
Minsk †	Belarus	1,589,000
Nizhniy Novgorod	Russia	1,438,000
Novosibirsk	Russia	1,436,000
Yekaterinburg	Russia	1,367,000

† denotes national capital

INDUSTRY

The former Soviet Union built up a huge industrial sector based on its abundant natural resources. It invested in engineering and defense industries rather than the production of consumer goods. These newer industries are now being developed.

INDUSTRIAL OUTPUT (US$ billion)

Total	Mining and Manufacturing	Average annual change since 1960
752.6	752.6	+5.7%

INDUSTRIAL WORKERS (millions)
(Figures in parentheses are percentages of total labor force.)

Total	Mining and Manufacturing	Construction
54.7	41.6 (31.8%)	13.1 (10%)

MAJOR PRODUCTS (Figures in parentheses are percentages of world production.)

Energy and minerals	Output	Change since 1960
Coal (mil. m.t.)	662.4 (14.1%)	+35.2%
Oil (mil. barrels)	4452.9 (19.7%)	+311%
Natural gas (billion cu meters)	711.7 (37.1%)	+1471%
Iron ore (mil. m.t.)	138.2 (24.3%)	+31%
Nickel (1,000 m.t.)	189.6 (23.5%)	+38.5%
Vanadium (1,000 m.t.)	9.6 (31.1%)	No data
Phosphate rock (mil. m.t.)	12.0 (22.6%)	+83%

Manufactures		
Steel (mil. m.t.)	163.0 (22.3%)	+149.6%
Cement (mil. m.t.)	134.9 (12.3%)	+196.6%
Sulfuric acid (mil. m.t.)	29.4 (20.5%)	+132.2%
Linen fabric (mil. sq ft)	8,490 (77.4%)	No data
Footwear (mil. pairs)	819.1 (18.4%)	+141.2%
Refrigerators (mil.)	6.2 (11.5%)	+167.3%

AGRICULTURE

Only about 10 percent of the former Soviet Union is suitable for arable farming, while livestock raising is the main occupation in Mongolia. Productivity on the communist state farms and collectives was generally low, and food often had to be imported.

LAND (million acres)

Total	Agricultural	Arable	Forest/woodland
6,890 (100%)	1,801 (31%)	568 (10%)	2,369 (40%)

FARMERS

20.7 million employed in agriculture (14% of workforce)
27 acres of arable land per person employed in agriculture

MAJOR CROPS
Numbers in parentheses are percentages of world average yield and total world production.

	Area mil. acres	Yield 100lbs/acre	Production mil. m.t.	Change since 1963
Wheat	116	15.8	83.9 (16)	+30%
Barley	76	16.9	58.5 (32)	+188%
Oats	29	14	18.5 (43)	+205%
Rye	23.9	16.6	18.1 (53)	+20%

MAJOR LIVESTOCK

	Number in mil.	Production mil. m.t.	Change since 1963
Sheep	155.4 (14)	—	+6%
Cattle	124.6 (10)	—	+46%
Pigs	79.6 (9)	—	+38%
Milk	—	103.1 (22)	+61%
Fish catch	—	11.2 (12)	—

Population density

(National capital is underlined.)

◆	over 5,000,000
■	1,000,000–5,000,000
●	600,000–999,999
×	national capital less than 600,000

persons per square mi	persons per square km
260	100
130	50
26	10
2.6	1

POPULATION

The tundra and taiga regions are sparsely populated, as also are the southern deserts and mountain areas. The greatest concentrations of population are in the southwestern part of the region.

1 GEORGIA
2 AZERBAIJAN
3 ARMENIA
4 TURKMENISTAN
5 UZBEKISTAN
6 TAJIKISTAN
7 KYRGYZSTAN

INDUSTRY

ARCTIC OCEAN

Provideniya
Pevek
Anadyr
Korf
Bering
Sea
Ust
Kamchatsk
Petropavlovsk-
Kamchatskiy
Magadan
Okhotsk
Sea of Okhotsk
Okha
Nikolayevsk-
na-Amure
PACIFIC
OCEAN
Poronaysk
Kholmsk
Blagoveshchensk
Vladivostok

Murmansk
Baltic Sea
Ventspils
Tallinn
RUSSIA
Klaipeda
LITHUANIA
Riga
ESTONIA
LATVIA
St Petersburg
L. Ladoga
Onega
Archangel
Mezen
N. Dvina
L. Onega
Dikson
Tiksi
Norilsk
BELARUS
Moscow
Yenisey
Ob
MOLDOVA
UKRAINE
Kiev
Nizhniy Novgorod
Odessa
Kharkov
Dnepropetrovsk
Perm
Sevastopol
Samara
Yekaterinburg
Black
Sea
Sea
of Azov
Don
Saratov
Volga
RUSSIA
Novorossiysk
Volgograd
Chelyabinsk
Batumi
Magnitogorsk
Leninakan
Ural
Aktyubinsk
Novosibirsk
3
Guryev
KAZAKHSTAN
Novokuznetsk
2 2
Baku
Karaganda
Semipalatinsk
Chita
Caspian
Sea
Aral
Sea
Syr Darya
Ust-Kamenogorsk
L. Baikal
4
5
L. Zaisan
L. Balkhash
Ulan Bator
Amur
Ussuri
7
Tashkent
Alma-Ata
MONGOLIA
Amu Darya
Dushanbe
6

Resources and industry

♦ industrial center
○ major port
• other town
── major road
── major railroad

mineral resources and fossil fuels
  iron and other ferroalloy
♦ metal ores
• other metal ores
▪ nonmetallic minerals

	coal
	iron ore
	lignite (brown coal)
	natural gas
	oil
	potash

1 GEORGIA
2 AZERBAIJAN
3 ARMENIA
4 TURKMENISTAN
5 UZBEKISTAN
6 TAJIKISTAN
7 KYRGYZSTAN

The region is rich in
natural resources, including
oil and natural gas and a wide
variety of minerals. But many
of the resources are in remote
areas and are costly to
extract and transport.

AGRICULTURE

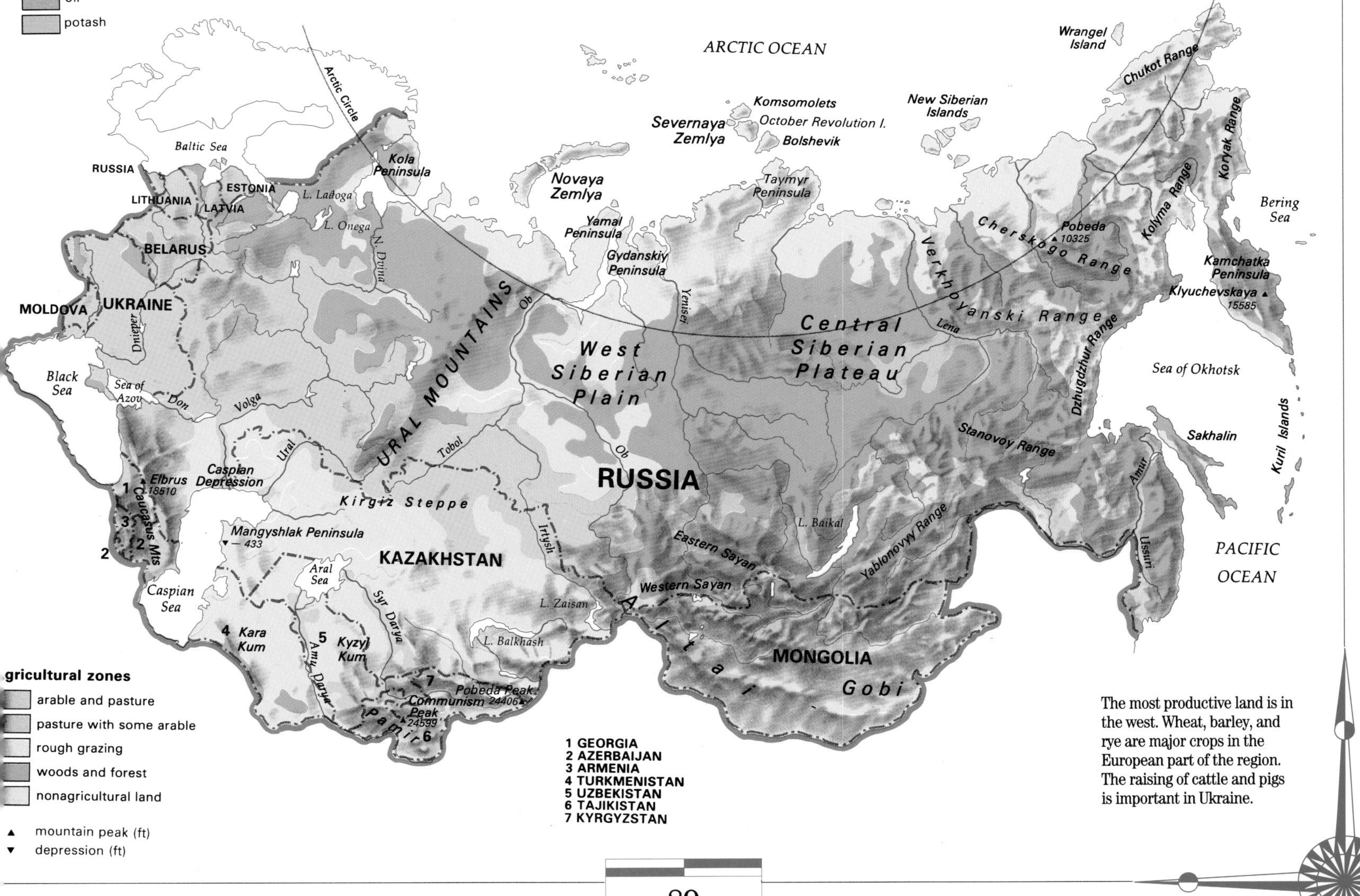

ARCTIC OCEAN
Wrangel
Island
Chukot Range
Komsomolets
Severnaya
October Revolution I.
New Siberian
Zemlya
Bolshevik
Islands
Koryak Range
Kolyma Range
RUSSIA
Kola
Peninsula
Novaya
Zemlya
Taymyr
Peninsula
Bering
Sea
Baltic Sea
ESTONIA
Yamal
Peninsula
Pobeda
▲10325
Kamchatka
Peninsula
LITHUANIA
LATVIA
L. Ladoga
Gydanskiy
Peninsula
Cherskogo Range
Klyuchevskaya ▲
15585
BELARUS
L. Onega
N. Dvina
Verkhoyanski Range
MOLDOVA
UKRAINE
Ob
Yenisey
Central
Dhugdzhur Range
Dnieper
URAL MOUNTAINS
West
Siberian
Siberian
Sea of Okhotsk
Black
Sea
Sea of
Azov
Don
Volga
Plain
Plateau
Lena
Tobol
Sakhalin
Caspian
Ural
RUSSIA
Kuril Islands
Elbrus
Caspian
Ob
1
18510
Depression
Stanovoy Range
3
Caucasus Mts
Kirgiz Steppe
Irtysh
2
Mangyshlak Peninsula
Yablonovyy Range
PACIFIC
— 433
Western Sayan
Eastern Sayan
OCEAN
Aral
Sea
KAZAKHSTAN
Syr Darya
L. Baikal
4 Kara
Kum
5 Kyzyl
L. Zaisan
Amur
Caspian
Sea
Kum
L. Balkhash
Ussuri
7 Pobeda Peak
Communism 24406
Altai
MONGOLIA
Amu Darya
Peak
24599
Gobi
Pamir
6

agricultural zones

	arable and pasture
	pasture with some arable
	rough grazing
	woods and forest
	nonagricultural land

▲ mountain peak (ft)
▼ depression (ft)

1 GEORGIA
2 AZERBAIJAN
3 ARMENIA
4 TURKMENISTAN
5 UZBEKISTAN
6 TAJIKISTAN
7 KYRGYZSTAN

The most productive land is in
the west. Wheat, barley, and
rye are major crops in the
European part of the region.
The raising of cattle and pigs
is important in Ukraine.

MIDDLE EAST

The Middle East contains some of the world's hottest and driest deserts. The two major rivers, the Tigris and Euphrates, rise in the well-watered mountains of Turkey and flow across the deserts of Syria and Iraq.

The mountains of Turkey are part of a long chain of folded mountains that extends across the northern Middle East to the Hindu Kush in northeastern Afghanistan.

The Middle East contains several oil-rich nations, but most of the region is economically underdeveloped. It is the home of three religions —Judaism, Christianity, and Islam—but religion has divided people and has been the cause of both international and civil wars. Politically, the Middle East is an unstable region, whose conflicts periodically involve the world community.

The Middle East is the meeting place of three continents. Here early peoples began to plant crops, build cities, and found civilizations. Today the region is important economically and strategically because of its large reserves and production of oil and natural gas.

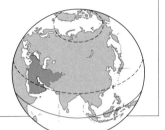

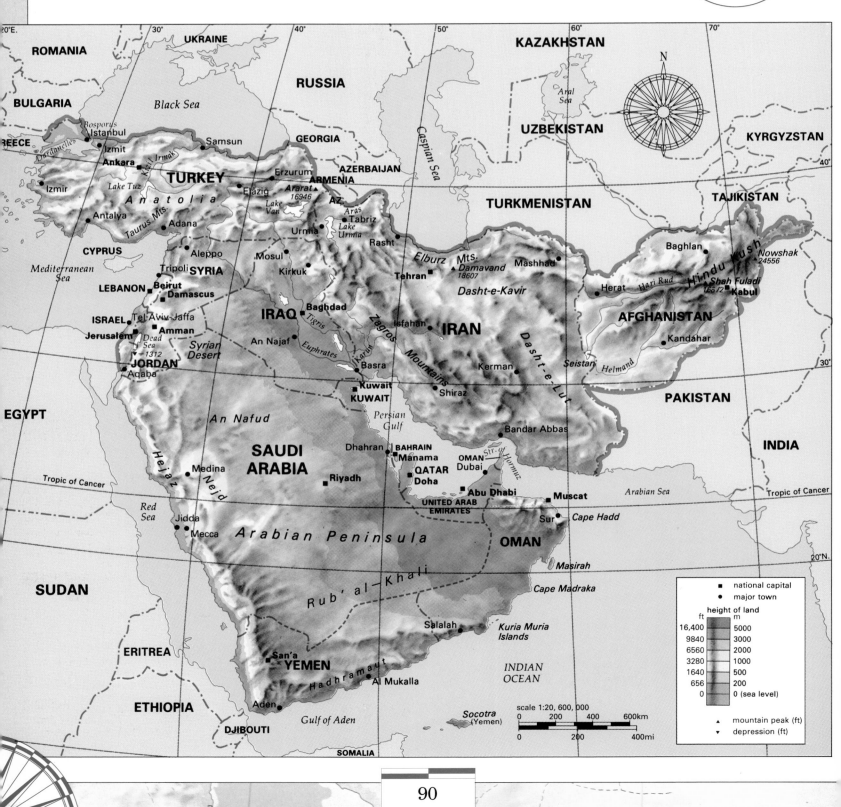

| | national capital |
| | major town |

height of land

ft	m
16,400	5000
9840	3000
6560	2000
3280	1000
1640	500
656	200
0	0 (sea level)

▲ mountain peak (ft)
▼ depression (ft)

scale 1:20, 600, 000

0   200   400   600km
0   200   400mi

THE POLITICAL AND CULTURAL WORLD

Islam, spread throughout the area by Arabs from the seventh century A.D., is the dominant religion in the Middle East. Israel, the only country in which Muslims are not a majority, has been in conflict with Arab nations since it was created as a homeland for Jews in 1948.

Other conflicts have arisen because of rivalries between ethnic, cultural, and religious groups, as in Lebanon, and the aspirations of minorities, such as the Kurds, who would like to establish their own country in parts of Iraq, Iran, and Turkey. Territorial disputes have led to war between Iraq and Iran (1980–1988) and Iraq's invasion of Kuwait (1990–1991).

COUNTRIES IN THE REGION

Afghanistan, Bahrain, Iran, Iraq, Israel, Jordan, Kuwait, Lebanon, Oman, Qatar, Saudi Arabia, Syria, Turkey, United Arab Emirates, Yemen

LANGUAGE

Countries with one official language Arabic: Bahrain, Iraq, Jordan, Kuwait, Lebanon, Oman, Qatar, Saudi Arabia, Syria, U.A.E., Yemen; Farsi: Iran; Turkish: Turkey
Countries with two official languages Arabic, Hebrew: Israel; Dari, Pushtu: Afghanistan

RELIGION

Countries with one major religion Afghanistan, Bahrain, Iran, Iraq, Jordan, Kuwait, Oman, Qatar, Saudi Arabia, Syria, Turkey, U.A.E., Yemen (I)
Countries with more than one major religion Israel (C,I,J); Lebanon (C,D,I and other)

Key: C-various Christian, D-Druze, I-Islam, J-Jewish

STYLES OF GOVERNMENT

Republics Afghanistan, Iran, Iraq, Israel, Lebanon, Syria, Turkey, U.A.E., Yemen
Monarchies Bahrain, Jordan, Kuwait, Oman, Qatar, Saudi Arabia
Federal state U.A.E.
Multiparty states Afghanistan, Israel, Lebanon, Turkey
One-party states Iran, Iraq, Syria
States without parties Bahrain, Jordan, Kuwait, Oman, Qatar, Saudi Arabia, U.A.E., Yemen

ECONOMIC INDICATORS: 1990

	UAE	S.Arabia	Jordan
GDP(US$ billions)	28.27	80.89	3.3329
GNP per capita (US$)	19,860	7,050	1,240
Annual rate of growth of GDP, 1980–1990	–4.5%	–1.8%	4.3%
Manufacturing as % of GDP	9%	9%	12%
Central government spending as % of GNP	13%	N/A	39%
Merchandise exports (US$ billions)	15.0	44.4	1.15
Merchandise imports (US$ billions)	9.6	24	2.66
% of GNP donated as development aid	2.65%	3.9%	-1%

WELFARE INDICATORS

Infant mortality rate (per 1,000 live births)			
1965	103	148	114
1990	23	65	51
Daily food supply available (calories per capita, 1989)	3,309	2,874	2,634
Population per physician (1984)	1,020	730	860
Teacher-pupil ratio (elementary school, 1989)	1 : 18	1 : 16	1 : 28

Afghanistan
Area 251,825 sq mi (652,225 sq km)
Population 16,557,000
Capital Kabul

Bahrain
Area 267 sq mi (691 sq km)
Population 516,000
Capital Manama

Iran
Area 634,559 sq mi (1,643,503 sq km)
Population 54,607,000
Capital Tehran

Iraq
Area 169,235 sq mi (438,317 sq km)
Population 18,920,000
Capital Baghdad

Israel
Area 7,992 sq mi (20,700 sq km)
Population 4,600,000
Capital Jerusalem

Jordan
Area 34,443 sq mi (89,206 sq km)
Population 4,009,000
Capital Amman

Kuwait
Area 6,880 sq mi (17,818 sq km)
Population 2,039,000
Capital Kuwait

Lebanon
Area 3,950 sq mi (10,230 sq km)
Population 2,701,000
Capital Beirut

Oman
Area 82,000 sq mi (212,500 sq km)
Population 1,502,000
Capital Muscat

Qatar
Area 4,400 sq mi (11,400 sq km)
Population 368,000
Capital Doha

Saudi Arabia
Area 865,000 sq mi (2,240,000 sq km)
Population 14,134,000
Capital Riyadh

Syria
Area 71,498 sq mi (185,180 sq km)
Population 12,530,000
Capital Damascus

Turkey
Area 300, 948 sq mi (779,452 sq km)
Population 58,687,000
Capital Ankara

United Arab Emirates (U.A.E.)
Area 30,000 sq mi (77,700 sq km)
Population 1,589,000
Capital Abu Dhabi

Yemen
Area 182,276 sq mi (472,099 sq km)
Population 11,282,000
Capital San'a

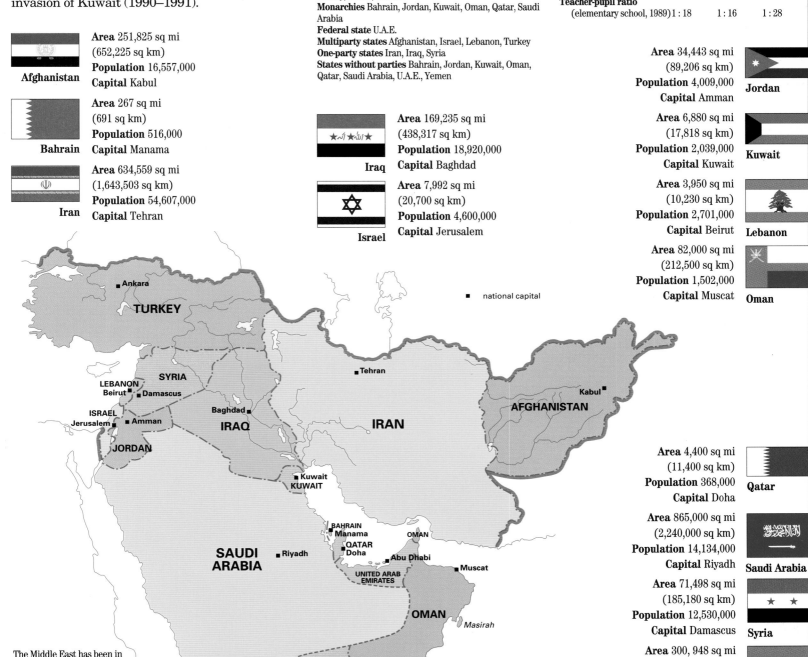

- national capital

The Middle East has been in ferment since 1945. Israel has fought four wars against its Arab foes, while the Palestinians in Israel continue their protests against Israeli rule. The Iran-Iraq war was the longest in the twentieth century, while the expulsion of Iraqi forces from Kuwait in 1991 involved many world powers.

HABITATS

Mountains, plateaus, and deserts dominate the Middle East. The Arabian Peninsula is almost completely surrounded by sea, yet much of the peninsula consists of desert and semidesert. The plains of the Tigris and Euphrates are fertile.

LAND

Highest point Mount Nowshak 24,556 ft (7,485 m)
Lowest point Dead Sea, −1,312 ft (−400 m), lowest point on land surface of the earth
Major features plateaus of Anatolia and Iran, Hindu Kush, Zagros and Elburz mountains, deserts of Arabia and Iran

WATER

Longest river Euphrates, 1,700 mi (2,720 km)
Largest lake Caspian Sea, 143,240 sq mi (371,000 sq km), largest area of inland water in the world

NOTABLE THREATENED SPECIES

Mammals mountain gazelle (Gazella gazella), Arabian oryx (Oryx leucoryx), Arabian tahr (Hemitragus jayakari)
Birds Yemen thrush (Turdus menachensis)
Plants Alkanna macrophylla; Anthemis brachycarpa; Ceratonia oreothauma subsp. oreothauma; Dionysia mira; Erodium subintegrifolium; Ferulago longistylis; Iris calcarea; Iris lortetii; Rumex rothschildianus; Wissmannia carinensis
Others Latifi's viper (Vipera latifi), cicek fish (Acanthorutilus handlirschi)

CLIMATE

The coasts of Turkey and the eastern Mediterranean have hot, dry summers and mild, moist winters. Inland is a hot desert region. The mountains and plateaus of the Turkish interior, Iran, and Afghanistan are subtropical and dry, though it snows in the mountains.

TEMPERATURE AND PRECIPITATION

	Temperature °F (°C) January	July	Altitude ft	(m)
Samsun	45 (7)	71 (22)	131	(40)
Haifa	57 (14)	81 (27)	32	(10)
Amman	46 (8)	77 (25)	2,547	(777)
Basra	54 (12)	93 (34)	7	(2)
Riyadh	59 (15)	93 (34)	1,935	(590)
Kandahar	42 (6)	84 (29)	3,460	(1,055)

	Precipitation in (mm) January	July	Year
Samsun	2.9 (74)	1.5 (39)	28.8 (731)
Haifa	6.8 (175)	0 (0)	19.6 (499)
Amman	2.7 (68)	0 (0)	10.7 (273)
Basra	1.4 (36)	0 (0)	6.5 (164)
Riyadh	0.1 (3)	0 (0)	3.2 (82)
Kandahar	3.1 (79)	0.1 (3)	8.9 (225)

ENVIRONMENTAL ISSUES

Soil erosion and the buildup of salt in the soil caused by poor drainage of irrigated land have damaged the area in the past. There is overgrazing and deforestation. Industrial and urban growth, together with oil extraction and war, have caused recent damage.

POPULATION AND WEALTH

	Highest	Middle	Lowest
Population (in millions)	54.6 (Iran)	4.0 (Jordan)	0.4 (Qatar)
Population increase (annual population growth rate, % 1960–1990)	10.0 (U.A.E.)	3.4 (Iraq)	1.3 (Lebanon)
Energy use (gigajoules/person)	642 (Qatar)	39 (Lebanon)	4 (Afghanistan)
Real purchasing power (US$/person)	19,440 (Qatar)	9,290 (Oman)	710 (Afghanistan)

ENVIRONMENTAL INDICATORS

CO2 emissions (mil. m.t. carbon/year)	42 (S. Arabia)	4.7 (Oman)	0.6 (Yemen)
Artificial fertilizer use (lbs/acre/year)	669 (Bahrain)	82 (Oman)	5.3 (Yemen)
Automobiles (per 1,000 population)	207 (Kuwait)	48 (Turkey)	2 (Yemen)
Access to safe drinking water (% population)	100 (Bahrain)	83 (Turkey)	21 (Afghanistan)

MAJOR ENVIRONMENTAL PROBLEMS AND SOURCES

Air pollution: urban high
Coastal pollution: medium/high; *sources*: oil; war
Land degradation: *types*: desertification, salinization; oil pollution, *causes*: agriculture; war
Resource problems: fuelwood shortage; inadequate drinking water and sanitation
Population problems: population explosion; war
Major events: Persian Gulf (1991), oil spills and oil well fires during and after the Gulf War

HABITATS

Some of the world's hottest and driest deserts are found in the region. Here the main sources of water are found at scattered oases or along such rivers as the Tigris and Euphrates.

Physical zones
- mountains/barren land
- forest
- grassland
- semidesert
- desert

▲ mountain peak (ft)
▼ depression (ft)
☀ climate station

ENVIRONMENTAL ISSUES

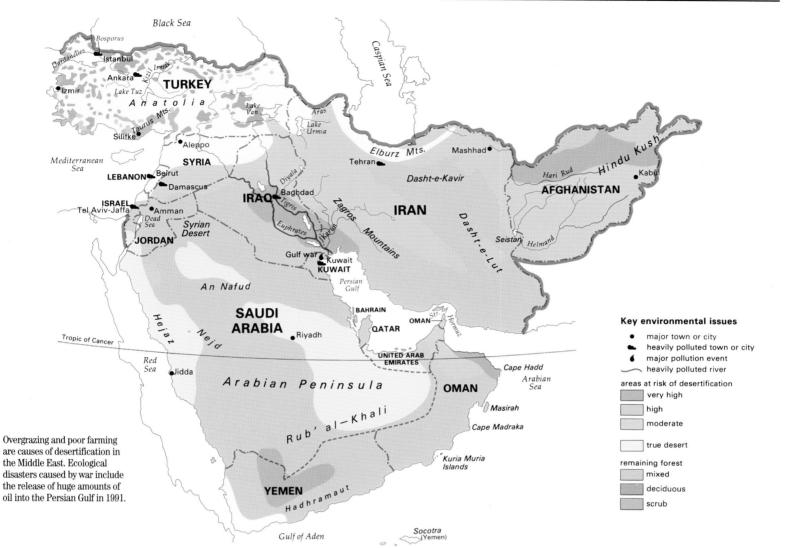

Black Sea
Bosporus
Dardanelles
Istanbul
Ankara
Kızıl Irmak
Izmir
Lake Tuz
TURKEY
A n a t o l i a
Taurus Mts.
Silifke
Aleppo
Mediterranean
Sea
SYRIA
LEBANON Beirut
Damascus
ISRAEL
Tel Aviv-Jaffa
Amman
Dead
Sea
*Syrian
Desert*
JORDAN
Diyala
Baghdad
IRAQ
Tigris
Euphrates
Karun
*Zagros
Mountains*
Lake
Van
Lake
Urmia
Aras
Elburz Mts.
Tehran
Mashhad
Dasht-e-Kavir
Hari Rud
Hindu Kush
Kabul
AFGHANISTAN
IRAN
D a s h t - e - L u t
Seistan
Helmand
Gulf war
Kuwait
KUWAIT
*Persian
Gulf*
Caspian Sea
An Nafud
**SAUDI
ARABIA**
Riyadh
Hejaz
Nejd
BAHRAIN
QATAR
OMAN
Str. of
Hormuz
**UNITED ARAB
EMIRATES**
Tropic of Cancer
Red
Sea
Jidda
A r a b i a n   P e n i n s u l a
Rub' al–Khali
Cape Hadd
Arabian
Sea
OMAN
Masirah
Cape Madraka
Kuria Muria
Islands
YEMEN
Hadhramaut
Socotra
(Yemen)
Gulf of Aden

Key environmental issues
- • major town or city
- heavily polluted town or city
- major pollution event
- heavily polluted river

areas at risk of desertification
- very high
- high
- moderate
- true desert

remaining forest
- mixed
- deciduous
- scrub

Overgrazing and poor farming
are causes of desertification in
the Middle East. Ecological
disasters caused by war include
the release of huge amounts of
oil into the Persian Gulf in 1991.

CLIMATE

height above sea level of climate stations

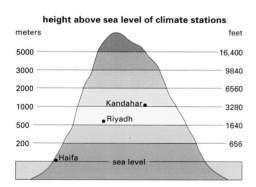

meters   feet
5000 ————   16,400
3000 ————   9840
2000 ————   6560
1000 ————   Kandahar   3280
500 ————   Riyadh   1640
200 ————   656
Haifa   sea level

Haifa
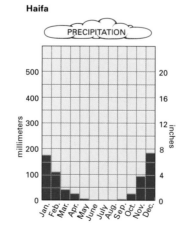
PRECIPITATION
millimeters — inches
500 / 20
400 / 16
300 / 12
200 / 8
100 / 4
0 / 0
Jan. Feb. Mar. Apr. May June July Aug. Sep. Oct. Nov. Dec.

Riyadh
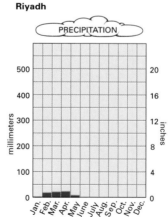
PRECIPITATION
millimeters — inches
500 / 20
400 / 16
300 / 12
200 / 8
100 / 4
0 / 0
Jan. Feb. Mar. Apr. May June July Aug. Sep. Oct. Nov. Dec.

Kandahar
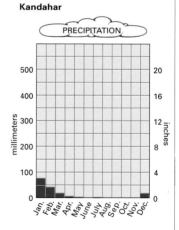
PRECIPITATION
millimeters — inches
500 / 20
400 / 16
300 / 12
200 / 8
100 / 4
0 / 0
Jan. Feb. Mar. Apr. May June July Aug. Sep. Oct. Nov. Dec.

Haifa
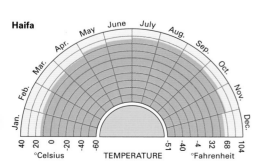
°Celsius   TEMPERATURE   °Fahrenheit
40 20 0 -20 -40 -60   -51 -40 -4 32 68 104

Riyadh
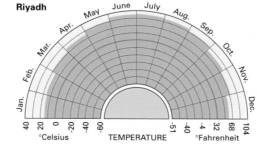
°Celsius   TEMPERATURE   °Fahrenheit
40 20 0 -20 -40 -60   -51 -40 -4 32 68 104

Kandahar
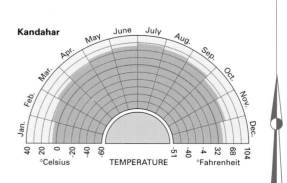
°Celsius   TEMPERATURE   °Fahrenheit
40 20 0 -20 -40 -60   -51 -40 -4 32 68 104

POPULATION

Cities developed in the Middle East more than 5,000 years ago. Today about half of the population is urban, and city populations are rising quickly because of natural increase and the movement of poor people from the countryside, looking for work.

POPULATION

Total population of region (in millions)	202.8
Population density (persons per sq mi)	80.8
Population change (average annual percent 1960–1990)	
Urban	+5.2
Rural	+0.8

URBAN POPULATION

As percentage of total population	
1960	36.8
1990	52.4
Percentage in cities of more than 1 million	16.8

TEN LARGEST CITIES

	Country	Population
Tehran †	Iran	6,043,000
Istanbul	Turkey	5,495,000
Baghdad †	Iraq	4,649,000
Ankara †	Turkey	2,252,000
Riyadh †	Saudi Arabia	2,000,000
Izmir	Turkey	1,490,000
Mashhad	Iran	1,464,000
Kabul †	Afghanistan	1,424,000
Jidda	Saudi Arabia	1,400,000
Damascus †	Syria	1,361,000

† denotes national capital

INDUSTRY

In the Middle East, only Israel and Turkey have built up broad-based manufacturing sectors. Foreign investment and expertise are now helping to build industries in the oil-rich nations, which are seeking to achieve more balanced economies.

INDUSTRIAL OUTPUT (US$ billion)

Total	Mining	Manufacturing	Average annual change since 1960
237.3	83.4	55.6	+4.9%

INDUSTRIAL WORKERS (millions)
(Figures in parentheses are percentages of total labor force.)

Total	Mining	Manufacturing	Construction
11.77	1.33 (2.5%)	5.55 (10.6%)	4.9 (9.3%)

MAJOR PRODUCTS (Figures in parentheses are percentages of world production.)

Energy and minerals	Output	Change since 1960
Oil (mil. barrels)	5966.6 (26.3%)	+288.5%
Natural gas (billion cu meters)	102.2 (5.3%)	+604%
Marble (mil. cu meters)	3.9 (40%)	No data
Magnesite (mil. m.t.)	3.4 (18.8%)	No data
Borate (mil. m.t.)	2.04 (52.8%)	No data

Manufactures		
Wool yarn (1,000 m.t.)	33.9 (10.3%)	-38.4%
Cement (mil. m.t.)	66.5 (6.1%)	+1724%
Steel (mil. m.t.)	9.8 (1.3%)	+2700%
Nitrogenous fertilizer (mil. m.t.)	5.1 (5.5%)	N/A
Polyethylene (1,000 m.t.)	357 (1.6%)	N/A
Jet fuels (mil. m.t.)	7.4 (5.2%)	N/A
Motor gasoline (mil. m.t.)	26.0 (3.6%)	N/A
Liquefied petroleum gas (mil. m.t.)	20.1 (13.1%)	N/A

N/A means production had not begun in 1960.

AGRICULTURE

Much of the farming in the Middle East, when conditions make it possible, is still traditional in character. But new high-technology farming now exists in some places, notably Israel, which has used large-scale irrigation systems and new technology to make the deserts bloom.

LAND (million acres)

Total	Agricultural	Arable	Forest/woodland
1,680 (100%)	654 (39%)	150 (9%)	116 (7%)

FARMERS

23.7 million employed in agriculture (38% of workforce)
7.4 acres of arable land per person employed in agriculture

MAJOR CROPS

	Area mil. acres	Yield 100lbs/acre	Production mil. m.t.	Change since 1963
Wheat	52.3	14.8	35.2 (7)	+119%
Barley	21	11.8	11.3 (6)	+76%
Lentils	2.7	8.3	1.1 (41)	+373%
Cotton	2.4	7.8	0.9 (5)	+45%
Grapes	2.7	53.7	6.5 (10)	+45%
Other fruit	—	—	12.7 (5)	+138%
Vegetables	—	—	31.3 (7)	+138%

MAJOR LIVESTOCK

	Number in mil.	Production mil. m.t.	Change since 1963
Sheep/goats	170.2 (10)	—	+10%
Cattle	28.6 (2)	—	+15%
Milk	—	7.7 (2)	+80%
Fish catch	—	1.2 (1)	

FOOD SECURITY (grain exports minus imports)

mil. m.t.	% domestic production	% world trade
−23.0	43	11

Numbers in parentheses are percentages of world total.

POPULATION

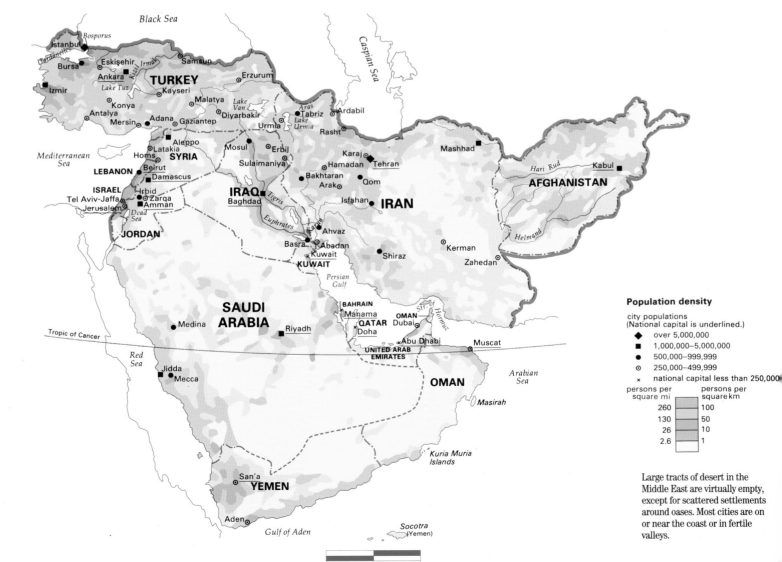

Population density

city populations
(National capital is underlined.)

◆	over 5,000,000
■	1,000,000–5,000,000
●	500,000–999,999
⊙	250,000–499,999
×	national capital less than 250,000

persons per square mi	persons per square km
260	100
130	50
26	10
2.6	1

Large tracts of desert in the Middle East are virtually empty, except for scattered settlements around oases. Most cities are on or near the coast or in fertile valleys.

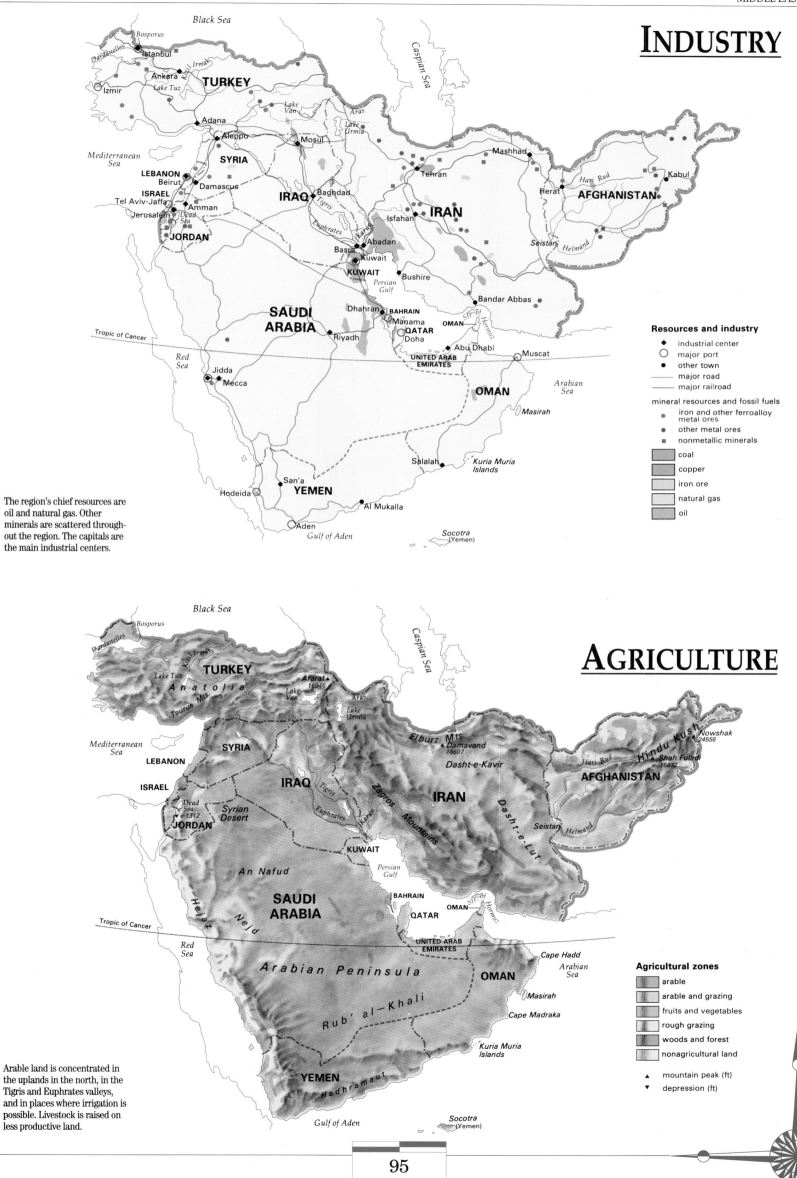

INDUSTRY

Black Sea

Bosporus
Dardanelles Istanbul
Ankara *Kızıl Irmak*
Izmir *Lake Tuz* **TURKEY**
Lake Van
Mediterranean Sea Adana *Aras*
Aleppo Mosul *Lake Urmia*
SYRIA Mashhad
LEBANON Tehran
Beirut Damascus *Hari Rud* Kabul
ISRAEL Amman Baghdad **IRAN** Herat **AFGHANISTAN**
Tel Aviv-Jaffa **IRAQ** *Tigris*
Jerusalem *Dead Sea* Isfahan
JORDAN *Euphrates* *Karun* *Seistan* *Helmand*
Abadan
Basra Kuwait
KUWAIT Bushire
Persian Gulf Bandar Abbas
SAUDI ARABIA Dhahran **BAHRAIN**
Manama *Str. of Hormuz*
Tropic of Cancer Riyadh **QATAR OMAN**
Doha
Red Sea Abu Dhabi Muscat
UNITED ARAB EMIRATES *Arabian Sea*
Jidda
Mecca **OMAN** *Masirah*

Salalah *Kuria Muria Islands*
San'a
Hodeida **YEMEN**
Al Mukalla
Aden *Socotra (Yemen)*
Gulf of Aden

Resources and industry
◆ industrial center
○ major port
● other town
— major road
— major railroad

mineral resources and fossil fuels
● iron and other ferroalloy metal ores
● other metal ores
■ nonmetallic minerals
coal
copper
iron ore
natural gas
oil

The region's chief resources are oil and natural gas. Other minerals are scattered throughout the region. The capitals are the main industrial centers.

AGRICULTURE

Black Sea

Bosporus
Dardanelles
Lake Tuz *Kızıl Irmak* **TURKEY** *Ararat ▲ 16946*
Anatolia *Lake Van*
Taurus Mts. *Aras*
Lake Urmia
Mediterranean Sea *Elburz Mts.* *Hindu Kush* *Nowshak 24556*
SYRIA *Damavand ▲ 18607* *Shah Fuladi 16872*
LEBANON *Dasht-e-Kavir* *Hari Rud*
ISRAEL **IRAQ** **IRAN** **AFGHANISTAN**
Tigris
Dead Sea ▼ -1312 *Syrian Desert* *Zagros Mountains* *Dasht-e-Lut*
JORDAN *Euphrates* *Karun* *Seistan* *Helmand*
KUWAIT
Persian Gulf
An Nafud **BAHRAIN**
QATAR **OMAN** *Str. of Hormuz*
Tropic of Cancer **SAUDI ARABIA**
Neid **UNITED ARAB EMIRATES**
Red Sea *Cape Hadd*
Arabian Sea
Hejaz *Arabian Peninsula* **OMAN**
Masirah
Rub' al-Khali *Cape Madraka*

Kuria Muria Islands
YEMEN *Hadhramaut*
Socotra (Yemen)
Gulf of Aden

Agricultural zones
arable
arable and grazing
fruits and vegetables
rough grazing
woods and forest
nonagricultural land

▲ mountain peak (ft)
▼ depression (ft)

Arable land is concentrated in the uplands in the north, in the Tigris and Euphrates valleys, and in places where irrigation is possible. Livestock is raised on less productive land.

NORTHERN AFRICA

The northern part of Africa consists largely of a low plateau broken by shallow basins and rugged volcanic highlands. The main land feature in the far northwest is the Atlas Mountain range. The other main highlands are in Ethiopia, though there are also mountain peaks in Algeria, Niger, Chad, and Sudan. Running through these highlands is a section of the Rift Valley, the world's longest geological depression, which runs from Syria to Mozambique.

South of the Mediterranean coastlands and the Atlas Mountains lies the Sahara, the world's largest desert. Only two major rivers, the Nile and the Niger, flow across North Africa throughout the year. But North Africa is not completely arid. South of the Sahara is a dry grassland region called the Sahel, which merges into tropical grassland, or savanna, and forest.

North Africa contains two main groups of people: Arabs and Berbers in the north and black Africans in the lands south of the Sahara. Nomadism is the traditional way of life in the Sahara, though it is now under threat. Most of the people are Muslims, though Christianity, introduced between the fourth and sixth centuries A.D., survived the spread of Islam in the inaccessible highlands of Ethiopia. All the countries of the region except Ethiopia were colonized by the French, British, Italians, and Spanish between 1830 and 1914. (Ethiopia was only briefly conquered and ruled by Italy from 1935 to 1941.) Arabic is the official language in the northern states, though some people speak Berber dialects. By contrast, many languages are spoken in the lands south of the Sahara. The former colonial language is used in many countries as an official language or for business and trade.

Northern Africa is part of the ancient landmass of Gondwanaland, which broke up between 200 and 100 million years ago. About 70 million years ago, Africa consisted of two land plates: North Africa was tilted downward, while Southern Africa was tilted upward. This divided Africa into a high plateau in the south and a low plateau in the north, which was flooded by the sea. New rocks were formed on the seabed. These rocks now contain water, oil, and natural gas.

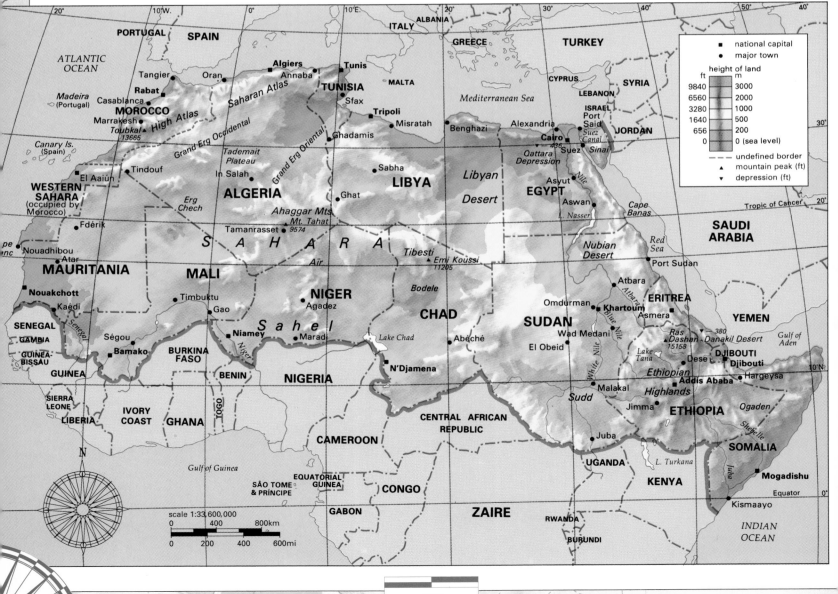

THE POLITICAL AND CULTURAL WORLD

L ike many other parts of the developing world, Northern Africa has faced many problems since the countries of the region became independent from colonial rule.

Egypt was in the front line of the Arab-Israeli wars until it agreed to a peace treaty with Israel in 1979. To the south, Chad, Sudan, Ethiopia, and Somalia have suffered bitter civil wars, while Libya has fought with Chad over their disputed border.

Western Sahara (formerly Spanish Sahara), a thinly populated desert territory, was annexed by Morocco in the face of opposition from nationalist Saharan guerrillas.

COUNTRIES IN THE REGION

Algeria, Chad, Djibouti, Egypt, Eritrea, Ethiopia, Mali, Mauritania, Morocco, Niger, Somalia, Sudan, Tunisia

MEMBERSHIP OF INTERNATIONAL ORGANIZATIONS

Arab League Algeria, Djibouti, Egypt, Libya, Mauritania, Morocco, Somalia, Sudan, Tunisia
Organization for African Unity (OAU) All countries except Eritrea and Morocco
Organization of Petroleum Exporting Countries (OPEC) Algeria, Libya

LANGUAGE

Countries with one official language Amharic: Ethiopia; Arabic: Algeria, Egypt, Libya, Morocco, Sudan, Tunisia; French: Mali, Niger
Countries with two official languages Arabic, French: Chad, Djibouti, Mauritania; Arabic, Somali: Somalia

RELIGION

Countries with one major religion Algeria, Djibouti, Libya, Mauritania, Morocco, Niger, Somalia, Tunisia (I)
Countries with more than one major religion Egypt (C,IR); Eritrea (C,I); Ethiopia (EO,I,IR); Chad, Mali, Sudan (C,I,IR)

Key: C-various Christian, EO-Ethiopian Orthodox, I-Islam, IR-indigenous religions

SYTLES OF GOVERNMENT

Republics All countries in the region except Morocco
Monarchy Morocco
Federal state (since 1991) Sudan
Multiparty states Chad, Egypt, Ethiopia, Mali, Mauritania, Morocco, Sudan, Tunisia
One-party states Algeria, Djibouti, Libya, Somalia
State without parties Niger
Military influence Algeria, Libya, Mauritania, Niger, Sudan
State without effective government (since 1991) Somalia

ECONOMIC INDICATORS: 1990

	Algeria	Egypt	Ethiopia
GDP (US$ billions)	42.15	33.21	5.49
GNP per capita (US$)	2,060	600	120
Annual rate of growth of GDP, 1980–1990	3.1%	5.0%	1.8%
Manufacturing as % of GDP	12%	16%	11%
Central government spending as % of GNP	N/A	40	35
Merchandise exports (US$ billions)	9.5	10.3	1.08
Merchandise imports (US$ billions)	9.5	10.3	1.08
% of GNP received as development aid	0.4%	15.9%	14.6%
Total external debt as % of GNP	53.1%	126.5%	54.2%

WELFARE INDICATORS

Infant mortality rate (per 1,000 live births)			
1965	154	145	165
1990	67	66	132
Daily food supply available (calories per capita, 1989)	2,866	3,336	1,667
Population per physician (1984)	2,340	770	78,780
Teacher-pupil ratio (elementary school, 1989)	1 : 28	1 : 24	1 : 43

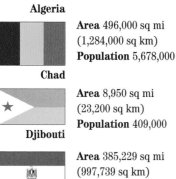

Area 919,595 sq mi (2,381,741 sq km)
Population 24,960,000
Algeria

Area 496,000 sq mi (1,284,000 sq km)
Population 5,678,000
Chad

Area 8,950 sq mi (23,200 sq km)
Population 409,000
Djibouti

Area 385,229 sq mi (997,739 sq km)
Population 53,153,000
Egypt

Area 45,405 sq mi (117,600 sq km)
Population 3,200,000
Eritrea

Area 472,400 sq mi (1,223,500 sq km)
Population 49,240,000
Ethiopia

Area 678,400 sq mi (1,757,000 sq km)
Population 4,545,000
Libya

Area 478,841 sq mi (1,240,192 sq km)
Population 8,156,000
Mali

Area 177,117 sq mi (458,730 sq km)
Population 25,061,000
Morocco

Area 458,075 sq mi (1,186,408 sq km)
Population 7,731,000
Niger

Area 246,201 sq mi (637,657 sq km)
Population 7,497,000
Somalia

Area 966,757 sq mi (2,503,890 sq km)
Population 25,203,000
Sudan

Area 59,664 sq mi (154,530 sq km)
Population 8,180,000
Tunisia

The boundaries of Northern Africa were drawn by the European colonial powers. The boundaries they mandated for many countries have caused friction in recent years. For example, the world's ninth largest country, Sudan, is divided into two cultural regions: the Arab north and the black African south. Tension between the ethnic regions has led to civil war.

national capital

Area 389,000 sq mi (1,030,700 sq km)
Population 2,024,000
Mauritania

Tunis
Algiers
Rabat
TUNISIA
Tripoli
MOROCCO
Cairo
El Aaiún
ALGERIA
LIBYA
EGYPT
WESTERN SAHARA (occupied by Morocco)
MAURITANIA
Nouakchott
MALI
NIGER
Bamako
Niamey
CHAD
N'Djamena
Khartoum
SUDAN
ERITREA
Asmera
DJIBOUTI
Djibouti
Addis Ababa
ETHIOPIA
SOMALIA
Mogadishu

HABITATS

The desert that dominates Northern Africa is spreading southward into the Sahel region. This is the result of severe droughts and human misuse of the land, including overgrazing by livestock and the cutting down of trees and shrubs for fuel.

LAND
Area 5,747,919 sq mi (14,887,110 sq km)
Highest point Ras Dashan, 15,158 ft (4,620 m)
Lowest point Lake Assal, Djibouti, −492 ft (−150 m)
Major features Atlas ranges; Ethiopian highlands; Sahara, world's greatest desert; northern part of East African Rift Valley

WATER
Longest river most of the Nile's 4,160 mile (6,690 km) length, the world's greatest for a river, and 1,082,000 sq mi (2,802,000 sq km) basin is in the region
Highest average flow Niger, 201,000 cu ft/sec (5,700 cu m/sec) on lower section
Largest lake Chad, 10,000 sq mi (25,900 sq km)

NOTABLE THREATENED SPECIES
Mammals Barbary macaque (Macaca sylvanus), Simien jackal (Canis simensis), Cuvier's gazelle (Gazella cuvieri), beira (Dorcatragus megalotis), addax (Addax nasomaculatus)
Birds Prince Ruspoli's turaco (Tauraco ruspoli), Djibouti francolin (Francolinus ochropectus), Algerian nuthatch (Sitta ledanti)
Plants Allium crameri; Biscutella elbensis; Centaurea cyrenaica; ye-eb (Cordeauxia edulis); Cupressus dupreziana; Cyclamen rohlfsianum; Cyperus papyrus subsp. hadidii; Euphorbia cameronii; Gillettiodendron glandulosum; Olea laperrinei

CLIMATE

Northern Africa contains the Sahara and other deserts in the east. The northern coasts have a Mediterranean climate. To the south is the Sahel, a hot, semiarid zone. The far south has wet and dry seasons. Mountains in the far east have a moderate climate.

POPULATION AND WEALTH

	Highest	Middle	Lowest
Population (in millions)	53.2 (Egypt)	8.2 (Tunisia)	0.41 (Djibouti)
Population increase (annual population growth rate, % 1960–1990)	5.6 (Djibouti)	2.6 (Morocco)	2.1 (Chad)
Energy use (gigajoules/person)	83 (Libya)	10 (Morocco)	1 (Ethiopia)
Real purchasing power (US$/person)	3,170 (Tunisia)	970 (Sudan)	500 (Mali)

ENVIRONMENTAL INDICATORS

	Highest	Middle	Lowest
CO₂ emissions (mil. m.t. carbon/year)	25 (Algeria)	3 (Tunisia)	below 0.1 (Djibouti)
Artificial fertilizer use (lbs/acre/year)	313 (Egypt)	12.4 (Mali)	below 0.9 (Niger)
Automobiles (per 1,000 population)	90 (Libya)	8 (Mauritania)	below 1.0 (Ethiopia)
Access to safe drinking water (% population)	97 (Libya)	61 (Morocco)	19 (Ethiopia)

MAJOR ENVIRONMENTAL PROBLEMS AND SOURCES

Air pollution: urban high
Land degradation: types: desertification, soil erosion, salinization; causes: agriculture, industry, population pressure
Resource problems: fuelwood shortage; inadequate drinking water and sanitation
Population problems: population explosion; urban overcrowding; famine; war

ENVIRONMENTAL ISSUES

The main environmental issue in the region is water. Intensive agriculture and the rapid expansion of city populations have added to the strain on Northern Africa's limited water resources. Desertification has already taken place in large areas.

TEMPERATURE AND PRECIPITATION

	Temperature °F (°C) January	July	Altitude ft (m)
Ouarzazate	48 (9)	86 (30)	3,726 (1,136)
Timbuktu	71 (22)	90 (32)	987 (301)
Tripoli	53 (12)	78 (26)	72 (22)
Alexandria	59 (15)	79 (26)	104 (32)
Wadi Halfa	55 (13)	90 (32)	508 (155)
Addis Ababa	61 (16)	59 (15)	8,057 (2,450)

	Precipitation in (mm) January	July	Year
Ouarzazate	0.2 (6)	0.1 (2)	4.8 (123)
Timbuktu	0 (0)	3.1 (79)	8.9 (225)
Tripoli	3.2 (81)	0 (0)	10.0 (253)
Alexandria	1.8 (48)	0 (0)	6.7 (169)
Wadi Halfa	0 (0)	0.04 (1)	0.1 (3)
Addis Ababa	0.5 (13)	11.0 (279)	42.9 (1,089)

World's highest recorded temperature, 136.4°F (58°C), Al Aziziyah, Libya; Wadi Halfa is one of the world's driest places.

NATURAL HAZARDS

Drought, earthquakes in mountains of northwest

HABITATS

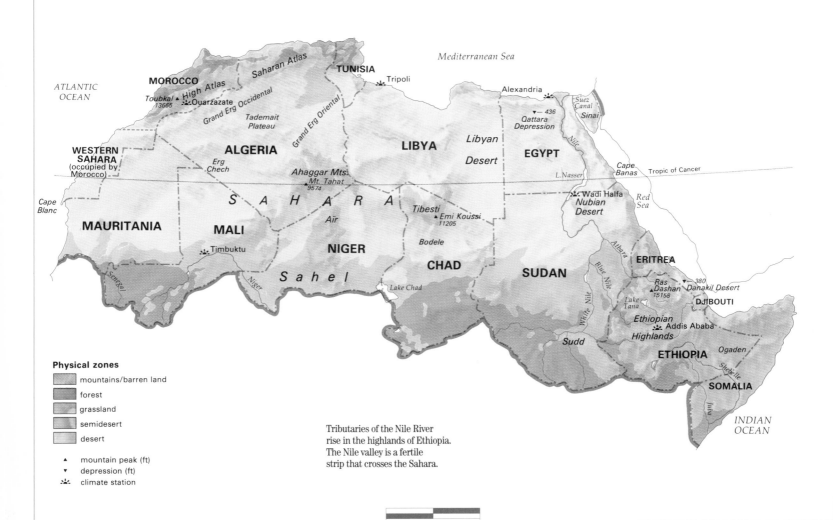

Physical zones
- mountains/barren land
- forest
- grassland
- semidesert
- desert

- ▲ mountain peak (ft)
- ▼ depression (ft)
- ⛰ climate station

Tributaries of the Nile River rise in the highlands of Ethiopia. The Nile valley is a fertile strip that crosses the Sahara.

ENVIRONMENTAL ISSUES

Key environmental issues

- major town or city
- heavily polluted town or city
- former nuclear test site
- heavily polluted river
- main area of coastal tourism

areas at risk of desertification
- very high
- high
- moderate
- true desert

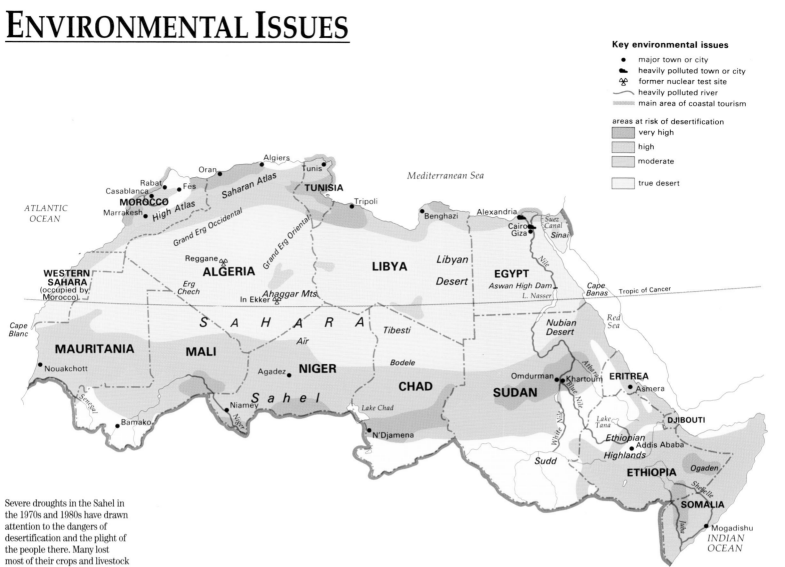

Severe droughts in the Sahel in the 1970s and 1980s have drawn attention to the dangers of desertification and the plight of the people there. Many lost most of their crops and livestock and had to flee their homelands.

CLIMATE

height above sea level of climate stations

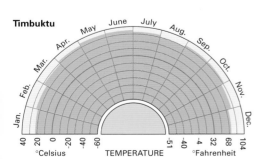

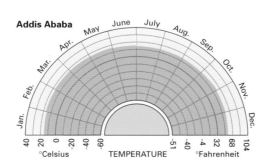

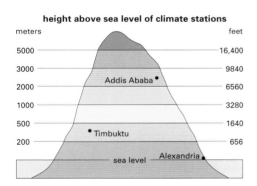

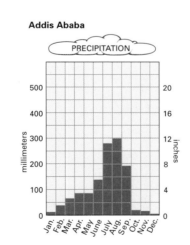

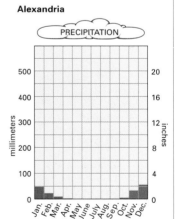

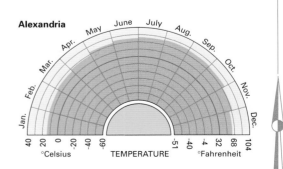

POPULATION

Much of Northern Africa is either uninhabited or sparsely populated. The population is mainly rural, though cities are growing quickly as people move into them from the countryside. Greater Cairo is one of the world's largest conurbations.

POPULATION

Total population of region (in millions)	175.8
Population density (persons per sq mi)	34
Population change (average annual percent 1960–1990)	
Urban	+4.3
Rural	+1.6

URBAN POPULATION

As percentage of total population	
1960	31.2
1990	44.3
Percentage in cities of more than 1 million	8.1

TEN LARGEST CITIES

	Country	Population
Cairo †	Egypt	6,325,000
Alexandria	Egypt	2,893,000
Casablanca	Morocco	2,409,000
Giza	Egypt	1,858,000
Addis Ababa †	Ethiopia	1,739,000
Algiers †	Algeria	1,722,000
Tunis †	Tunisia	1,395,000
Mogadishu †	Somalia	1,000,000
Tripoli †	Libya	980,000
Rabat †	Morocco	893,000

† denotes national capital

INDUSTRY

Northern Africa's natural resources include oil and gas in Algeria, Egypt, and Libya, uranium in Niger, phosphates in Morocco and Western Sahara, and iron ore in Mauritania. The main industrial areas are in northern Egypt.

INDUSTRIAL OUTPUT (US$ billion)

Total	Mining	Manufacturing	Average annual change since 1960
59.8	19.4	30.1	2.6%

INDUSTRIAL WORKERS (millions)
(Figures in parentheses are percentages of total labor force.)

Total	Mining	Manufacturing	Construction
7.34	0.62 (1.0%)	4.32 (7.1%)	2.4 (3.9%)

MAJOR PRODUCTS (Figures in parentheses are percentages of world production.)

Energy and minerals	Output	Change since 1960
Oil (mil. barrels)	1133.2 (5.0%)	+1193%
Natural gas (billion cu meters)	50.0 (2.9%)	+333.3%
Iron Ore (mil. m.t.)	9.5 (1.7%)	+42%
Natural phosphate (mil. m.t.)	10.4 (19.6%)	+211%

Manufactures		
Cotton yarn (1,000 m.t.)	329 (2.1%)	+86%
Cotton woven fabrics (mil. yd)	992 (1.8%)	+134%
Silk fabrics (mil. sq yd)	29.3 (1.0%)	No data
Manufactured tobacco (1,000 m.t.)	46.6 (20.7%)	No data
Footwear (mil. pairs)	151.2 (3.4%)	+47%
Superphosphate fertilizer (mil. m.t.)	1.5 (7.0%)	N/A
Liquefied petroleum gas (mil. m.t.)	6.8 (4.4%)	N/A
Cement (mil. m.t.)	27.2 (0.25%)	+938%

N/A *means production had not begun in 1960.*

AGRICULTURE

In the past, most people were subsistence farmers or nomadic herders. But today intensive farming is becoming common. Major products include grain, citrus fruits, cotton, dates, groundnuts, potatoes and other vegetables, and rice.

LAND (million acres)

Total	Agricultural	Arable	Forest/woodland
3,617 (100%)	946 (26%)	143 (4%)	328 (9%)

Farmers

39.3 million employed in agriculture (57% of workforce)
3.7 acres of arable land per person employed in agriculture

MAJOR CROPS

	Area mil. acres	Yield 100lbs/acre	Production mil. m.t.	Change since 1963
Millet/sorghum	32	4.5	6.6 (7)	+4%
Wheat	15.8	12.4	8.8 (2)	+67%
Barley	12.3	7.2	4.1 (2)	+17%
Corn	5.9	20.7	5.7 (1)	+76%
Cotton	2.9	5.1	0.7 (4)	+6%
Vegetables	—	—	17.6 (4)	+149%
Fruit	—	—	8.7 (3)	+49%

MAJOR LIVESTOCK

	Number in mil.	Production mil. m.t.	Change since 1963
Sheep/goats	175.7 (11)	—	+36%
Cattle	77.9 (6)	—	+40%
Milk	—	6.3 (1)	+147%
Fish catch	—	1.2 (1)	—

FOOD SECURITY (grain exports minus imports)

mil. m.t.	% domestic production	% world trade
−20.3	63	9

Numbers in parentheses are percentages of world total.

POPULATION

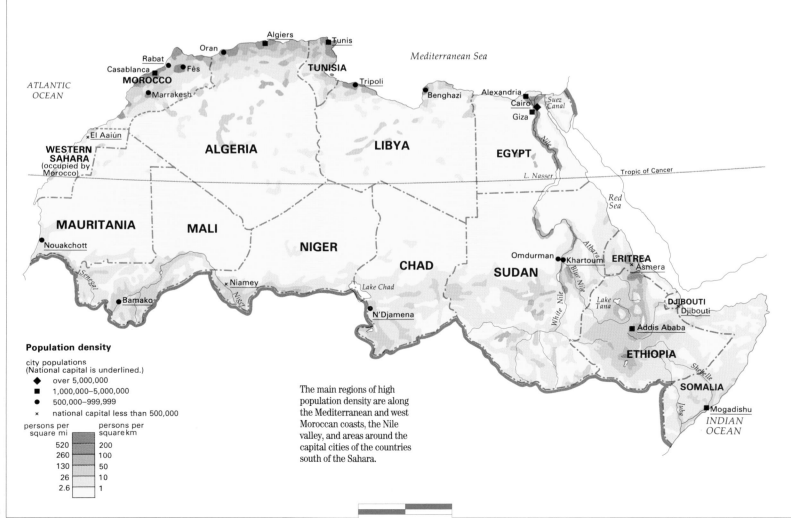

Population density

city populations
(National capital is underlined.)

- ◆ over 5,000,000
- ■ 1,000,000–5,000,000
- ● 500,000–999,999
- × national capital less than 500,000

persons per square mi	persons per square km
520	200
260	100
130	50
26	10
2.6	1

The main regions of high population density are along the Mediterranean and west Moroccan coasts, the Nile valley, and areas around the capital cities of the countries south of the Sahara.

INDUSTRY

Resources and industry
- ◆ industrial center
- ○ major port
- ● other town
- — major road
- — major railroad

mineral resources and fossil fuels
- ● iron and other ferroalloy metal ores
- ● other metal ores
- ■ nonmetallic minerals

natural gas
oil
phosphates

Tangier, Algiers, Annaba, Tunis, Oran, TUNISIA, Sfax, Casablanca, Rabat, Tripoli, Benghazi, Tobruk, Alexandria, Port Said, *Mediterranean Sea*, Marrakesh, Tendrara, Touggourt, Misratah, Al Jaghbub, Cairo, Suez Canal, Suez, Agadir, Hun

ATLANTIC OCEAN

MOROCCO

El Aaiún, Boukra, WESTERN SAHARA, Dakhla, ALGERIA, LIBYA, EGYPT, El Kharga, Aswan, *L. Nasser*, Tropic of Cancer

Nouadhibou, Wadi Halfa, *Red Sea*, Port Sudan, Nouakchott, MAURITANIA, MALI, Timbuktu, Agadez, NIGER, CHAD, SUDAN, Khartoum, Karima, ERITREA, Mitsiwa (Massawa), Asmera, Aseb

Bamako, Niamey, *Niger*, Lake Chad, N'Djamena, Nyala, *White Nile*, *Blue Nile*, *Lake Tana*, DJIBOUTI, Djibouti, Berbera, Addis Ababa, Dire Dawa, Wau, ETHIOPIA, Juba, SOMALIA, Mogadishu, INDIAN OCEAN, Kismaayo

Manufacturing is increasing in the countries bordering the Mediterranean Sea. Tourism is also important in Egypt, Morocco, and Tunisia.

AGRICULTURE

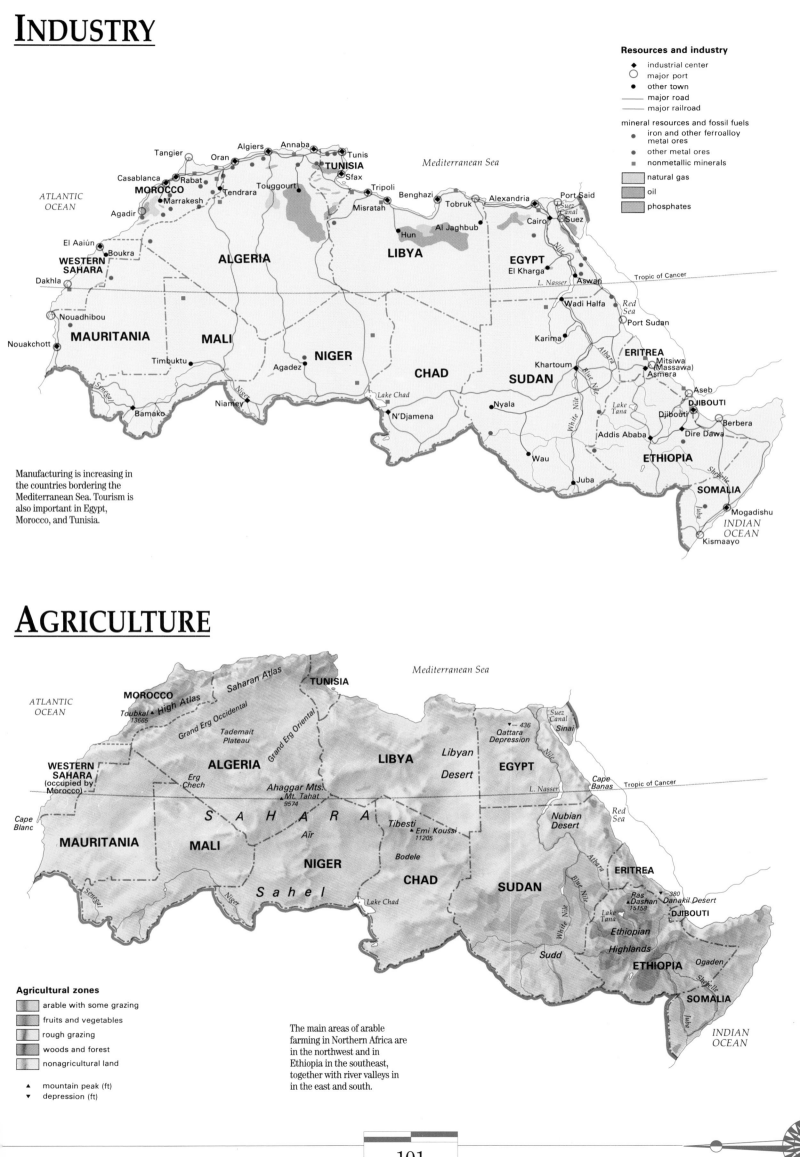

Mediterranean Sea

ATLANTIC OCEAN

MOROCCO, Saharan Atlas, TUNISIA, Toubkal 13665, High Atlas, Grand Erg Occidental, Tademait Plateau, Grand Erg Oriental, LIBYA, Libyan Desert, EGYPT, Qattara Depression −436, Suez Canal, Sinai, L. Nasser, Cape Banas, Tropic of Cancer

WESTERN SAHARA (occupied by Morocco), ALGERIA, Erg Chech, Ahaggar Mts. Mt. Tahat 9574

Cape Blanc, MAURITANIA, MALI, S A H A R A, Aïr, NIGER, Sahel, CHAD, Tibesti, Emi Koussi 11205, Bodele, SUDAN, Nubian Desert, Red Sea, Athara, ERITREA, Ras Dashan 15158, Danakil Desert −380, DJIBOUTI

Senegal, *Niger*, Lake Chad, *White Nile*, *Blue Nile*, *Lake Tana*, Ethiopian Highlands, Ogaden, Sudd, ETHIOPIA, Shebelle, SOMALIA, *Juba*, INDIAN OCEAN

Agricultural zones
- arable with some grazing
- fruits and vegetables
- rough grazing
- woods and forest
- nonagricultural land

- ▲ mountain peak (ft)
- ▼ depression (ft)

The main areas of arable farming in Northern Africa are in the northwest and in Ethiopia in the southeast, together with river valleys in in the east and south.

CENTRAL AFRICA

Central Africa is made up of 26 countries, stretching from Cape Verde, an island nation in the Atlantic Ocean west of Senegal, to the Seychelles, another island nation, east of Kenya in the Indian Ocean.

West Africa, which extends from Senegal to Nigeria, consists of coastal plains that rise inland to low plateaus. Cameroon has some volcanic highlands, but the Zaire basin is a shallow depression in the central plateaus. Beyond the Zaire basin are mountains that overlook the Rift Valley, which contains Lakes Tanganyika, Edward, and Albert. East of the Rift Valley lie the high plateaus of East Africa. This region contains Africa's largest lake, Victoria, the source of the White Nile. Ancient volcanic mountains include Kilimanjaro, Africa's highest peak. These volcanoes were formed while earth movements were fracturing the continent, creating the Rift Valley.

Central Africa straddles the Equator, and the climate is generally hot and humid, though temperatures are much lower in the highlands. The world's second largest rain forest (after the Amazon basin) occupies parts of the Zaire basin. But Central Africa also contains large areas of savanna, home of much wildlife, especially in the national parks on the plateaus of East Africa. Most of the people are black Africans, who are divided into many ethnic groups. Each group has its own language, art, customs, and traditional religion, though Islam has made inroads into northern West Africa and also East Africa. Christianity was introduced by European missionaries during the colonial period in the nineteenth and twentieth centuries.

Subsistence farming is the main activity, and manufacturing is generally limited to producing basic items such as cement, clothes, and processed food and drink for the home market.

Central Africa is part of the vast plateau of extremely old rocks that make up the African plateau. In places, the ancient rocks are overlaid by young sedimentary rocks and elsewhere by volcanic rocks. The volcanic rocks in East Africa reached the surface 35 to 25 million years ago through cracks formed when the plateaus were stretched by earth movements. These movements tore open the Rift Valley, which runs north-south through eastern Africa. The ancient rocks of Africa are rich in minerals.

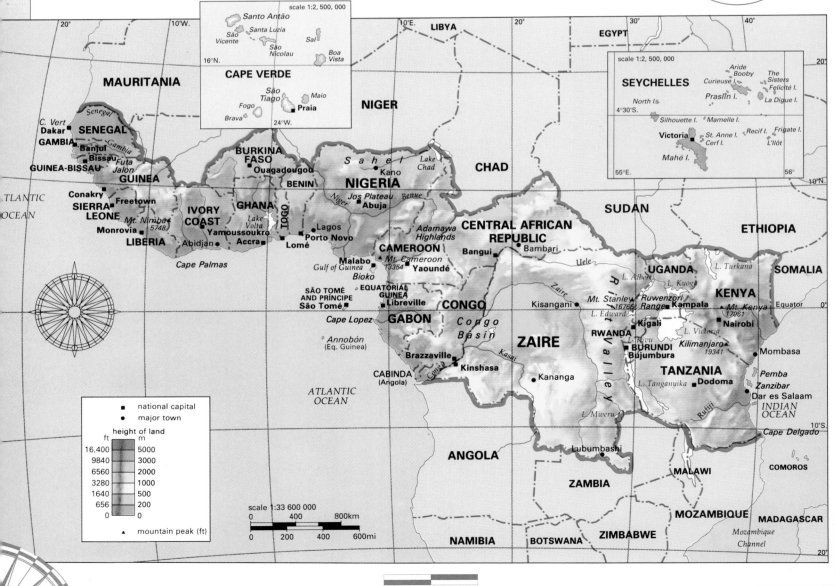

national capital

major town

height of land

ft	m
16,400	5000
9840	3000
6560	2000
3280	1000
1640	500
656	200
0	0

mountain peak (ft)

scale 1:33 600 000

THE POLITICAL AND CULTURAL WORLD

The European colonizers drew Africa's boundaries with little regard for existing ethnic groups. One result of this policy is that the nations of Central Africa contain many cultural groups.

Nigeria, for example, has more than 200 ethnic groups, and no local language is used widely enough for it to be the official language. Hence Nigeria, like most countries in the region, has adopted the former colonial language, in this case English, for official purposes. Several of the groups in Nigeria are rivals. In 1967, when one of these groups, the Ibo, tried to set up its own state, civil war ensued. Similar ethnic tensions are common in Central Africa.

COUNTRIES IN THE REGION

Benin, Burkina Faso, Burundi, Cameroon, Cape Verde, Central African Republic, Congo, Equatorial Guinea, Gabon, Gambia, Ghana, Guinea, Guinea-Bissau, Ivory Coast, Kenya, Liberia, Nigeria, Rwanda, São Tomé and Príncipe, Senegal, Seychelles, Sierra Leone, Tanzania, Togo, Uganda, Zaire

Dependencies of other states British Indian Ocean Territory (U.K.)

MEMBERSHIP OF INTERNATIONAL ORGANIZATIONS

Economic Community of West African States (ECOWAS) Benin, Burkina Faso, Cape Verde, Gambia, Ghana, Guinea, Guinea-Bissau, Ivory Coast, Kenya, Rwanda, Seychelles, Tanzania

RELIGION

Countries with one major religion Gambia (I); Cape Verde, Equatorial Guinea (RC)
Countries with two major religions Nigeria (I,P); São Tomé and Príncipe, Seychelles (P,RC)
Countries with three or more major religions Benin, Burkina Faso, Gabon, Guinea, Guinea-Bissau, Ivory Coast, Liberia, Senegal (I,IR,RC); Kenya, Zaire; (I,IR,P,RC) Cameroon, Burundi, Central African Republic, Congo, Ghana, Rwanda, Sierra Leone, Tanzania, Togo, Uganda (C,I,IR,P,RC)

Key: C-various Christian, I-Islam, IR-indigenous religions, P-Protestant, RC-Roman Catholic

LANGUAGE

Countries with one official language Gambia, Ghana, Liberia, Nigeria, Sierra Leone, Uganda (E); Benin, Burkina Faso, Central African Republic, Congo, Gabon, Guinea, Ivory Coast, Senegal, Togo, Zaire (F); Cape Verde, Guinea-Bissau, São Tomé and Príncipe (P); Equatorial Guinea (S)
Countries with two official languages Cameroon(E,F); Kenya, Tanzania (E,Sw); Burundi (F,K); Rwanda (F,R)
Country with three official languages Seychelles (C,E,F)

Key: C-Creole, E-English, F-French, K-Kirundi, P-Portuguese, R-Rwandan, S-Spanish, Sw-Swahili

Numerous indigenous languages are spoken in the region.

STYLES OF GOVERNMENT

Republics All countries in the region
Federal state Nigeria
Multiparty states Benin, Burkina Faso, Cameroon, Cape Verde, Congo, Gambia, Liberia, Nigeria, São Tomé and Príncipe, Senegal, Sierra Leone, Togo, Uganda, Zaire
One-party states Burundi, Central African Republic, Equatorial Guinea, Guinea-Bissau, Ivory Coast, Kenya, Rwanda, Seychelles, Tanzania
States without parties Ghana, Guinea
Military influence Burundi, Equatorial Guinea, Ghana, Guinea, Guinea-Bissau, Liberia, Nigeria, Sierra Leone, Togo

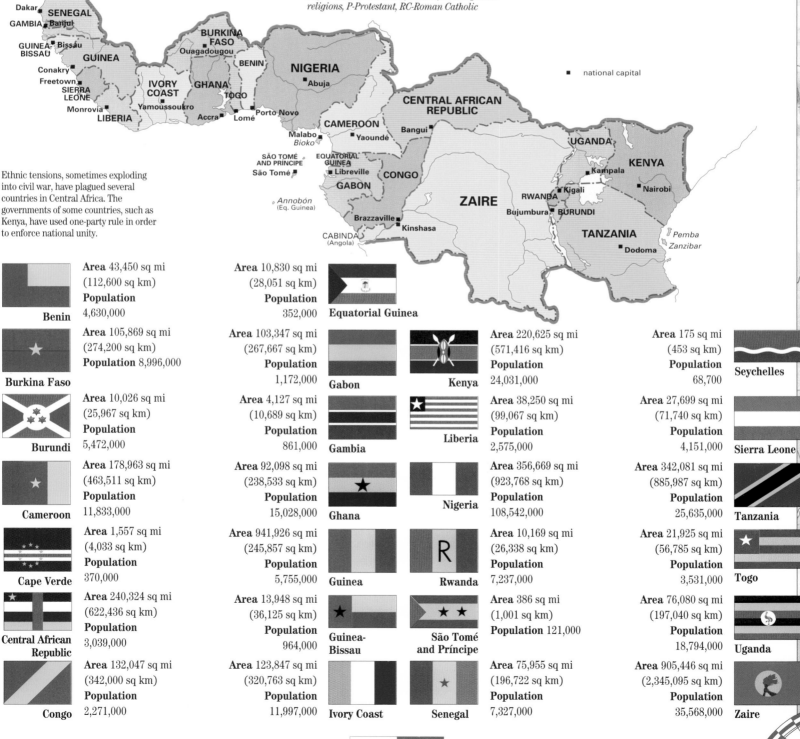

■ national capital

Ethnic tensions, sometimes exploding into civil war, have plagued several countries in Central Africa. The governments of some countries, such as Kenya, have used one-party rule in order to enforce national unity.

Benin Area 43,450 sq mi (112,600 sq km) Population 4,630,000

Burkina Faso Area 105,869 sq mi (274,200 sq km) Population 8,996,000

Burundi Area 10,026 sq mi (25,967 sq km) Population 5,472,000

Cameroon Area 178,963 sq mi (463,511 sq km) Population 11,833,000

Cape Verde Area 1,557 sq mi (4,033 sq km) Population 370,000

Central African Republic Area 240,324 sq mi (622,436 sq km) Population 3,039,000

Congo Area 132,047 sq mi (342,000 sq km) Population 2,271,000

Area 10,830 sq mi (28,051 sq km) Population 352,000 **Equatorial Guinea**

Gabon Area 103,347 sq mi (267,667 sq km) Population 1,172,000

Gambia Area 4,127 sq mi (10,689 sq km) Population 861,000

Ghana Area 92,098 sq mi (238,533 sq km) Population 15,028,000

Guinea Area 941,926 sq mi (245,857 sq km) Population 5,755,000

Guinea-Bissau Area 13,948 sq mi (36,125 sq km) Population 964,000

Ivory Coast Area 123,847 sq mi (320,763 sq km) Population 11,997,000

Kenya Area 220,625 sq mi (571,416 sq km) Population 24,031,000

Liberia Area 38,250 sq mi (99,067 sq km) Population 2,575,000

Nigeria Area 356,669 sq mi (923,768 sq km) Population 108,542,000

Rwanda Area 10,169 sq mi (26,338 sq km) Population 7,237,000

São Tomé and Príncipe Area 386 sq mi (1,001 sq km) Population 121,000

Senegal Area 75,955 sq mi (196,722 sq km) Population 7,327,000

Seychelles Area 175 sq mi (453 sq km) Population 68,700

Sierra Leone Area 27,699 sq mi (71,740 sq km) Population 4,151,000

Tanzania Area 342,081 sq mi (885,987 sq km) Population 25,635,000

Togo Area 21,925 sq mi (56,785 sq km) Population 3,531,000

Uganda Area 76,080 sq mi (197,040 sq km) Population 18,794,000

Zaire Area 905,446 sq mi (2,345,095 sq km) Population 35,568,000

HABITATS

Central Africa contains rain forests and grasslands called savanna. The savanna merges in the north into dry grassland. The altitude, especially on the high plateaus of East Africa, has a marked, moderating influence on the tropical climate.

LAND

Area 3,465,907 sq mi (8,979,034 sq km)
Highest point Kilimanjaro, 19,340 ft (5,895 m)
Lowest point sea level
Major features Jos Plateau and Adamawa Highlands in west, Congo basin, Ruwenzori Range, mountains and Rift Valley in east

WATER

Longest river Congo (Zaire), 2,880 mi (4,630 km)
Largest basin Congo, 1,476,000 sq mi (3,822,000 sq km)
Highest average flow Congo, 1,377,000 cu ft/sec (39,000 cu m/sec)
Largest lake Victoria, 24,300 sq mi (62,940 sq km)

NOTABLE THREATENED SPECIES

Mammals Nimba otter-shrew *(Micropotamogale lamottei)*, mountain gorilla *(Gorilla gorilla beringei)*, chimpanzee *(Pan troglodytes)*, bonobo *(Pan paniscus)*, drill *(Mandrillus leucophaeus)*, Pygmy hippopotamus *(Choeropsis liberiensis)*, Ader's duiker *(Cephalophus adersi)*
Birds white-breasted guinea fowl *(Agelastes meleagrides)*, Bannerman's turaco *(Tauraco bannermani)*, Sokoke scops owl *(Otus ireneae)*, Seychelles magpie robin *(Copsychus sechellarum)*
Plants *Aeschynomene batekensis; Drypetes singroboensis; Justicia hepperi; Memecylon fragrans; Pitcairnia feliciana;* African violet *(Saintpaulia ionantha); Scleria sheilae; Temnopteryx sericea; Uvariodendron gorgonis; Vernonia sechellensis*
Others Goliath frog *(Conraua goliath)*, Lake Victoria cichlid fish (250 species), African blind barbfish *(Caecobarbus geertsi)*

CLIMATE

Central Africa lies on the Equator, and much of the region has a tropical rainy climate, though temperatures vary with altitude. To the east, the mountains have moderate temperatures, giving many places a pleasant, mild climate. To the north is a hot semiarid area.

TEMPERATURE AND PRECIPITATION

	Temperature °F (°C) January	July	Altitude ft	(m)
Dakar	69 (22)	81 (27)	131	(40)
Ngaoundéré	72 (22)	70 (21)	3,670	(1,119)
Lisala	77 (25)	75 (24)	1,509	(460)
Bukoba	70 (21)	68 (20)	3,729	(1,137)
Lodwar	84 (29)	82 (28)	1,660	(506)
Mombasa	82 (28)	75 (24)	52	(16)

	Precipitation in (mm) January		July		Year	
Dakar	0	(0)	3.5	(88)	22.8	(578)
Ngaoundéré	0.1	(2)	10.1	(256)	59.9	(1,511)
Lisala	2.5	(63)	7.5	(190)	64.0	(1,626)
Bukoba	5.9	(151)	1.9	(49)	80.4	(2,043)
Lodwar	0.3	(8)	0.6	(15)	6.4	(162)
Mombasa	0.9	(25)	3.5	(89)	45.8	(1,163)

NATURAL HAZARDS

Drought, floods, earthquakes

ENVIRONMENTAL ISSUES

Human adaptation of the environment of Central Africa has been going on for thousands of years. Today, the fast-increasing population and the devastation of wars are adding to the pressure on the region's fragile resources, such as soils and vegetation.

POPULATION AND WEALTH

	Highest	Middle	Lowest
Population (in millions)	108.5 (Nigeria)	5.8 (Guinea)	0.4 (Equ. Guinea)
Population increase (annual population growth rate, % 1960–1990)	3.6 (Kenya)	2.8 (Zaire)	1.1 (Equ. Guinea)
Energy use (gigajoules/person)	34 (Gabon)	2 (Guinea)	below 0.1 (C. Verde)
Real purchasing power (US$/person)	3,960 (Gabon)	910 (Guinea)	410 (Uganda)

ENVIRONMENTAL INDICATORS

CO$_2$ emissions (mil. m.t. carbon/year)	53 (Nigeria)	24 (Burkina)	9 (C. Verde)
Deforestation ('000s acres/year 1980s)	1,260 (Ivory C)	136 (C.A.R.)	2 (Burundi)
Artificial fertilizer use (lbs/acre/year)	101 (Kenya)	9 (Ghana)	below 2 (Guinea)
Automobiles (per 1,000 population)	15 (Tanzania)	5 (Kenya)	below 1.0 (Rwanda)
Access to safe drinking water (% population)	75 (Gambia)	34 (Zaire)	12 (C.A.R.)

MAJOR ENVIRONMENTAL PROBLEMS AND SOURCES

Land degradation: *types:* desertification, soil erosion, salinization, deforestation, habitat destruction; *causes:* agriculture, population pressure
Resource problems: fuelwood shortage; inadequate drinking water and sanitation; land use competition
Population problems: population explosion; urban overcrowding; inadequate health facilities; disease; famine; war
Major event: Lake Nyos (1986), gas cloud released

HABITATS

Physical zones

- mountains/barren land
- forest
- grassland
- semidesert

▲ mountain peak (ft)
⁂ climate station

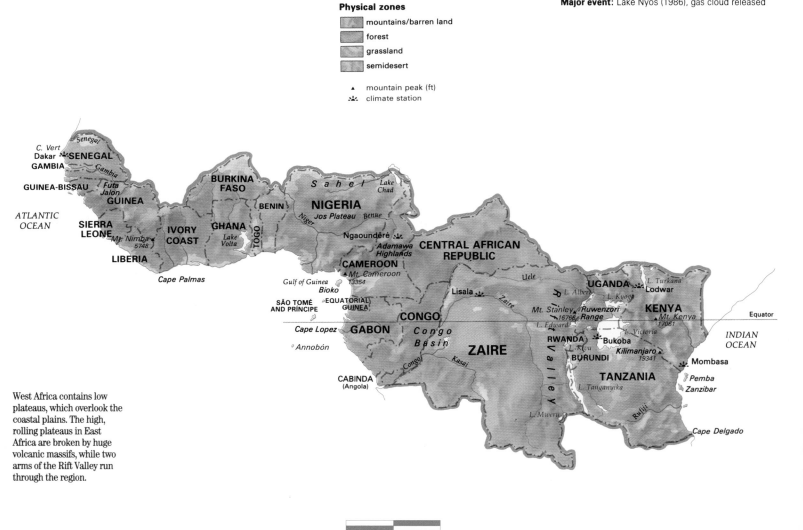

West Africa contains low plateaus, which overlook the coastal plains. The high, rolling plateaus in East Africa are broken by huge volcanic massifs, while two arms of the Rift Valley run through the region.

ENVIRONMENTAL ISSUES

Key environmental issues

- • major town or city
- 🖢 heavily polluted town or city
- ✛ major natural disaster
- ○ port receiving toxic waste
- 〜 heavily polluted river
- ▨ remaining tropical rain forest

areas of fuelwood shortage

- ▨ severe
- ▨ acute
- ▨ prospective

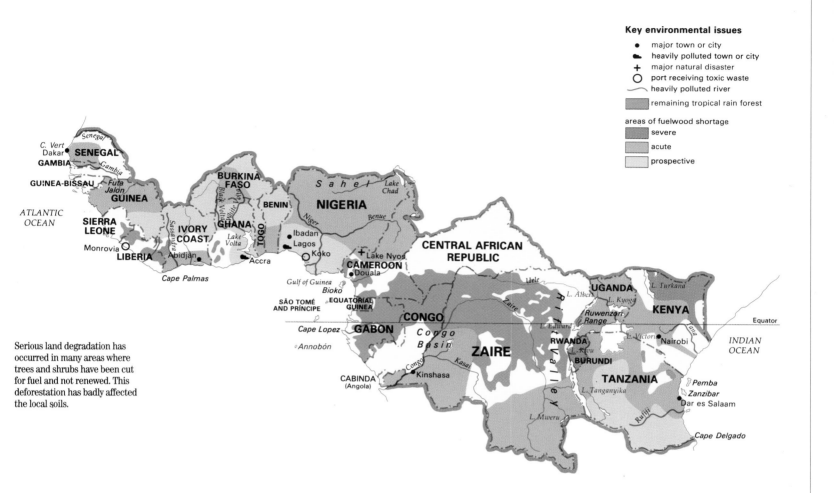

Serious land degradation has occurred in many areas where trees and shrubs have been cut for fuel and not renewed. This deforestation has badly affected the local soils.

CLIMATE

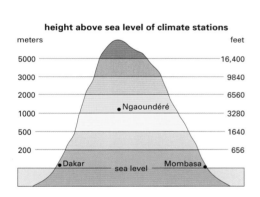

height above sea level of climate stations

Dakar

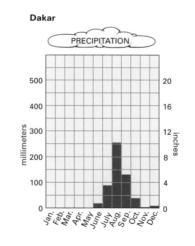

Ngaoundéré

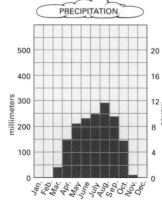

Mombasa

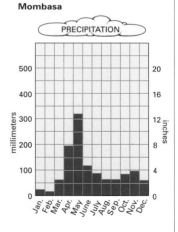

Dakar

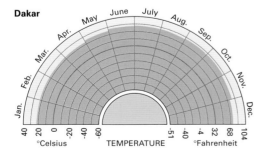

Ngaoundéré

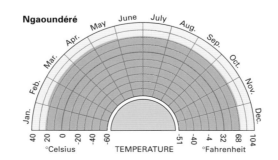

Mombasa

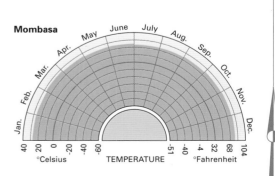

POPULATION

About three out of every four people in Central Africa live in rural areas, in scattered communities or in villages. But during this century, as the countries became independent, the cities have expanded rapidly as people arrive looking for jobs and better education.

POPULATION

Total population of region (in millions)	310.8
Population density (persons per sq mi)	195
Population change (average annual percent 1960–1990) Urban	+5.2
Rural	+1.9

URBAN POPULATION

As percentage of total population	
1960	15.2
1990	24.3
Percentage in cities of more than 1 million	2.1

TEN LARGEST CITIES

	Country	Population
Kinshasa †	Zaire	2,654,000
Abidjan	Ivory Coast	1,850,000
Nairobi †	Kenya	1,429,000
Dakar †	Senegal	1,382,000
Dar es Salaam	Tanzania	1,100,000
Lagos	Nigeria	1,097,000
Ibadan	Nigeria	1,060,000
Douala	Cameroon	1,030,000
Accra †	Ghana	965,000
Libreville †	Gabon	830,000

† denotes national capital

INDUSTRY

Central Africa's rich natural resources are mainly exported, because the region lacks manufacturing industries. Most industries are small-scale, except in Kenya and Nigeria, where larger-scale manufacturing is growing. Nigeria and Tanzania have coal deposits.

INDUSTRIAL OUTPUT (US$ billion)

Total	Mining	Manufacturing	Average annual change since 1960
22.8	10.6	12.2	+2.3%

INDUSTRIAL WORKERS (millions)

Total (mining, manufacturing, & utilities)	% of labor force
6.6	7.1%

MAJOR PRODUCTS (Figures in parentheses are percentages of total world production.)

Energy and minerals	Output	Change since 1960
Oil (mil. barrels)	700	+70%
Bauxite (mil. m.t.)	18.0 (20%)	+350%
Copper (mil. m.t.)	0.5 (6%)	+8%
Diamonds (mil. carats)	25.9 (27%)	+28%

Manufactures		
Textiles (mil. sq yd)	810 (1.0%)	+123%
Palm oil (mil. m.t.)	1.5 (8.1%)	No data
Tobacco products (billion units)	9.7 (2.1%)	+79%

AGRICULTURE

Agriculture employs about 70 percent of the people, with most farmers producing enough to meet the basic needs of their families. There is some nomadic herding. Commercial crops include cocoa, coffee, cotton, groundnuts, palm oil, rubber, and tea.

LAND (million acres)

Total	Agricultural	Arable	Forest/woodland
2,033 (100%)	538 (27%)	185 (9%)	971 (48%)

FARMERS

84 million employed in agriculture (70% of workforce)
2.2 acres of arable land per person employed in agriculture

MAJOR CROPS

	Area mil. acres	Yield 100lbs/acre	Production mil. m.t.	Change since 1963
Millet/ sorghum	37.5	8.8	15.0 (17)	+49%
Corn	19.7	10.4	9.4 (2)	+119%
Cassava	15.5	76.4	53.9 (40)	+100%
Groundnuts	9.1	8	3.4 (16)	−9%
Cocoa beans	9.1	2.8	1.2 (59)	+27%
Palm kernels	—		0.6 (22)	−21%
Palm oil	—		1.5 (18)	+59%
Bananas	—	—	21.2 (32)	+90%

MAJOR LIVESTOCK

	Number in mil.	Production mil. m.t.	Change since 1963
Sheep/goats	110.5 (7)	—	+67%
Cattle	58.3 (5)	—	+50%
Milk	—	2.6 (1)	+36%
Fish catch	—	2.2 (2)	—

FOOD SECURITY (grain exports minus imports)

mil. m.t.	% domestic production	% world trade
−4.6	15	2

Numbers in parentheses are percentages of world total.

POPULATION

Population density

city populations
(National capital is underlined.)
- ■ 1,000,000–5,000,000
- ● 500,000–999,999
- × national capital less than 500,000

persons per square mi	persons per square km
520	200
260	100
130	50
26	10
2.6	1

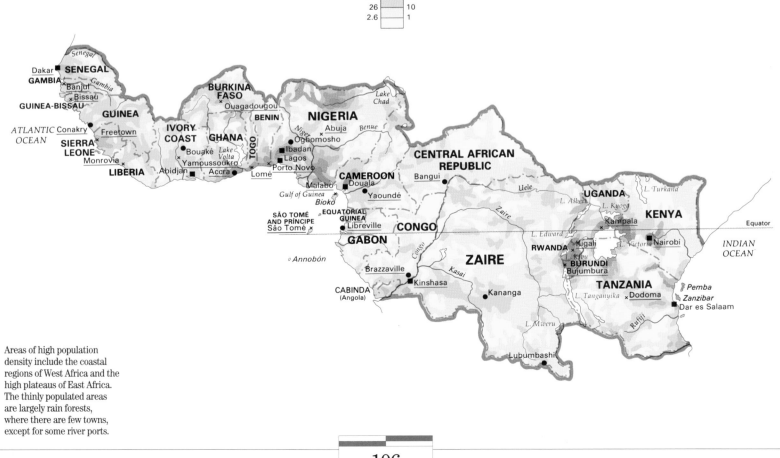

Areas of high population density include the coastal regions of West Africa and the high plateaus of East Africa. The thinly populated areas are largely rain forests, where there are few towns, except for some river ports.

INDUSTRY

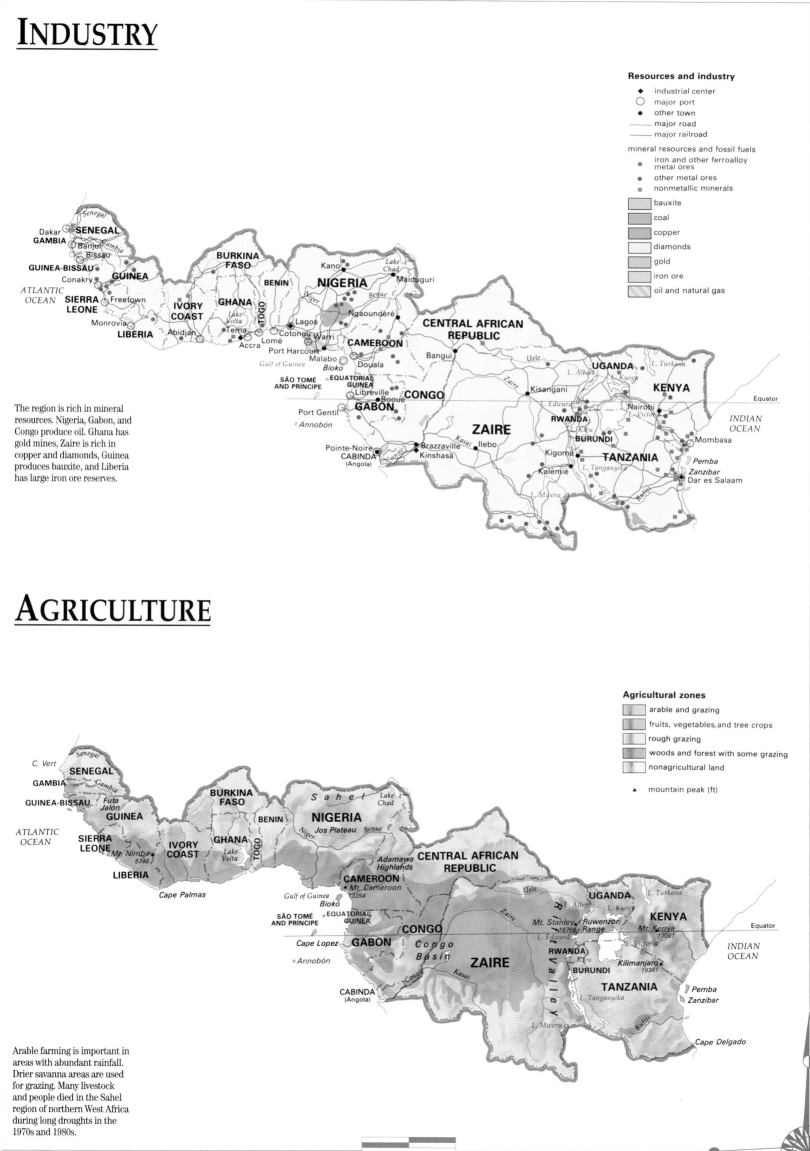

Resources and industry

- ◆ industrial center
- ○ major port
- ● other town
- —— major road
- —— major railroad

mineral resources and fossil fuels
- • iron and other ferroalloy metal ores
- ● other metal ores
- ■ nonmetallic minerals

bauxite
coal
copper
diamonds
gold
iron ore
oil and natural gas

The region is rich in mineral resources. Nigeria, Gabon, and Congo produce oil. Ghana has gold mines, Zaire is rich in copper and diamonds, Guinea produces bauxite, and Liberia has large iron ore reserves.

AGRICULTURE

Agricultural zones

arable and grazing
fruits, vegetables, and tree crops
rough grazing
woods and forest with some grazing
nonagricultural land

▲ mountain peak (ft)

Arable farming is important in areas with abundant rainfall. Drier savanna areas are used for grazing. Many livestock and people died in the Sahel region of northern West Africa during long droughts in the 1970s and 1980s.

SOUTHERN AFRICA

Southern Africa consists of ten mainland countries and three island nations – Madagascar, the Comoros, and Mauritius. The mainland is a high, saucer-shaped plateau bordered by mostly narrow coastal plains. The Drakensberg contains the highest peaks. The region also contains the most southerly part of the Rift Valley, enclosing Lake Malawi.

Forests and savanna are found in the north, but the south is dry grassland, merging into the Kalahari, a semidesert, and the Namib Desert, one of the driest places on the earth.

Colonization, involving the introduction of commercial farming, the exploitation of natural resources and the setting up of manufacturing industries, has made a great impact on the black African cultures of Southern Africa.

Nowhere has the impact been greater than in South Africa. Its history of racial conflict has become an international political issue. In the early 1990s, talks began between the ethnic groups aimed at creating a society in which all adults can vote. South Africa's first ever multi-racial elections took place in 1994.

Southern Africa is a region of ancient, often mineral-rich rocks, which once formed part of the supercontinent of Gondwanaland. Younger rocks occur around the central plateau, which have been folded and faulted, notably in the southwest. Apart from the Atlas Mountains, these ranges are Africa's only recently formed fold mountains.

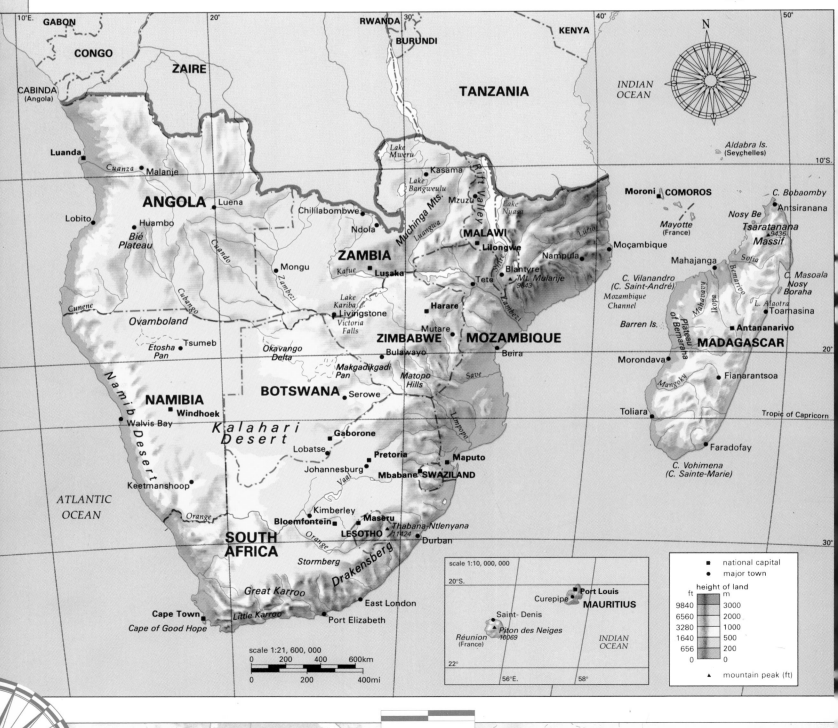

THE POLITICAL AND CULTURAL WORLD

Descendants of the region's earliest people, the Khoi-San (Hottentots and Bushmen), now make up extremely small groups. Most people are black Africans, who speak one of the many Bantu languages, including Tswana and Zulu.

The other main groups are the descendants of European settlers, including the Afrikaaners (descendants of early Dutch settlers in South Africa) and the British. Relationships between European settlers and black Africans have underlain the political problems of the region. In several countries, including Angola, Namibia, Mozambique, and Zimbabwe, independence was achieved only after long colonial conflicts.

COUNTRIES IN THE REGION

Angola, Botswana, Comoros, Lesotho, Madagascar, Malawi, Mauritius, Mozambique, Namibia, South Africa, Swaziland, Zambia, Zimbabwe

MEMBERSHIP OF INTERNATIONAL ORGANIZATIONS

Organization for African Unity (OAU) Angola, Botswana, Lesotho, Madagascar, Malawi, Mauritius, Mozambique, Namibia, Swaziland, Zambia, Zimbabwe
Southern Africa Development Coordination Conference (SADCC) Angola, Botswana, Lesotho, Malawi, Mozambique, Swaziland, Zambia, Zimbabwe

STYLES OF GOVERNMENT

Republics Angola, Botswana, Comoros, Madagascar, Malawi, Mozambique, Namibia, South Africa, Zambia, Zimbabwe
Monarchies Lesotho, Swaziland
Federal states Comoros
Multiparty states Angola, Botswana, Mauritius, Mozambique, Namibia, South Africa, Zambia, Zimbabwe
One-party states Comoros, Madagascar, Malawi, Swaziland
State without parties Lesotho
Military influence Lesotho

LANGUAGE

Countries with one official language English: Botswana, Mauritius, Zambia, Zimbabwe; Malagasy: Madagascar; Portuguese: Angola, Mozambique
Countries with two official languages Arabic, French: Comoros; Afrikaans, English: South Africa, Namibia; Chewa, English: Malawi; English, Sotho: Lesotho; English, Swazi: Swaziland

Other significant languages in the region include Comorian (the majority language of the Comoros), ChiSona, Kimbundu, Lunda, Makua, Setwana, Si Ndebele, Tombuka, Umbundu, and numerous other indigenous languages.

RELIGION

Countries with one major religion Lesotho, Namibia (C); Mauritius (H); Comoros (I)
Countries with two major religions Angola, Botswana, Malawi, Swaziland, Zambia, Zimbabwe (C,IR)
Countries with three major religions Madagascar, Mozambique (C,I,IR)
Country with more than three major religions South Africa (C,DR,H,I,IR,RC)

Key: C-various Christian, DR-Dutch Reformed, H-Hindu, I-Islam, IR-indigenous religions, RC-Roman Catholic

Angola Area 481,354 sq mi (1,246,700 sq km) Population 10,020,000

Botswana Area 224,607 sq mi (581,730 sq km) Population 1,304,000

Comoros Area 719 sq mi (1,862 sq km) Population 550,000

Lesotho Area 11,720 sq mi (30,355 sq km) Population 1,774,000

Madagascar Area 226,658 sq mi (587,041 sq km) Population 12,004,000

Malawi Area 36,400 sq mi (94,276 sq km) Population 8,754,600

Mauritius Area 788 sq mi (2,040 sq km) Population 1,082,000

Mozambique Area 308,642 sq mi (799,379 sq km) Population 15,656,000

Namibia Area 317,818 sq mi (823,144 sq km) Population 1,781,000

South Africa Area 473,290 sq mi (1,225,815 sq km) Population 35,282,000

Swaziland Area 6,704 sq mi (17,364 sq km) Population 788,000

Zambia Area 290,586 sq mi (752,614 sq km) Population 8,452,000

Zimbabwe Area 150,873 sq mi (390,759 sq km) Population 9,709,000

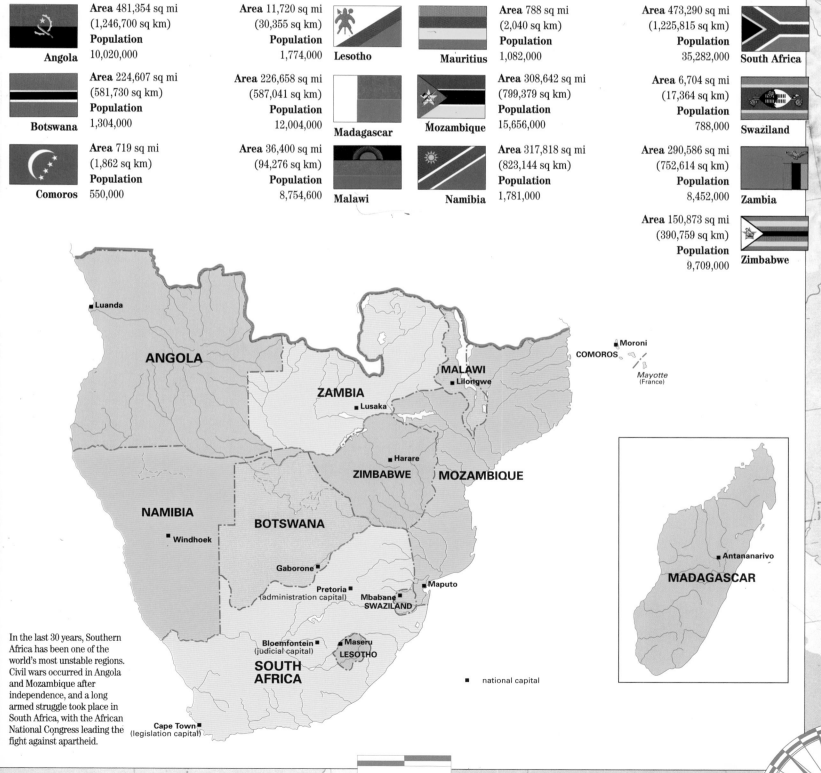

In the last 30 years, Southern Africa has been one of the world's most unstable regions. Civil wars occurred in Angola and Mozambique after independence, and a long armed struggle took place in South Africa, with the African National Congress leading the fight against apartheid.

■ national capital

HABITATS

The plateau that forms the heart of Southern Africa is largely enclosed by mountain ranges. Some rivers, such as the Orange and Zambezi, cut through the rim and reach the sea. Others flow into inland drainage basins. In the southwest are desert areas.

LAND

Area 2,220,194 sq mi (5,751,800 sq km)
Highest point Thabana Ntlenyana, 11,424 ft (3,482 m)
Lowest point sea level
Major features interior plateau, salt pans and deltas, Kalahari and Namib Deserts, Karoo tableland, Cape ranges in southwest, Drakensberg range, Madagascar

WATER

Longest river Zambezi, 1,650 mi (2,650 km)
Largest basin Zambezi, 514,000 sq mi (1,331,000 sq km)
Highest average flow Zambezi, 565,000 cu ft/sec (16,000 cu m/sec)
Largest lake Malawi, 11,400 sq mi (29,600 sq km)

NOTABLE THREATENED SPECIES

Mammals Juliana's golden mole (Amblysomus julianae), golden bamboo lemur (Hapalemur aureus), indri (Indri indri), brown hyena (Hyaena brunnea), Mauritian flying fox (Pteropus niger), Riverine rabbit (Bunolagus monticularis), mountain zebra (Equus zebra)
Birds Madagascar serpent eagle (Eutriorchis astur), Cape vulture (Gyps coprotheres), pink pigeon (Nesoenas mayeri)
Plants Allophylus chirindensis; spiral aloe (Aloe polyphylla); Dasylepis burttdavyi; Encephalartos chimanimaniensis; Hyophorbe amaricaulis; Jubaeopsis caffra; Kniphofia umbrina; St. Helena olive (Nesiota elliptica); Protea odorata; Ramosmania heterophylla
Others Angonoka tortoise (Geochelone yniphora), Cape platana or clawed toad (Xenopus gilli), fiery redfin (Pseudobarbatus phlegethon)

CLIMATE

The northern part of the region has a tropical climate, with dry and wet seasons. The southwest is largely desert. The southwestern tip has dry summers and mild, moist winters. The southeastern coasts of South Africa have hot, humid summers and mild, dry winters.

TEMPERATURE AND PRECIPITATION

	Temperature °F (°C)		Altitude
	January	July	ft (m)
Lusaka	72 (22)	61 (16)	4,188 (1,277)
Bulawayo	70 (21)	57 (14)	4,398 (1,341)
Cape Town	69 (21)	53 (12)	55 (17)
Toliara	81 (27)	68 (20)	30 (9)
Antananarivo	69 (21)	59 (15)	4,499 (1,372)

	Precipitation in (mm)		
	January	July	Year
Lusaka	9.0 (231)	0 (0)	32.6 (829)
Bulawayo	5.6 (142)	0 (0)	23.2 (589)
Cape Town	0.5 (15)	3.5 (89)	25.7 (652)
Toliara	2.8 (71)	0.2 (4)	13.5 (342)
Antananarivo	11.8 (300)	0.3 (8)	50.0 (1,270)

World's greatest recorded 24-hour rainfall, 73.6 in (1,870 mm), Réunion island

NATURAL HAZARDS

Drought

ENVIRONMENTAL ISSUES

Many problems in Southern Africa are related to the population explosion, which puts pressure on habitats and their wildlife. Pollution caused by urbanization and industry are evident in South Africa, while the ravages of war are widespread.

POPULATION AND WEALTH

	Highest	Middle	Lowest
Population (in millions)	35.3 (S. Africa)	8.5 (Zambia)	0.8 (Swaziland)
Population increase (annual population growth rate, % 1960–1990)	3.4 (Botswana)	2.6 (Namibia)	1.7 (Mauritius)
Energy use (gigajoules/person)	83 (S. Africa)	2 (Comoros)	1 (Madagascar)
Real purchasing power (US$/person)	5,480 (S. Africa)	1,370 (Zimbabwe)	570 (Comoros)

ENVIRONMENTAL INDICATORS

CO₂ emissions (mil. m.t. carbon/year)	47 (S. Africa)	3.4 (Angola)	0.3 (Comoros)
Deforestation ('000s acres/ year 1980s)	385 (Madagascar)	197 (Zimbabwe)	1.2 (Mauritius)
Artificial fertilizer use (lbs/acre/year)	274 (Mauritius)	16 (Zambia)	below 1 (Botswana)
Automobiles (per 1,000 population)	3,079 (S. Africa)	49 (Madagascar)	6 (Lesotho)
Access to safe drinking water (% population)	98 (Mauritius)	50 (Swaziland)	24 (Mozambique)

MAJOR ENVIRONMENTAL PROBLEMS AND SOURCES

Air pollution: locally high
Land degradation: *types:* desertification, soil erosion, deforestation, habitat destruction; *causes:* agriculture, population pressure
Resource problems: fuelwood shortage; inadequate drinking water, and sanitation
Population problems: population explosion; urban overcrowding; inadequate health facilities; famine; war

HABITATS

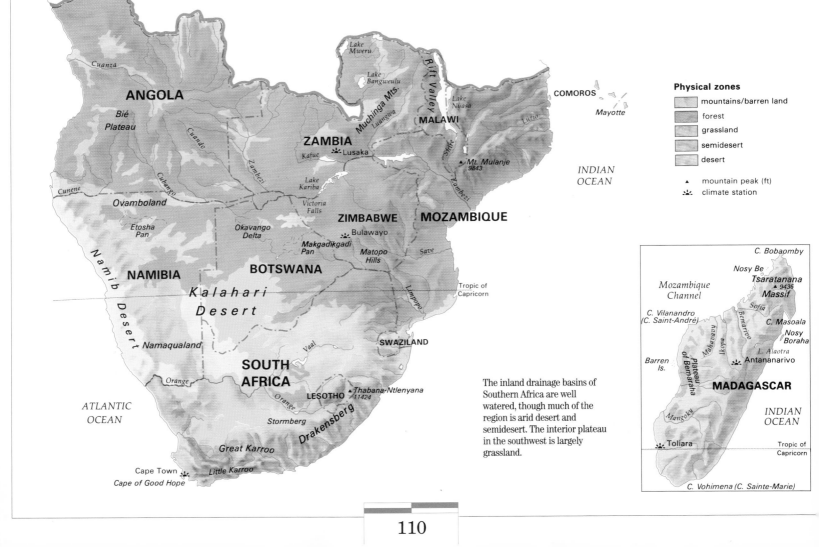

The inland drainage basins of Southern Africa are well watered, though much of the region is arid desert and semidesert. The interior plateau in the southwest is largely grassland.

Physical zones
- mountains/barren land
- forest
- grassland
- semidesert
- desert
- ▲ mountain peak (ft)
- ⛅ climate station

ENVIRONMENTAL ISSUES

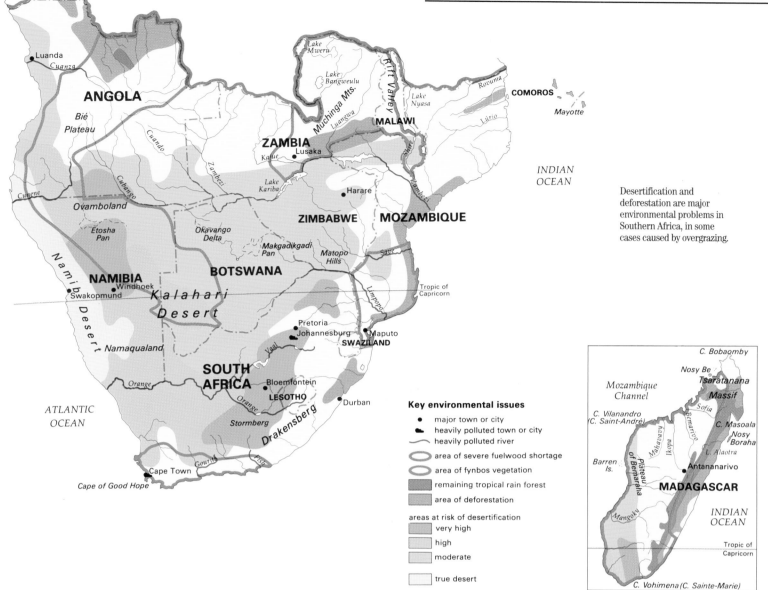

Desertification and deforestation are major environmental problems in Southern Africa, in some cases caused by overgrazing.

Key environmental issues

- • major town or city
- ● heavily polluted town or city
- ⌇ heavily polluted river
- ◯ area of severe fuelwood shortage
- ◯ area of fynbos vegetation
- ▨ remaining tropical rain forest
- ▨ area of deforestation

areas at risk of desertification
- ▨ very high
- ▨ high
- ▨ moderate
- ☐ true desert

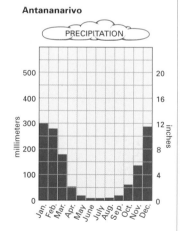

CLIMATE

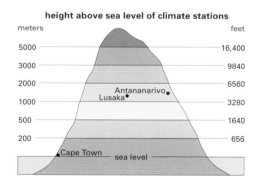

height above sea level of climate stations

Cape Town

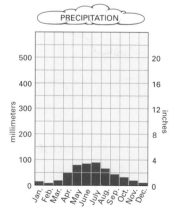

Lusaka

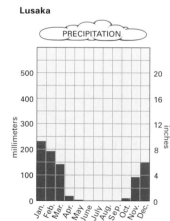

Antananarivo

PRECIPITATION

Cape Town

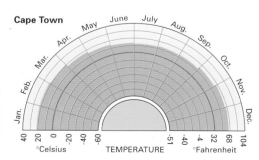

Lusaka

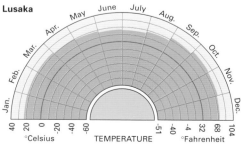

Antananarivo

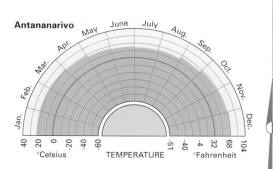

TEMPERATURE

POPULATION

Europeans founded most of the cities in Southern Africa. Today the cities are expanding quickly. They are magnets that attract people from the less populated rural areas who are seeking jobs and better health and education services for their families.

POPULATION

Total population of region (in millions)	108.3
Population density (persons per sq mi)	55.9
Population change (average annual percent 1960–1990)	
Urban	+5.9
Rural	+1.6

URBAN POPULATION

As percentage of total population	
1960	22.1
1990	39.6
Percentage in cities of more than 1 million	4.1

TEN LARGEST CITIES

	Country	Population
Johannesburg	South Africa	3,411,000
Cape Town †	South Africa	1,912,000
Luanda †	Angola	1,200,000
Maputo †	Mozambique	1,070,000
Durban	South Africa	982,000
Lusaka †	Zambia	900,000
Pretoria †	South Africa	823,000
Antananarivo †	Madagascar	703,000
Harare †	Zimbabwe	681,000
Port Elizabeth	South Africa	652,000

† denotes national capital

INDUSTRY

South Africa is Africa's leading industrialized nation. It attracts migrant workers from the black African states. Some countries, such as Madagascar, have little industry except commercial farming, though Namibia and Botswana export minerals.

INDUSTRIAL OUTPUT (US$ billion)

Total	Mining	Manufacturing	Average annual change since 1960
50.9	13.9	30.6	+2.3%

INDUSTRIAL WORKERS (millions)
(Figures in parentheses are percentages of total labor force.)

Total	Mining	Manufacturing	Construction
4.7	1.0 (3.3%)	2.95 (9.8%)	0.73 (2.4%)

MAJOR PRODUCTS (Figures in parentheses are percentages of world production.)

Energy and minerals		Output	Change since 1960
Bituminous coal (mil. m.t.)		183.3 (5.3%)	+358%
Oil (mil. barrels)		169.3 (0.7%)	N/A
Copper (1,000 m.t.)		770.0 (9.0%)	-22.3%
Nickel (1,000 m.t.)		69.5 (8.6%)	+124%
Chrome (mil. m.t.)		2.17 (51.5%)	+153%
Vanadium (1,000 m.t.)		16.4 (53%)	N/A
Zirconium (1,000 m.t.)		154.5 (21.1%)	N/A
Gold (m.t.)		639.0 (35.9%)	-18%
Diamonds (mil. carats)		25.6 (43.1%)	+86.2%

Manufactures			
Canned fruits (1,000 m.t.)		264.2 (5.1%)	No data
Ladies' dresses (mil.)		19.1 (4.1%)	No data
Ferroalloys and chrome (mil. m.t.)		3.4 (26.6%)	N/A
Household hardware (1,000 units)		10.3 (4.6%)	No data

N/A means production had not begun in 1960.

AGRICULTURE

Subsistence farming is the main occupation in the region. Malawi exports sugarcane. In South Africa and Zimbabwe, there is successful commercial farming. Both of these countries export food, while the other countries are food importers.

LAND (million acres)

Total	Agricultural	Arable	Forest/woodland
1,606 (100%)	904 (56%)	84 (5%)	395 (25%)

FARMERS

23.3 million employed in agriculture (56% of workforce)
3.4 acres of arable land per person employed in agriculture

MAJOR CROPS

	Area mil. acres	Yield 100lbs/acre	Production mil. m.t.	Change since 1963
Corn	21.9	11.6	11.6 (3)	+36%
Wheat	4.9	15.1	3.4 (1)	+270%
Roots/tubers	4.9	49.5	11.0 (2)	+79%
Groundnuts	2.2	5.4	0.5 (3)	-17%
Sugarcane	1.4	646	42.9 (4)	+101%
Tobacco	0.4	10.5	0.2 (4)	+45%
Fruits	—	—	5.9 (2)	+105%

MAJOR LIVESTOCK

	Number in mil.	Production mil. m.t.	Change since 1963
Sheep/goats	55.7 (3)	—	0%
Cattle	42.1 (3)	—	+24%
Milk	—	3.5 (1)	+13%
Fish catch	—	1.8 (2)	—

FOOD SECURITY (grain exports minus imports)

mil. m.t.	% domestic production	% world trade
-0.2	1	0.1

Numbers in parentheses are percentages of world total.

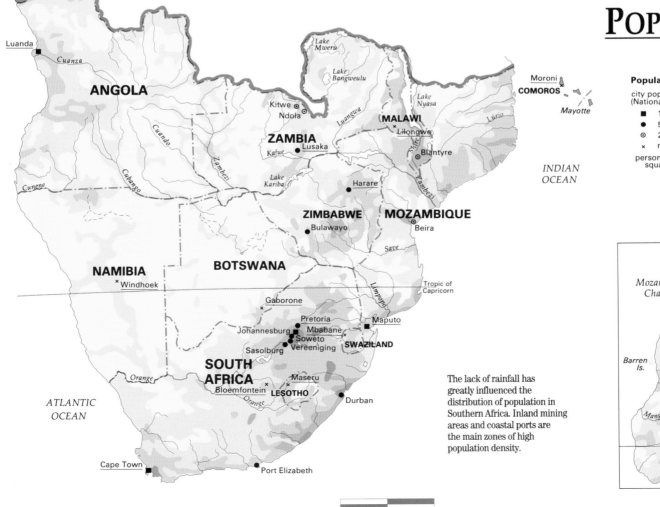

POPULATION

Population density

city populations
(National capital is underlined.)

- ■ 1,000,000–5,000,000
- ● 500,000–999,999
- ◉ 250,000–499,999
- × national capital less than 250,000

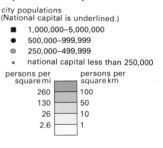

persons per square mi	persons per square km
260	100
130	50
26	10
2.6	1

The lack of rainfall has greatly influenced the distribution of population in Southern Africa. Inland mining areas and coastal ports are the main zones of high population density.

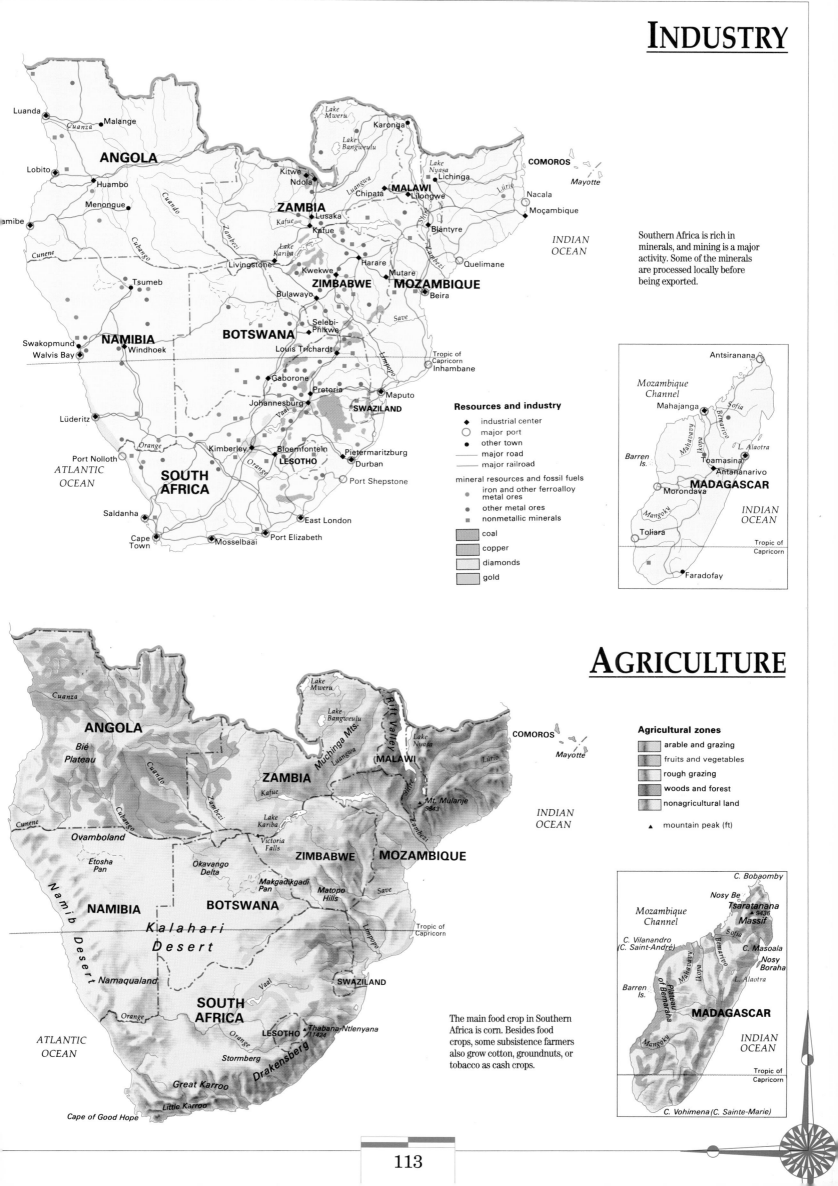

INDUSTRY

Southern Africa is rich in minerals, and mining is a major activity. Some of the minerals are processed locally before being exported.

Resources and industry
- ◆ industrial center
- ○ major port
- ● other town
- — major road
- — major railroad

mineral resources and fossil fuels
- ● iron and other ferroalloy metal ores
- ● other metal ores
- ■ nonmetallic minerals
- coal
- copper
- diamonds
- gold

AGRICULTURE

Agricultural zones
- arable and grazing
- fruits and vegetables
- rough grazing
- woods and forest
- nonagricultural land
- ▲ mountain peak (ft)

The main food crop in Southern Africa is corn. Besides food crops, some subsistence farmers also grow cotton, groundnuts, or tobacco as cash crops.

INDIAN SUBCONTINENT

The region is a pendant-shaped landmass, extending from the world's highest mountain ranges in the north to the islands of Sri Lanka and the Maldives in the south.

The climate ranges from polar conditions on the mountains to hot tropical weather on the plains. The influence of monsoon winds, which bring rain between June and September, are felt throughout much of the region.

Over the centuries, many waves of migrants have settled in the subcontinent. Today the region has many languages and religions, reflecting its complex past. Cultural rivalries and religious differences sometimes cause conflict and violence. However, despite such pressures and the poverty in which many people live, India remains the world's largest parliamentary democracy.

The Indian subcontinent was once part of the ancient continent of Gondwanaland. Plate movements propelled the landmass north until it collided with Eurasia, thrusting up the rocks on the intervening seabed into high fold mountains, the Himalayas, with the world's highest peak.

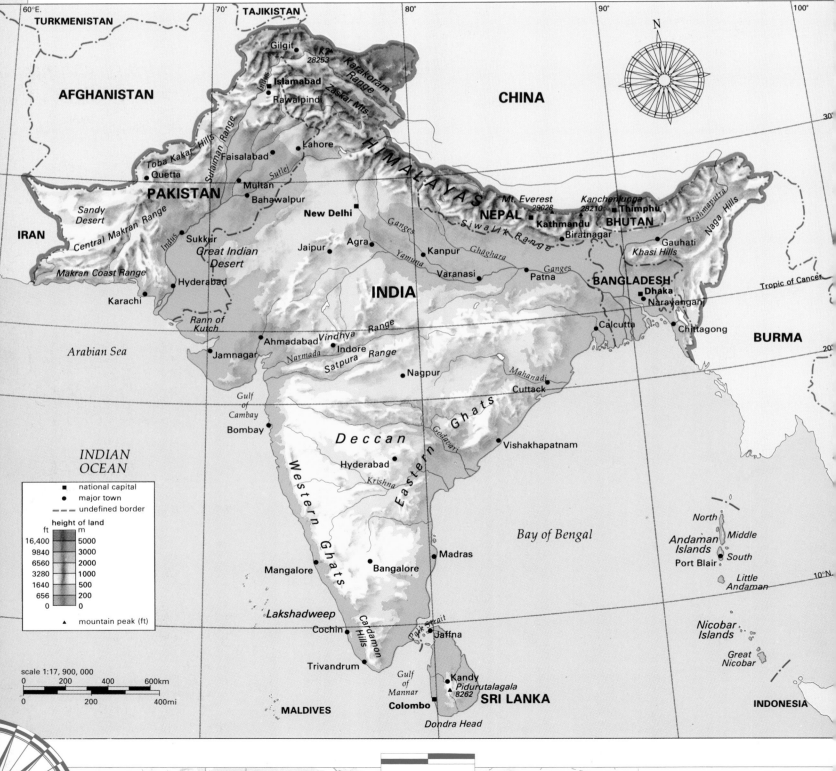

Legend:
- ■ national capital
- ● major town
- – – – undefined border

height of land

ft	m
16,400	5000
9840	3000
6560	2000
3280	1000
1640	500
656	200
0	0

▲ mountain peak (ft)

scale 1:17, 900, 000

0   200   400   600km

0   200   400mi

THE POLITICAL AND CULTURAL WORLD

In the mid-nineteenth century, most of the Indian subcontinent, apart from the remote mountain kingdoms of Bhutan and Nepal, was under British rule. But when British India became independent in 1947, the region split into two countries: the mainly Hindu India and Islamic Pakistan. Pakistan consisted of two parts: West and East Pakistan. After a civil war, East Pakistan broke away from West Pakistan in 1971 and proclaimed its independence as Bangladesh.

Tensions between India and the Islamic Republic of Pakistan (formerly West Pakistan) continue, and the boundaries in the Jammu and Kashmir region in the northwest are disputed.

COUNTRIES IN THE REGION
Bangladesh, Bhutan, India, Maldives, Nepal, Pakistan, Sri Lanka
Island territories
Andaman Islands, Nicobar Islands, Lakshadweep (India)

MEMBERSHIP OF INTERNATIONAL ORGANIZATIONS
Colombo Plan Bangladesh, Bhutan, India, Maldives, Nepal, Pakistan, Sri Lanka
South Asia Regional Cooperation Committee (SARC) All countries of the region

LANGUAGE
Countries with one official language Bengali: Bangladesh; Divehi: Maldives; Nepali: Nepal; Sinhalese: Sri Lanka; Urdu: Pakistan
Country with two official languages English, Hindi: India
Country with three official languages Dzongkha, English, Lhotsam: Bhutan

India has 14 officially recognized languages. As well as Hindi and Urdu, the most significant languages in the region include Gujarati, Malayalam, Marathi, Punjabi, Tamil, and Telugu. There are hundreds of local languages and dialects.

RELIGION
Countries with one major religion Maldives, Pakistan (I)
Countries with two major religions Bhutan (B,H); Bangladesh (H,I)
Countries with three or more major religions Nepal (B,H,I); Sri Lanka (B,C,H,I); India (B,C,H,I,J,S)

Key: B-Buddhist, C-various Christian, H-Hindu, I-Islam, J-Jain, S-Sikh

ECONOMIC INDICATORS: 1990

	Bangladesh	India	Pakistan
GNP(US$ billions)	22.88	254.54	35.5
GNP per capita (US$)	210	350	380
Annual rate of growth of GDP, 1980-1990 (%)	4.3	5.3	6.3
Manufacturing as % of GDP	9	19	17
Central government spending as % of GNP	15	18	24
Merchandise exports (US$ billions)	1.49	16.1	4.95
Merchandise imports (US$ billions)	3.38	20.5	6.95
% of GNP received as development aid	9.2	0.6	2.9
Total external debt as % of GNP	53.8	25.0	52.1

WELFARE INDICATORS

Infant mortality rate (per 1,000 live births)			
1965	144	150	149
1990	105	92	103
Daily food supply available (calories per capita, 1989)	2,021	2,229	2,219
Population per physician (1984)	6,390	2,520	2,900
Teacher-pupil ratio (elementary school, 1989)	1 : 60	1 : 61	1 : 41

Pakistan
Area 307,374 sq mi (796,095 sq km)
Population 112,050,000
Capital Islamabad
Currency 1 Pakistan rupee (Pre; plural PRs) = 100 paisa

India is a nonaligned state and did not take sides in the Cold War. It possesses nuclear weapons. One family dominated Indian politics for many years. The country was led by the Nehru-Gandhi family from its independence in 1947 until prime minister Rajiv Gandhi was assassinated in May 1991.

■ national capital

Area 55,598 sq mi (143,998 sq km)
Population 115,593,000
Capital Dhaka
Currency 1 Bangladesh taka (Yk) = 100 paisa

Bangladesh

Area 18,150 sq mi (47,000 sq km)
Population 1,516,000
Capital Thimphu
Currency 1 gnultrum (Nu) = 100 chetrum

Bhutan

Area 1,222,559 sq mi (3,166,414 sq km)
Population 853,094,000
Capital New Delhi
Currency I Indian rupee (Re; plural Rs) = 100 paisa

India

Area 115 sq mi (298 sq km)
Population 215,000
Capital Male
Currency 1 Maldivian rufiyaa (Rf) = 100 laair

Maldives

Area 56,827 sq mi (147,181 sq km)
Population 19,143,000
Capital Kathmandu
Currency 1 Nepalese rupee (NRe; plural NRs) = 100 paisa

Nepal

Area 25,332 sq mi (65,610 sq km)
Population 17,217,000
Capital Colombo
Currency 1 Sri Lanka rupee (SL Re; plural SL Rs) = 100 cents

Sri Lanka

Habitats

The mountains in the north and the deserts in the northwest are barren. The rivers that rise in the mountains, especially the Indus, Ganges, and Brahmaputra, drain the fertile river valleys and deltas south of the mountains.

LAND

Area 1,727,276 sq mi (4,476,064 sq km)
Highest point Mount Everest, 29,028 ft (8,848 m), highest on earth
Major features Himalayas, world's highest mountain range, plains and deltas in north, Thar Desert, Deccan plateau

WATER

Longest river Brahmaputra and Indus both 1,800 mi (2,900 km)
Largest basin Ganges, 409,000 sq mi (1,059,000 sq km)
Largest lake Manchhar, Pakistan, 100 sq mi (260 sq km); reservoirs in India are larger

NOTABLE THREATENED SPECIES

Mammals lion-tailed macaque *(Macaca silenus)*, Hispid hare *(Caprolagus hispidus)*, Indus river dolphin *(Platanista minor)*, Indian rhinoceros *(Rhinoceros unicornis)*, pygmy hog *(Sus salvanius)*, swamp deer *(Cervus duvauceli)*
Birds lesser florican *(Sypheotides indica)*, Jerdon's courser *(Cursorius bitorquatus)*, western tragopan *(Tragopan melanocephalus)*, forest owlet *(Athene blewitii)*, great Indian bustard *(Choriotis nigriceps)*
Plants Beddomes cycad (*Cycas beddomei*); kin (*Dioscorea deltoidea*); opposite-leaved ebony *(Diospyros oppositifolia)*; frerea *(Frerea indica)*; Shirhoy lily *(Lilium macklineae)*; Drury's slipper orchid *(Paphiopedilum druryi)*; Himilayan cherry *(Prunus himalaica)*; Royle's saussurea *(Saussurea roylei)*; Wallich's elm *(Ulmus wallichiana)*; blue vanda *(Vanda coerulea)*

Climate

South of the towering Himalayas, with their polar and subarctic climates, the Indian subcontinent is a warm tropical region. Dry climates include the hot Great Indian Desert on the India-Pakistan border. Other areas have hot monsoon climates with heavy rains between late June and September.

TEMPERATURE AND PRECIPITATION

	Temperature January	°F (°C) July	Altitude ft (m)
Jacobabad	59 (15)	98 (37)	187 (57)
Simla	66 (19)	41 (5)	6,636 (2,022)
New Delhi	57 (14)	90 (32)	714 (218)
Kathmandu	50 (10)	75 (24)	4,388 (1,338)
Chittagong	68 (20)	82 (28)	88 (27)
Trincomalee	79 (26)	86 (30)	23 (7)

	Precipitation January	in (mm) July	Year
Jacobabad	0.2 (5)	1.1 (23)	3.5 (88)
Simla	2.4 (61)	16.7 (424)	62.1 (1,577)
New Delhi	0.9 (23)	7.1 (180)	28.2 (715)
Kathmandu	0.6 (15)	13.5 (345)	52.3 (1,328)
Chittagong	0.2 (5)	23.5 (597)	112.5 (2,858)
Trincomalee	6.8 (173)	2.0 (51)	68.0 (1,727)

World's highest recorded annual rainfall, 1,042.1 in (26,470 mm), Cherrapunji, northeast India

NATURAL HAZARDS

Cyclones, storm surges, flooding of great river deltas

Environmental Issues

The Indian subcontinent is subject to such natural disasters as floods, drought, storms, and earthquakes. Population pressures have led to deforestation and soil erosion, while urban and industrial pollution are mounting problems.

POPULATION AND WEALTH

	Highest	Middle	Lowest
Population increase (annual population growth rate, % 1960–1990)	3.0 (Pakistan)	2.4 (Nepal)	1.9 (Sri Lanka)
Energy use (gigajoules/person)	8 (India)	2 (Bangladesh)	1 (Nepal)
Real purchasing power (US$/person)	2,120 (Sri Lanka)	870 (Nepal)	720 (Bangladesh)

ENVIRONMENTAL INDICATORS

CO_2 emissions (mil. m.t. carbon/year)	230 (India)	6.8 (Nepal)	0.2 (Bhutan)
Deforestation ('000s acres/year 1980s)	37.6 (India)	143 (Sri Lanka)	2.4 (Bhutan)
Artificial fertilizer use (lbs/acre/year)	100 (Sri Lanka)	68.7 (Bangladesh)	0.8 (Bhutan)
Automobiles (per 1,000 population)	7 (Sri Lanka)	2 (India)	0.4 (Bangladesh)
Access to safe drinking water (% population)	57 (India)	41 (Sri Lanka)	36 (Nepal)

MAJOR ENVIRONMENTAL PROBLEMS AND SOURCES

Air pollution: generally high, urban very high; acid rain prevalent; high greenhouse gas emissions
River pollution: medium; *sources*: agricultural, sewage
Land degradation: *types*: desertification, soil erosion, salinization, deforestation, habitat destruction; *causes*: agriculture, industry, population pressure
Resource problems: fuelwood shortage; inadequate drinking water and sanitation; coastal flooding
Population problems: population explosion; urban overcrowding; inadequate health facilities; famine
Major events: Bhopal (1984), leak of poisonous chemicals; Bangladesh (1988, 1991), major floods

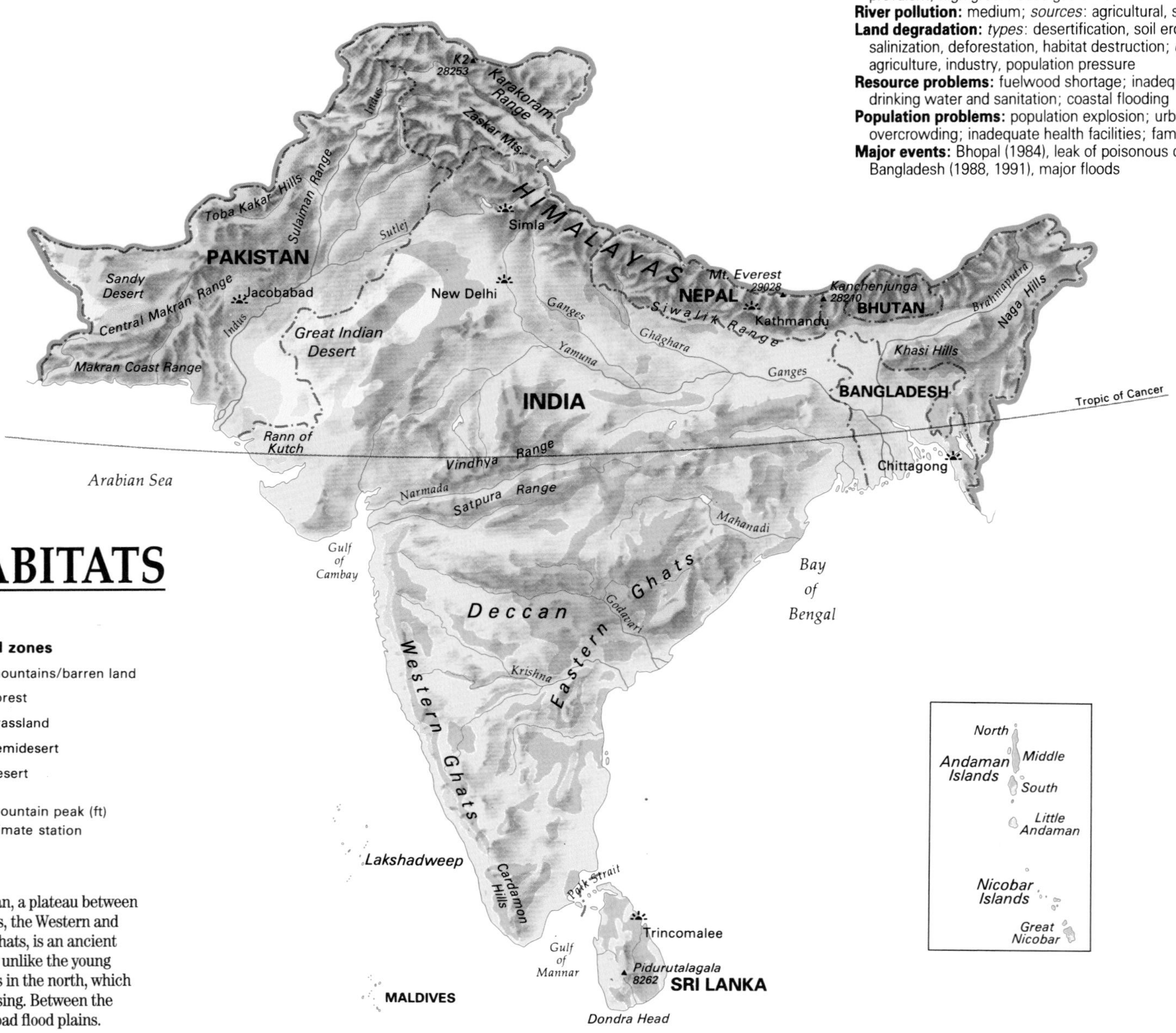

Habitats

Physical zones
- mountains/barren land
- forest
- grassland
- semidesert
- desert

▲ mountain peak (ft)
climate station

The Deccan, a plateau between two ranges, the Western and Eastern Ghats, is an ancient landmass, unlike the young mountains in the north, which are still rising. Between the two lie broad flood plains.

ENVIRONMENTAL ISSUES

The original forests of the Indian subcontinent have largely been destroyed. The arid northwest and the west-central Deccan plateau are at risk of desertification.

Key environmental issues

- major town or city
- heavily polluted town or city
- major pollution event
- major natural disaster
- heavily polluted river
- area liable to flood
- remaining tropical rain forest
- area of deforestation

areas at risk of desertification
- very high
- high
- moderate
- true desert

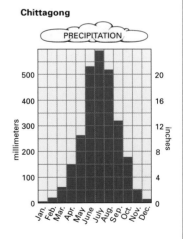

CLIMATE

height above sea level of climate stations

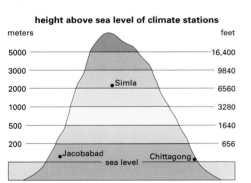

meters / feet

5000	16,400
3000	9840
2000	6560
1000	3280
500	1640
200	656

Simla
Jacobabad
Chittagong
sea level

Jacobabad

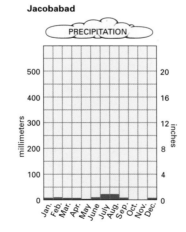

PRECIPITATION

Simla

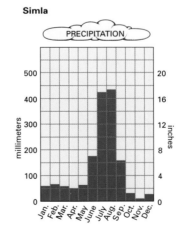

PRECIPITATION

Chittagong

PRECIPITATION

Jacobabad

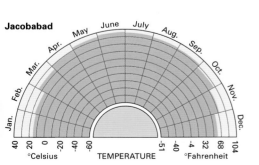

°Celsius   TEMPERATURE   °Fahrenheit

Simla

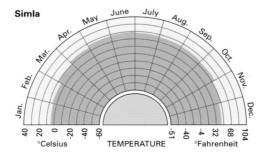

°Celsius   TEMPERATURE   °Fahrenheit

Chittagong

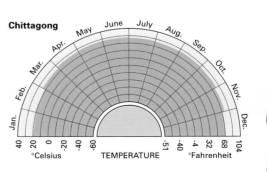

°Celsius   TEMPERATURE   °Fahrenheit

POPULATION

The subcontinent is one of the world's most populous regions. Most people in the subcontinent live in rural areas, but there are many large cities, including some of the world's most crowded, with over 1,200 people per square mile. India alone has more than 200 large cities.

POPULATION

Total population of region (in millions)	1,129.5
Population density (persons per sq mi)	750
Population change (average annual percent 1960–1990) Urban	+4.5
Rural	+2.3

URBAN POPULATION

As percentage of total population	
1960	19.2
1990	28.6
Percentage in cities of more than 1 million	4.8

TEN LARGEST CITIES

	Country	Population
Calcutta	India	9,194,000
Bombay	India	8,243,000
New Delhi †	India	5,729,000
Karachi	Pakistan	5,181,000
Dhaka †	Bangladesh	4,770,000
Madras	India	4,289,000
Lahore	Pakistan	2,953,000
Bangalore	India	2,922,000
Ahmadabad	India	2,548,000
Hyderabad	India	2,546,000

† denotes national capital

INDUSTRY

The countries of the Indian subcontinent are, according to the World Bank, "low-income developing nations." The region has plenty of resources and huge potential, but its industrial development has been extremely slow.

INDUSTRIAL OUTPUT (US$ billion)

Total	Mining	Manufacturing	Average annual change since 1960
86.33	7.53	68.0	+5%

MAJOR PRODUCTS (Figures in parentheses are percentages of world production.)

Energy and minerals	Output	Change since 1960
Coal (mil. m.t.)	205.3 (4.3%)	+271%
Oil (mil. barrels)	266.8 (1.2%)	+7900%
Iron ore (mil. m.t.)	32.8 (5.8%)	+77%
Bauxite (mil. m.t.)	4.0 (4.1%)	+255%

Manufactures		
Refined sugar (mil. m.t.)	10.5 (16.4%)	+193%
Cotton woven fabrics (mil. sq yd)	20,295 (14.2%)	+263%
Jute fabrics (mil. sq yd)	4,467 (92%)	+48%
Footwear (mil. pairs)	197.4 (4.4%)	+1368%
Broadleaved lumber (mil. cu yd)	533.2 (12.1%)	+647%
Cement (mil. m.t.)	45.5 (4.1%)	+415%
Transistors (mil.)	3,560 (5.2%)	N/A
Bicycles (mil.)	7.4 (7.3%)	+662%

N/A means production had not begun in 1960.

AGRICULTURE

Farming is the main activity throughout the subcontinent. The best farmland is in the densely populated northern plains. Rice is the main food crop throughout the subcontinent, although wheat is also important in many areas.

LAND (million acres)

Total	Agricultural	Arable	Forest/woodland
1,020 (100%)	551 (54%)	489 (48%)	197 (19%)

FARMERS

258.7 million people employed in agriculture (66% of work force)
2.2 acres of arable land per person employed in farming

MAJOR CROPS

	Area mil. acres	Yield 100lbs/acre	Production mil. m.t.	Change since 1963
Paddy rice	130	19.9	117.7 (25)	+61%
Wheat	79	16.2	58.2 (11)	+274%
Millet/ sorghum	74.8	5.6	19.1 (21)	+10%
Pulses	61.5	4.7	13.2 (24)	+3%
Cotton	22.4	2.4	2.6 (16)	+81%
Corn	17.7	9.7	7.8 (2)	+30%
Groundnuts	16.8	7.4	5.8 (27)	+11%
Sugarcane	10.1	481.5	222.4 (23)	+73%
Vegetables	—	—	53.0 (13)	+107%
Fruit	—	—	30.3 (9)	+94%

MAJOR LIVESTOCK

	Number in mil.	Production mil. m.t.	Change since 1963
Cattle	247.4 (19)	—	+15%
Sheep/goats	235.8 (14)	—	+74%
Buffaloes	93.7 (68)	—	+48%
Milk	—	25.2 (5)	+158%
Fish catch	—	4.4 (5)	—

Numbers in parentheses are percentages of world total.

POPULATION

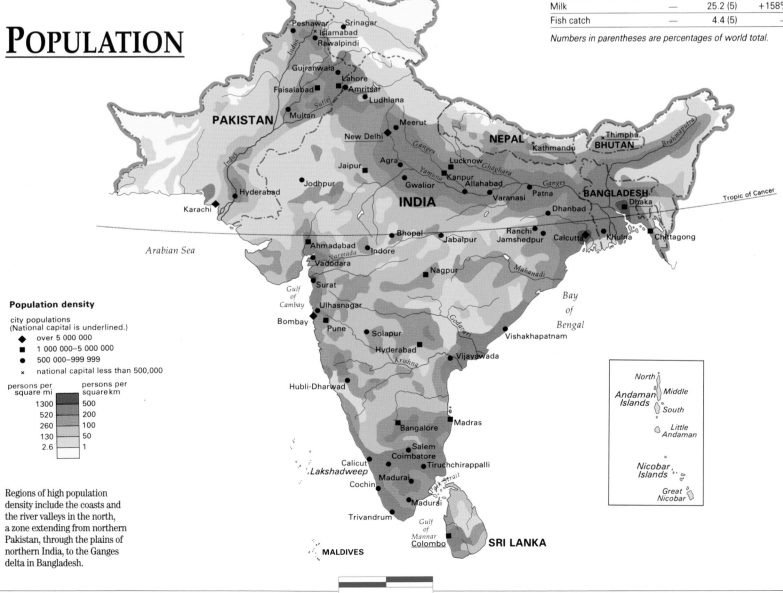

Population density

city populations
(National capital is underlined.)

◆   over 5 000 000
■   1 000 000–5 000 000
●   500 000–999 999
✕   national capital less than 500,000

persons per square mi	persons per square km
1300	500
520	200
260	100
130	50
2.6	1

Regions of high population density include the coasts and the river valleys in the north, a zone extending from northern Pakistan, through the plains of northern India, to the Ganges delta in Bangladesh.

INDUSTRY

India has coal and iron reserves, while oil and gas fields are being developed. Pakistan and Bangladesh have large gas reserves.

Resources and industry

◆ industrial center
○ major port
● other town
— major road
— major railroad

mineral resources and fossil fuels
● iron and other ferroalloy metal ores
● other metal ores
■ nonmetallic minerals
▨ coal
▨ iron ore
▨ natural gas

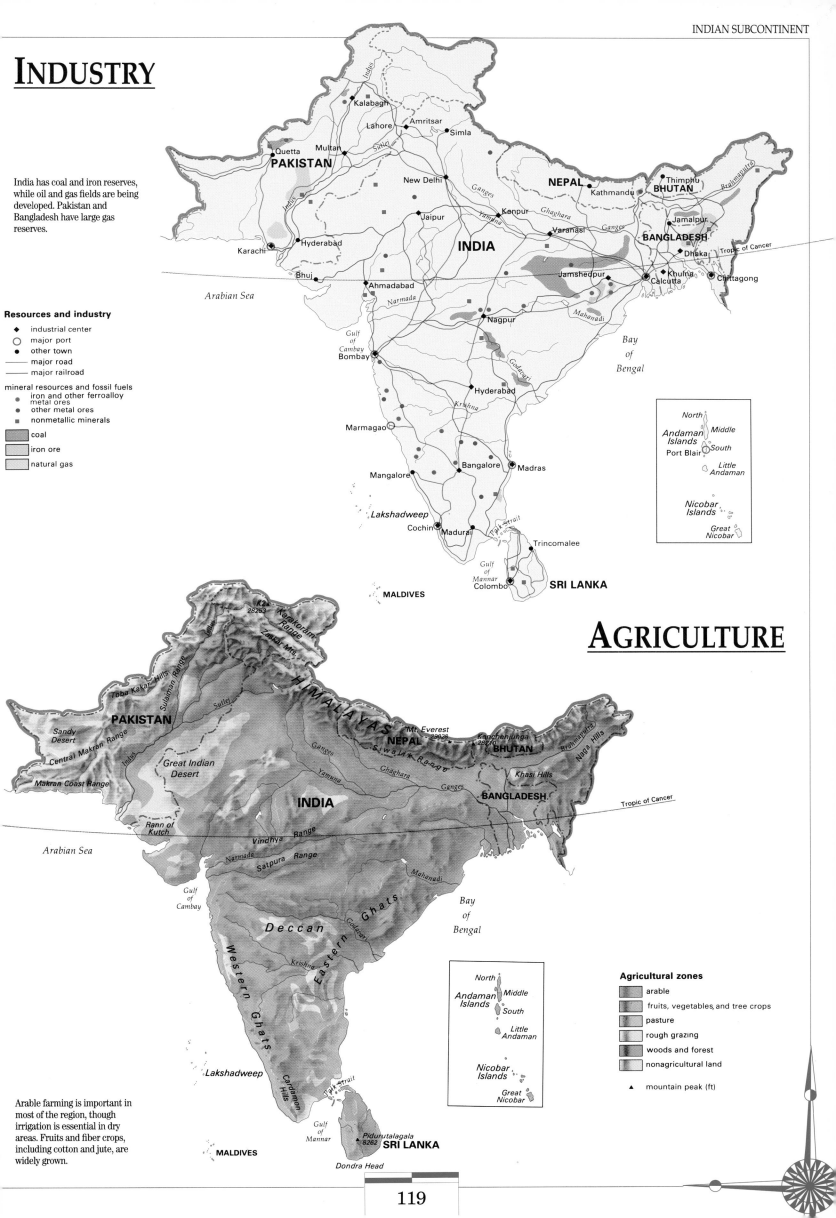

PAKISTAN
Kalabagh
Lahore Amritsar Simla
Quetta Multan
Sutlej
New Delhi
Karachi
Hyderabad
Bhuj
Ahmadabad
Narmada
Gulf of Cambay
Bombay
Marmagao
Mangalore
Lakshadweep
Cochin Madurai
MALDIVES

NEPAL BHUTAN Thimphu
Kathmandu
Ganges Ghaghara Jamalpur
Kanpur Ganges
Jaipur Yamuna Varanasi
BANGLADESH
INDIA Dhaka Chittagong
Khulma
Jamshedpur Calcutta
Tropic of Cancer
Nagpur Mahanadi
Bay of Bengal
Godavari
Hyderabad
Krishna
Bangalore Madras
Park Strait
Trincomalee
Gulf of Mannar
Colombo SRI LANKA

Arabian Sea

North
Andaman Islands Middle
Port Blair South
Little Andaman
Nicobar Islands
Great Nicobar

AGRICULTURE

K2 28253 Karakoram Range
Zaskar Mts.
Toba Kakar Hills Sulaiman Range
PAKISTAN
Sandy Desert
Central Makran Range
Makran Coast Range
Indus
Rann of Kutch
Great Indian Desert
Sutlej
HIMALAYAS
Ganges
Yamuna Siwalik Range
Mt. Everest 29028
Kanchenjunga 28210
NEPAL BHUTAN
Ghaghara Ganges
Khasi Hills
Naga Hills
Brahmaputra
BANGLADESH
INDIA
Tropic of Cancer
Vindhya Range
Narmada Satpura Range
Mahanadi
Deccan
Western Ghats
Eastern Ghats
Godavari
Krishna
Bay of Bengal
Gulf of Cambay
Lakshadweep
Cardamon Hills
Park Strait
Gulf of Mannar
Pidurutalagala 8262 SRI LANKA
MALDIVES
Dondra Head

Arabian Sea

North
Andaman Islands Middle
South
Little Andaman
Nicobar Islands
Great Nicobar

Agricultural zones
▨ arable
▨ fruits, vegetables, and tree crops
▨ pasture
▨ rough grazing
▨ woods and forest
▨ nonagricultural land

▲ mountain peak (ft)

Arable farming is important in most of the region, though irrigation is essential in dry areas. Fruits and fiber crops, including cotton and jute, are widely grown.

CHINA AND TAIWAN

China is the world's third largest country in area and the largest in population. It contains great mountain ranges, high plateaus, deserts, grasslands, and fertile valleys.

The climate in the southwest Plateau of Tibet is very harsh. The deserts in the northwest have an arid climate with temperatures that may soar to 100°F (38°C) in summer and plunge to −29°F (−34°C) during winter nights. Most people live in the east, where the climate ranges from temperate to subtropical.

About 93 percent of the people in China belong to the Han group, a name that comes from the Han dynasty (206 B.C.–A.D. 220). The other 7 percent belong to minority groups.

Civilization in China dates back around 5,000 years. The Chinese empire became weak in the nineteenth century, and in 1912, the country became a republic. A communist regime has ruled since 1949, though from the late 1980s, the government began to introduce free enterprise economic policies.

China is bordered by Mongolia and Russia to the north and the Indian subcontinent and Southeast Asia in the south. It shares Everest, the world's highest mountain, with Nepal. It also has deep basins, one reaching 505 ft (154 m) below sea level. The great plains of China are drained by the great rivers Huang and Chang.

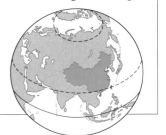

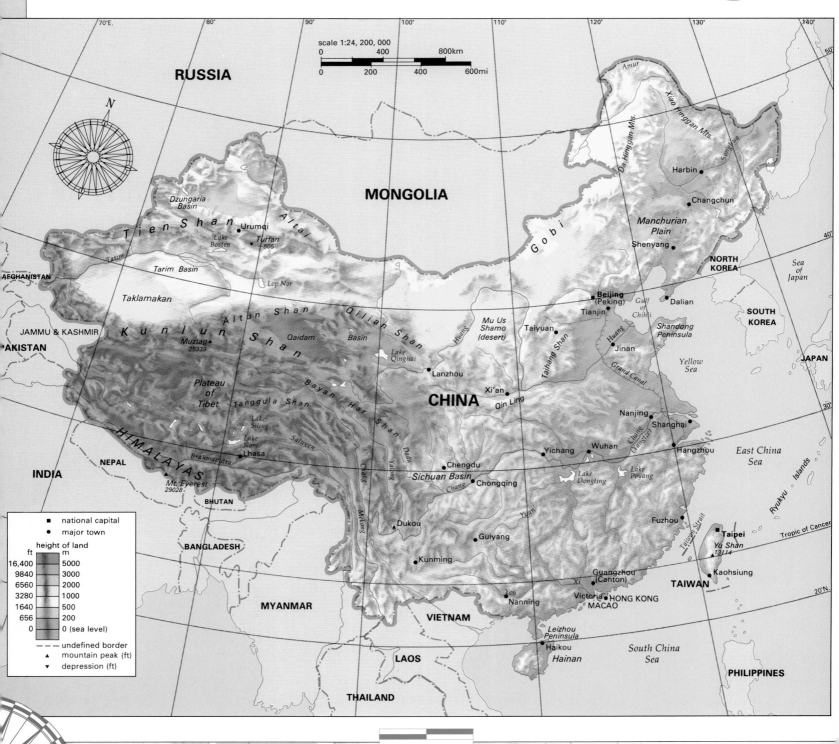

THE POLITICAL AND CULTURAL WORLD

The region includes the small British territory of Hong Kong, a financial and industrial center on the southeast coast of China, which Britain will return to China in 1997. Near Hong Kong is the even smaller Portuguese territory of Macao, which Portugal will return to China in 1999.

A third territory is the island of Taiwan, on which Chinese nationalist forces set up a rival government after the communists took power in 1949. China would also like to reunite with Taiwan, now a successful industrial economy, and has promised the Taiwanese a high degree of autonomy if they agree. But this seems unlikely until after the return of the dependencies of Hong Kong and Macao.

Since the death of China's communist leader Mao Zedong (1949–1976), China's leadership has tried to make friendlier relations with other countries, notably Russia and the United States. China was opened to foreign investment and free enterprise, and this led in the late 1980s to demands for political reform. Demonstrators for such changes were brutally suppressed.

COUNTRIES IN THE REGION

China, Taiwan

Island territories Hainan (China)
Dependencies of other states Hong Kong (U.K.: due to be returned to China in 1997); Macao (Portugal: due to be returned to China in 1999)

LANGUAGE

Countries with one official language Mandarin Chinese: China, Taiwan

RELIGION

China Although religion is officially discouraged, many people practice a combination of Confucianist, Taoist, and traditional folk belief. There are smaller groups of Buddhists, Muslims, and Christians.
Taiwan Confucianist-Taoist-traditional (48.5%), Buddhist (43%), Christian (7.4%), Islam (0.5%)

STYLES OF GOVERNMENT

Republics China, Taiwan
Federal state China
Multiparty state Taiwan
One-party state China
One-chamber assembly China, Taiwan

ECONOMIC INDICATORS

	China
GDP (US$ billions)	364.9
GNP per capita (US$)	370
Annual rate of growth of GDP, 1980–1990	9.5%
Manufacturing as % of GDP	38.0%
Central government spending as % of GNP	N/A
Merchandise exports (US$ billions)	61.3
Merchandise imports (US$ billions)	52.6
% of GNP received as development aid	0.6%
Total external debt as a % of GNP	14.4%

WELFARE INDICATORS

Infant mortality rate (per 1,000 live births)	
1965	90
1990	29
Daily food supply available (calories per capita, 1989)	2,639
Population per physician (1984)	1,010
Teacher-pupil ratio (elementary school, 1989)	1 : 22

Area 3,676,300 sq mi (9,526,900 sq km)
Population 1,139,060,000
China **Capital** Beijing
Currency 1 yuan (Y) = 10 jiao = 100 fen

Area 13,900 sq mi (36,000 sq km)
Population 20,100,000
Capital Taipei **Taiwan**
Currency 1 new Taiwan dollar (NT$) = 100 cents

- ■ national capital
- • provincial or municipal capital
- province
- municipality
- autonomous region

Locales are given in present-day Pinyin spelling.

HABITATS

The landscape of China falls into three main areas. In the west is the immense Plateau of Tibet, the "roof of the world," the highest and largest plateau on earth. Its average height is 13,000 ft (4,000 m). In the far south of the plateau are the Himalayas.

The next main area, to the north and east, is a vast region of plateaus and river basins. It includes the Gobi Desert, and the basin of the Tarim River and the Sichuan Basin. This area is bordered to the west by mountain ranges.

The great plains of China form the third main area, stretching east and southeast from the plateaus to the sea. They were formed from the deposited soils washed down by great rivers flowing from the higher land. The plains are generally below 1,600 ft (500 m), and broken by occasional hills.

The boundaries between these three main areas follow the lines of deep-seated faults in the underlying crust of the earth. Tectonic activity continues—there are frequent earthquakes, particularly in the mountains of the west and on the island of Taiwan.

LAND

Area 3,690,246 sq mi (9,562,904 sq km)
Highest point Mount Everest, 29,028 ft (8,848 m) highest on earth
Lowest point Turfan depression, −505 ft (−154 m)
Major features Plateau of Tibet, Himalayas, world's highest mountain chain, Red and Tarim basins, Takla Makan and Gobi deserts, river plains in east

WATER

Longest river Chang, 3,720 mi (5,980 km)
Largest basin Chang, 705,000 sq mi (1,827,000 sq km)
Highest average flow Chang, 1,137,000 cu ft/sec (32,190 cu m/sec)
Largest lake Qinghai, 1,721 sq mi (4,460 sq km)

NOTABLE THREATENED SPECIES

Mammals Kozlov's pika (Ochotona koslowi), golden monkey (Rhinopithecus roxellana), Yunnan snub-nosed monkey (Rhinopithecus bieti), baiji (Lipotes vexillifer), giant panda (Ailuropoda melanoleuca), Thorold's deer (Cervus albirostris)
Birds white-eared night heron (Gorsachius magnificus), crested ibis (Nipponia nippon), Chinese monal (Lophophorus lhuysii)
Plants Baishanzhu mountain fir (Abies beshanzhuensis); xianmu (Burretiodendron hsienmu); Camellia granthamiana; Coptis teeta; Cycas taiwaniana; dove tree (Davidia involucrata); maidenhair tree (Ginkgo biloba); Kirengeshoma palmata; dawn redwood (Metasequoia glyptostroboides); ginseng (Panax ginseng)
Others Chinese alligator (Alligator chinensis), Chinese giant salamander (Andrias davidianus), Chinese paddlefish (Psephurus gladius), Chinese three-tailed swallowtail butterfly (Bhutanitis thaidina)

HABITATS

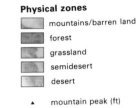

Physical zones

- mountains/barren land
- forest
- grassland
- semidesert
- desert

▲ mountain peak (ft)
▼ depression (ft)
☀ climate station

China contains barren regions of mountain, desert, and semidesert. There are also grassy plains in the northwest and fertile areas of valleys and plains in the southeast.

CLIMATE

There are three main climatic zones in the region, corresponding to the three major physical regions. The Plateau of Tibet has a harsh, cold, dry climate, and has been called the "earth's third pole." The height of the mountains prevents warmer air from moving north. Above 13,000 ft (4,000 m), it is always freezing. The remote arid steppes and deserts of northwest China are far from the ocean and its rain-bearing winds, and have less than 4 in (100 mm) of rain a year.

The lowlands and hills of eastern China occupy almost half the country and have a great range of climates. The northeast lies in a temperate zone; farther south there are both warm temperate and subtropical zones, while southern Yunnan in the southwest and also the island of Hainan are tropical. Throughout eastern China the monsoon brings high rainfall in summer. Cold, dry, northerly winds (the winter monsoon) blow outward over much of China. When the land warms in spring, a great current of warm, humid air reaches inland from the south and east, bringing rain. This is the wet summer monsoon.

TEMPERATURE AND PRECIPITATION

| | Temperature °F (°C) | | Altitude |
	January	July	ft (m)
Lhasa	28 (−2)	60 (16)	12,088 (3,685)
Hami	10 (−12)	82 (28)	2,421 (738)
Guangzhou	56 (13)	82 (28)	201 (63)
Beijing	23 (−5)	79 (26)	170 (52)
Shanghai	38 (3)	82 (28)	22 (7)
Harbin	−4 (−20)	73 (23)	564 (172)

| | Precipitation in (mm) | | |
	January	July	Year
Lhasa	0.01 (0.2)	4.8 (122)	17.9 (454)
Hami	0.1 (2)	0.2 (6)	1.3 (33)
Guangzhou	1.5 (39)	8.6 (220)	66.2 (1,681)
Beijing	0.1 (4)	9.5 (243)	26.9 (683)
Shanghai	1.8 (48)	5.8 (147)	44.4 (1,129)
Harbin	0.2 (4)	4.9 (127)	21.8 (554)

NATURAL HAZARDS

Large rivers in flood, earthquakes in interior and on Taiwan, typhoons in coastal areas, landslides

CLIMATE

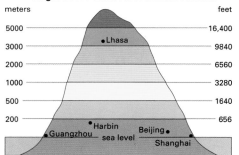

height above sea level of climate stations

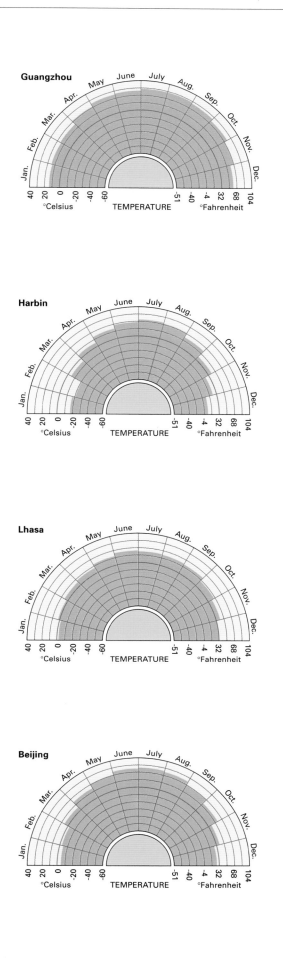

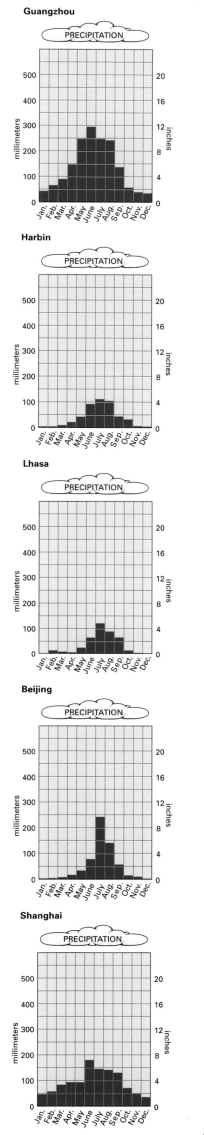

ENVIRONMENTAL ISSUES

The region's environmental problems arise largely from one factor—China's huge and still growing population. Attempts to tackle the problems are linked with the government's policy of reducing the overall population.

In recent decades pressure on the land from farming has contributed to the southward spread of the Gobi Desert. Farming land has been terraced since prehistoric times, but overirrigation in some areas has led to salinization and waterlogging, greatly reducing the productivity of the land. Only about 11 percent of China's forests remain. Also, the country has seen rapid growth of cities and industries since the 1970s, causing severe air and water pollution.

Those industries that still rely on fossil fuels also contribute to pollution. Coal-burning steam engines are still in production and use, and coal is also the chief freight carried on Chinese trains.

The village system of agriculture has encouraged the growth of small-scale environmental projects. These include the recycling of waste water and the conservation of naturally produced methane for domestic use.

POPULATION AND WEALTH

Population (in millions)	1,139.1
Population increase (annual population growth rate, % 1960–1990)	1.8
Energy use (gigajoules/person)	22
Real purchasing power (US$/person)	2,470

ENVIRONMENTAL INDICATORS

CO₂ emissions (mil. m.t. carbon/year)	380
Municipal waste (lbs/person/year)	N/A
Nuclear waste (cumulative m.t. heavy metal)	N/A
Artificial fertilizer use (lbs/acre/year)	20.5
Automobiles (per 1,000 population)	0.9
Access to safe drinking water (% population)	72

N/A = not available

MAJOR ENVIRONMENTAL PROBLEMS AND SOURCES

Air pollution: generally high, urban very high; acid rain prevalent; high greenhouse gas emissions
River/lake pollution: local/medium; *sources:* agricultural, sewage, soil erosion
Land pollution: local/medium; *sources:* industrial, agricultural
Land degradation: *types:* desertification, soil erosion, salinization, deforestation; *causes:* agriculture, industry, population pressure
Waste disposal problems: domestic; industrial
Resource problems: inadequate sanitation; land use competition; coastal flooding
Population problems: population explosion; urban overcrowding; inadequate health facilities

ENVIRONMENTAL ISSUES

Key environmental issues

- • major town or city
- ⬤ heavily polluted town or city
- ⌒ heavily polluted river

soil degradation

- severe
- high
- moderate
- low

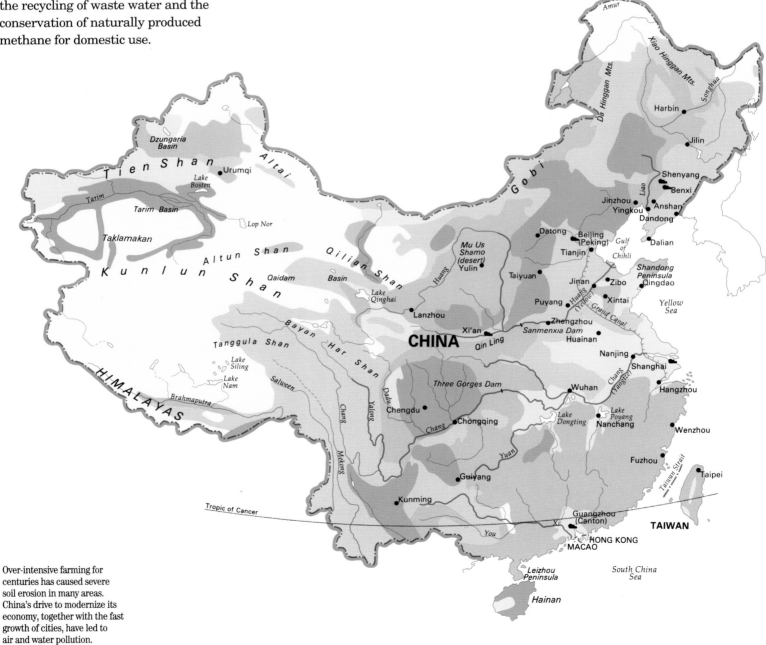

Over-intensive farming for centuries has caused severe soil erosion in many areas. China's drive to modernize its economy, together with the fast growth of cities, have led to air and water pollution.

POPULATION

China is the world's third largest country and the most populous. As early as 800 B.C., it had a population of nearly 14 million. Most of the people lived in country villages until the late twentieth century. Peasant life was almost unchanged through several thousand years of political change and war, flood, famine, and invasion. European traders boosted the growth of the coastal cities in the eighteenth century, but the interior remained thinly populated. Changing patterns of settlement during the twentieth century have been the result of government policy.

China's population doubled between 1949 and 1979, and in the 1980s, it passed the one billion mark. But as a result of government policies, the population growth rate fell from 3 percent a year in the 1960s to 1.5 percent in the 1980s.

The heaviest concentrations of people, and most of the major cities, are found on the east coast and along the Huang and Chang rivers, especially around Shanghai. Western China remains sparsely settled because of its harsh climate and terrain.

POPULATION

Total population of region (in millions)	1,162
Population density (persons per sq mi)	312.9
Population change (average annual percent 1960–1990) Urban Rural	+2.2 +1.7

URBAN POPULATION

As percentage of total population 1960 1990	19.0 21.4
Percentage in cities of more than 1 million	15.4

TEN LARGEST CITIES

	Population
Shanghai	12,320,000
Beijing †	9,750,000
Tianjin	7,790,000
Chongqing	6,511,000
Wenzhou	5,948,000
Guangzhou	5,669,000
Hangzhou	5,234,000
Shenyang	5,055,000
Dalian	4,619,000
Jinzhou	4,448,000

† denotes national capital

POPULATION

Population density

city populations
(National capital is underlined.)
◆ over 5,000,000
■ 1,000,000–5,000,000

persons per square mi	persons per square km
520	200
260	100
130	50
26	10
2.6	1

Western China, with its harsh climate and rugged terrain, contains few people. The areas of highest population density are on the east coast and along the Huang and Chang rivers, especially around Shanghai.

INDUSTRY

China has huge resources of both fuel and minerals and many industries. On a per capita basis, however, it is one of the world's poorer nations. Many of the resources are underdeveloped. They include coal, petroleum, natural gas, iron ore, bauxite, tin, antimony, and manganese in major reserves. There is great potential for hydroelectric power projects as the country has many large rivers and a hilly landscape.

The economy is centrally planned, with all industries owned by the state until very recently. Some private enterprise is now being encouraged. Petrochemical products account for nearly 25 percent of China's exports. Other major industries include iron and steel, cement, vehicles, fertilizers, food processing, clothing, and textiles.

The most recent government plans have promoted modernization of industry and reform of its organization. Joint ventures with other countries and foreign loans have been encouraged. Much of this overseas investment went into light industry and textiles. Special Economic Zones were created to foster industrial contact with the west.

INDUSTRIAL OUTPUT (US$ billion)

Total	Mining and Manufacturing	Average annual change since 1960
255.8	255.8	+14.3%

INDUSTRIAL WORKERS (millions)
(Figures in parentheses are percentages of total labor force.)

Total	Mining	Manufacturing	Construction
127.6	1.1 (0.2%)	100.4 (18.5%)	26.1 (4.7%)

MAJOR PRODUCTS (Figures in parentheses are percentages of world production.)

Energy and minerals	Output	Change since 1960
Coal (mil. m.t.)	1,040.0 (22.1%)	+281%
Oil (mil. barrels)	1,013.7 (4.5%)	+2,415%
Iron Ore (mil. m.t.)	77.2 (13.7%)	+175.5%
Tungsten (1,000 m.t.)	21.0 (51.2%)	No data

Manufactures		
Cotton fabrics (mil. sq yd)	25,435 (33.1%)	+179%
Silk fabrics (mil. sq yd)	2,257.3 (82.1%)	+231%
Shirts (mil.)*	189.1 (25%)	+88%
Nitrogenous fertilizers (mil. m.t.)	13.8 (14.9%)	+452%
Cement (mil. m.t.)	228.2 (20.8%)	+1,567%
Steel (mil. m.t.)	62.2 (8.5%)	+345%
Sewing machines (mil.)	9.8 (55.5%)	+504%
Televisions (mil.)	27.3 (24.9%)	N/A
Bicycles (mil.)	44.4 (44.3%)	+685%

* Hong Kong only
N/A means production had not begun in 1960.

INDUSTRY

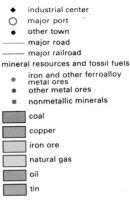

Resources and industry

- ◆ industrial center
- ○ major port
- ● other town
- —— major road
- —— major railroad

mineral resources and fossil fuels
- ● iron and other ferroalloy metal ores
- ● other metal ores
- ■ nonmetallic minerals

- coal
- copper
- iron ore
- natural gas
- oil
- tin

China's resources include coal, oil, and natural gas, together with many metals and nonmetallic minerals. The smaller territories have few resources but are extremely important for manufacturing.

AGRICULTURE

China covers only 7 percent of the world's land area, but succeeds in feeding its people, amounting to 20 percent of the world's population. Some 80 percent of people belong to peasant or rural households, and traditional farming life continues, despite reforms introduced by communism since 1949.

Much of China, particularly in the north and west, will only grow scrub and provides poor pasture. Only 10 percent of the land can be used for growing crops, mainly in the valleys and plains in the east and south.

The main crops are wheat and rice. Small family plots have always been used to grow vegetables, a key part of the Chinese diet. Pigs, chickens, and ducks are also raised in the villages. Water control is essential to prevent flooding and to provide irrigation in the plains, while in the foothills, terracing conserves both soil and water.

The northern plains also produce corn, millet, and potatoes. South of the Chang River, paddy rice predominates. Tea, tobacco, and mulberry trees (for silkworm production) are also commercially important.

LAND (million acres)

Total	Agricultural	Arable	Forest/woodland
2,305 (100%)	1,022 (45%)	232 (10%)	289 (12%)

FARMERS

451 million people employed in agriculture (69% of workforce)
0.49 acres of arable land per person employed in agriculture

MAJOR CROPS

	Area mil. acres	Yield 100lbs/acre	Production mil. m.t.	Change since 1963
Paddy rice	80.8	48.2	177.0 (38)	+106%
Wheat	71.7	27.2	30.5 (131)	+295%
Corn	50.1	35.2	80.1 (17)	+254%
Roots/tubers	22.7	141	146.1 (25)	+32%
Soybeans	21	12.8	12.2 (12)	+14%
Rapeseed	13	11.1	6.6 (29)	+538%
Cotton	11.8	7.8	4.2 (26)	+246%
Millet/sorghum	11.3	19.6	10.1 (11)	−41%
Pulses	10.8	10.7	5.3 (10)	+27%
Vegetables	—	—	110.0 (26)	+134%

MAJOR LIVESTOCK

	Number in mil.	Production mil. m.t.	Change since 1963
Pigs	344.6 (41)	—	+75%
Sheep/goats	166.5 (10)	—	+41%
Cattle	71.3 (6)	—	+16%
Milk	—	3.4 (1)	+25%
Fish catch	—	9.6 (10)	—

FOOD SECURITY (grain exports minus imports)

mil. m.t.	% domestic production	% world trade
−8.6	2	4

Numbers in parentheses are percentages of world total.

AGRICULTURE

Agricultural zones

- arable
- pasture with some arable
- rough grazing
- woods and forest
- nonagricultural land

▲ mountain peak (ft)
▼ depression (ft)

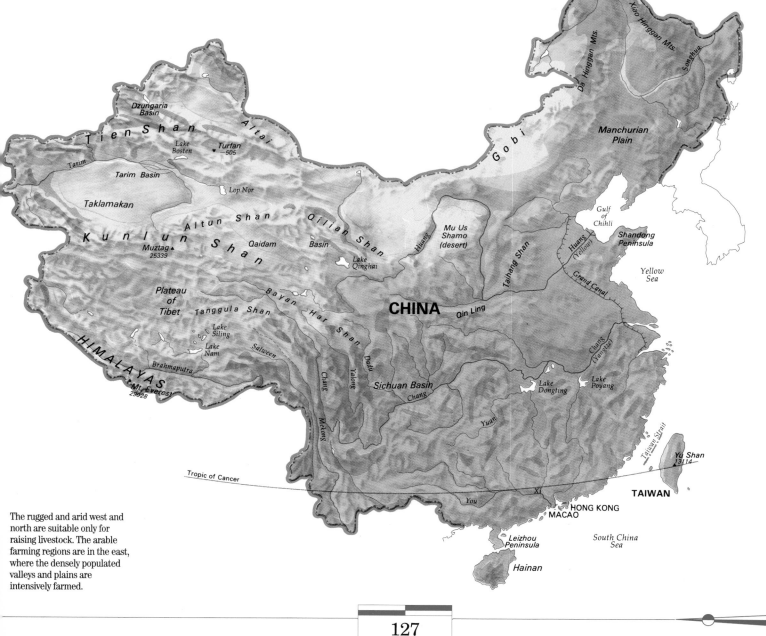

The rugged and arid west and north are suitable only for raising livestock. The arable farming regions are in the east, where the densely populated valleys and plains are intensively farmed.

SOUTHEAST ASIA

Southeast Asia includes a peninsula and a vast archipelago, comprising over 20,000 islands. The region contains two zones where volcanic eruptions and earthquakes are caused by collisions between the huge plates that form the earth's crust. One zone runs east-west through southern Indonesia and the other from eastern Indonesia to the Philippines.

The region is humid and tropical. The south has rainfall throughout the year, but the north has a monsoon climate, with most rain coming in the summer months (June through August).

Small groups of Negritos, descendants of the earliest inhabitants, live in remote areas, but most Southeast Asians are of Malay or Chinese descent. The diversity of cultures shows how many outside influences have affected the region. Of the region's ten countries, only Thailand remained free. Wars in Europe marred the area's chances for independence, and the postcolonial years have been marked by civil wars and political instability. Agriculture is the main activity. Industry is limited to a few cities, such as Manila and Singapore.

Southeast Asia lies between the eastern end of the Himalayas and northern Australia. Most of the region lies on the southeastern edge of the huge Eurasian plate and is bordered by deep ocean trenches. As the plates descend into the mantle, their edges melt, forming the molten rock that fuels Southeast Asia's volcanoes.

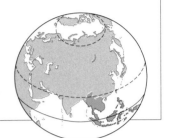

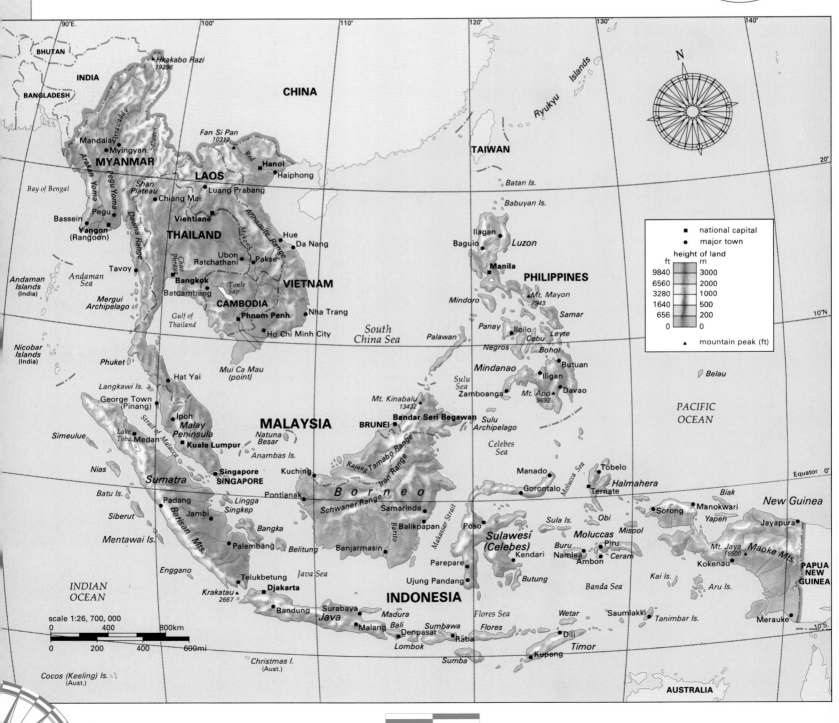

THE POLITICAL AND CULTURAL WORLD

After the defeat of Japan in 1945, communist forces began a long struggle for power in Southeast Asia. The British defeated them in Malaya, but after a long struggle in Vietnam, involving first France and then the United States, the communists emerged victorious in 1975. Cambodia and Laos also became communist countries.

In Myanmar (formerly Burma), Indonesia, and Thailand, army rulers have suppressed political parties, while Brunei's sultan has allowed no opposition to his government. The only countries with elements of parliamentary democracy are Malaysia, Singapore, and the Philippines.

COUNTRIES IN THE REGION

Brunei, Cambodia, Indonesia, Laos, Malaysia, Myanmar, Philippines, Singapore, Thailand, Vietnam

LANGUAGE

Countries with one official language Khmer: Cambodia; Indonesian: Indonesia; Bahasa Malaysian: Malaysia; Myanmar: Myanmar; Lao: Laos; Thai: Thailand; Vietnamese: Vietnam
Countries with two official languages English, Malay: Brunei; English, Pilipino: Philippines
Country with four official languages Bahasa Malay, Chinese, English, Tamil: Singapore

RELIGION

Country with one major religion Cambodia (B)
Countries with two major religions Laos (B,IR); Thailand (B,I)
Countries with three or more major religions Vietnam (B,C,T); Indonesia (B,C,H,I); Brunei, Myanmar (B,C,IR,I); Philippines (B,I,P,RC); Singapore, Malaysia (B,C,H,I,T)

Key: B-Buddhist, C-various Christian, H-Hindu, I-Islam, IR-indigenous religions, P-Protestant, RC-Roman Catholic, T-Taoist

ECONOMIC INDICATORS

	Singapore	Thailand	Indonesia
GDP(US$ billions)	34.6	80.17	107.29
GNP per capita (US$)	11,160	1,420	570
Annual rate of growth of GDP, 1980–1990	6.4%	7.6%	5.5%
Manufacturing as % of GDP	18%	26%	20%
Central government spending as % of GNP	23%	15%	20%
Merchandise exports (US$ billions)	52.6	22.9	25.7
Merchandise imports (US$ billions)	60.5	32.9	21.8
% of GNP received as development aid	–	1.0%	1.6%
Total external debt as % of GNP	–	32.6%	66.4%

WELFARE INDICATORS

Infant mortality rate (per 1,000 live births)	Singapore	Thailand	Indonesia
1965	26	145	128
1990	7	44	61
Daily food supply available (calories per capita, 1989)	3,198	3,121	2,750
Population per physician (1984)	1,410	2,150	9,410
Teacher-pupil ratio (elementary school, 1989)	1 : 26	1 : 18	1 : 23

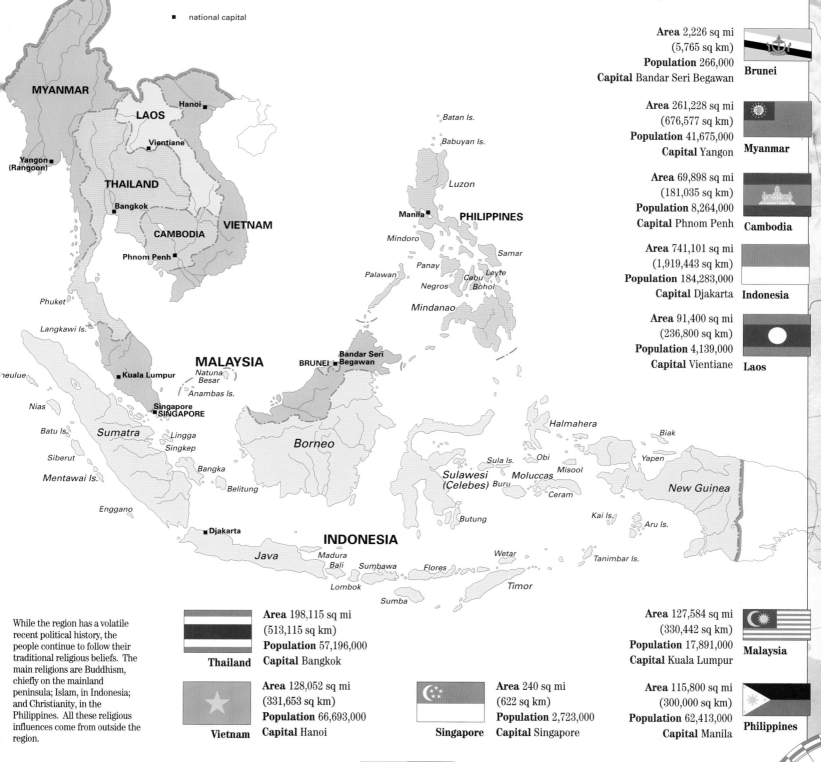

■ national capital

Area 2,226 sq mi
(5,765 sq km)
Population 266,000
Capital Bandar Seri Begawan — Brunei

Area 261,228 sq mi
(676,577 sq km)
Population 41,675,000
Capital Yangon — Myanmar

Area 69,898 sq mi
(181,035 sq km)
Population 8,264,000
Capital Phnom Penh — Cambodia

Area 741,101 sq mi
(1,919,443 sq km)
Population 184,283,000
Capital Djakarta — Indonesia

Area 91,400 sq mi
(236,800 sq km)
Population 4,139,000
Capital Vientiane — Laos

While the region has a volatile recent political history, the people continue to follow their traditional religious beliefs. The main religions are Buddhism, chiefly on the mainland peninsula; Islam, in Indonesia; and Christianity, in the Philippines. All these religious influences come from outside the region.

Area 198,115 sq mi
(513,115 sq km)
Population 57,196,000
Capital Bangkok — Thailand

Area 128,052 sq mi
(331,653 sq km)
Population 66,693,000
Capital Hanoi — Vietnam

Area 240 sq mi
(622 sq km)
Population 2,723,000
Capital Singapore — Singapore

Area 127,584 sq mi
(330,442 sq km)
Population 17,891,000
Capital Kuala Lumpur — Malaysia

Area 115,800 sq mi
(300,000 sq km)
Population 62,413,000
Capital Manila — Philippines

HABITATS

Rain forest flourishes in the south, with deciduous forest and tropical savanna grassland in the north. The fertile lowlands and broad deltas of the great rivers on the mainland peninsula, including the Irrawaddy, Mekong, and Salween, are cultivated.

LAND

Major features mountain chains and flood plains, deltas of great rivers in north of region, mountainous and volcanic islands of Malaysia, Indonesia, Philippines, world's largest archipelago

WATER

Longest river Mekong, 2,600 mi (4,180 km)
Largest lake Tonle Sap, 3,860 sq mi (10,000 sq km)

NOTABLE THREATENED SPECIES

Mammals pileated gibbon (Hylobates pileatus), orangutan (Pongo pygmaeus), flat-headed cat (Felis planiceps), Malayan tapir (Tapirus indicus), Javan rhinoceros (Rhinoceros sondaicus), kouprey (Bos sauveli), tamaraw (Bubalus mindorensis)
Birds Philippine eagle (Pithecophaga jefferyi), giant ibis (Pseudibis gigantea), Gurney's pitta (Pitta gurneyi), salmon-crested cockatoo (Cacatua moluccensis)
Plants Allobunkillia species; titan arum (Amorphopallus titanumm); umbrella leaf palm (Johannesteijsmannia lanceolata); Maingaya species; Maxburretia rupicola; pitcher plant (Nepenthes) – Mount Kinabulu species; Rothschild's slipper orchid (Paphiopedilum rothschildianum); Phyllagathis magnifica; Rafflesia species; jade vine (Strongylodon macrobotrys)
Others river terrapin (Batagur baska), false gharial (Tomistoma schlegelii), Komodo dragon (Varanus komodoensis)

CLIMATE

Malaysia and Indonesia, which straddle the equator, have a tropical climate, also called a rain-forest climate. The coastal areas in the north of the region have a marked summer monsoon. Other inland areas in the northwest have a distinct dry season in winter.

TEMPERATURE AND PRECIPITATION

	Temperature °F (°C)		Altitude
	January	July	ft (m)
Yangon	77 (25)	81 (27)	19 (6)
Ho Chi Minh City	79 (26)	81 (27)	29 (9)
Manila	77 (25)	82 (28)	45 (14)
Cameron Highlands	64 (18)	64 (18)	4,753 (1,449)
Singapore	79 (26)	81 (27)	33 (10)
Djakarta	79 (26)	81 (27)	19 (6)

	Precipitation in (mm)		
	January	July	Year
Yangon	0.1 (3)	22.8 (580)	103.1 (2,618)
Ho Chi Minh City	0.5 (15)	12.3 (315)	71.2 (1,808)
Manila	0.9 (23)	17.0 (432)	70.5 (1,791)
Cameron Highlands	6.6 (168)	4.8 (122)	104.0 (2,640)
Singapore	9.9 (252)	6.7 (170)	89.8 (2,282)
Djakarta	11.8 (300)	2.5 (64)	69.1 (1,755)

ENVIRONMENTAL ISSUES

Natural hazards include earthquakes, hurricanes (locally called typhoons), floods, and volcanic eruptions. But human activity, including the rapid destruction of forests, the population explosion, and urban expansion are causing new problems.

POPULATION AND WEALTH

	Highest	Middle	Lowest
Population increase (annual population growth rate, % 1960–1990)	2.8 (Philippines)	2.2 (Laos)	1.4 (Cambodia)
Energy use (gigajoules/person)	140 (Singapore)	8 (Philippines)	1 (Cambodia)
Real purchasing power (US$/person)	10,540 (Singapore)	2,170 (Philippines)	660 (Myanmar)

ENVIRONMENTAL INDICATORS

CO_2 emissions (mil. m.t. carbon/year)	140 (Indonesia)	40 (Philippines)	5 (Cambodia)
Deforestation ('000s acres/ year 1980s)	2,273 (Indonesia)	427 (Vietnam)	74 (Cambodia)
Artificial fertilizer use (lbs/acre/year)	1,636 (Singapore)	56 (Vietnam)	0.17 (Cambodia)
Automobiles (per 1,000 population)	87 (Singapore)	6 (Philippines)	0.6 (Indonesia)
Access to safe drinking water (% population)	78 (Singapore)	51 (Malaysia)	30 (Myanmar)

MAJOR ENVIRONMENTAL PROBLEMS AND SOURCES

Air pollution: urban high; high greenhouse gas emissions
Marine/coastal pollution: medium; *sources:* industrial, agricultural, sewage, oil
Land degradation: *types:* soil erosion, deforestation, habitat destruction; *causes:* agriculture, industry, population pressure
Resource problems: fuelwood shortage; inadequate drinking water and sanitation
Population problems: population explosion; urban overcrowding; inadequate health facilities
Major events: Burkit Suharto (1982–1983), fire in coal seams and peat; Bangkok (1991), chemical explosion and fire

HABITATS

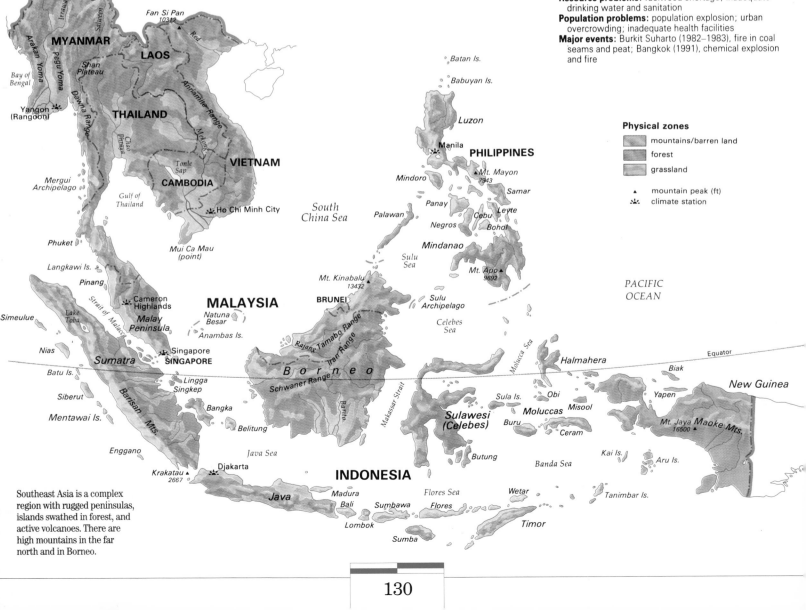

Southeast Asia is a complex region with rugged peninsulas, islands swathed in forest, and active volcanoes. There are high mountains in the far north and in Borneo.

Physical zones
- mountains/barren land
- forest
- grassland

▲ mountain peak (ft)
☀ climate station

ENVIRONMENTAL ISSUES

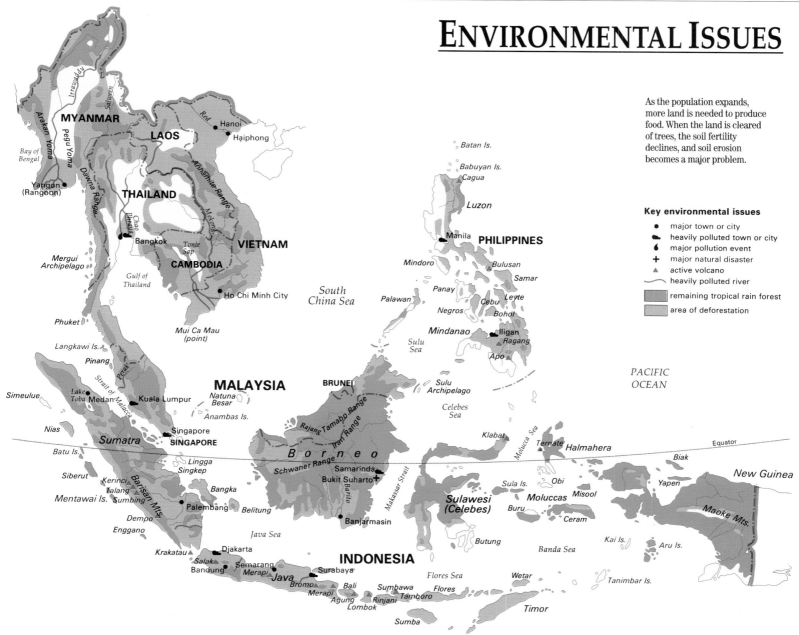

As the population expands, more land is needed to produce food. When the land is cleared of trees, the soil fertility declines, and soil erosion becomes a major problem.

Key environmental issues

- • major town or city
- 🖑 heavily polluted town or city
- 🝆 major pollution event
- ✛ major natural disaster
- ▲ active volcano
- 〰 heavily polluted river
- ▨ remaining tropical rain forest
- ▨ area of deforestation

Map labels:

MYANMAR, LAOS, THAILAND, VIETNAM, CAMBODIA, Hanoi, Haiphong, Yangon (Rangoon), Bangkok, Ho Chi Minh City, Irrawaddy, Salween, Red, Annamite Range, Mekong, Dawna Range, Pegu Yoma, Arakan Yoma, Chao Phraya, Tonle Sap, Bay of Bengal, Gulf of Thailand, Mergui Archipelago, Phuket, Mui Ca Mau (point), Langkawi Is.

Batan Is., Babuyan Is., Cagua, Luzon, Manila, PHILIPPINES, Mindoro, Bulusan, Samar, Panay, Leyte, Cebu, Negros, Bohol, Mindanao, Iligan, Ragang, Apo, South China Sea, Sulu Sea, Sulu Archipelago, Celebes Sea, PACIFIC OCEAN

Pinang, Simeulue, Lake Toba, Medan, Kuala Lumpur, MALAYSIA, Natuna Besar, BRUNEI, Anambas Is., Nias, Siberut, Kerinci, Talang, Sumbing, Barisan Mts., Sumatra, Batu Is., Singapore, SINGAPORE, Lingga, Singkep, Bangka, Belitung, Palembang, Mentawai Is., Dempo, Enggano, Strait of Malacca, Perak, Borneo, Rajang, Tamabo Range, Iran Range, Schwaner Range, Barito, Samarinda, Bukit Suharto, Banjarmasin, Klabat, Ternate, Halmahera, Biak, Yapen, New Guinea, Maoke Mts., Sula Is., Obi, Misool, Sulawesi (Celebes), Moluccas, Buru, Ceram, Butung, Banda Sea, Kai Is., Aru Is., Molucca Sea, Makassar Strait, Equator, Java Sea, Krakatau, Djakarta, Salak, Bandung, Semarang, Merapi, Java, Surabaya, Bali, Bromo, Merapi, Agung, Lombok, Rinjani, Sumbawa, Tambora, Flores, Sumba, Flores Sea, Wetar, Tanimbar Is., Timor, INDONESIA

CLIMATE

height above sea level of climate stations

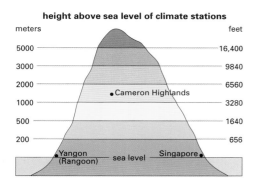

meters		feet
5000		16,400
3000		9840
2000		6560
1000	Cameron Highlands	3280
500		1640
200		656
	Yangon (Rangoon) sea level Singapore	

Yangon (Rangoon)

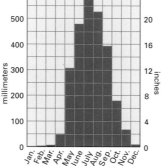

PRECIPITATION

Cameron Highlands

PRECIPITATION

Singapore

PRECIPITATION

Yangon (Rangoon)

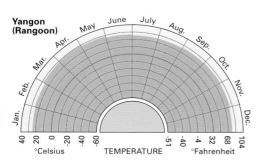

TEMPERATURE

Cameron Highlands

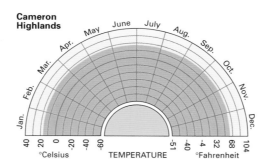

TEMPERATURE

Singapore

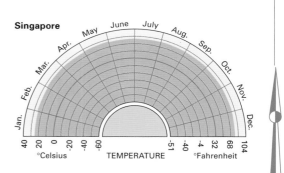

TEMPERATURE

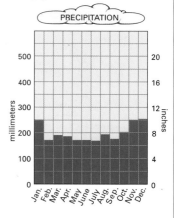

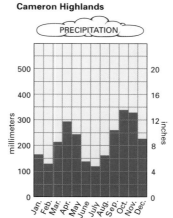

POPULATION

The mountains and forest areas in Southeast Asia are thinly populated. Most people live on the cultivated lowlands and around the leading port cities. The percentage of people living in urban areas is low, but the cities are growing at a rapid rate.

POPULATION

Total population of region (millions)	454.6
Population density (persons per sq mi)	470.9
Population change (average annual percent 1960–1990)	
Urban	+4.5
Rural	+2.0

TEN LARGEST CITIES

	Country	Population
Djakarta †	Indonesia	7,886,000
Manila †	Philippines	6,720,000
Bangkok †	Thailand	5,609,000
Ho Chi Minh City	Vietnam	3,420,000
Singapore †	Singapore	2,704,000
Hanoi †	Vietnam	2,571,000
Yangon †	Myanmar	2,513,000
Surabaya	Indonesia	2,224,000
Medan	Indonesia	1,806,000
Quezon City	Philippines	1,546,000

† denotes national capital

INDUSTRY

Political instability has restricted development in Southeast Asia. Some countries, such as Laos and Cambodia, are among the world's poorest. But Malaysia is developing quickly, and Singapore has become a prosperous industrial center.

INDUSTRIAL OUTPUT (US$ billion)

Total	Mining	Manufacturing	Average annual change since 1960
89.5	16.7	68.4	+7.2%

MAJOR PRODUCTS (Figures in parentheses are percentages of world production.)

Energy and minerals	Output	Change since 1960
Coal (mil. m.t.)	14.3 (0.3%)	+610%
Oil (mil. barrels)	785.8 (3.5%)	+312%
Natural gas (billion cu meters)	78.9 (4.1%)	+1073%
Tin (1,000 m.t.)	92.3 (46.0%)	-22.4%
Nickel (1,000 m.t.)	63.4 (7.8%)	+199%

Manufactures		
Processed palm and coconut oil (mil. m.t.)	6.5 (35.3%)	+413%
Canned fruits (1,000 m.t.)	665.0 (12.9%)	+302%
Lumber (mill cu ft)*	688.6 (15.6%)	+123%
Natural and synthetic rubber (mil. m.t.)	3.9 (27.1%)	+54%
Rubber footwear (mil. pairs)	47.2 (19.9%)	N/A
Jet fuels (mil. m.t.)**	7.8 (5.5%)	N/A
Cement (mil. m.t.)	36.3 (3.3%)	+1,628%
Radios and sound recorders (mil.)	57.7 (20.3%)	N/A

* Hardwood timber only (coniferous excluded)
** Mainly Singapore
N/A means production had not begun in 1960.

AGRICULTURE

Agriculture employs about half of the people of Southeast Asia. The region has large commercial plantations growing such things as oil palms, pineapples, rubber, and sugarcane, together with small plots worked by subsistence farmers to feed their families.

LAND (million acres)

Total	Agricultural	Arable	Forest/woodland
1,077 (100%)	222 (21%)	145 (13%)	593 (55%)

FARMERS

97 million people employed in agriculture (54% of workforce)
1.48 acres of arable land per person employed in agriculture

MAJOR CROPS

	Area mil. acres	Yield 100lbs/acre	Production mil. m.t.	Change since 1963
Paddy rice	86.9	25.4	100.2 (22)	+103%
Corn	20.5	14.1	13.2 (3)	+140%
Cassava	8.4	103.8	39.3 (29)	+153%
Pulses	4.9	6.9	1.5 (3)	+126%
Soybeans	3.9	9.1	1.6 (2)	+255%
Sugarcane	3.2	489	71.2 (7)	+143%
Bananas	—	—	9.7 (15)	+128%
Other fruit	—	—	14.3 (6)	+196%

MAJOR LIVESTOCK

	Number in mil.	Production mil. m.t.	Change since 1963
Cattle	28.9 (2)	—	+36%
Fish catch	—	9.0 (10)	

FOOD SECURITY (grain exports minus imports)

mil. m.t.	% domestic production	% world trade
+1.5	1	1

Numbers in parentheses are percentages of world total.

POPULATION

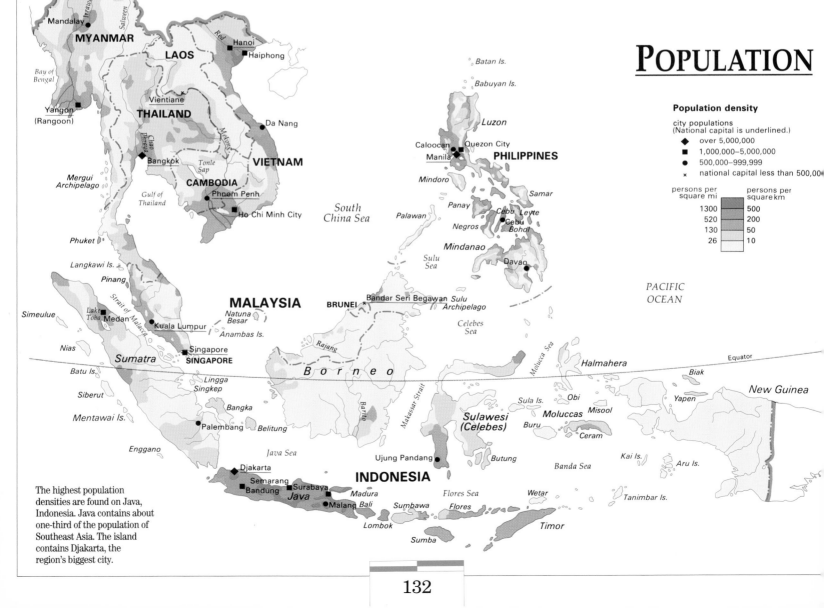

Population density

city populations
(National capital is underlined.)

◆ over 5,000,000
■ 1,000,000–5,000,000
● 500,000–999,999
× national capital less than 500,000

persons per square mi	persons per square km
1300	500
520	200
130	50
26	10

The highest population densities are found on Java, Indonesia. Java contains about one-third of the population of Southeast Asia. The island contains Djakarta, the region's biggest city.

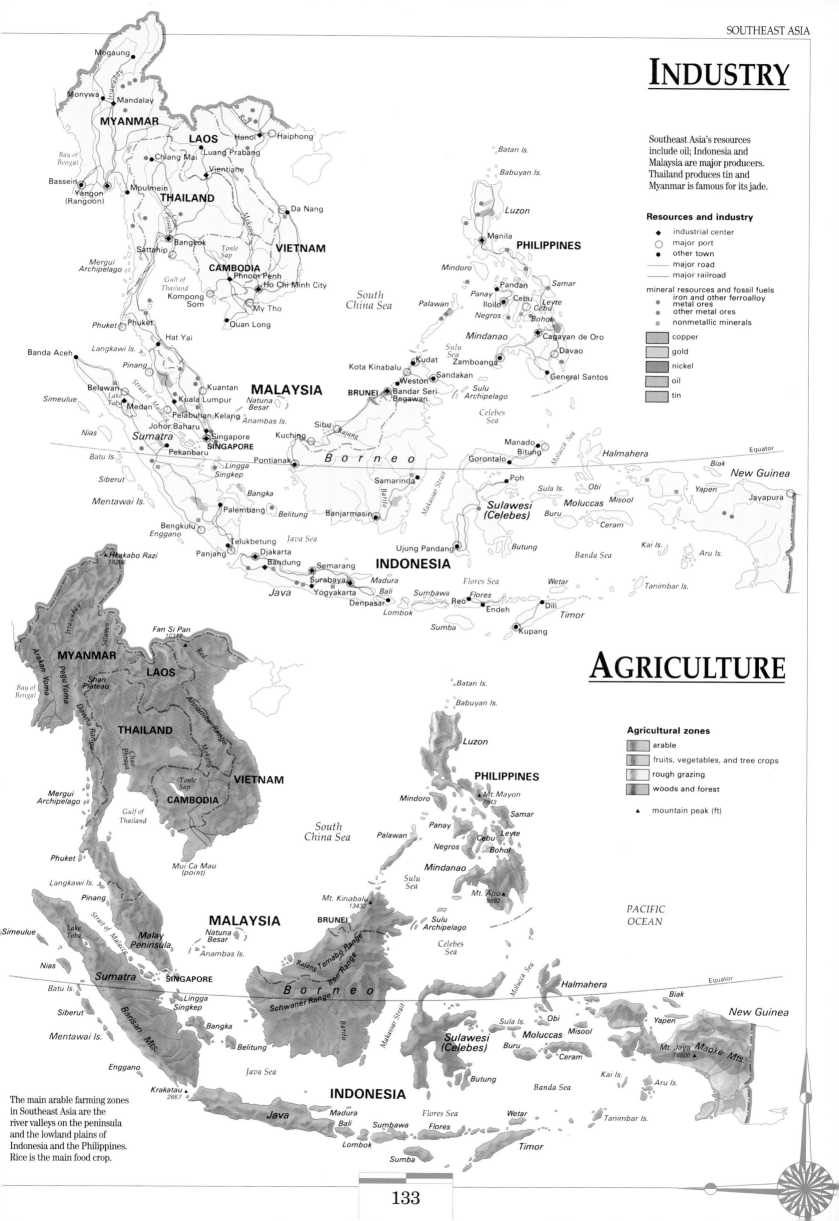

JAPAN AND KOREA

Rugged mountains interspersed with lowlands dominate the landscapes of Japan and Korea. The Korean mountains are old and stable, but most of Japan's highest peaks are volcanic. Japan lies in an unstable zone. Earthquakes and tsunamis (powerful sea waves triggered by earth movements) are constant threats. The region has a monsoon climate, with hot, wet summers and cold winters.

Until fairly recent times, Japan and Korea were cut off from the rest of the world. But from the late 1860s, Japan began to modernize and become a world power. Its defeat in World War II proved a challenge. With help from the United States, it has become a major industrial power. Korea, which had been occupied by Japan from 1910 to 1945, is now split into free-enterprise South Korea and the communist North.

Japan and Korea occupy a frontier zone between Eurasia and the Pacific Ocean. Japan forms part of the Pacific "ring of fire," a zone of crustal instability that encircles the Pacific Ocean. Japan has 60 active volcanoes and has over a thousand earthquakes every year.

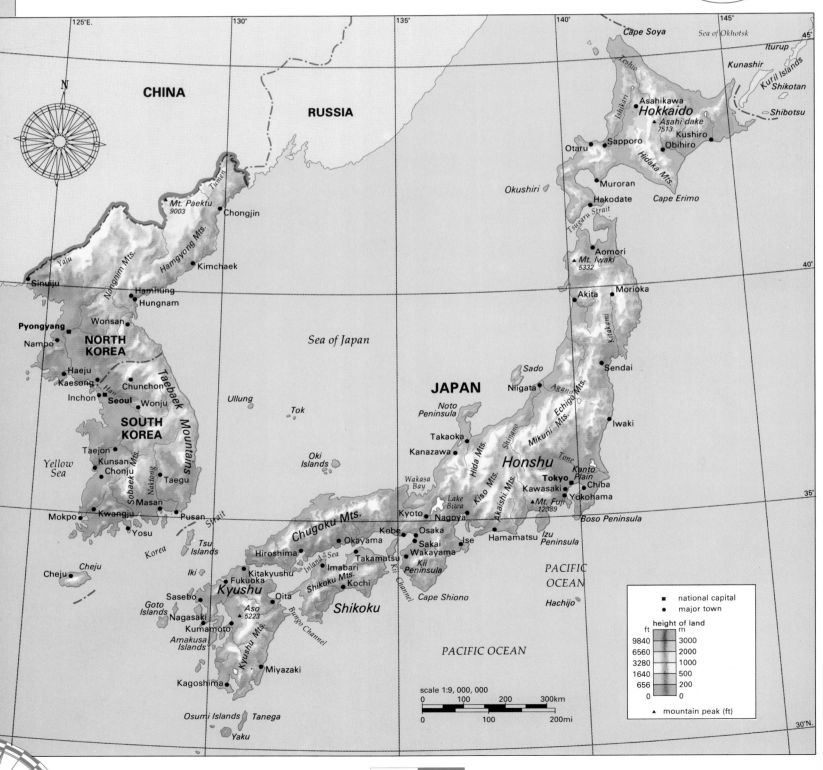

THE POLITICAL AND CULTURAL WORLD

Before World War II, Japan was a military dictatorship. After the war, the Allied forces occupied the country from 1945 to 1952. During this time a new constitution was adopted in which power was vested in a prime minister and cabinet, who were answerable to the Diet (parliament). The emperor was subsequently given a symbolic role in the country's leadership.

Korea was split into two parts in 1945. Separate governments for North and South Korea were set up in 1947. This action triggered the Korean War (1948–1953). In recent years, talks have been held about reunification, but little progress has been made.

ECONOMIC INDICATORS: 1990

	Japan	S. Korea
GDP (US$ billions)	2,942.89	236.4
GNP per capita (US$)	25,430	5,400
Annual rate of growth of GDP, 1980–1990	4.1%	9.7%
Manufacturing as % of GDP	29.0%	31.0%
Central government spending as % of GNP	17.0%	16.0%
Merchandise exports (US$ billions)	280.4	65.0
Merchandise imports (US$ billions)	216.8	69.8
% of GNP donated as development aid	0.31%	N/A

WELFARE INDICATORS

	Japan	S. Korea
Infant mortality rate (per 1,000 live births)		
1965	18	62
1990	5	17
Daily food supply available (calories per capita, 1989)	2,956	2,852
Population per physician (1984)	660	1,160
Teacher-pupil ratio (elementary school, 1989)	1 : 21	1 : 36

Area 145,875 sq mi
(377,815 sq km)
Population 123,460,000
Capital Tokyo
Currency 1 yen
¥= 100 sen

Japan

Area 47,300 sq mi
(122,400 sq km)
Population 21,773,000
Capital Pyongyang
Currency 1 won
(W) = 100 chon

North Korea

Area 38,291 sq mi
(99,173 sq km)
Population 42,793,000
Capital Seoul
Currency 1 won
(W) = 100 chon

South Korea

Japan is a constitutional monarchy. An emperor is the ceremonial head of state. The country is divided into 47 prefectures. South Korea is a republic, divided into nine provinces and five cities with the rank of province. North Korea is a communist state, divided into nine provinces and four city areas.

- ■ national capital

HABITATS

Both Japan and Korea are largely mountainous, with uplands extending to the sea and with few large coastal lowlands. There are extensive forests throughout the region on the mountain slopes and cultivation of crops in the fertile valleys.

LAND

Area 232,141 sq mi (601,241 sq km)
Highest point Mount Fuji, 12,388 ft (3,776 m)
Lowest point sea level
Major features Mountains of moderate height cover most of Japan and Korea; over 3,900 islands in Japan

WATER

Longest river Yalu, 503 mi (810 km)
Largest basin Yalu, 24,000 sq mi (63,000 sq km)
Highest average flow Yalu, 19,000 cu ft/sec (526 cu m/sec)
Largest lake Biwa, 268 sq mi (695 sq km)

NOTABLE THREATENED SPECIES

Mammals Amami rabbit (Pentalagus furnessi), Iriomote cat (Felis iriomotensis)
Birds short-tailed albatross (Diomeda albatrus), Okinawa rail (Rallus okinawae), Amami thrush (Zoothera amami)
Plants Korean fir (Abies koreana); Arisaema heterocephalum; Chrysanthemum zawadskii; Cyclobalanopsis hondae; Cymbidium koran; Euphrasia omiensis; Fritillaria shikokiana; Gentiana yakusimensis; Magnolia pseudokobus; Rhododendron mucronulatum
Others Japanese giant salamander (Andrias japonicus), Tokyo bitterling (Tanakia tanago)

CLIMATE

During the winter, North Korea and northern Japan are cooled by polar air, producing low temperatures and heavy snowfalls. In the summer, wet monsoon winds bring hot and humid weather, especially in the south. Typhoons, or hurricanes, often strike eastern Japan.

TEMPERATURE AND PRECIPITATION

	Temperature °F (°C) January	July	Altitude ft (m)
Wonsan	25 (−4)	73 (23)	121 (37)
Seoul	23 (−5)	75 (25)	282 (86)
Sapporo	21 (−6)	68 (20)	59 (18)
Niigata	36 (2)	75 (24)	13 (4)
Tokyo	37 (3)	77 (25)	20 (6)

	Precipitation in (mm) January	July	Year
Wonsan	1.2 (31)	10.7 (273)	51.6 (1,310)
Seoul	1.2 (31)	14.7 (376)	49.5 (1,258)
Sapporo	4.4 (111)	3.9 (100)	44.7 (1,136)
Niigata	7.6 (194)	7.6 (193)	72.5 (1,841)
Tokyo	1.9 (48)	5.6 (142)	61.5 (1,563)

NATURAL HAZARDS

Earthquakes and associated sea waves (tsunami) in Japan, floods, typhoons, landslides

ENVIRONMENTAL ISSUES

Concern about environmental issues is increasing, especially in Japan. Most problems are caused by overcrowding and the rapid development of industry, such as Minamata disease, caused by eating seafood that had absorbed mercury from toxic industrial wastes.

POPULATION AND WEALTH

	Japan	N. Korea	S. Korea
Population increase (annual population growth rate, % 1960–1990)	0.9	2.4	1.8
Energy use (gigajoules/person)	110	79	52

ENVIRONMENTAL INDICATORS

CO_2 emissions (mil. m.t. carbon/year)	220	20	29
Municipal waste (lbs/person/year)	758	N/A	873
Nuclear waste (cumulative m.t. heavy metal)	5,600	0	700
Artificial fertilizer use (lbs/acre/year)	386	278	376

MAJOR ENVIRONMENTAL PROBLEMS AND SOURCES

Air pollution: locally high, urban high; acid rain prevalent; high greenhouse gas emissions
River/lake pollution: medium; sources: industrial, agricultural, sewage
Marine/coastal pollution: medium; sources: industrial, agricultural, sewage, oil
Population problems: urban overcrowding

HABITATS

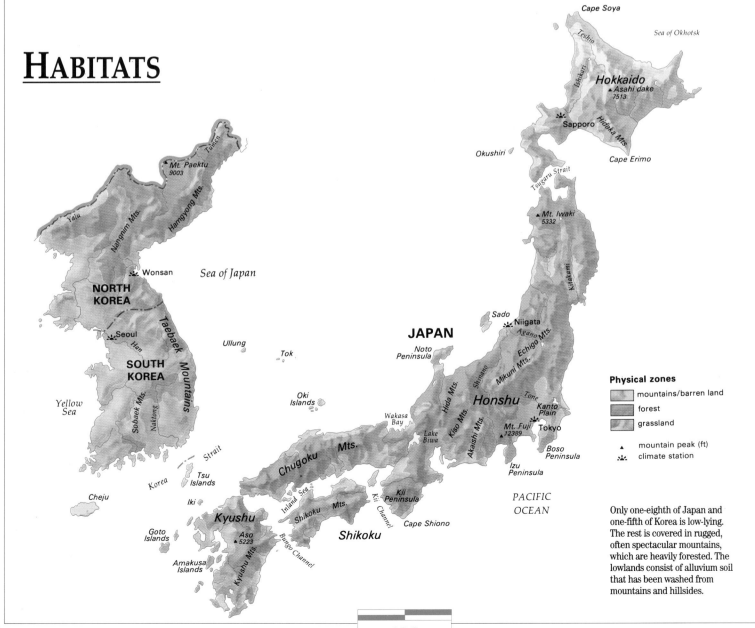

Physical zones
- mountains/barren land
- forest
- grassland
- ▲ mountain peak (ft)
- �▲ climate station

Only one-eighth of Japan and one-fifth of Korea is low-lying. The rest is covered in rugged, often spectacular mountains, which are heavily forested. The lowlands consist of alluvium soil that has been washed from mountains and hillsides.

ENVIRONMENTAL ISSUES

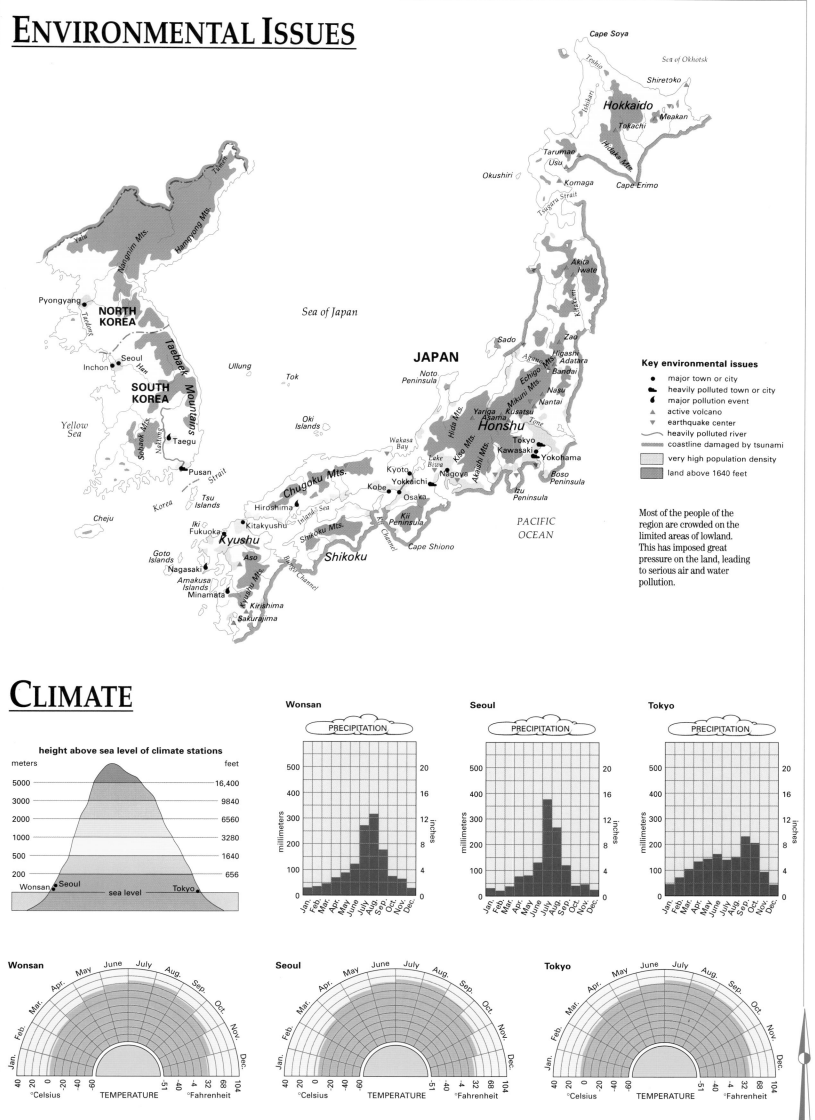

Key environmental issues

- • major town or city
- ✎ heavily polluted town or city
- ◗ major pollution event
- ▲ active volcano
- ▽ earthquake center
- ～ heavily polluted river
- ▬ coastline damaged by tsunami
- ▢ very high population density
- ▨ land above 1640 feet

Most of the people of the region are crowded on the limited areas of lowland. This has imposed great pressure on the land, leading to serious air and water pollution.

CLIMATE

height above sea level of climate stations

POPULATION

Between 1870 and 1970, Japan's population rose from 30 million to over 100 million. The annual growth rate has now dropped, averaging 0.5 percent between 1980 and 1991. The growth rate in North and South Korea is also below the world average of 1.7 percent.

POPULATION

Total population of region (in millions)	190
Population density (persons per sq mi)	834
Population change (average annual percent 1960–1990)	
Urban	+2.1
Rural	-0.2

URBAN POPULATION

As percentage of total population	
1960	62.5
1990	74.2
Percentage in cities of more than 1 million	14.2

TEN LARGEST CITIES

	Country	Population
Tokyo †	Japan	11,936,000
Seoul †	South Korea	9,646,000
Pusan	South Korea	3,517,000
Yokohama	Japan	3,220,000
Pyongyang †	North Korea	2,639,000
Osaka	Japan	2,624,000
Nagoya	Japan	2,155,000
Taegu	South Korea	2,031,000
Sapporo	Japan	1,672,000
Kyoto	Japan	1,461,000

† denotes national capital

INDUSTRY

The region has limited natural resources, and the countries import many raw materials. And by developing modern technology, they have become world leaders in manufacturing. Their technical expertise ensures the quality and saleability of their products.

INDUSTRIAL OUTPUT (US$ billion)

Total	Mining	Manufacturing	Average annual change since 1960
1,100.9	19.4	1,081.5	+8.0%

INDUSTRIAL WORKERS (in millions)
(Figures in parentheses are percentages of total labor force.)

Total	Mining	Manufacturing	Construction
29.6	0.2 (0.23%)	22.6 (25.6%)	6.8 (7.7%)

MAJOR PRODUCTS (Figures in parentheses are percentages of world production.)

Energy and minerals	Output	Change since 1960
Coal (mil. m.t.)	86.9 (1.8%)	+29.5%
Limestone (mil. m.t.)	231.0 (9%)	+407%
Graphite (1,000 m.t.)	129.8 (12.7%)	+36%

Manufactures		
Steel (mil. m.t.)	129.1 (17.7%)	+481.3%
Automobiles (mil.)	17.2 (36.2%)	+2,163%
Ships (mil. gross m.t.)	24.1 (57.7%)	+590%
Excavators (1,000)	115.3 (65.2%)	No data
Clocks and watches (mil.)	382.9 (31.8%)	No data
Semiconductors/ transistors (mil.)	60,455.0 (88.9%)	N/A
Calculators (mil.)	72.3 (85%)	N/A
Televisions (mil.)	28.1 (25.7%)	+540%
Radios and audiocassette recorders/players (mil.)	88.4 (29.5%)	+534%
Pianos and organs (1,000)	543.0 (53.8%)	No data
Industrial robots (1,000)	55.8 (70%)	N/A

N/A means production had not begun in 1960.

AGRICULTURE

Because only 14 percent of the land can be cultivated, farming is generally intensive and scientific, using irrigation, fertilizers, farm machinery, and improved seeds. Mountainous land is terraced along traditional lines to control soil erosion from rain and wind.

LAND (million acres)

Total	Agricultural	Arable	Forest/woodland
148 (100%)	24.7 (17%)	24.7 (17%)	9.8 (14%)

MAJOR CROPS

	Area mil. acres	Yield 100lbs/acre	Production mil. m.t.	Change since 1963
Paddy rice	10.6	56.4	27.1 (6)	+14%
Soybeans	1.4	13.1	0.9 (1)	+43%
Barley	1.4	23.1	1.5 (1)	−46%
Pulses	1.2	9.1	0.5 (1)	−2%
Wheat	1.2	30.8	1.7 (—)	+5%
Corn	1.2	56.4	3.0 (1)	+105%
Millet	0.9	11.2	0.6 (2)	+39%
Vegetables	—	—	26.8 (6)	+71%
Fruit	—	—	8.8 (3)	+117%

MAJOR LIVESTOCK

	Number in mil.	Production mil. m.t.	Change since 1963
Pigs	17.8 (2)	—	+182%
Cattle	8.7 (1)	—	+66%
Milk	—	8.8 (2)	+222%
Fish catch	—	16.4 (18)	—

POPULATION

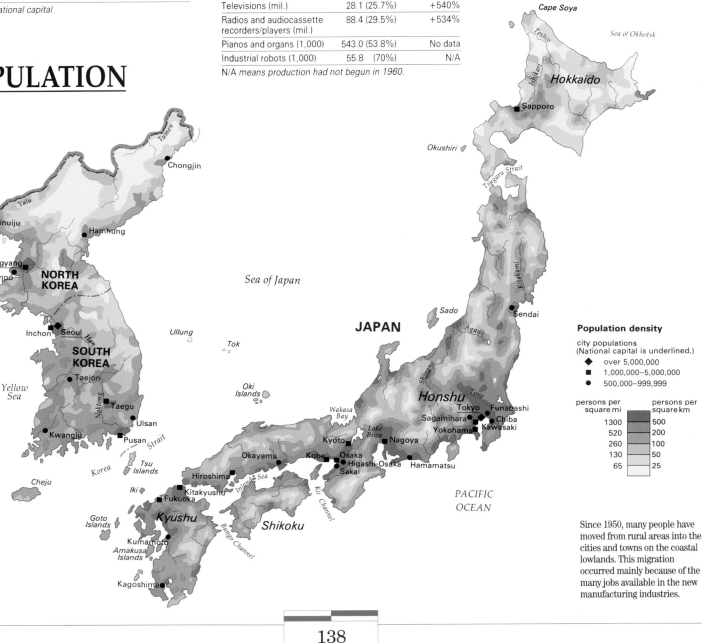

Population density

city populations
(National capital is underlined.)

◆ over 5,000,000
■ 1,000,000–5,000,000
● 500,000–999,999

persons per square mi	persons per square km
1300	500
520	200
260	100
130	50
65	25

Since 1950, many people have moved from rural areas into the cities and towns on the coastal lowlands. This migration occurred mainly because of the many jobs available in the new manufacturing industries.

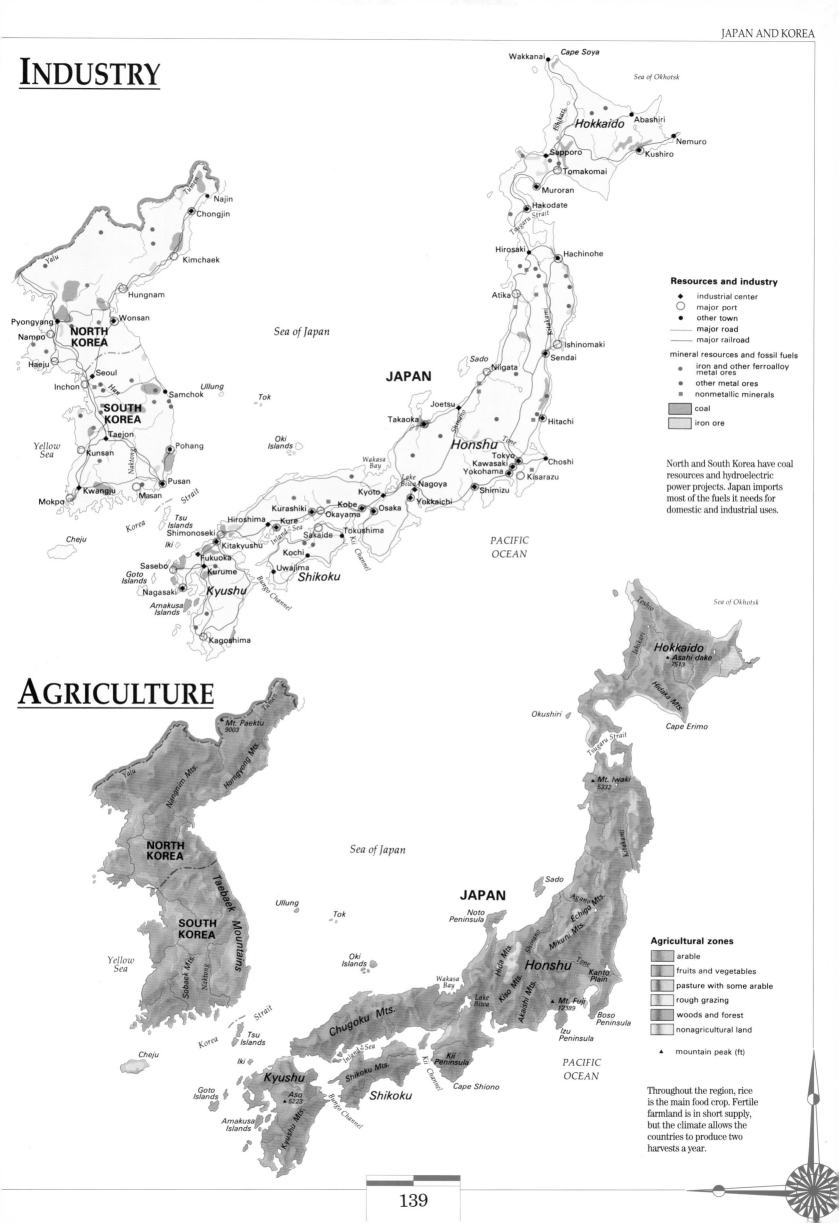

INDUSTRY

Resources and industry
- ◆ industrial center
- ○ major port
- ● other town
- —— major road
- —— major railroad

mineral resources and fossil fuels
- ● iron and other ferroalloy metal ores
- ● other metal ores
- ■ nonmetallic minerals
- ▨ coal
- ▨ iron ore

North and South Korea have coal resources and hydroelectric power projects. Japan imports most of the fuels it needs for domestic and industrial uses.

AGRICULTURE

Agricultural zones
- arable
- fruits and vegetables
- pasture with some arable
- rough grazing
- woods and forest
- nonagricultural land
- ▲ mountain peak (ft)

Throughout the region, rice is the main food crop. Fertile farmland is in short supply, but the climate allows the countries to produce two harvests a year.

Industry map labels

NORTH KOREA — Najin, Chongjin, Kimchaek, Hungnam, Wonsan, Pyongyang, Nampo, Haeju, Yalu, Tumen

SOUTH KOREA — Seoul, Inchon, Samchok, Taejon, Kunsan, Pohang, Mokpo, Kwangju, Masan, Pusan, Yellow Sea, Naktong, Han, Korea Strait, Cheju

JAPAN — Wakkanai, Cape Soya, Sea of Okhotsk, Hokkaido, Abashiri, Nemuro, Kushiro, Sapporo, Tomakomai, Muroran, Hakodate, Tsugaru Strait, Ishikari, Hirosaki, Hachinohe, Atika, Kitakami, Ishinomaki, Sendai, Sado, Niigata, Honshu, Joetsu, Takaoka, Shinano, Hitachi, Tokyo, Kawasaki, Yokohama, Choshi, Kisarazu, Nagoya, Shimizu, Yokkaichi, Tone, Lake Biwa, Kyoto, Osaka, Kobe, Kurashiki, Okayama, Hiroshima, Kure, Shimonoseki, Sakaide, Tokushima, Kii Channel, Inland Sea, Kochi, Uwajima, Shikoku, Kitakyushu, Fukuoka, Kurume, Sasebo, Nagasaki, Kyushu, Kagoshima, Goto Islands, Amakusa Islands, Iki, Tsu Islands, Oki Islands, Ullung, Tok, Wakasa Bay, Sea of Japan, Pacific Ocean

Agriculture map labels

Mt. Paektu 9003, Nangnim Mts., Hamgyong Mts., Taebaek Mountains, Sobaek Mts., Naktong, NORTH KOREA, SOUTH KOREA, Yellow Sea, Yalu, Tumen, Cheju, Iki, Tsu Islands, Korea Strait, Ullung, Tok, Oki Islands, Kyushu, Aso 5223, Kyushu Mts., Amakusa Islands, Goto Islands, Bungo Channel, Shikoku, Shikoku Mts., Inland Sea, Kii Channel, Cape Shiono, Kii Peninsula, Chugoku Mts., Hida Mts., Kiso Mts., Akaishi Mts., Lake Biwa, Wakasa Bay, Noto Peninsula, Honshu, Shinano, Agano, Mikuni Mts., Echigo Mts., Tone, Kanto Plain, Mt. Fuji 12389, Izu Peninsula, Boso Peninsula, JAPAN, Sea of Japan, Pacific Ocean, Mt. Iwaki 5332, Kitakami, Tsugaru Strait, Okushiri, Teshio, Ishikari, Hidaka Mts., Asahi dake 7513, Cape Erimo, Hokkaido, Sea of Okhotsk

AUSTRALIA AND ITS NEIGHBORS

Australia is an ancient landmass that once formed part of the supercontinent of Gondwanaland. Australia is a stable continent, and its scenery is the result of constant erosion and deposition rather than great land movements.

Australia is the world's sixth largest country and its smallest continent. Most of the land is flat—plains or level plateaus make up nine-tenths of Australia. Papua New Guinea is more mountainous but has large lowlands.

The climate ranges from tropical in the north to Mediterranean in the south, though the interior is semiarid or desert. The southeast and Tasmania have a mild temperate climate.

Australia's Aboriginal people arrived from Southeast Asia at least 40,000 years ago. A nomadic people, they developed complex cultural and religious traditions. Most Australians today are of European descent, especially from Britain. Recent arrivals include Asians. Australia is a leading exporter of agricultural products, although the most important part of the economy is manufacturing.

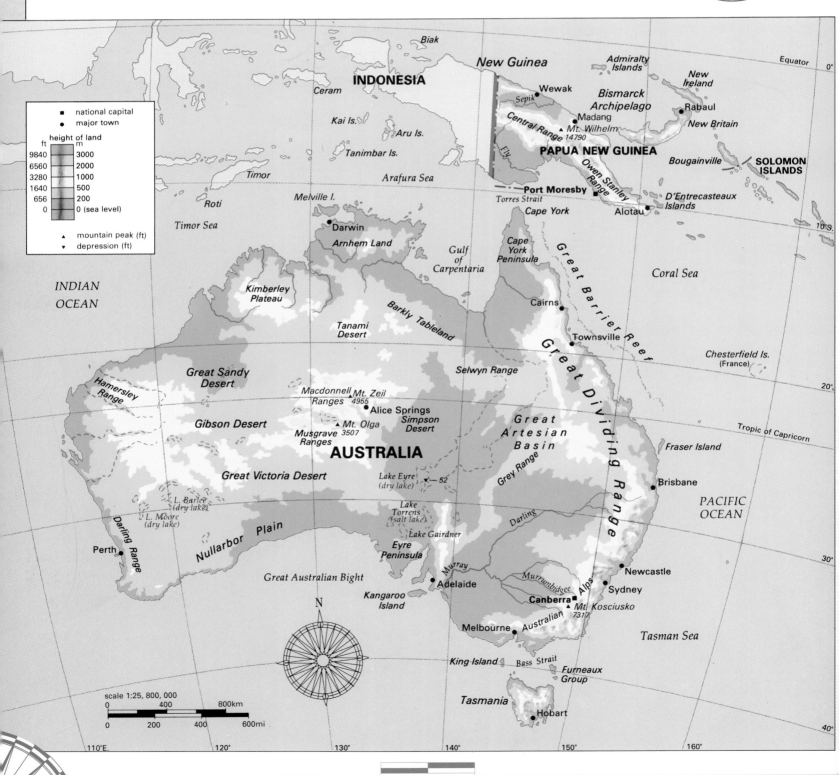

THE POLITICAL AND CULTURAL WORLD

In 1901, the former British colonies of New South Wales, Queensland, South Australia, Tasmania, Victoria, and Western Australia became states and federated to become the independent Commonwealth of Australia. Northern Territory was transferred from South Australia as a territory in 1911.

Today Australia remains a constitutional monarchy – its head of state is the British monarch, who is represented by a governor-general. Papua New Guinea, which was under Australian control during the colonial period, is another constitutional monarchy. Both countries are members of the Commonwealth.

COUNTRIES IN THE REGION

Australia, Papua New Guinea

Island territories
Cocos Islands, Christmas Island, Norfolk Island, Heard Island and the McDonald Islands (Australia)

MEMBERSHIP OF INTERNATIONAL ORGANIZATIONS

Colombo Plan Australia, Papua New Guinea
Organization for Economic Cooperation and Development (OECD) Australia
South Pacific Forum Australia, Papua New Guinea

LANGUAGE

Countries with one official language English: Australia, Papua New Guinea

RELIGION

Australia Roman Catholic (26%), Anglican (24%), other Protestants (17%), nonreligious (13%), other Christians (6%), others (14%)
Papua New Guinea Protestant (64%), Roman Catholic (33%), indigenous religions (2%), Bahai (0.6%), others (0.3%)

STYLES OF GOVERNMENT

Monarchies Australia, Papua New Guinea
Federal state Australia
Multiparty states Australia, Papua New Guinea

ECONOMIC INDICATORS

	Australia
GDP (US$ billions)	296.3
GNP per capita (US$)	17,000
Annual rate of growth of GDP, 1980–1990	3.4%
Manufacturing as % of GDP	15.0%
Central government spending as % of GDP	26.0%
Merchandise exports (US$ billions)	41.2
Merchandise imports (US$ billions)	38.4
% of GNP donated as development aid	0.34%

WELFARE INDICATORS

Infant mortality rate (per 1,000 live births)	
1965	19
1990	8
Daily food supply available (calories per capita, 1989)	3,216
Population per physician (1984)	440
Teacher-pupil ratio (elementary school, 1989)	1 : 17

- ■ national capital
- ● state capital

Area 178,703 sq mi
(462,840 sq km)
Population 3,874,000
Capital Port Moresby
Currency 1 Papua New Guinea kina
(K) = 100 toea

Papua New Guinea

Area 2,966,200 sq mi
(7,682,300 sq km)
Population 16,873,000
Capital Canberra
Currency 1 Australian dollar
($A) = 100 cents

Australia

Although Australia is a constitutional monarchy, political power is vested in the federal government, led by the prime minister. Each state also has its own parliament to deal with such matters as education and public welfare. Some Australians would like to see constitutional changes to make their country a republic.

Habitats

Northern Australia is tropical, with much savanna grassland that merges into the country's arid center. The east coast has tropical forests, with a range of mountains extending north to south. There are large grassland areas in the southwest and southeast.

LAND

Area 3,144,903 sq mi (8,145,140 sq km)
Highest point Mount Wilhelm, Papua New Guinea 14,790 ft (4,508 m)
Lowest point Lake Eyre, Australia, −52 ft (−16 m)
Major features Australia, 2,966,200 sq mi (7,682,300 sq km), is the world's lowest continent

WATER

Longest river Murray–Darling, 2,330 mi (3,780 km)
Largest basin Murray–Darling, 414,100 sq mi (1,072,000 sq km)
Highest average flow Murray, 14,000 cu ft/sec (400 cu m/sec)
Largest lake Eyre, 3,400 sq mi (8,900 sq km)

NOTABLE THREATENED SPECIES

Mammals northern hairy-nosed wombat (*Lasiorhinus krefftii*), numbat (*Myrmecobius fasciatus*), great bilby (*Macrotis lagotis*)
Birds paradise parrot (*Psephotus pulcherrimus*)
Plants Good's banksia (*Banksia goodii*), Huon pine (*Dacrydium franklinii*), caesia (*Eucalyptus caesia*), stag's horn fern (*Platycerium grande*)
Others western swamp turtle (*Pseudemydura umbrina*), baw baw frog (*Philoria frosti*)

Climate

Papua New Guinea and northern Australia have a tropical climate. The interior of Australia is very dry. Mediterranean climates occur in the south. The east is subtropical, while the southeast and Tasmania have warm summers and cool winters.

CLIMATE

	Temperature °F (°C)		Altitude ft (m)
	January	July	
Darwin	82 (28)	77 (25)	98 (30)
Perth	73 (23)	55 (13)	197 (60)
Alice Springs	82 (28)	54 (12)	1,900 (579)
Sydney	72 (22)	54 (12)	138 (42)
Port Moresby	82 (28)	77 (25)	126 (38)

	Precipitation in (mm)		
	January	July	Year
Darwin	15.1 (386)	0 (0)	65.4 (1,661)
Perth	0.3 (8)	7.1 (180)	34.4 (873)
Alice Springs	1.7 (43)	0.3 (8)	9.9 (252)
Sydney	3.5 (89)	4.6 (117)	47.3 (1,214)
Port Moresby	7.0 (178)	1.1 (28)	39.8 (1,012)

NATURAL HAZARDS

Drought, storms and flooding, bush fires

Environmental Issues

While the Aboriginal people generally live in harmony with nature, the rapid population increase in the last 200 years and the spread of livestock farming has led to a depletion of plants and animals. Introduced species, such as rabbits, have caused much damage.

POPULATION AND WEALTH

	Australia
Population (in millions)	16.9
Population increase (annual population growth rate, % 1960–1990)	1.7
Energy use (gigajoules/person)	201
Real purchasing power (US$/person)	14,530

ENVIRONMENTAL INDICATORS

CO$_2$ emissions (mil. m.t. carbon/year)	63
Deforestation ('000s acres/year 1980s)	1,677
Artificial fertilizer use (lbs/acre/year)	25.8
Automobiles (per 1,000 population)	424
Access to safe drinking water (% population)	90

MAJOR ENVIRONMENTAL PROBLEMS AND SOURCES

Air pollution: urban high
Marine/coastal pollution: medium; *sources:* industrial, agricultural, sewage
Land degradation: *types:* desertification, soil erosion, salinization, deforestation, coastal degradation, habitat destruction; *causes:* agriculture, industry, population pressure
Resource problems: inadequate drinking water; inadequate sanitation; coastal flooding

HABITATS

Physical zones

- mountains/barren land
- forest
- grassland
- semidesert
- desert

▲ mountain peak (ft)
▼ depression (ft)
�▪ climate station

Behind the narrow coastal plain in the east lies the Great Dividing Range of mountains. Beyond lie the grasslands, which merge to the west into the semideserts and deserts of the vast western plateaus.

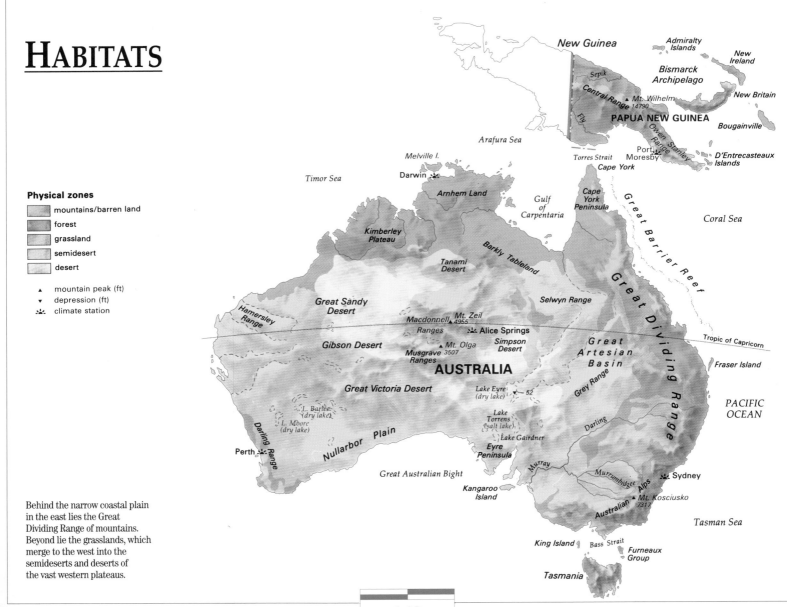

ENVIRONMENTAL ISSUES

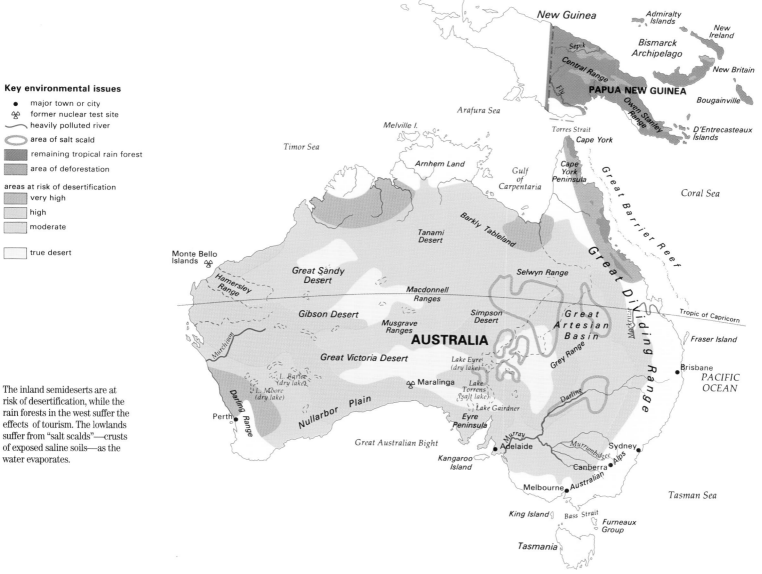

Key environmental issues

- •   major town or city
- ☢   former nuclear test site
- ⌒   heavily polluted river
- ◯   area of salt scald
- ▓   remaining tropical rain forest
- ▒   area of deforestation

areas at risk of desertification

- ▓   very high
- ▒   high
- ░   moderate
- ☐   true desert

The inland semideserts are at risk of desertification, while the rain forests in the west suffer the effects of tourism. The lowlands suffer from "salt scalds"—crusts of exposed saline soils—as the water evaporates.

CLIMATE

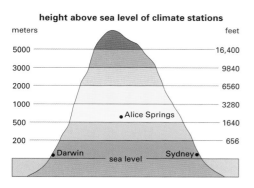

height above sea level of climate stations

Darwin

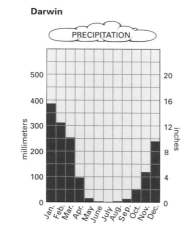

Alice Springs

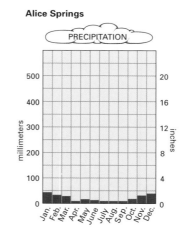

Sydney

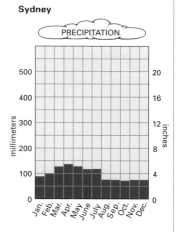

Darwin

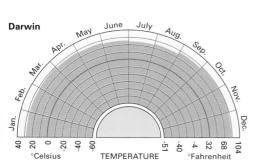

Alice Springs

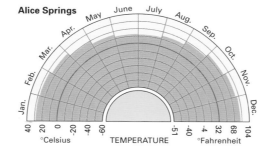

Sydney

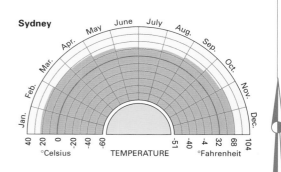

POPULATION

Australia has one of the world's lowest average population densities, but 86 percent of its people live in cities and towns on the coasts, making it one of the more urbanized countries. In Papua New Guinea, 84 percent of the people live in rural areas.

POPULATION

Total population of the region (in millions)	20.74
Population density (persons per sq mi)	6.5
Population change (average annual percent 1960–1990)	−4%

URBAN POPULATION

As percentage of total population	
1970	47.5
1990	50

TEN LARGEST CITIES

	Country	Population
Melbourne	Australia	2,965,000
Sydney	Australia	3,531,000
Brisbane	Australia	1,215,000
Perth	Australia	1,083,000
Adelaide	Australia	1,013,000
Newcastle	Australia	419,000
Canberra †	Australia	289,000
Gold Coast	Australia	220,000
Hobart	Australia	180,000
Port Moresby †	Papua New Guinea	152,000

† denotes national capital

INDUSTRY

Mining is a major industry in Australia. Some raw materials are exported to Japan and elsewhere, but other materials are used in local manufacturing industries. Australia's industries concentrate on producing consumer goods for domestic use and for export.

INDUSTRIAL OUTPUT (US$ billion)

Total	Mining	Manufacturing
40.50	7.9	32.5

INDUSTRIAL WORKERS ('000s)

Total	Mining	Manufacturing
1,559	419	1,140

MAJOR PRODUCTS

Energy and minerals	output
Coal (mil. m.t.)	162
Iron ore (mil. m.t.)	96.7
Copper (1,000 m.t.)	375.8
Nickel (1,000 m.t.)	42
Bauxite (1,000 m.t.)	38.88
Uranium (1,000 m.t.)	3.5
Gold (m.t.)	284
Diamonds (mil. carats)	36

Manufactures	
Wool carpets (mil. sq ft)	446.2
Cement (mil. m.t.)	7.0
Steel (mil. m.t.)	6.6
Aluminum (mil. m.t.)	1.3

AGRICULTURE

Australia's prosperity was based on farming. Cattle, wheat, and wool are major products, as are dairy products, fruit, and sugarcane. Australia now exports mainly in the Pacific region since its trade with Britain, its main trading partner, declined in the 1970s.

LAND (million acres)

	Australia	Papua New Guinea
Total	1,898 (100%)	114 (100%)
Agricultural	1,119.8 (59%)	0.88 (0.8%)
Arable	81.6 (4.3%)	0.22 (0.2%)
Forest/woodland	–	96.8 (84.8%)

MAJOR CROPS

	Area mil. acres	Yield lbs/acre	Production mil. m.t.
Wheat	28.4	667.6	8.6
Sugarcane	0.79	55,253	25.9
Fruit	–	–	3.23
Grain, total	40.17	791.6	14.62

MAJOR LIVESTOCK

	Number in mil.	Production mil. m.t.
Sheep	137.9	–
Cattle	24.68	–
Pigs	–	252
Milk	–	5.19
Fish catch	–	0.15

POPULATION

Population density

city populations
(National capital is underlined.)

- ■ 1,000,000–5,000,000
- ● 500,000–999,999
- ◉ 250,000–499,999
- ○ 100,000–249,999

persons per square mi		persons per square km
260		100
130		50
26		10
2.6		1

The cities of Sydney, Melbourne, Brisbane, Perth, and Adelaide together contain about 60 percent of Australia's population. Most of the interior is uninhabited. Papua New Guinea is also thinly populated.

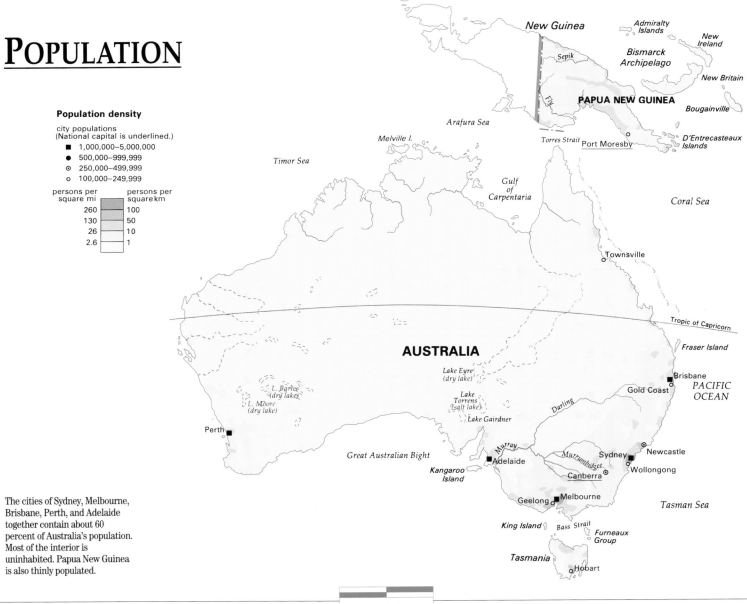

INDUSTRY

Australia has many valuable reserves of metals, coal, oil, and precious stones, including opals. Papua New Guinea has some gold and copper.

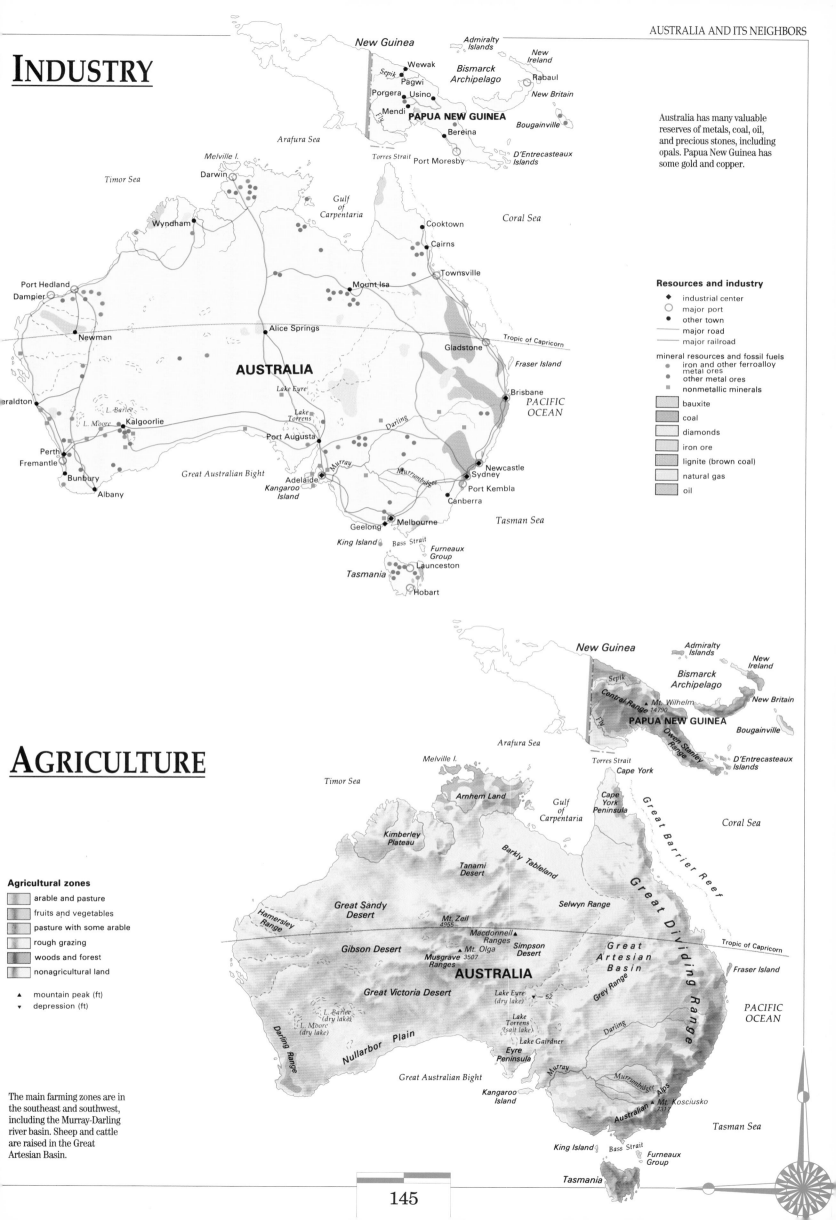

New Guinea

Admiralty Islands

New Ireland

Bismarck Archipelago

Wewak

Sepik

Pagwi

Porgera   Usino

Fly

Mendi   **PAPUA NEW GUINEA**

Rabaul

New Britain

Bougainville

Bereina

Arafura Sea

Torres Strait   Port Moresby

D'Entrecasteaux Islands

Melville I.

Darwin

Timor Sea

Wyndham

Gulf of Carpentaria

Coral Sea

Cooktown

Cairns

Townsville

Mount Isa

Port Hedland

Dampier

Newman

Alice Springs

AUSTRALIA

Tropic of Capricorn

Gladstone

Fraser Island

Brisbane

PACIFIC OCEAN

Geraldton

Lake Eyre

L. Barlee

L. Moore   Kalgoorlie

Lake Torrens

Darling

Port Augusta

Perth

Fremantle

Bunbury

Albany

Great Australian Bight

Adelaide

Kangaroo Island

Murray

Murrumbidgee

Newcastle

Sydney

Port Kembla

Canberra

Geelong   Melbourne

Tasman Sea

King Island   *Bass Strait*

Furneaux Group

Launceston

Tasmania

Hobart

Resources and industry

- ◆ industrial center
- ○ major port
- ● other town
- —— major road
- —— major railroad

mineral resources and fossil fuels
- iron and other ferroalloy metal ores
- other metal ores
- nonmetallic minerals

- bauxite
- coal
- diamonds
- iron ore
- lignite (brown coal)
- natural gas
- oil

AGRICULTURE

The main farming zones are in the southeast and southwest, including the Murray-Darling river basin. Sheep and cattle are raised in the Great Artesian Basin.

Agricultural zones

- arable and pasture
- fruits and vegetables
- pasture with some arable
- rough grazing
- woods and forest
- nonagricultural land

- ▲ mountain peak (ft)
- ▼ depression (ft)

New Guinea

Admiralty Islands

New Ireland

Bismarck Archipelago

Sepik

Central Range

Mt. Wilhelm ▲ 14790

New Britain

Fly

PAPUA NEW GUINEA

Owen Stanley Range

Bougainville

D'Entrecasteaux Islands

Arafura Sea

Torres Strait

Cape York

Melville I.

Timor Sea

Arnhem Land

Gulf of Carpentaria

Cape York Peninsula

Great Barrier Reef

Coral Sea

Kimberley Plateau

Barkly Tableland

Hamersley Range

Tanami Desert

Great Sandy Desert

Selwyn Range

Great Dividing Range

Mt. Zeil 4955

Macdonnell Ranges ▲

Gibson Desert

Mt. Olga ▲

Simpson Desert

Great Artesian Basin

Tropic of Capricorn

Musgrave Ranges ▲ 3507

AUSTRALIA

Fraser Island

Great Victoria Desert

Lake Eyre (dry lake) ▼ −52

Grey Range

PACIFIC OCEAN

L. Barlee (dry lake)

L. Moore (dry lake)

Lake Torrens (salt lake)

Darling

Darling Range

Nullarbor Plain

Lake Gairdner

Eyre Peninsula

Murray

Murrumbidgee

Great Australian Bight

Kangaroo Island

Australian Alps

Mt. Kosciusko ▲ 7317

Tasman Sea

King Island   *Bass Strait*

Furneaux Group

Tasmania

NEW ZEALAND AND ITS NEIGHBORS

New Zealand is an island nation with snow-capped mountains, fertile green plains, forested hills, and volcanic regions famous for their bubbling hot springs and explosive geysers. The climate varies from subtropical in North Island to wet temperate on South Island. The Southern Alps on South Island have a severe mountain climate.

The Maoris, a Polynesian people, settled in New Zealand (called Aotearoa, or "Land of the Long White Cloud") about A.D. 750. Dutch sailors reached the islands in 1642, but Europeans did not settle there until the early 1800s. Most New Zealanders are descendants of British immigrants. The country's economy was founded on farming and foreign trade.

New Zealand lies in the southwestern Pacific Ocean, 994 miles (1,600 km) southeast of Australia. It is in an unstable zone, characterized by earthquakes and volcanic eruptions. Glacial action has carved scenic fiords into the southwest coast of South Island.

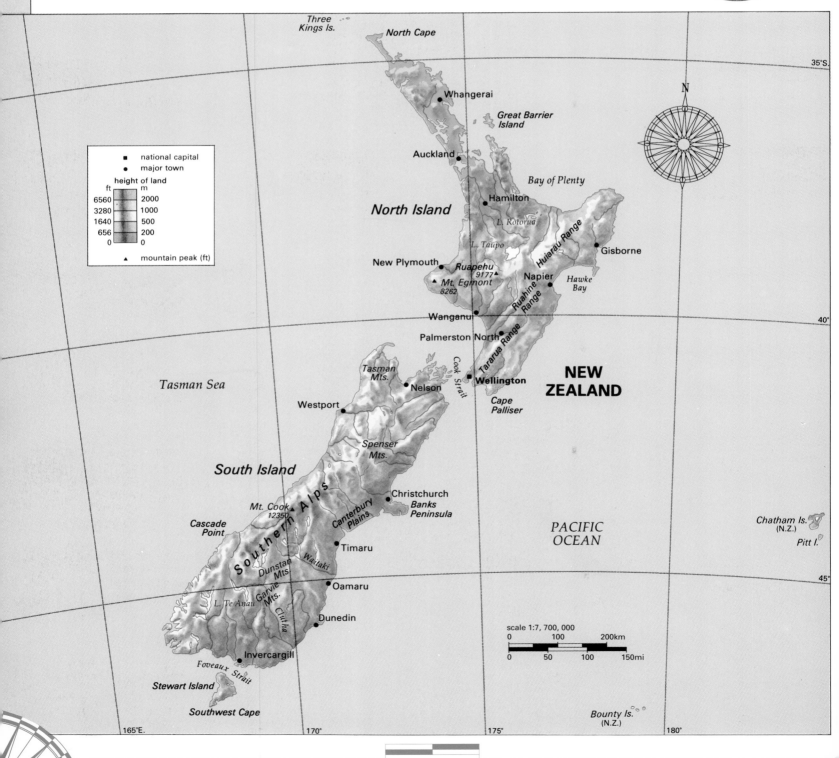

THE POLITICAL AND CULTURAL WORLD

With its Maori population, New Zealand is regarded as part of Polynesia, which also includes the independent island nations of Tonga, Tuvalu, and Western Samoa, as well as the American state of Hawaii.

Micronesia lies mainly in the North Pacific and includes Kiribati, Nauru, the Marshall Islands, and the Federated States of Micronesia. Kiribati contains both Polynesians and Micronesians. Melanesia includes Papua New Guinea, the Solomon Islands, Vanuatu, and Fiji.

COUNTRIES IN THE REGION

Fiji, Kiribati, Marshall Islands, Nauru, New Zealand, Solomon Islands, Tonga, Tuvalu, Vanuatu, Western Samoa

Island territories Cook Islands, Niue, Tokelau (N.Z.)
Dependencies of other states American Samoa, Guam, Johnston Atoll, Midway Islands, Northern Marianas, U.S. Trust Territory of the Pacific Islands (Federated States of Micronesia, Belau) Wake Island (U.S.A.); French Polynesia, New Caledonia, Wallis and Futuna Islands (France)

LANGUAGE

Countries with one official language Fiji, Kiribati, New Zealand, Solomon Islands (E); Nauru (N)
Countries with two official languages Marshall Islands (E,Ma); Tonga (E,To); Western Samoa (E,Sa)
Country with three or more official languages Vanuatu (B,E,F)
Country with no official language Tuvalu

Key: B-Bislama, E-English, F-French, Ma-Marshallese, N-Nauruan, Sa-Samoan, To-Tongan

Other significant languages in the region include French and a great variety of indigenous Melanesian and Polynesian languages

RELIGION

Countries with one major religion Marshall Islands, Tuvalu (P)
Countries with two major religions Kiribati, Nauru, Tonga, Western Samoa (P,RC); Vanuatu (C,IR)
Countries with three or more major religions Fiji (C,H,I); Solomon Islands (A,I,P,RC); New Zealand (A,N,P,RC)

Key: A-Anglican, C-various Christian, H-Hindu, I-Islam, IR-indigenous religions, N-nonreligious, P-Protestant, RC-Roman Catholic

ECONOMIC INDICATORS

	New Zealand
GDP (US$ billions)	42.76
GNP per capita (US$)	12,680
Annual rate of growth of GDP, 1980–1990	1.9%
Manufacturing as % of GDP	19.0%
Central government spending as % of GNP	35.0%
Merchandise exports (US$ billions)	9.5
Merchandise imports (US$ billions)	7.12
% of GNP donated as development aid	0.23%

WELFARE INDICATORS

Infant mortality rate (per 1,000 live births)	
1965	20
1990	10
Daily food supply available (calories per capita, 1989)	3,362
Population per physician (1984)	580
Teacher-pupil ratio (elementary school, 1989)	1 : 19

Fiji
Area 7,056 sq mi (18,274 sq km)
Population 764,000
Capital Suva

Kiribati
Area 328 sq mi (849 sq km)
Population 72,000
Capital Bairiki

Marshall Islands
Area 70 sq mi (181 sq km)
Population 30,870
Capital Majuro

Nauru
Area 8 sq mi (21 sq km)
Population 9,000
Capital Yaren

New Zealand
Area 103,288 sq mi (267,515 sq km)
Population 3,392,000
Capital Wellington

Solomon Islands
Area 10,954 sq mi (28,370 sq km)
Population 320,000
Capital Honiara

Tonga
Area 310 sq mi (780 sq km)
Population 95,000
Capital Nuku'alofa

Tuvalu
Area 9 sq mi (24 sq km)
Population 9,000
Capital Funafuti

Vanuatu
Area 5,700 sq mi (14,763 sq km)
Population 158,000
Capital Port-Vila

Western Samoa
Area 1,093 sq mi (2,831 sq km)
Population 168,000
Capital Apia

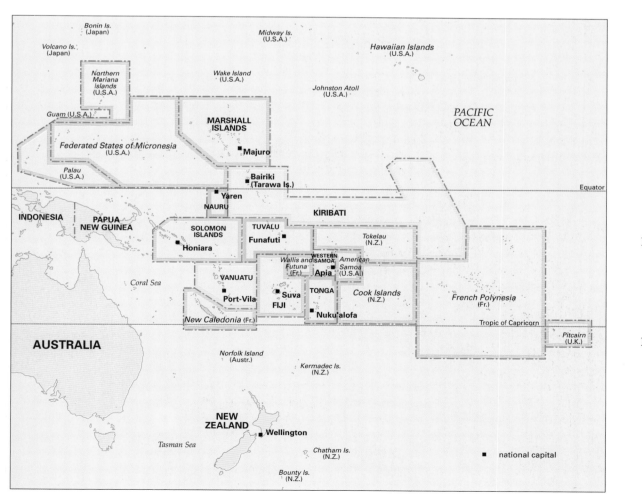

Oceania contains thousands of islands scattered across the Pacific Ocean. Some are mountainous and volcanic, while others are made up of coral that has accumulated on the tops of submerged volcanoes.

Habitats

Scenic mountains and wilderness cover much of the country, providing habitats for New Zealand's wildlife. Forests run the length of the country from northeast to southwest. There are volcanoes, fiords, and geysers. The island countries have a range of tropical habitats.

LAND

Area 127,744 sq mi (330,854 sq km)
Highest point Mount Cook, New Zealand 12,349 ft (3,764 m)
Major features Mountain ranges of New Zealand; coral, volcanic, and continental islands in the Pacific Ocean

WATER

Longest river Waikato, New Zealand 270 mi (434 km)
Largest lake Lake Taupo, New Zealand 234 sq mi (606 sq km)

NOTABLE THREATENED SPECIES

Mammals woodland island cuscus (*Phalanger lullulae*), Pohnpei flying fox (*Pteropus molossinus*), Samoan flying fox (*Pteropus samoensis*)
Birds kagu (*Rhynochetos jubatus*), black stilt (*Himantopus novaezelandiae*), rapa fruit-dove (*Ptilinopus huttoni*), kakapo (*Strigops habroptilus*), Guam flycatcher (*Myiagra freycineti*)
Plants Kau silverwood (*Argyroxiphium kauense*), lobster claw (*Clianthus puniceus*), Philip Island hibiscus (*Hibiscus insularis*), Chatham Island forget-me-not (*Myosotium hortensia*), vuleito (*Noeveitchia storckii*), toromiro (*Sophora toromiro*), *Tecomanthe speciosa*
Others tuatara (*Sphenodon punctatus*), short Samoan tree snail (*Samoana abbreviata*), Stephens Island weta beetle (*Deinacrida rugosa*), Queen Alexandra's birdwing butterfly (*Ornithoptera alexandrae*)

Climate

New Zealand has a mild, wet climate. North Island is warm and humid in the north, but the central plateau has frosts. South Island is cooler, and the Southern Alps contain large snowfields and glaciers. The west is rainy, while the eastern plains are much drier.

CLIMATE

| | Temperature °F (°C) | | Altitude |
	January	July	ft (m)
Auckland	66 (19)	51 (10)	85 (26)
Hokitika	59 (15)	45 (7)	12 (4)
Wellington	62 (17)	47 (9)	415 (127)
Dunedin	58 (14)	42 (6)	240 (73)
Christchurch	61 (16)	42 (6)	32 (10)

| | Precipitation in (mm) | | |
	January	July	Year
Auckland	3.1 (79)	5.7 (145)	49.1 (1,249)
Hokitika	10.3 (262)	8.6 (218)	114.4 (2,907)
Wellington	3.2 (81)	5.4 (137)	47.4 (1,205)
Dunedin	3.4 (86)	3.1 (79)	36.9 (936)
Christchurch	2.2 (56)	2.7 (69)	25.1 (637)

Environmental Issues

New Zealanders are concerned that local trees are being replaced by imported species. The country has its own supply of energy from hot water geysers. Many people oppose the testing of nuclear weapons on Pacific islands, where deforestation also occurs.

POPULATION AND WEALTH

	New Zealand	Fiji	Solomon Is
Population (in millions)	3.4	0.7	0.36
Population increase (annual population growth rate, % 1960–1990)	1.2	No data	No data
Energy use (gigajoules/person)	No data	11	7
Real purchasing power (US$/person)	No data	3,900	No data

ENVIRONMENTAL INDICATORS

CO$_2$ emissions (mil. m.t. carbon/year)	No data	0.2	No data
Artificial fertilizer use (lbs/acre/year)	632.8	79.4	No data
Automobiles (per 1,000 population)	44	N/A	N/A
Access to safe drinking water (% population)	No data	No data	75

MAJOR ENVIRONMENTAL PROBLEMS AND SOURCES

Air pollution: urban high
Marine/coastal pollution: medium; *sources:* industrial, agricultural, sewage
Land degradation: *types:* desertification, soil erosion, salinization, deforestation, coastal degradation, habitat destruction; *causes:* agriculture, industry, population pressure
Resource problems: inadequate drinking water; inadequate sanitation; coastal flooding

N/A means production had not begun in 1960.

HABITATS

Physical zones

- mountains/barren land
- forest
- grassland

▲ mountain peak (ft)
☀ climate station

North Island contains the long, mountainous northern peninsula and a volcanic region around lakes Taupo and Rotorua. The mountain range extends southwest across South Island, though both islands have fertile coastal plains.

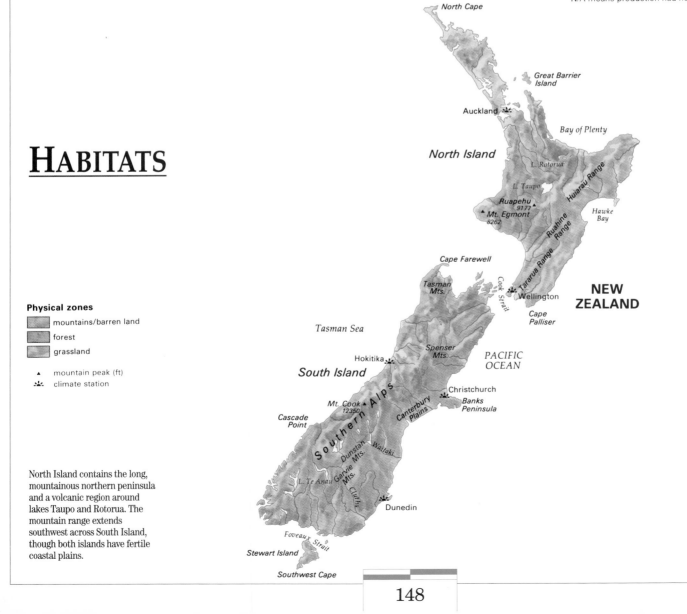

North Cape

Great Barrier Island

Auckland

Bay of Plenty

North Island

L. Rotorua

Huiarau Range

L. Taupo

Ruapehu 9177

Mt. Egmont 8262

Rushine Range

Hawke Bay

Cape Farewell

Tararua Range

Tasman Mts.

Cook Strait

Wellington

NEW ZEALAND

Tasman Sea

Cape Palliser

Spenser Mts.

PACIFIC OCEAN

Hokitika

South Island

Christchurch

Southern Alps

Banks Peninsula

Mt. Cook 12350

Canterbury Plains

Cascade Point

Dunstan Mts.

Waitaki

L. Te Anau

Garvie Mts.

Clutha

Dunedin

Foveaux Strait

Stewart Island

Southwest Cape

ENVIRONMENTAL ISSUES

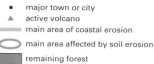

Key environmental issues

- major town or city
- ▲ active volcano
- main area of coastal erosion
- main area affected by soil erosion
- remaining forest
- area of deforestation

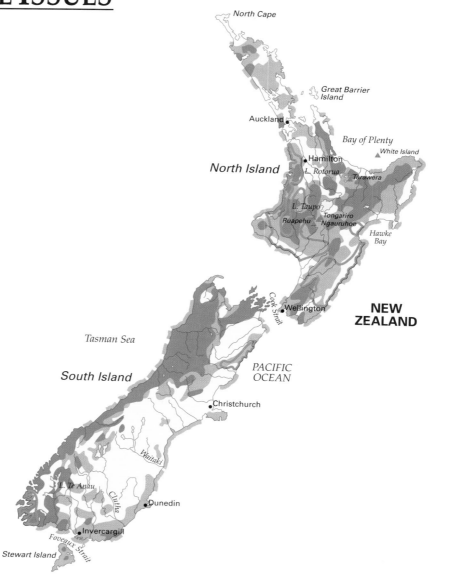

North Cape

Great Barrier Island

Auckland

Bay of Plenty

Hamilton
L. Rotorua
White Island
North Island
Tarawera

L. Taupo
Tongariro
Ruapehu
Ngauruhoe

Hawke Bay

Cook Strait
Wellington

NEW ZEALAND

Tasman Sea

South Island

PACIFIC OCEAN

Christchurch

Waitaki

L. Te Anau
Clutha
Dunedin

Invercargill

Foveaux Strait
Stewart Island

New Zealand has strong conservationist groups concerned with protecting national parks and nature reserves. Plans to build hydroelectric projects have been opposed because they may damage the environment.

CLIMATE

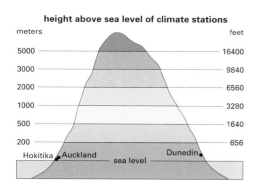

height above sea level of climate stations

meters		feet
5000		16400
3000		9840
2000		6560
1000		3280
500		1640
200		656

Hokitika Auckland Dunedin
sea level

Hokitika
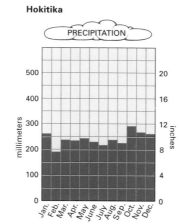

Auckland
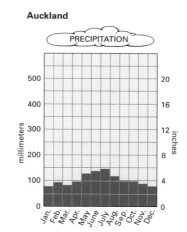

Dunedin
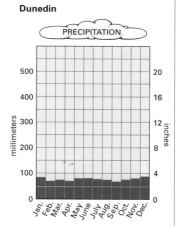

Hokitika
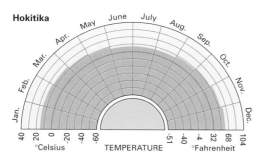

Auckland
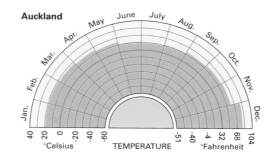

Dunedin
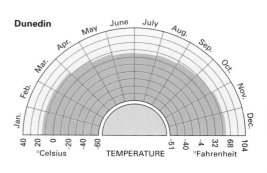

POPULATION

North Island has more than 70 percent of the population of New Zealand and the two largest cities, Auckland and Wellington. South Island has attracted fewer people. Populations in the Pacific Islands tend to be small but concentrated.

POPULATION

Total population of the region (in millions)	4.9
Population density (persons per sq mi)	38.3
Population change (average annual percent 1960–1990)	−20.4%

URBAN POPULATION

As percentage of total population 1970	31.0
1990	35.5
Percentage in cities of more than 1 million	N/A

TEN LARGEST CITIES

	Country	Population
Auckland	New Zealand	885,000
Wellington †	New Zealand	325,000
Christchurch	New Zealand	307,000
Hamilton	New Zealand	148,000
Suva †	Fiji	141,000
Dunedin	New Zealand	109,000
Palmerston North	New Zealand	69,300
Tauranga	New Zealand	64,000
Hastings	New Zealand	55,800
Rotorua	New Zealand	54,200

† denotes national capital

INDUSTRY

Water power used in hydroelectric power plants is the main source of electricity. Many industries process agricultural products, but New Zealand's cities have many other industries. Auckland is the leading industrial city. There is little other industry in the region.

INDUSTRIAL OUTPUT (US$ billion)

Total	Mining	Manufacturing
21.6	5.93	15.32

INDUSTRIAL WORKERS ('000s)

Total	Mining	Manufacturing
334	7	327

MAJOR PRODUCTS

Energy and minerals	output
Gold (m.t.)	6.9

Manufactures	
Cement (mil. m.t.)	0.8
Aluminum (mil. m.t.)	0.26

AGRICULTURE

New Zealand has plenty of grazing land, and sheep and cattle farming are still the chief agricultural activities. But forestry, fruit growing, and other kinds of farming have become increasingly important in recent years. The other countries export few farm products.

LAND (million acres)

Total	Agricultural	Arable	Forest/woodland
81.5 (100%)	10.8 (13%)	20 (24%)	26.4 (32%)

MAJOR CROPS

	Area mil. acre	Yield 100 lbs/acre	Production mil. m.t.
Wheat	0.18	37.5	0.32
Oats	0.037	33.9	0.057
Pulses	0.069	14	0.064
Sorghum	0.004	23	0.004
Sugarcane	0.17	52.6	4.2
Fruit	–	–	0.44

MAJOR LIVESTOCK

	Number in mil.	Production mil. m.t.
Sheep	74.30	–
Pigs	–	42
Cattle	8.5	–
Fish catch	–	0.18
Milk	–	6.7

POPULATION

More than 80 percent of the people of New Zealand live in urban areas. Nearly 50 percent live in one of three cities: Auckland, Wellington, and Christchurch. Large areas are thinly populated.

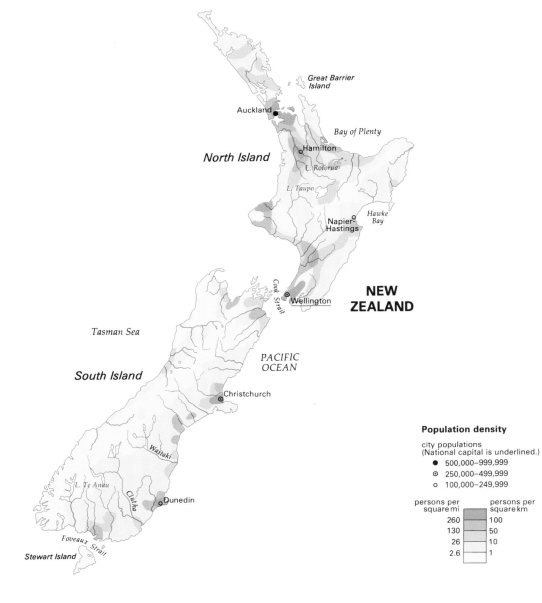

Population density

city populations
(National capital is underlined.)

- ● 500,000–999,999
- ⊙ 250,000–499,999
- ○ 100,000–249,999

persons per square mi	persons per square km
260	100
130	50
26	10
2.6	1

INDUSTRY

New Zealand's mineral resources include coal, natural gas, iron ore, and gold. Steam from geysers in North Island's volcanic area is used as a source of power.

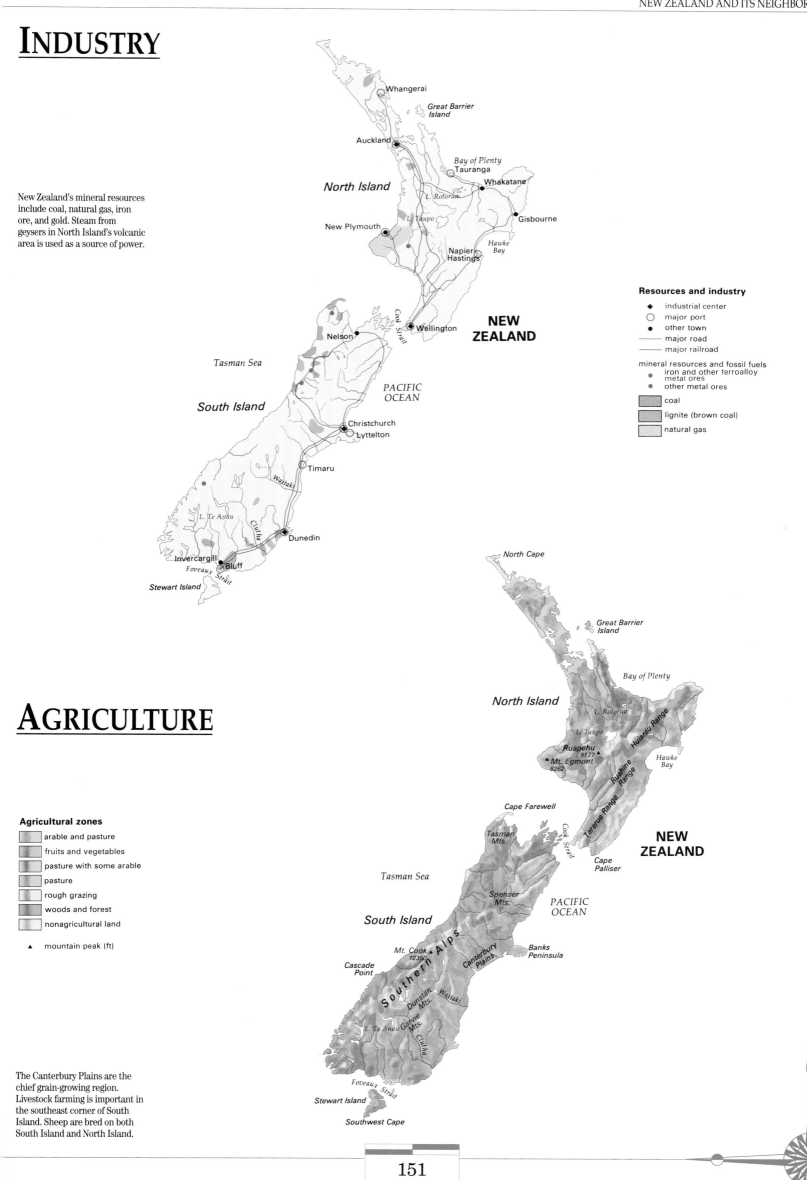

Resources and industry

◆ industrial center
○ major port
● other town
—— major road
—— major railroad

mineral resources and fossil fuels
● iron and other terroalloy metal ores
● other metal ores
coal
lignite (brown coal)
natural gas

Whangerai

Great Barrier Island

Auckland

Bay of Plenty
Tauranga
Whakatane

North Island
L. Rotorua
Gisbourne

L. Taupo
New Plymouth
Hawke Bay
Napier
Hastings

NEW ZEALAND

Nelson
Wellington

Tasman Sea

Cook Strait

PACIFIC OCEAN

South Island

Christchurch
Lyttelton

Timaru

Waitaki

L. Te Anau
Clutha

Dunedin

Invercargill Bluff
Foveaux Strait

Stewart Island

AGRICULTURE

Agricultural zones

arable and pasture
fruits and vegetables
pasture with some arable
pasture
rough grazing
woods and forest
nonagricultural land

▲ mountain peak (ft)

The Canterbury Plains are the chief grain-growing region. Livestock farming is important in the southeast corner of South Island. Sheep are bred on both South Island and North Island.

North Cape

Great Barrier Island

Bay of Plenty

North Island

L. Rotorua

L. Taupo
Ruapehu
9177
▲ Mt. Egmont
8262

Huiarau Range
Ruahine Range
Hawke Bay

Cape Farewell

Tasman Mts.

Cook Strait

Tararua Range

Cape Palliser

NEW ZEALAND

Tasman Sea

Spenser Mts.

PACIFIC OCEAN

South Island

Southern Alps
Mt. Cook ▲
12350

Canterbury Plains

Banks Peninsula

Cascade Point

Dunstan Mts.
Waitaki
Garvie Mts.
Clutha

L. Te Anau

Foveaux Strait

Stewart Island

Southwest Cape

ANTARCTICA

Antarctica is the coldest place on earth. It is a mountainous and mostly ice-covered continent surrounding the South Pole. It is also the driest continent, though it holds almost nine-tenths of the planet's ice. Much of the region is poorly mapped because it is difficult to reach and has a very harsh climate. But research on Antarctica has helped in the understanding of the way the southern continents have reached their present positions. Its climate influences weather systems all over the world. The ice sheet over Antarctica holds a record of recent climatic change and of pollution, including the presence of greenhouse gases. The ice sheet comprises so much of the world's ice and snow, that were it to melt, the world mean sea level would rise by 200 ft (60 m).

Antarctica has no permanent population although scientists carry out research there. In 1982, scientists located a hole in the ozone layer of the atmosphere over Antarctica. The ozone layer screens out 90 percent of the sun's ultraviolet radiation and damage to it has been attributed to chlorofluorocarbons, chemicals used as propellants in some aerosol spray cans. These chemicals are also used in industry and in the coolant system of refrigerators.

The ozone hole is seasonal, developing only in the Antarctic winter and spring, and its size also changes. An increase in ultraviolet radiation would decrease the yield of farmers' crops, change climates around the world, and also lead to an increase in the number of cases of skin cancer.

Antarctica was once part of the ancient supercontinent of Gondwanaland, which also comprised Australia, New Zealand, and the southwest Pacific islands. About 500 million years ago, it was near the equator and had a warm, wet climate. Coal deposits give evidence of this. As Gondwanaland broke up, the part that became Antarctica drifted toward the South Pole and remained there, while the other continents drifted away to the warmer north.

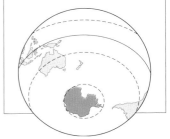

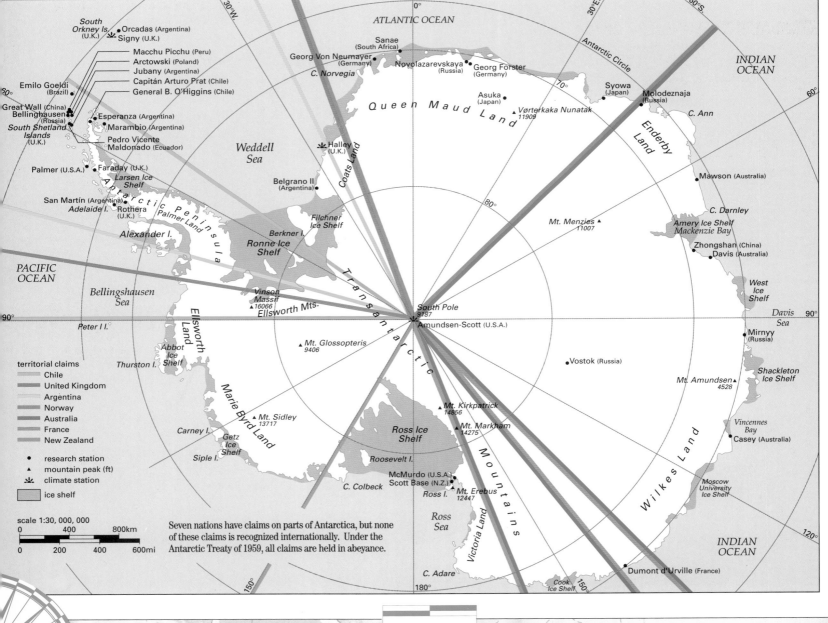

territorial claims
Chile
United Kingdom
Argentina
Norway
Australia
France
New Zealand

- research station
▲ mountain peak (ft)
�* climate station
ice shelf

scale 1:30,000,000
0   400   800km
0   200   400   600mi

Seven nations have claims on parts of Antarctica, but none of these claims is recognized internationally. Under the Antarctic Treaty of 1959, all claims are held in abeyance.

THE POLITICAL AND CULTURAL WORLD

Despite claims to parts of Antarctica by various nations, people from any part of the world can go anywhere in Antarctica, providing their purpose is peaceful, because under international agreement, Antarctica is a demilitarized, nuclear-free zone.

Under recent agreements, restrictions have been placed on the development of the continent. Under the 1991 Environmental Protocol, for example, mining was banned for a period of 50 years. Some campaigning conservationists would like to go further and declare that Antarctica should become a world park, dedicated to science and the preservation of this fragile wilderness. Early this century several sledge expeditions set out to reach the South Pole at the heart of the interior. A Norwegian, Roald Amundsen (1872–1928), was the first to arrive on December 14, 1911. He was followed a month later by Robert F. Scott (1868–1912), and a team of British explorers, who perished in a blizzard on the return journey. In 1929 the American Richard E. Byrd (1888–1957) became the first man to fly over the South Pole.

LAND

Area of exposed rock 18,650 sq mi (48,310 sq km)
Highest point Vinson Massif 16,066 ft (4,897 m)
Height of surface at South Pole 9,187 ft (2,800 m)
Maximum thickness of ice 15,669 ft (4,776 m)

HABITATS

The long chain of the Transantarctic Mountains runs across the whole of Antarctica, passing close to the South Pole and dividing the continent into two unequal parts: Lesser Antarctica and the massive semicircle of Greater Antarctica. From Lesser Antarctica the mountainous Antarctic Peninsula snakes northeast toward the southern tip of South America to the west of the Weddell Sea. The Ross Sea is a smaller gulf south of New Zealand. The southern end of both these seas is covered by permanent ice shelves.

The hostile conditions in Antarctica, combined with long months of darkness, limit plant life to lichens, mosses, algae, and molds in the few ice-free areas. There are no land mammals in Antarctica, but whales and seals feed on masses of tiny, shrimplike krill, while porpoises and dolphins are attracted by shoals of fish, especially Atlantic perch. With no land predators, the Antarctic coast is a haven for birds. Emperor penguins, Antarctic petrels, and South Polar skuas breed here and nowhere else, and more than 40 other species of birds live in Antarctica.

CLIMATE

Temperatures in Antarctica rarely rise above 32°F (0°C) in summer, and they plummet in winter from -40 to -94°F (-40 to -70°C). Strong winds sweep outward from the plateau at 43 mph (70 km/h), with gusts reaching 118 mph (190 km/h). The wind chill factor makes conditions even worse. On the Arctic Peninsula, milder winds from neighboring oceans raise summer temperatures slightly. High atmospheric pressure, giving clear winter skies, dominates the interior of the continent.

The winds blow loose snow across the surface, creating blinding blizzards. Yet Antarctica has little precipitation. With about 2 in (50 mm) of snow a year, it is classified as a desert. Only trace amounts of precipitation are recorded at climate stations in the region. By the end of March, the sun sets on Antarctica, and the continent is in freezing darkness for six months. Although the summer is very short, the land receives more sunlight than equatorial regions do throughout the year. However, the ice sheet reflects most of the sun's energy back into the atmosphere.

CLIMATE

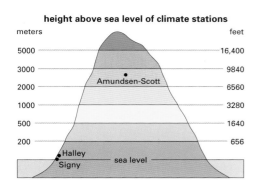

height above sea level of climate stations

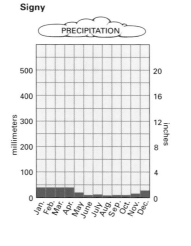

Signy — PRECIPITATION

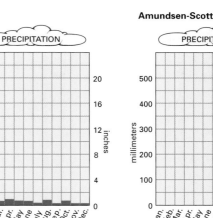

Halley — PRECIPITATION

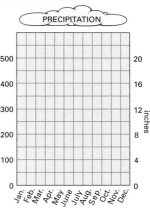

Amundsen-Scott — PRECIPITATION

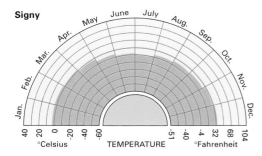

Signy — TEMPERATURE

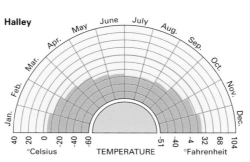

Halley — TEMPERATURE

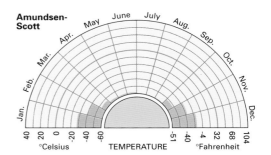

Amundsen-Scott — TEMPERATURE

GAZETTEER

This gazetteer lists places and features, such as rivers or mountains, found on the topographic map in each region. The first number (in **bold** type) is the page number, then coordinates give the latitude (distance north or south of 0°, the Equator) and longitude (distance east or west of 0°, the Greenwich Meridian).

Abbreviations:
b. bay, *c.* country, *d.* district, *des.* desert, *est.* estuary, *f.* feature, *i.* island, *isls.* islands, *l.* lake, *mt.* mountain, *mts.* mountains, *pen.* peninsula, *r.* river, *str.* strait

Aare (*r.*), **72**, 47.37N 8.13E
Abbot Ice Shelf, **152**, 73.00S 92.00W
Abéché, **96**, 13.49N 20.49E
Aberdeen, **52**, 57.08N 2.07W
Aberystwyth, **52**, 52.25N 4.06W
Abidjan, **102**, 2.19N 4.01W
Abu Dhabi, **90**, 24.27N 54.23E
Abuja, **102**, 9.12N 7.11E
Acapulco, **30**, 16.51N 99.56W
Accra, **102**, 5.33N 0.15W
Achill Island, **52**, 53.57N 10.00W
Acklins Island, **31**, 22.30N 74.10W
Aconcagua (*mt.*), **38**, 32.37S 70.00W
Adamawa Highlands, **102**, 7.05N 12.00E
Adana, **90**, 37.00N 35.19E
Adare, Cape, **152**, 71.17S 170.14E
Adda (*r.*), **68**, 45.08N 9.55E
Addis Ababa, **96**, 9.03N 38.42E
Adelaide, **140**, 34.56S 138.36E
Adelaide Island, **152**, 67.15S 68.30W
Aden, **90**, 12.50N 45.00E
Aden, Gulf of, **90**, 13.00N 47.00E
Adige (*r.*), **68**, 45.10N 12.20E
Admiralty Islands, **140**, 2.00S 147.20E
Adour (*r.*), **58**, 43.32N 1.32W
Afghanistan (*c.*), **90**, 33.00N 65.30E
Agadez, **96**, 17.00N 7.56E
Agano (*r.*), **134**, 37.58N 139.02E
Agra, **114**, 27.09N 78.00E
Ahaggar (*mts.*), **96**, 24.00N 5.50E
Ahmadabad, **114**, 23.03N 72.40E
Ahvenamaa (*isls.*), **46**, 60.15N 20.00E
Air (*mts.*), **96**, 20.00N 8.30E
Ajaccio, **58**, 41.55N 8.43E
Akaishi Mts., **134**, 35.20N 138.10E
Akita, **134**, 39.44N 140.05E
Akureyri, **46**, 65.41N 18.04W
Al Mukalla, **90**, 14.34N 49.09E
Alaotra, Lake, **108**, 17.30S 48.30E
Alaska (*d.*), **22**, 66.00N 153.00W
Alaska Peninsula, **22**, 56.00N 160.00W
Alaska Range, **22**, 62.10N 152.00W
Albacete, **64**, 39.00N 1.52W
Albania (*c.*), **78**, 41.00N 20.00E
Albany (*r.*), **16**, 52.10N 82.00W
Albert, Lake, **102**, 1.45N 31.00E
Ålborg, **46**, 57.03N 9.56E
Albuquerque, **22**, 35.05N 106.40W
Aldabra Islands, **108**, 9.00S 47.00E
Aleppo, **90**, 36.14N 37.10E
Aleutian Is., **22**, 52.00N 170.00W
Alexander Archipelago, **22**, 56.30N 134.30W
Alexander Island, **152**, 71.00S 70.00W
Alexandria, **96**, 31.13N 29.55E
Algeria (*c.*), **96**, 25.00N 3.00E
Algiers, **96**, 36.50N 3.00E
Aliakmon (*r.*), **68**, 40.30N 22.38E
Alicante, **64**, 38.21N 0.29W
Alice Springs, **140**, 23.42S 133.52E
Allegheny Mts., **22**, 40.00N 80.00W
Aller (*r.*), **72**, 52.57N 9.11E
Allier (*r.*), **58**, 46.58N 3.30E
Alma-Ata, **84**, 43.19N 76.55E
Almeriía, **64**, 36.50N 2.26W
Alotau, **140**, 10.20S 150.23E
Alps (*mts.*), **72**, 46.00N 6.50E
Altai (*mts.*), **84**, 46.30N 93.30E
Altun Shan (*mts.*), **120**, 38.10N 87.50E
Amakusa (*i.*), **134**, 32.30N 130.00E
Amazon (*r.*), **38**, 2.00S 50.00W
Ambon, **128**, 3.50S 128.10E
Amery Ice Shelf, **152**, 69.30S 72.00E
Amiens, **58**, 49.54N 2.18E
Amman, **90**, 31.57N 35.56E
Amsterdam, **72**, 52.22N 4.54E
Amu Darya (*r.*), **84**, 43.50N 59.00E
Amundsen, Mt., **152**, 67.14S 100.00E
Amundsen-Scott, **152**, 90.00S 0.00
Amur (*r.*), **120**, 53.17N 140.00E
An Nafud (*des.*), **90**, 28.40N 41.30E
An Najaf, **90**, 31.59N 44.19E
Anambas Islands, **128**, 3.00N 106.10E
Anatolia (*f.*), **90**, 38.00N 35.00E
Anchorage, **22**, 61.10N 150.00W
Andaman Islands, **114**, 12.00N 93.00E
Andes (*mts.*), **38**, 15.00S 72.00W
Andorra (*c.*), **58**, 42.30N 1.32E
Andorra la Vella, **58**, 42.30N 1.31E
Andreas, Cape, **68**, 35.40N 34.35E
Andros (*i.*), **30**, 24.30N 78.00W
Andros (*i.*), **68**, 37.50N 24.50E
Aneto Peak, **64**, 42.38N 0.40W
Angerman (*r.*), **46**, 63.00N 17.43E
Angers, **58**, 47.29N 0.32W
Anglesey (*i.*), **52**, 53.16N 4.25W
Angola (*c.*), **108**, 11.45S 18.00E
Ankara, **90**, 39.55N 32.50E
Annaba, **96**, 36.55N 7.47E
Annamite Range, **128**, 17.40N 105.30E
Annobóon (*i.*), **102**, 1.25S 5.36E
Antalya, **90**, 36.53N 30.42E
Antananarivo, **108**, 18.55S 47.31E
Antarctic Peninsula, **152**, 69.30S 65.00W
Antigua (*i.*), **31**, 17.09N 61.49W
Antigua and Barbuda (*c.*), **31**, 17.30N 61.49W
Antofagasta, **38**, 23.40S 70.23W
Antrim, Mts. of, **52**, 55.00N 6.10W
Antsiranana, **108**, 12.19S 49.17E
Antwerp, **72**, 51.13N 3.14E
Aomori, **134**, 40.50N 140.43E
Apennines (*mts.*), **68**, 42.00N 13.30E
Apo, Mt., **128**, 6.58N 125.17E
Appalachian Mts., **22**, 39.30N 80.00W
Aqaba, **90**, 29.32N 35.00E
Arabian Peninsula, **90**, 21.20N 46.44E
Araguaia (*r.*), **38**, 5.30S 48.05W
Arakan Yoma (*mts.*), **128**, 20.00N 94.00E
Aran Is., **52**, 53.07N 9.38W
Ararat (*mt.*), **90**, 39.45N 44.15E
Aras (*r.*), **90**, 40.00N 48.28E
Ardennes (*mts.*), **58**, 49.40N 5.00E
Arequipa, **38**, 17.58S 63.14W
Argentina (*c.*), **38**, 35.00S 65.00W
Århus, **46**, 56.09N 10.13E
Arica, **38**, 18.30S 70.20W
Arkansas (*r.*), **22**, 33.50N 91.00W
Armenia (*c.*), **84**, 40.00N 45.00E
Arnhem Land (*f.*), **140**, 13.10S 134.30E
Arno (*r.*), **68**, 43.43N 10.17E
Arran (*i.*), **52**, 55.35N 5.14W
Aru Islands, **128**, 6.00S 134.30E
Aruba (*i.*), **31**, 12.30N 70.00W
Asahidake (*mt.*), **134**, 43.42N 142.54E
Asahikawa, **134**, 43.46N 142.23E
Ashkhabad, **84**, 37.58N 58.24E
Asmera, **96**, 15.20N 38.58E
Aso (*mt.*), **134**, 32.55N 131.02E
Aswan, **96**, 24.05N 32.56E
Asyut, **96**, 27.14N 31.07E
Atacama Desert, **38**, 21.00S 69.00W
Atar, **96**, 20.32N 13.08W
Atbara, **96**, 17.42N 34.00E
Atbara (*r.*), **96**, 17.47N 34.00E
Athabasca (*r.*), **16**, 58.40N 110.50W
Athabasca Lake, **16**, 59.07N 110.00W
Athens, **68**, 37.59N 23.42E
Atlanta, **22**, 33.45N 84.23W
Aube (*r.*), **58**, 48.34N 3.43E
Auckland, **146**, 36.55S 174.45E
Australia (*c.*), **140**, 27.00S 135.00E
Australian Alps, **140**, 36.30S 148.30E
Austria (*c.*), **72**, 47.30N 14.00E
Axios (*r.*), **68**, 40.31N 22.43E
Azerbaijan (*c.*), **84**, 40.10N 47.50E

Babuyan Islands, **128**, 19.20N 121.30E
Back (*r.*), **16**, 66.37N 96.00W
Badajoz, **64**, 38.53N 6.58W
Baffin Bay, **16**, 72.00N 63.00W
Baffin Island, **16**, 68.05N 70.00W
Baghdad, **90**, 33.20N 44.26E
Baghlan, **90**, 36.11N 68.44E
Baguio, **128**, 16.25N 120.37E
Bahamas (*c.*), **31**, 23.30N 75.00W
Bahawalpur, **114**, 29.24N 71.36E
Bahía Blanca, **38**, 38.45S 62.15W
Bahrain (*c.*), **90**, 26.00N 50.35E
Baikal, Lake, **84**, 53.30N 108.00E
Baja California (*pen.*), **30**, 25.00N 112.00W
Baku, **84**, 40.22N 49.53E
Balaton, Lake, **78**, 46.55N 17.50E
Balearic Islands, **64**, 39.30N 2.30W
Bali (*i.*), **128**, 8.30S 115.05E
Balikpapan, **128**, 1.15S 116.50E
Balkan Mountains, **78**, 42.50N 24.30E
Balkhash, Lake, **84**, 46.40N 75.00E
Balsas (*r.*), **30**, 18.10N 102.05W
Baltimore, **22**, 39.17N 76.37W
Bamako, **96**, 12.40N 7.59W
Bambari, **102**, 5.45N 20.40E
Banas, Cape, **96**, 23.54N 35.48E
Bandar Abbas, **90**, 27.10N 56.15E
Bandar Seri Begawan, **128**, 4.56N 114.58E
Bandung, **128**, 6.57S 107.34E
Bangalore, **114**, 12.58N 77.35E
Bangka (*i.*), **128**, 2.20S 106.10E
Bangkok, **128**, 13.45N 100.35E
Bangladesh (*c.*), **114**, 24.00N 90.00E
Bangui, **102**, 4.23N 18.37E
Bangweulu, Lake, **108**, 11.15S 29.45E
Banjarmasin, **128**, 3.22S 114.36E
Banjul, **102**, 13.28N 16.39W
Banks Island, **16**, 73.00N 122.00W
Banks Peninsula, **146**, 43.45S 173.10E
Barbados (*c.*), **31**, 13.20N 59.40W
Barbuda (*i.*), **31**, 17.41N 61.48W
Barcelona, **64**, 41.25N 2.10E
Bari, **68**, 41.08N 16.52E
Barisan Mts., **128**, 3.30S 102.30E
Barito (*r.*), **128**, 3.35S 114.35E
Barkly Tableland (*f.*), **140**, 19.00S 136.40E
Barlee, Lake (dry), **140**, 29.30S 119.30E
Barra (*i.*), **52**, 56.59N 7.28W
Barranquilla, **38**, 11.00N 74.50W
Barren Islands, **108**, 18.55S 44.15E
Barrow, **22**, 71.16N 156.50W
Barrow (*r.*), **52**, 52.17N 7.00W
Basra, **90**, 30.33N 47.50E
Bass Strait, **140**, 39.45S 146.00E
Bassein, **128**, 16.45N 94.30E
Basseterre, **31**, 17.17N 62.43W
Bastia, **58**, 42.41N 9.26E
Batan Islands, **128**, 20.50N 121.55E
Batdambang, **128**, 13.06N 103.13E
Batu Islands, **128**, 0.30S 98.20E
Bavarian Alps (*mts.*), **72**, 47.38N 11.30E
Bayan Har Shan (*mts.*), **120**, 34.00N 97.20E
Beijing (Peking), **120**, 39.55N 116.25E
Beira, **108**, 19.49S 34.52E
Beirut, **90**, 33.52N 35.30E
Belarus (*c.*), **84**, 53.00N 27.00E
Belém, **38**, 1.27S 48.29W
Belfast, **52**, 54.36N 5.57W
Belgium (*c.*), **72**, 51.00N 4.30E
Belgrade, **78**, 44.49N 20.28E
Belitung (*i.*), **128**, 3.00S 108.00E
Belize (*c.*), **30**, 17.00N 88.30W
Belle-Ile (*i.*), **58**, 47.20N 3.10W
Bellingshausen Sea, **152**, 71.00S 85.00W
Belmopan, **30**, 17.25N 88.46W
Belo Horizonte, **38**, 19.45S 43.53W
Bemaraha, Plateau of, **108**, 20.00S 45.15E
Bemarivo (*r.*), **108**, 15.27S 47.40E
Ben Nevis (*mt.*), **52**, 56.48N 5.00W
Bengal, Bay of, **114**,, 13.00N 85.00E
Benghazi, **96**, 32.07N 20.05E
Benin (*c.*), **102**, 9.00N 2.30E
Benue (*r.*), **102**, 7.52N 6.45E
Bergen, **46**, 60.23N 5.20E
Bering Strait, **22**, 65.30N 169.00W
Berkner (*i*), **152**, 79.30S 49.30W
Berlin, **72**, 52.31N 13.24E
Bermuda (*i.*), **31**, 32.18N 65.00W
Bern, **72**, 46.57N 7.26E
Bernese Alps (*mts.*), **72**, 46.30N 7.37E
Besançon, **58**, 47.14N 6.02E
Bhutan (*c.*), **114**, 27.25N 90.00E
Biak (*i.*), **128**, 0.55S 136.00E
Bialystok, **78**, 53.09N 23.01E
Bié Plateau, **108**, 13.00S 16.00E
Bihor Mts., **78**, 46.26N 22.43E
Bilbao, **64**, 43.15N 2.56W
Bioko (*i.*), **102**, 3.25N 8.45E
Biratnagar, **114**, 26.18N 87.17E
Birmingham, **52**, 52.30N 1.55W
Biscay, Bay of, **58**, 45.00N 3.00W
Bishkek, **84**, 42.53N 74.46E
Bismarck Archipelago, **140**, 3.35S 147.00E
Bissau, **102**, 11.52N 15.39W
Bitterroot Range, **22**, 47.06N 115.00W
Biwa, Lake, **134**, 35.20N 136.10E
Black Forest, **72**, 48.00N 8.00E
Black Hills, **22**, 44.17N 103.28W
Blanc, Cape, **96**, 20.44N 17.05W
Blanc, Mont, **58**, 45.50N 6.52E
Blantyre, **108**, 15.46S 35.00E
Bloemfontein, **108**, 29.07S 26.14E
Blönduós, **46**, 65.39N 20.18W
Blue Ridge Mts., **22**, 36.30N 80.15W
Bobaomby, Cape, **108**, 11.48S 49.19E
Bodele (*f.*), **96**, 16.50N 17.10E
Bogotá, **38**, 4.38N 74.05W
Bohemian Forest, **72**, 49.20N 13.10E
Bohol (*i.*), **128**, 9.45S 124.10E
Bokn Fjord, **46**, 59.10N 5.35E
Bolivia (*c.*), **38**, 17.00S 65.00W
Bolmen (*l.*), **46**, 56.55N 13.40E
Bologna, **68**, 44.30N 11.20E
Bolshevik (*i.*), **84**, 78.30N 102.00E
Bombay, **114**, 18.56N 72.51E
Bonaire (*i.*), **31**, 12.15N 68.27W
Bonn, **72**, 50.44N 7.05E
Boothia Peninsula, **16**, 70.30N 95.00W
Borås, **46**, 57.43N 12.55E
Bordeaux, **58**, 44.50N 0.34W
Borneo (*i.*), **128**, 1.00N 114.00E
Bornholm (*i.*), **46**, 55.10N 15.00E
Bosnia and Herzegovina (*c.*), **78**, 44.20N 17.50E
Boso Peninsula, **134**, 35.20N 140.00E
Bosporus (*str.*), **78**, 41.07N 29.04E
Bosten, Lake, **120**, 42.00N 87.00E
Boston, **22**, 42.21N 71.04W
Bothnia, Gulf of, **46**, 63.30N 20.30E
Botrange (*mt.*), **72**, 50.30N 6.04E
Botswana (*c.*), **108**, 21.00S 24.00E
Bougainville (*i.*), **140**, 6.00S 155.00E
Bounty Islands, **146**, 48.20S 179.00E
Bracč (*i.*), **78**, 43.20N 16.38E
Braga, **64**, 41.32N 8.26W
Brahmaputra (*r.*), **114**, 23.50N 89.45E
Brasília, **38**, 15.54S 47.50W
Brasov, **78**, 45.40N 25.35E
Bratislava, **78**, 48.10N 17.10E
Brazil (*c.*), **38**, 10.00S 52.00W
Brazil, Plateau of, **38**, 14.00S 45.00W
Brazzaville, **102**, 4.14S 15.14E
Brecon Beacons (*mts.*), **52**, 51.53N 3.27W
Breidhafjördhur, **46**, 65.15N 23.00W
Bremen, **72**, 53.05N 8.49E
Brest, **58**, 48.24N 4.29W
Bridgetown, **31**, 13.06N 59.37W
Brighton, **52**, 50.50N 0.09W
Brisbane, **140**, 27.30S 153.00E
Bristol, **52**, 51.26N 2.35W
Bristol Channel, **52**, 51.17N 3.20W
Brno, **78**, 49.11N 16.39E
Brooks Range, **22**, 68.50N 152.00W
Bruges, **72**, 51.13N 3.14E
Brunei (*c.*), **128**, 4.56N 114.58E
Brussels, **72**, 50.50N 4.23E
Bucharest, **78**, 44.25N 26.06E
Budapest, **78**, 47.30N 19.03E
Buenos Aires, **38**, 34.40S 58.30W
Bug (*r.*), **78**, 52.29N 21.11E
Bujumbura, **102**, 3.22S 29.21E
Bulawayo, **108**, 20.10S 28.43E
Bulgaria (*c.*), **78**, 42.30N 25.00E
Bungo Channel, **134**, 32.52N 132.30E
Burgas, **78**, 42.30N 27.29E
Burgos, **64**, 42.21N 3.41W
Burkina Faso (*c.*), **102**, 12.15N 1.30W
Burren, **52**, 53.00N 9.00W
Buru (*i.*), **128**, 3.30S 126.30E
Burundi (*c.*), **102**, 3.30S 30.00E
Butuan, **128**, 8.56N 125.31E
Butung (*i.*), **128**, 5.00S 122.50E

Cabinda (*d.*), **102**, 5.34S 12.12E
Cádiz, **64**, 36.32N 6.18W
Caen, **58**, 49.11N 0.22W
Cagliari, **68**, 39.14N 9.07E
Caicos Islands, **31**, 21.30N 72.00W
Cairngorm Mts., **52**, 57.04N 3.30W
Cairns, **140**, 16.51S 145.43E
Cairo, **96**, 30.03N 31.15E
Calcutta, **114**, 22.35N 88.21E
Calgary, **16**, 51.00N 114.10W
Cali, **38**, 3.24N 76.30W
California, Gulf of, **30**, 28.30N 111.00W
Camagüey, **30**, 21.25N 77.55W
Cambay, Gulf of, **114**, 20.30N 72.00E
Cambodia (*c.*), **128**, 12.00N 105.00E
Cambrian Mountains, **52**, 52.33N 3.33W
Cameroon (*c.*), **102**, 6.00N 12.30E
Cameroon, Mt., **102**, 4.20N 9.05E
Campeche, Bay of, **30**, 20.58N 94.00W
Canada (*c.*), **16**, 55.00N 100.00W
Canadian (*r.*), **22**, 35.20N 95.40W
Canadian Shield (*f.*), **16**, 54.00N 82.00W
Canary Islands, **96**, 29.00N 15.00W
Canberra, **140**, 35.18S 149.08E
Cantabrian Mountains, **64**, 42.55N 5.10W
Canterbury Plains, **146**, 43.50S 171.40E
Cape Breton Island, **16**, 46.00N 60.30W
Cape Cod, **22**, 42.08N 70.01W
Cape Town (*town*), **108**, 33.56S 18.28E
Cape York Peninsula, **140**, 12.405S 142.20E
Capri (*i.*), **68**, 40.33N 14.13E
Caprivi Strip (*f.*), **108**, 17.50S 23.10E
Caracas, **38**, 10.35N 66.56W
Carbonara, Cape, **68**, 39.06N 9.32E
Cardamon Hills, **114**, 9.30N 76.55E
Cardiff, **52**, 51.28N 3.11W
Carnic Alps, **68**, 46.40N 12.48E
Carpathian Mts., **78**, 46.20N 25.40E
Carpentaria, Gulf of, **140**, 14.00S 139.00E
Casablanca, **96**, 33.39N 7.35W
Cascade Point, **146**, 44.01S 168.22E
Cascade Range, **22**, 44.00N 121.30W
Caspian Depression, **84**, 47.00N 48.00E
Castries, **31**, 14.01N 60.59W
Catania, **68**, 37.31N 15.05E
Caucasus Mts., **84**, 43.00N 44.00E
Cayenne, **38**, 4.55N 52.18W
Cayman Islands, **30**, 19.00N 81.00W
Cebu (*i.*), **128**, 10.15N 123.45E
Central African Republic (*c.*), **102**, 6.30N 20.00E
Central Makran Range, **114**, 26.30N 65.00E
Central Range, **140**, 6.00S 144.00E
Central Siberian Plateau, **84**, 66.00N 108.00E
Cephalonia (*i.*), **68**, 38.15N 20.33E
Ceram (*i.*), **128**, 3.10S 129.30E
Ceuta, **64**, 35.53N 5.19W
Cévennes (*mts.*), **58**, 44.00N 3.30E
Chad (*c.*), **96**, 13.00N 19.00E
Chad, Lake, **96**, 13.30N 14.00E
Chalcidice (*i.*), **68**, 40.30N 23.40E
Chang (Yangtze) (*r.*), **120**, 31.40N 121.15E
Changchun, **120**, 43.50N 125.20E
Channel Islands, **58**, 49.28N 2.13E
Chao Phraya (*r.*), **128**, 13.34N 100.35E
Charente (*r.*), **58**, 45.57N 1.05W
Chattahoochee (*r.*), **22**, 30.52N 84.57W
Chatham Islands, **146**, 44.00S 176.40W
Cheju, **134**, 33.31N 126.32E
Cheju (*i.*), **134**, 33.30N 126.35E
Chelyabinsk, **84**, 55.10N 61.25E
Chengdu, **120**, 30.37N 104.06E
Cherskogo Range, **84**, 65.50N 143.00E
Chesapeake Bay, **22**, 38.00N 76.00W
Chesterfield, Islands), **140**, 19.30S 158.00E
Cheviot Hills, **52**, 55.22N 2.24W
Chiang-Mai, **128**, 18.48N 98.59E
Chiba, **134**, 35.38N 140.07E
Chicago, **22**, 41.50N 87.45W
Chiclayo, **38**, 6.47S 79.47W
Chihli, Gulf of, **120**, 38.30N 119.30E
Chile (*c.*), **38**, 26.00S 71.00W
Chililabombwe, **108**, 12.29S 27.53E
Chiloé Isla de, **38**, 43.00S 73.00W
Chiltern Hills, **52**, 51.40N 0.53W
China (*c.*), **120**, 33.00N 105.00E
Chios (*i.*), **68**, 38.23N 26.04E
Chirripo (*mt.*), **30**, 9.31N 83.30W
Chişinău, **84**, 47.00N 28.50E
Chita, **84**, 52.03N 113.35E
Chittagong, **114**, 22.20N 91.48E
Chongjin, **134**, 41.55N 129.50E
Chongqing, **120**, 29.31N 106.35E
Chonju, **134**, 36.39N 127.31E
Chonos Archipelago, **38**, 45.00S 73.00W
Christchurch, **146**, 43.32S 172.37E
Christmas Island, **128**, 10.30S 105.40E
Chugoku Mts., **134**, 35.00N 133.00E
Chukot Range, **84**, 68.13N 179.55E
Chunchon, **134**, 37.52N 127.43E
Churchill, **16**, 58.46N 94.10W
Churchill (*r.*), **16**, 58.47N 94.12W
Cincinnati, **22**, 39.10N 84.30W
Cinto, Mt., **58**, 42.23N 8.56E
Citlaltépetl (*mt.*), **30**, 19.00N 97.20W
Ciudad Bolivár, **38**, 8.06N 1.59W
Ciudad Juárez, **30**, 31.42N 106.29W
Clermont-Ferrand, **58**, 45.47N 3.05E
Clervaux, **72**, 50.04N 6.01E
Cleveland, **22**, 41.30N 81.41W
Clipperton Island, **30**, 10.17N 109.13W
Cluj-Napoca, **78**, 46.47N 23.37E
Clutha (*r.*), **146**, 46.18S 169.05E
Clyde (*r.*), **52**, 55.58N 4.53W
Coast Mountains, **16**, 55.00N 129.00W
Coast Range, **22**, 40.00N 123.00W
Coats Land, **152**, 77.00S 28.00W
Cochin, **114**, 9.56N 76.15E
Coco (*r.*), **30**, 14.58N 83.15W
Cocos (*isls.*), **38**, 5.32N 87.04W
Cocos Islands, **128**, 12.10S 96.55E
Coimbra, **64**, 40.12N 8.25W
Colbeck, Cape, **152**, 77.06S 157.48W
Cologne, **72**, 50.56N 6.59E
Colombia (*c.*), **38**, 5.00N 75.00W
Colombo, **114**, 6.55N 79.52E
Colorado (*r.*), **38**, 39.50S 62.02W
Colorado (*r.*), **22**, 31.45N 114.40W
Colorado (*r.*), **22**, 28.36N 95.58W
Colorado Plateau, **22**, 36.00N 112.00W
Columbia (*r.*), **22**, 46.15N 124.05W
Communism Peak, **84**, 38.39N 72.01E
Como, Lake, **68**, 46.05N 9.17E
Comoros (*c.*), **108**, 12.15S 44.00E
Conakry, **102**, 9.30N 13.43W
Concepción, **38**, 36.50S 73.03W
Conchos (*r.*), **30**, 29.34N 104.30W

Islay (*i.*), **52**, 55.45N 6.20W
Israel (*c.*), **90**, 32.0N 34.50E
Istanbul, **90**, 41.02N 28.58E
Istra (*pen.*), **78**, 45.12N 13.55E
Italy (*c.*), **68**, 44.30N 11.00E
Iturup (*i.*), **134**, 44.54N 147.30E
Ivory Coast (*c.*), **102**, 7.00N 5.30W
Iwaki, **134**, 36.58N 140.58E
Iwaki, Mt., **134**, 41.20N 140.20E
Izmir, **90**, 38.24N 27.09E
Izmit, **90**, 40.48N 29.55E
Izu Peninsula, **134**, 34.55N 139.00E

Jacksonville, **22**, 30.20N 81.40W
Jacmel, **31**, 18.14N 72.32W
Jaffna, **114**, 9.38N 80.02E
Jaipur, **114**, 26.53N 75.50E
Jakobstad, **46**, 63.40N 22.42E
Jamaica (*c.*), **30**, 18.00N 77.00W
Jambi, **128**, 1.36S 103.39E
Jamnagar, **114**, 22.28N 70.06E
Japan (*c.*), **134**, 38.00N 137.00E
Japurá (*r.*), **38**, 3.00S 64.50W
Java (*i.*), **128**, 7.30S 111.00E
Jaya, Mt., **128**, 4.00S 137.15E
Jayapura, **128**, 2.28S 140.38E
Jerusalem, **90**, 31.47N 35.13E
Jeidda, **90**, 21.30N 39.10E
Jimma, **96**, 7.39N 36.47E
Jinan, **120**, 36.50N 117.00E
Johannesburg, **108**, 26.11S 28.04E
Jönköping, **46**, 57.47N 14.11E
Jordan (*c.*), **90**, 31.00N 36.00E
Jos Plateau, **102**, 10.00N 9.00E
Jotunheimen (*mts.*), **46**, 61.38N 8.18E
Juan Fernandez Islands, **38**, 34.20S 80.00W
Juba, **96**, 4.50N 31.35E
Juba (*r.*), **96**, 0.20S 42.53E
Júcar (*r.*), **64**, 39.10N 0.15W
Juneau, **22**,, 58.26N 134.30W
Jura (*i.*), **52**, 55.58N 5.55W
Jura Mts., **58**, 46.50N 5.50E
Juruá (*r.*), **38**, 2.33S 65.50W
Jutland (*pen.*), **46**, 56.12N 9.20E
Juventud, Isla de la, **30**, 21.40N 82.40W
Jyväskylä, **46**, 62.14N 25.44E

K2 (*mt.*), **114**, 35.53N 76.32E
Kabul, **90**, 34.30N 69.10E
Kaédi, **96**, 16.09N 13.30W
Kaesong, **134**, 37.59N 126.30E
Kafue (*r.*), **108**, 15.43S 28.55E
Kagoshima, **134**, 31.37N 130.32E
Kai Islands, **128**, 5.45S 132.55E
Kalahari Desert, **108**, 23.55S 23.00E
Kalámai, **68**, 37.02N 22.05E
Kallanesi (*l.*), **46**, 62.40N 27.45E
Kalmar, **46**, 56.40N 16.00E
Kamchatka Peninsula, **84**, 56.00N 160.00E
Kampala, **102**, 0.19N 32.35E
Kanaga, **102**, 5.53S 22.26E
Kanazawa, **134**, 36.35N 136.40E
Kanchenjunga (*mt.*), **114**, 27.44N 88.11E
Kandahar, **90**, 31.36N 65.47E
Kandy, **114**, 7.18N 80.43E
Kangaroo Island, **140**, 35.50S 137.06E
Kano, **102**, 12.00N 8.31E
Kanpur, **114**, 26.27N 80.14E
Kansas City, **22**, 39.05N 94.35W
Kanto Plain, **134**, 36.00N 140.00E
Kaohsiung, **120**, 22.36N 120.17E
Kara Kum (*des.*), **84**, 38.45N 58.00E
Karachi, **114**, 24.51N 67.02E
Karakoram Range, **114**, 35.30N 76.30E
Kariba, Lake, **108**, 16.50S 28.00E
Karpathos (*i.*), **68**, 35.35N 27.08E
Karun (*r.*), **90**, 30.25N 48.12E
Kasai (*r.*), **102**, 3.10S 16.13E
Kasana, **108**, 10.10S 31.11E
Kathmandu, **114**, 27.42N 85.19E
Kattegat (*str.*), **46**, 57.25N 11.30E
Kauai (*i.*), **22**, 22.05N 159.30W
Kawasaki, **134**, 35.30N 139.45E
Kazakhstan (*c.*), **84**, 48.00N 70.00E
Kebnekaise (*mt.*), **46**, 67.53N 18.33E
Keetmanshoop, **108**, 26.34S 18.07E
Kékes (*mt.*), **78**, 47.52N 20.01E
Kemi, **46**, 65.49N 24.32E
Kemi (*r.*), **46**, 65.47N 24.30E
Kendari, **128**, 3.57S 122.36
Kenya (*c.*), **102**, 0.00 38.00E
Kenya, Mt., **102**, 0.10S 37.19E
Kerman, **90**, 30.18N 57.05E
Khabarovsk, **84**, 48.32N 135.08E
Khalkis, **68**, 38.27N 23.36E
Khanía, **68**, 35.30N 24.02E
Khartoum, **96**, 15.33N 32.35E
Khasi Hills, **114**, 25.30N 91.00E
Khios, **68**, 38.23N 26.04E
Kiev, **84**, 50.28N 30.29E
Kigali, **102**, 1.59S 30.05E
Kii Channel, **134**, 34.00N 135.00E
Kii Peninsula, **134**, 34.00N 135.30E
Kilimanjaro (*mt.*), **102**, 3.02S 37.20E
Kimberley, **108**, 28.44S 24.44E
Kimberley Plateau, **140**, 17.20S 127.20E
Kimchaek, **134**, 40.41N 129.12E
Kinabalu, Mt., **128**, 6.10N 116.40E
King Island, **140**, 39.50S 144.00E
Kingston, **30**, 17.58N 76.48W
Kingstown, **31**, 13.12N 61.14W
Kinshasa, **102**, 4.18S 15.18E
Kirgiz Steppe, **84**, 50.00N 57.10E
Kirkpatrick, Mt., **152**, 84.20S 166.19E
Kirkuk, **90**, 35.28N 44.26E
Kirkwall, **52**, 58.59N 2.58W
Kiruna, **46**, 67.51N 20.16E
Kisangani, **102**, 0.33N 25.14E
Kismaayo, **96**, 0.25S 42.31E
Kiso Mts., **134**, 35.20N 137.30E
Kitakami (*r.*), **134**, 38.25N 141.18E
Kitakyushu, **134**, 35.50N 130.50E
Kíthira (*i.*), **68**, 36.15N 23.00E
Kivu, Lake, **102**, 1.50S 29.10E
Kizil Irmak (*r.*), **90**, 41,45N 35.57E
Kjolen Mountains, **46**, 67.30N 17.30E
Klar (*r.*), **46**, 59.23N 13.32E
Klyuchevskaya, (*mt.*) **84**, 55.00N 159.30E
Kobe, **134**, 34.42N 135.15E
Kochi, **134**, 33.33N 133.52E
Kodiak Island, **22**, 57.00N 153.50W
Kokenau, **128**, 4.42S 136.25E
Kola Peninsula, **84**, 67.00N 38.00E
Kolyma Range, **84**, 68.50N 161.00E
Korčula (*i.*), **78**, 42.56N 16.53E
Korea Strait, **134**, 35.00N 129.20E
Koryak Range, **84**, 62.20N 171.00E
Kos (*i.*), **68**, 36.48N 27.10E
Kosciusko, Mt., **140**, 36.28S 148.17E
Košice, **78**, 48.44N 21.15E
Krakatau (*i.*), **128**, 6.11S 105.26E
Kraków, **78**, 50.03N 19.55E
Krasnoyarsk, **84**, 56.05N 92.46E
Krishna (*r.*), **114**, 16.00N 81.00E
Kristiansand, **46**, 58.10N 8.00E
Krk (*i.*), **78**, 45.04N 14.36E
Kuala Lumpur, **128**, 3.08N 101.42E
Kuching, **128**, 1.32N 110.20E
Kumamoto, **134**, 32.50N 130.42E
Kunashir (*i.*), 44.10N 146.00E
Kunlun Shan (*mts.*), **120**, 36.40N 88.00E
Kunming, **120**, 25.04N 102.41E
Kunsan, **134**, 35.58N 126.41E
Kuopio, **46**, 62.51N 27.30E
Kupang, **128**, 10.13S 123.38E
Kuria Muria Islands, **90**, 17.30N 56.00E
Kuril Islands, **84**, 46.00N 150.30E
Kushiro, **134**, 42.58N 144.24E
Kuskokwim Mts., **22**, 62.00N 156.00W
Kutch, Rann of, (*f.*), **114**, 23.50N 69.50E
Kuwait (*c.*), **90**, 29.20N 47.40E
Kwangju, **134**, 35.01N 126.44E
Kyoga, Lake, **102**, 1.30N 33.00E
Kyoto, **134**, 35.04N 135.50E
Kyrgygstan (*c.*), **84**, 41.30N 75.00E
Kyushu (*i.*), **134**, 33.30N 131.00E
Kyushu Mts., **134**, 32.20N 131.20E
Kyzyl Kum (*des.*), **84**, 42.00N 64.30E

La Camargue (*f.*), **58**, 43.40N 4.35E
La Coruña, **64**, 43.22N 8.24W
La Paz, **38**, 16.30S 68.10W
La Spezia, **68**, 44.07N 9.49E
Labrador (*f.*), **16**, 57.00N 62.00W
Ladoga, Lake, **84**, 61.00N 32.00E
Lagos, **102**, 6.27N 3.28E
Lahn (*r.*), **72**, 50.18N 7.36E
Lahore, **114**, 31.34N 74.22E
Lakshadweep (*isls.*), **114**, 11.00N 72.00E
Lanai (*i.*), **22**, 20.50N 156.55W
Land's End, **52**, 50.03N 5.45W
Langjökull (*mt.*), **46**, 63.43N 20.03W
Langkawi Islands, **128**, 6.20N 99.30E
Langres Plateau, **58**, 47.41N 5.00E
Lanzhou, **120**, 36.01N 103.45E
Laos (*c.*), **128**, 19.00N 104.00E
Lapland (*f.*), **46**, 68.10N 24.10E
Larisa, **68**, 39.36N 22.24E
Larsen Ice Shelf, **152**, 68.30S 62.30W
Las Vegas, **22**, 36.11N 115.08W
Latvia (*c.*), **84**, 57.00N 25.00E
Laurentian Mts., **16**, 52.15N 70.00W
Lausanne, **72**, 46.31N 6.38E
Le Havre, **58**, 49.30N 0.06E
Lebanon (*c.*), **90**, 34.00N 36.00E
Leeds, **52**, 53.48N 1.34W
Leipzig, **72**, 51.19N 12.20E
Leizhou Peninsula, **120**, 20.40N 109.30E
Lena (*r.*), **84**, 72.00N 127.10E
León, **30**, 21.10N 101.42W
León, **64**, 42.35N 5.34W
Lérida, **64**, 41.37N 0.38E
Lerwick, **52**, 60.09N 1.09W
Les Landes (*f.*), **58**, 44.00N 1.00W
Lesbos (*i.*), **68**, 39.10N 26.16E
Lesotho (*c.*), **108**, 29.30S 28.00E
Lesser Antilles (*isls.*), **31**, 16.00N 62.00W
Levkas (*i.*), **68**, 38.44N 20.37E
Lewis (*i.*), **52**, 58.10N 6.40W
Leyte (*i.*), **128**, 10.40N 124.50E
Lhasa, **120**, 29.41N 91.10E
Liberia (*c.*), **102**, 6.30N 9.30W
Libreville, **102**, 0.30N 9.25E
Libya (*c.*), **96**, 26.30N 17.00E
Libyan Desert, **96**, 26.00N 24.00E
Liechtenstein (*c.*), **72**, 47.09N 9.32E
Liège, **72**, 50.38N 5.35E
Lille, **58**, 50.39N 3.05E
Lilongwe, **108**, 13.58S 33.49E
Lima, **38**, 12.06S 77.03W
Limassol, **68**, 34.40N 33.03E
Limerick, **52**, 52.40N 8.37W
Límnos (*i.*), **68**, 39.55N 25.14E
Limoges, **58**, 45.50N 1.15E
Limpopo (*r.*), **108**, 25.14S 33.33E
Lingga (*i.*), **128**, 0.20S 104.30E
Linz, **72**, 48.18N 14.18E
Lipari Islands, **68**, 38.35N 14.45E
Lisbon, **64**, 38.44N 9.08W
Lithuania (*c.*), **84**, 55.00N 24.00E
Little Andaman (*i.*), **114**, 10.50N 92.38E
Little Karroo (*f.*), **108**, 33.40S 21.40E
Liverpool, **52**, 53.25N 3.00W
Livingstone, **108**, 17.50S 25.53E
Livorno (Leghorn), **68**, 43.33N 10.18E
Ljubljana, **78**, 46.04N 14.28E
Ljungan (*r.*), **46**, 61.12N 17.08E
Llanos (*f.*), **38**, 7.30N 70.00W
Llullaillaco (*mt.*), **38**, 24.38S 68.38W
Lobatse, **108**, 25.12S 25.39E
Lobito, **108**, 12.20S 13.34E
Łódź, **78**, 51.49N 19.28E
Lofoten (*isls.*), **46**, 68.15N 13.50E
Logan, Mt., **16**, 60.34N 140.24W
Loire (*r.*), **58**, 47.16N 2.11W
Lolland (*i.*), **46**, 54.46N 11.30E
Lombok (*i.*), **128**, 8.30S 116.20E
Lomé, **102**, 6.10N 1.21E
London, **52**, 51.32N 0.06W
Londonderry, **52**, 55.00N 7.20W
Long Island, **22**, 40.50N 73.00W
Long Island, **31**, 23.00N 75.00W
Lop Nor (*l.*), **120**, 40.30N 90.30E
Lopez, Cape, **102**, 0.36S 8.45E
Los Angeles, **22**, 34.00N 118.17W
Lot (*r.*), **58**, 44.18N 0.20E
Luanda, **108**, 8.50S 13.20E
Luang Prabang, **128**, 19.53N 102.10E
Luangwa (*r.*), **108**, 15.32S 30.28E
Lublin, **78**, 51.18N 22.31E
Lubumbashi, **102**, 11.41S 27.29E
Lucania, Mt., **16**, 61.01N 140.28W
Luena, **108**, 11.46S 19.55E
Lugano, **72**, 46.01N 8.58E
Lule (*r.*), **46**, 65.35N 22.03E
Luleå, **46**, 65.34N 22.10E
Lüneburg Heide (*f.*), **72**, 53.06N 10.30E
Lúrio (*r.*), **108**, 13.32S 40.31E
Lusaka, **108**, 15.26S 28.20E
Luxembourg, **72**, 49.37N 6.08E
Luxembourg (*c.*), **72**, 49.50N 6.15E
Luzon (*i.*), **128**, 17.50N 121.00E
Lyon, **58**, 45.46N 4.50E
Maas (*r.*), **72**, 51.44N 4.42E
Maastricht, **72**, 50.51N 5.42E
Macao, **120**, 22.13N 113.36E
Macdonnell Ranges, **140**, 23.45S 133.20E
Macedonia (*c.*), **78**, 41.30N 21.30E
Macgillycuddy's Reeks (*mts.*), **52**, 52.00N 9.45W
Mackenzie (*r.*), **16**, 69.20N 134.00W
Mackenzie Mts., **16**, 64.00N 130.00W
Madagascar (*c.*), **108**, 20.00S 47.30E
Madang, **140**, 5.14S 145.45E
Madeira (*i.*), **96**, 32.45N 17.00W
Madeira (*r.*), **38**, 3.20S 59.00W
Madraka, Cape, **90**, 19.00N 57.50E
Madras, **114**, 13.05N 80.18E
Madrid, **64**, 40.25N 3.43W
Madura (*i.*), **128**, 7.00S 113.30E
Madurai, **114**, 9.55N 78.07E
Magdeburg, **72**, 52.08N 11.38E
Magellan, Strait of, **38**, 53.00S 71.00W
Maggiore, Lake, **68**, 45.57N 8.37E
Mahajangu, **108**, 15.43S 46.19E
Mahanadi (*r.*), **114**, 20.17N 86.43E
Mahavavy (*r.*), **108**, 15.57S 45.54E
Mahón, **64**, 39.55N 4.18E
Main (*r.*), **72**, 50.00N 8.18E
Mainland (*i.*), **52**, 59.00N 3.10W
Mainland (*i.*), **52**, 60.15N 1.22W
Majorca (*i.*), **64**, 39.35N 3.00E
Makassar Strait, **128**, 3.00S 118.00E
Makgadikgadi Pan (*f.*), **108**, 20.50S 25.45E
Makran Coast Range, **114**, 25.40N 65.00E
Malabo, **102**, 3.45N 8.48E
Malacca, Strait of, **128**, 3.00N 100.30E
Málaga, **64**, 36.43N 4.25W
Malakal, **96**, 9.31N 31.40E
Malang, **128**, 7.59S 112.45E
Malanje, **108**, 9.36S 16.21E
Målaren (*l.*), **46**, 59.30N 17.12E
Malawi (*c.*), **108**, 13.00S 34.00E
Malay Peninsula, **128**, 4.00N 102.00E
Malaysia (*c.*), **128**, 5.00N 110.00E
Maldives (*c.*), **114**, 6.20N 73.00E
Malea, Cape, **68**, 36.27N 23.11E
Mali (*c.*), **96**, 18.00N 1.00W
Malin Head, **52**, 55.22N 7.24W
Malmö, **46**, 55.36N 13.00E
Malpelo Island, **38**, 2.00N 81.43W
Malta (*c.*), **68**, 35.55N 14.25E
Malta (*i.*), **68**, 35.55N 14.25E
Man, Isle of, **52**, 54.15N 4.30W
Manado, **128**, 1.30N 124.58E
Managua, **30**, 12.06N 86.18W
Managua, Lake, **30**, 12.10N 86.30W
Manama, **90**, 26.12N 50.36E
Manaus, **38**, 3.06S 60.00W
Manchester, **52**, 53.30N 2.15W
Manchurian Plain, **120**, 42.00N 122.00E
Mandalay, **128**, 21.57N 96.04E
Mangalore, **114**, 12.54N 74.51E
Mangoky (*r.*) **108**, 21.29S 43.41E
Mangyshlak Peninsula, **84**, 44.00N 52.30E
Manila , **128**, 14.36N 120.59E
Manitoba, Lake, **16**, 51.00N 98.45W
Mannar, Gulf of, **114**, 8.20N 79.00E
Manokwan, **128**, 0.53S 134.05E
Maoke Mts., **128**, 4.00S 137.30E
Maputo, **108**, 25.58S 32.35E
Maracaibo, **38**, 10.44S 71.37W
Maracaibo, Lake, **38**, 9.50N 71.30W
Maradi, **96**, 13.29N 7.10E
Marañón (*r.*), **38**, 4.40S 73.20W
Marie Byrd Land **152**, 79.30S 125.00W
Maritime Alpes (*mts.*), **58**, 44.30N 7.15E
Maritsa (*r.*), **78**, 41.40N 26.16E
Markham, Mt., **152**, 82.51S 161.21E
Marne (*r.*), **58**, 48.49N 2.24E
Marrakesh, **96**, 31.49N 8.00W
Marseille, **58**, 43.18N 5.24E
Martinique (*i.*), **31**, 14.40N 61.00W
Masan, **134**, 35.10N 128.35E
Maseru, **108**, 29.18S 27.28E
Mashhad, **90**, 36.16N 59.34E
Masirah (*i.*), **90**, 20.30N 58.50E
Mask, Lough, **52**, 53.38N 9.22W
Masoala, Cape, **108**, 15.59S 50.13E
Massif Central (*mts.*), **58**, 45.00N 3.10E
Mato Grosso, Plateau of, **38**, 16.00S 54.00W
Matopo Hills, **108**, 20.45S 28.30E
Matterhorn (*mt.*), **72**, 45.59N 7.43E
Maui (*i.*), **22**, 20.45N 156.15W
Mauna Kea (*mt.*), **22**, 19.50N 155.25W
Mauritania (*c.*), **96**, 19.00N 10.00W
Mauritius (*c.*), 20.08S 57.30E
Mayon, Mt., **128**, 13.14N 123.45E
Mayotte (*i.*), **108**, 12.50S 45.10E
Mbabane, **108**, 26.19S 31.08E
McKinley, Mt., **22**, 63.00N 151.00W
McMurdo, **152**, 77.50S 166.25E
Mecca, **90**, 21.26N 39.49E
Mecklenburg Bay, **72**, 54.20N 11.50E
Medan, **128**, 3.35N 98.39E
Medellín, **38**, 6.15N 75.36W
Medina, **90**, 24.30N 39.35E
Mekong (*r.*), **128**, 10.00N 106.20E
Melbourne, **140**, 37.45S 144.58E
Melilla, **64**, 35.17N 2.51W
Melville Island, **140**, 11.30S 131.00E
Melville Peninsula, **16**, 68.00N 84.00W
Memphis, **22**, 35.08N 90.03W
Mendip Hills, **52**, 51.15N 2.40W
Mentawai Islands, **128**, 2.50S 99.00E
Merauke, **128**, 8.30S 140.22E
Mergui Archipelago, **128**, 11.30N 98.30E
Meseta (*f.*), **64**, 40.15N 3.30W
Messina, **68**, 38.13N 15.34E
Metz, **58**, 49.07N 6.11E
Meuse (*r.*), **72**, 51.49N 5.01E
Mexico (*c.*), **30**, 22.00N 101.40W
Mexico City, **30**, 19.25N 99.10W
Mexico, Gulf of, **31**, 25.00N 90.00W
Miami, **22**, 25.45N 80.15W
Michigan, Lake, **22**, 44.00N 87.00W
Middle (*i.*), **114**, 12.35N 93.00E
Middlesbrough, **52**, 54.34N 1.13W
Mikuni Mts., **134**, 37.00N 139.20E
Milan, **68**, 45.28N 9.16E
Milos (*i.*), **68**, 36.40N 24.26E
Milwaukee, **22**, 43.02N 87.55W
Mindanao (*i.*), **128**, 7.30N 125.00E
Mindoro (*i.*), **128**, 13.00N 121.00E
Minho (*r.*), **64**, 41.52N 8.51W
Minneapolis, **22**, 44.59N 93.13W
Minorca (*i.*), **64**, 40.00N 4.00E
Minsk, **84**, 53.51N 27.30E
Miskolc, **78**, 48.07N 20.47E
Misool (i.), **128**, 1.50S 130.10E
Misratah, **96**, 32.24N 15.04E
Mississippi (*r.*), **22**, 29.00N 89.15W
Missouri (*r.*), **22**, 38.50N 90.08W
Mitchell, Mt., **22**, 35.47N 82.16W
Mitilíni, **68**, 39.06N 26.34E
Miyazaki, **134**, 31.58N 131.50E
Mjøsa (*l.*), **46**, 60.40N 11.00E
Mljet (*i.*), **78**, 42.45N 17.30E
Moçambique, **108**, 15.00S 40.55E
Mogadishu, **96**, 2.02N 45.21E
Mojave Desert, **22**, 35.00N 117.00W
Mokpo, **134**, 34.48N 126.22E
Molde, **46**, 62.44N 7.08E
Moldova (*c.*), **84**, 47.30N 28.30E
Moldooeanu (*mt.*), **78**, 45.36N 24.44E
Molokai (*i.*), **22**, 21.20N 157.00W
Moluccas (*isls.*), **128**, 4.00S 128.00E
Mombasa, **102**, 4.04S 39.40E
Monaco, **58**, 43.40N 7.25E
Monaco (*c.*), **58**, 43.40N 7.25E
Mongolia (*c.*), **84**, 46.30N 104.00E
Mongu, **108**, 15.10S 23.09E
Monrovia, **102**, 6.20N 10.46W
Montego Bay (*town*), **30**, 18.27N 77.56W
Montenegro (*d.*), **78**, 42.45N 19.20E
Monterrey, **30**, 25.40N 100.20W
Montevideo, **38**, 34.55S 56.10W
Montpellier, **58**, 43.36N 3.53E
Montreal, **16**, 45.31N 73.34W
Moore, Lake (*dry*), **140**, 29.30S 117.30E
Morava (*r.*), **78**, 44.43N 21.02E
Moray Firth (*est.*), **52**, 57.35N 3.50W
Morioka, **134**, 39.43N 141.10E
Morocco (*c.*), **96**, 32.00N 8.00W
Morondava, **108**, 20.17S 44.17E
Moroni, **108**, 11.40S 43.19E
Morvan (*f.*), **58**, 47.00N 4.50E
Moscow, **84**, 55.45N 37.42E
Moscow University Ice Shelf, **152**, 67.00S 120.00E
Moselle (*r.*), **72**, 50.22N 7.36E
Mostar, **78**, 43.20N 17.50E
Mosul, **90**, 36.21N 43.08E
Mourne Mts., **52**, 54.10N 6.02W
Mozambique (*c.*), **108**, 19.00S 35.00E
Mozambique Channel, **108**, 16.00S 42.30E
Muchinga Mts., **108**, 12.00S 31.00E
Mui Ca Mau (*point*), **128**, 8.30N 104.35E
Mulanje, Mt., **108**, 15.57S 35.33E
Mulhacén (*mt.*), **64**, 37.04N 3.22W
Mulhouse, **58**, 47.45N 7.21E
Mull (*i.*), **52**, 56.28N 5.56W
Multan, **114**, 30.10N 71.36E
Munich, **72**, 48.08N 11.34E
Mur (*r.*), **72**, 47.05N 15.27E
Mures (*r.*), **78**, 46.16N 20.10E
Müritz, Lake, **72**, 53.25N 12.43E
Muroran, **134**, 42.21N 140.59E
Murray (*r.*), **140**, 35.23S 139.20E
Murrumbidgee (*r.*), **140**, 34.38S 143.10E
Musala (*mt.*), **78**, 42.11N 23.35E
Muscat, **90**, 23.36N 58.37E
Musgrave Ranges, **140**, 26.10S 131.50E
Mutare, **108**, 18.58S 32.40E
MuUs Shamo (des.), **120**, 40.00N 109.00E
Muztag (*mt.*), **120**, 36.25N 87.25E
Mweru, Lake, **102**, 9.00S 28.40E
Myanmar (Burma) (*C.*), **102**, 22.00N 98.00E
Myingyan, **128**, 21.25N 95.20E
Mzuzu, **108**, 11.50S 33.39E

Naga Hills, **114**, 26.10N 94.30E
Nagasaki, **134**, 32.45N 129.52E
Nagoya, **134**, 35.08N 136.53E
Nagpur, **114**, 21.10N 79.12E
Nairobi, **102**, 1.17S 36.50E
Naktong (*r.*), **134**, 35.10N 128.18E
Nam, Lake, **120**, 30.40N 90.30E
Namib Desert, **108**, 22.50S 14.40E
Namibia (*c.*), **108**, 22.00S 17.00E
Namlea, **128**, 3.15S 127.07E
Nampo, **134**, 38.40N 125.30E
Nampula, **108**, 15.09S 39.14E
Namur, **72**, 50.28N 4.52E
Nancy, **58**, 48.42N 6.12E
Nangnim Mts., **134**, 40.30N 127.00E
Nanjing, **120**, 32.00N 118.40E

Sierra de Gredos *(mts.)*, **64**, 40.18N 5.20W
Sierra de Guadarrama *(mts.)*, **64**, 41.00N 3.50W
Sierra de la Demanda *(mts.)*, **64**, 42.10N 3.00W
Sierra de Segura *(mts.)*, **64**, 38.00N 2.50W
Sierra Leone *(c.)*, **102**, 8.30N 12.00W
Sierra Madre *(mts.)*, **30**, 15.00N 92.00W
Sierra Madre del Sur *(mts.)*, **30**, 17.00N 10.00W
Sierra Madre Occidental *(mts.)*, **30**, 25.00N 107.00W
Sierra Madre Oriental *(mts.)*, **30**, 23.00N 99.00W
Sierra Morena *(mts.)*, **64**, 38.10N 5.00W
Sierra Nevada *(mts.)*, **22**, 37.45N 119.30W
Sierra Nevada *(mts.)*, **64**, 37.04N 3.20W
Signy, **152**, 60.43S 45.36W
Silesian Plaain, **78**, 50.30N 19.30E
Siling, Lake, **120**, 31.40N 88.30E
Siljan *(l.)*, **46**, 60.50N 14.45E
Simeulue *(i.)*, **128**, 2.30N 96.00E
Simpson Desert, **140**, 25.00S 136.50E
Sinai *(pen.)*, **96**, 29.00N 34.00E
Singapore, **128**, 1.20N 103.45E
Singapore *(c.)*, **128**, 1.20N 103.45E
Singkep *(i.)*, **128**, 0.30S 104.20E
Sinuiju, **134**, 40.04N 124.25E
Siret *(r.)*, **78**, 45.28N 27.56E
Siwalik Range, **114**, 31.15N 77.45E
Sjaelland *(i.)*, **46**, 55.30N 11.45E
Skagerrak *(str.)*, **46**, 58.00N 9.30E
Skellefteå, **46**, 64.46N 20.57E
Skopje, **78**, 41.58N 21.29E
Skye *(i.)*, **52**, 57.20N 6.15W
Sligo, **52**, 54.17N 8.28W
Slovakia *(c.)*, **78**, 48.50N 20.00E
Slovenia *(c.)*, **78**, 45.50N 14.30E
Slovenské Mts., **78**, 48.50N 19.50E
Smolikas *(mt.)*, **68**, 40.06N 20.55E
Snake *(r.)*, **22**, 46.12N 119.02W
Sněžka, Mt., **78**, 50.45N 15.37E
Snowdon *(mt.)*, **52**, 53.05N 4.05W
Sobaek Mts., **134**, 35.50N 127.45E
Sochi, **84**, 43.35N 39.46E
Socotra *(i.)*, **90**, 12.30N 54.00E
Sofia, **78**, 42.41N 23.19E
Sofia *(r.)*, **108**, 15.27S 47.23E
Sogne Fjord, **46**, 61.06N 5.10E
Somalia *(c.)*, **96**, 4.00N 47.00E
Somerset Island, **16**, 73.00N 93.30W
Somes *(r.)*, **78**, 48.04N 22.30E
Songhua *(r.)*, **120**, 47.46N 132.30E
Sorong, **128**, 0.50S 131.17E
South *(i.)*, **114**, 11.41N 92.40E
South Africa *(c.)*, **108**, 30.00S 22.00E
South Georgia *(i.)*, **38**, 54.00S 37.00W
South Island, **146**, 43.00S 171.00E
South Korea *(c.)*, **134**, 37.00N 128.00E
South Orkney Islands, **152**, 60.35S 45.30W
South Shetland Islands, **152**, 62.00S 58.00W
Southampton, **52**, 50.54N 1.23W
Southampton Island, **16**, 64.30N 84.00W
Southern Alps, **146**, 43.20S 170.45E
Southern Uplands, **52**, 55.30N 3.30W
Southwest Cape, **146**, 47.15S 167.30E
Soya, Cape, **134**, 45.33N 141.58E
Spain *(c.)*, **64**, 40.00N 4.00W
Spartivento, Cape, **68**, 37.55N 16.04E
Spátha, Cape, **68**, 35.42N 23.43E
Spenser Mts., **146**, 42.12S 172.36E
Spessart *(mts.)*, **72**, 50.07N 9.35E
Split, **78**, 43.31N 16.28E
Spokane, **22**, 47.40N 117.23W
Sporades, Northern *(isls.)*, **68**, 39.20N 23.30E
Sri Lanka *(c.)*, **114**, 7.30N 80.50E
Stanley, Mt., **102**, 0.20N 30.50E
Stanovoy Range, **84**, 56.00N 125.40E
Stara Zagora, **78**, 42.26N 25.37E
Stavanger, **46**, 58.58N 5.45E
Stewart Island, **146**, 47.02S 167.51E
Stikine Mts., **16**, 59.00N 129.00W
Stockholm, **46**, 59.20N 18.03E
Stormberg *(mts.)*, **108**, 30.45S 25.00E
Storsjön *(l.)*, **46**, 63.10N 14.20E
Strasbourg, **58**, 48.35N 7.45E
Straumnes, **46**, 66.30N 23.05W
Struma *(r.)*, **68**, 40.45N 23.51E
Stuttgart, **72**, 48.46N 9.11E
Subotica, **78**, 46.04N 19.41E
Sucre, **38**, 19.05S 65.15W
Sudan *(c.)*, **96**, 14.00N 28.00E
Sudd *(f.)*, **96**, 7.50N 30.00E
Sudetic Mts., **78**, 50.30N 16.30E
Suez, **96**, 29.59N 32.33E
Suez Canal, **96**, 30.40N 32.20E
Suir *(r.)*, **52**, 52.17N 7.00W
Sukkur, **114**, 27.42N 68.54E
Sula Islands, **128**, 1.50S 125.10E
Sulaiman Range, **114**, 30.50N 70.20E
Sulawesi (Celebes) *(i.)*, **128**, 2.00S 120.30E
Sulu Archipelago, **128**, 5.30N 121.00E
Sumatra *(i.)*, **128**, 2.00S 102.00E
Sumba *(i.)*, **128**, 9.30S 119.55E
Sumbawa *(i.)*, **128**, 8.45S 117.50E
Sundsvall, **46**, 62.23N 17.18E
Superior, Lake, **16**, 48.00N 88.00W
Sur, **90**, 22.23N 59.32E
Surabaya, **128**, 7.14S 112.45E
Suriname *(c.)*, **38**, 4.00N 56.00W
Surtsey *(i.)*, **46**, 63.18N 20.30W
Sutlej *(r.)*, **114**, 29.26N 71.09E
Svartisen *(mt.)*, **46**, 66.40N 13.56E
Swabian Jura *(mts.)*, **72**, 48.30N 9.38E
Swansea, **52**, 51.37N 3.57W
Swaziland *(c.)*, **108**, 26.30S 32.00E
Sweden *(c.)*, **46**, 63.00N 16.00E
Switzerland *(c.)*, **72**, 46.45N 8.30E
Sydney, **140**, 33.55S 151.10E
Syr Darya *(r.)*, **84**, 46.00N 61.12E
Syracuse, **68**, 37.05N 15.17E
Syria *(c.)*, **90**, 35.00N 38.00E
Syrian Desert, **90**, 32.00N 39.00E
Szczecin, **78**, 53.25N 14.32E
Szeged, **78**, 46.16N 20.08E

Tabriz, **90**, 38.05N 46.18E
Tademait, Plateau of, **96**, 28.45N 2.10E
Taebaek Mountains, **134**, 36.40N 129.00E
Taegu, **134**, 35.52N 128.36E
Taejon, **134**, 36.20N 127.26E
Tagus *(r.)*, **64**, 39.00N 8.57W
Tahat, Mt., **96**, 23.20N 5.40E
Taihang Shan *(mts.)*, **120**, 36.40N 113.35E
Taipei,**120**, 25.05N 121.32E
Taiwan *(c.)*, **120**, 23.30N 121.00E
Taiwan Strait, **120**, 25.00N 120.00E
Taiyuan, **120**, 37.50N 112.30E
Tajikistan *(c.)*, **84**, 39.00N 70.30E
Tajumedco *(mt.)*, **30**, 15.02N 91.55W
Takamatsu, **134**, 34.28N 134.05E
Takaoka, **134**, 36.47N 137.00E
Taklamakan *(des.)*, **120**, 38.10N 82.00E
Tallinn, **84**, 59.22N 24.48E
Tamabo Range, **128**, 3.30N 115.23E
Tamanrasset, **96**, 22.50N 5.31E
Tampere, **46**, 61.30N 23.45E
Tampico, **30**, 22.18N 97.52W
Tana, Lake, **96**, 12.00N 37.20E
Tanami Desert, **140**, 19.50S 130.50E
Tanaro *(r.)*, **68**, 45.01N 8.46E
Tanega *(i.)*, **134**, 30.32N 131.00E
Tanganyika, Lake, **102**, 5.37S 29.30E
Tanggula Shan *(mts.)*, **120**, 32.40N 92.30E
Tangier, **96**, 35.48N 5.45W
Tanimbar Islands, **128**, 7.50S 131.30E
Tanzania *(c.)*, **102**, 5.00S 35.00E
Tapajós *(r.)*, **38**, 2.25S 54.40W
Taranto, **68**, 40.28N 17.14E
Taranto, Gulf of, **68**, 40.00N 17.20E
Tararua Range, **146**, 40.50S 175.25E
Tarim *(r.)*, **120**, 41.00N 83.30E
Tarim Basin, **120**, 40.00N 83.00E
Tarn *(r.)*, **58**, 44.05N 1.06E
Tarragona, **64**, 41.07N 1.15E
Tashkent, **84**, 41.16N 69.13E
Tasman Mts., **146**, 41.06S 172.30E
Tasmania *(i.)*, **140**, 42.00S 147.00E
Tatra Mountains, **78**, 49.10N 20.00E
Taunus *(mts.)*, **72**, 50.10N 8.30E
Taupo, Lake, **146**, 38.48S 175.55E
Taurus Mts., **90**, 37.15N 34.15E
Tavoy, 12, 14.07N 98.18E
Tay, Firth of *(est.)*, **52**, 56.24N 3.08W
Taymyr Peninsula, **84**, 74.50N 100.00E
Tbilisi, **84**, 41.43N 44.48E
Te Anau, Lake, **146**, 45.14S 167.46E
Tehran, **90**, 35.40N 51.26E
Tehuantepec, Gulf of, **30**, 16.00N 95.00W
Tehuantepec, Isthmus of, **30**, 17.00N 95.00W
Tel Aviv, **90**, 32.05N 34.46E
Telukbetung, **128**, 5.28S 105.16E
Tennessee *(r.)*, **22**, 37.04N 88.33W
Ternate, **128**, 0.48N 127.23E
Terni, **68**, 42.34N 12.44E
Teshio *(r.)*, **134**, 44.53N 141.44E
Tete, **108**, 16.10S 33.30E
Thabana-Ntlenyana *(mt.)*, **108**, 29.28S 29.17E
Thailand *(c.)*, **128**, 16.00N 101.00E
Thailand, Gulf of, **128**, 11.00N 101.00E
Thames *(r.)*, **52**, 51.30N 0.05E
Thar Desert, **114**, 28.00N 72.00E
Thasos *(i.)*, **68**, 40.40N 24.39E
Thimphu, **114**, 27.29N 89.40E
Thira *(i.)*, **68**, 36.24N 25.27E
Three Kings Islands, **146**, 34.09S 172.09E
Thule, **16**, 77.30N 69.29W
Thunder Bay *(town)*, **16**, 48.25N 89.14W
Thuringian Forest, **72**, 50.40N 10.52E
Tianjin, **120**, 39.08N 117.12E
Tiber *(r.)*, **68**, 41.45N 12.16E
Tibesti *(mts.)*, **96**, 21.00N 17.30E
Tibet, Plateau of, **120**, 34.00N 86.30E
Tien Shan *(mts.)*, **120**, 42.00N 80.30E
Tierra del Fuego *(i.)*, **38**, 54.00S 69.00W
Tigris *(r.)*, **90**, 31.00N 47.27E
Timaru, **146**, 44.24S 171.15E
Timbuktu, **96**, 16.49N 2.59W
Timişoara, **78**, 45.47N 21.15E
Timor *(i.)*, **128**, 9.30S 125.00E
Tindouf, **96**, 27.42N 8.09W
Tiranë, **78**, 41.20N 19.48E
Tirso *(r.)*, **68**, 39.52N 8.33E
Tisza *(r.)*, **78**, 45.09N 20.16E
Titicaca, Lake, **38**, 16.00S 69.00W
Toamasina, **108**, 18.10S 49.23E
Toba Kakar Hills, **114**, 31.15N 68.00E
Toba, Lake, **128**, 2.45N 98.50E
Tobago *(i.)*, **31**, 11.15N 60.40W
Tobelo, **128**, 1.45N 127.59E
Tobol *(r.)*, **84**, 58.15N 68.12E
Tocantins *(r.)*, **38**, 1.50S 49.15W
Togo *(c.)*, **102**, 8.30N 1.00E
Tok *(i.)*, **134**, 37.14N 132.00E
Tokyo, **134**, 35.40N 139.45E
Toliara, **108**, 23.21S 43.40E
Tone *(r.)*, **134**, 35.44N 140.51E
Tonle Sap *(l.)*, **128**, 12.50N 104.00E
Torne *(r.)*, **46**, 65.53N 24.07E
Toronto, **16**, 43.39N 79.23W
Torrens, Lake *(salt)*, **140**, 31.00S 137.50E
Torres Strait, **140**, 10.00S 142.20E
Toubkal *(mt.)*, **96**, 31.03N 7.57W
Toulon, **58**, 43.07N 5.53E
Toulouse, **58**, 43.33N 1.24E
Tours, **58**, 47.23N 0.42E
Townsville, **140**, 19.13S 146.48E
Transylvanian Alps *(mts.)*, **78**, 45.40N 24.40E
Trapani, **68**, 38.02N 12.30E
Trent *(r.)*, **52**, 53.41N 0.41W
Trieste, **68**, 45.40N 13.47E
Triglow *(mt.)* **78**, 46.23N 13.50E
Trinidad *(i.)*, **31**, 10.30N 61.15W
Trinidad and Tobago *(c.)*, **31**, 11.00N 61.20W
Trinidade *(i.)*, **38**, 20.30S 30.00W
Tripoli, **90**, 34.27N 35.50E
Tripoli, **96**, 32.58N 13.12E
Trivandrum, **114**, 8.41N 76.57E
Tromsø, **46**, 69.42N 19.00E
Trondheim, **46**, 63.36N 10.23E
Trondheim Fjord, **46**, 63.40N 10.30E
Tsaratanana Massif *(mts.)*, **108**, 14.00S 49.00E
Tsu Islands, **134**, 34.30N 129.20E
Tsugaru Strait, **134**, 41.30N 140.50E
Tsumeb, **108**, 19.12S 17.43E
Tumen *(r.)*, **134**, 42.18N 130.41E
Tunis, **96**, 35.47N 10.10E
Tunisia *(c.)*, **96**, 35.00N 10.00E
Turfan *(f.)*, **120**, 42.40N 89.00E
Turin, **68**, 45.04N 7.40E
Turkana, Lake, **102**, 4.00N 36.00E
Turkey *(c.)*, **90**, 39.00N 35.00E
Turkmenistan *(c.)*, **84**, 40.00N 60.00E
Turks Islands, **31**, 21.30N 71.10W
Turku, **46**, 60.27N 22.17E
Tuz, Lake, **90**, 38.45N 33.24E
Tweed *(r.)*, **52**, 55.46N 2.00W

Ubon Ratchathani, **128**, 15.15N 104.50E
Ucayali *(r.)*, **38**, 4.40S 73.20W
Uele *(r.)*, **102**, 4.08N 22.25E
Uganda *(c.)*, **102**, 1.00N 33.00E
Uist, North *(i.)*, **52**, 57.35N 7.20W
Uist, South *(i.)*, **52**, 57.15N 7.20W
Ujung Pandang, **128**, 5.09S 119.28E
Ukraine *(c.)*, **84**, 49.00N 30.00E
Ulan Bator, **84**, 47.54N 106.52E
Uliastay, **84**, 47.42N 96.52E
Ullung *(i.)*, **134**, 37.30N 131.00E
Ume *(r.)*, **46**, 63.47N 20.16E
Umeå, **46**, 63.45N 20.20E
Ungava Peninsula, **16**, 60.00N 74.00W
United Arab Emirates *(c.)*, **90**, 24.00N 54.00E
United Kingdom *(c.)*, **52**, 55.00N 3.00W
United States of America *(c.)*, **22**, 42.00N 96.00W
Unst *(i.)*, **52**, 60.45N 0.55W
Uppsala, **46**, 59.52N 17.38E
Ural *(r.)*, **84**, 47.00N 52.00E
Ural Mountains, **84**, 60.00N 60.00E
Urmia, **90**, 37.32N 45.02E
Urmia, Lake, **90**, 37.40N 45.28E
Uruguay *(c.)*, 38. 34.00S 56.00W
Uruguay *(r.)*, **38**, 34.00S 58.30W
Urumqi, **120**, 43.43N 87.38E
Ussuri *(r.)*, **84**, 48.30N 135.04E
Usumacinta *(r.)*, **30**, 18.44N 92.30W
Utrecht, **72**, 52.04N 5.07E
Uzbekistan *(c.)*, **84**, 42.00N 63.00E

Vaal *(r.)*, **108**, 29.04S 23.37E
Vaasa, **46**, 63.06N 21.36E
Vaduz, **72**, 47.09N 9.31E
Váh *(r.)*, **78**, 47.40N 18.09E
Valencia, **64**, 39.29N 0.24W
Valladolid, **64**, 41.39N 4.45W
Valletta, **68**, 35.53N 14.31E
Van, Lake, **90**, 38.35N 42.52E
Vancouver, **16**, 49.20N 123.10W
Vancouver Island, **16**, 49.45N 126.00W
Vänern *(l.)*, **46**, 58.55N 13.30E
Varanasi, **114**, 25.20N 83.00E
Varna, **78**, 43.13N 27.57E
Vatican City *(c.)*, **68**, 41.54N 12.27E
Vatnajökull *(mts.)*, **46**, 64.20N 17.00W
Vättern *(l.)*, **46**, 58.24N 14.36E
Venezuela *(c.)*, **38**, 7.00N 65.30W
Venice, **68**, 45.26N 12.20E
Venice, Gulf of, **68**, 45.20N 13.00E
Veracruz, **30**, 19.11N 96.10W
Verkhoyansk, **84**, 67.25N 133.25E
Verkhoyanski Range, **84**, 66.00N 130.00E
Verona, **68**, 45.27N 10.59E
Vert, Cape, **102**, 14.45N 17.25W
Vest Fjorden, **46**, 68.10N 15.00E
Vesterålen *(i.)*, **46**, 60.06N 15.50E
Vestmannaeyjar, **46**, 63.30N 20.20W
Vesuvius *(mt.)*, **68**, 40.48N 14.25E
Victoria, **120**, 22.16N 114.15E
Victoria Falls, **108**, 17.58S 25.45E
Victoria Island, **16**, 71.00N 110.00W
Victoria, Lake, **102**, 1.00S 33.00E
Victoria Land, **152**, 75.00S 163.00E
Vienna, **72**, 48.13N 16.22E
Vienne *(r.)*, **58**, 47.13N 0.05E
Vientiane, **128**, 18.01N 102.48E
Vietnam *(c.)*, **128**, 15.00N 108.00E
Vignemale Peak, **58**, 42.46N 0.08W
Vigo, **64**, 42.15N 8.44W
Vik, **46**, 63.25N 19.00W
Vilanandro, Cape (C. St.-André), **108**, 16.11S 44.29E
Vilnius, **84**, 54.40N 25.19E
Vincennes Bay, **152**, 66.30S 109.30E
Vindhya Range, **114**, 22.55N 76.00E
Vinson Massif, **152**, 78.35S 85.25W
Virgin Islands, **31**, 18.30N 64.40W
Vishakhapatnam, **114**, 17.42N 83.24E
Vistula *(r.)*, **78**, 54.23N 18.52E
Vladivostok, **84**, 43.09N 131.53E
Vlissingen, **72**, 51.27N 3.35E
Vlorë, **78**, 40.28N 19.27E
Vltava *(r.)*, **78**, 50.22N 14.28E
Vogelsberg *(mts.)*, **72**, 50.30N 9.15E
Vohimena, Cape (C. Ste.-Marie), **108**, 25.36S 45.08E
Volga *(r.)*, **84**, 45.45N 47.50E
Volgograd, **84**, 48.45N 44.30E
Volos, **68**, 39.22N 22.57E
Volta, Lake, **102**, 7.00N 0.00
Vørterkaka Nunatak, **152**, 72.20S 27.29E
Vosges *(mts.)*, **58**, 48.30N 7.10E
Vostok, **152**, 78.30S 106.50E

Wad Medani, **96**, 14.24N 33.30E
Waddenzee *(b.)*, **72**, 53.15N 5.05E
Waddington, Mt., **16**, 51.23N 125.15W
Waitaki *(r.)*, **146**, 44.56S 171.09E
Wakasa Bay, **134**, 35.50N 135.40E
Wakayama, **134**, 34.12N 135.10E
Walcheren, **72**, 51.32N 3.35E
Walvis Bay *(town)*, **108**, 22.57S 14.30E
Wanganui, **146**, 39.56S 175.02E
Warsaw, **78**, 52.15N 21.00E
Wash, The *(b.)*, **52**, 52.55N 0.15E
Washington D.C., **22**, 38.55N 77.00W
Waterford, **52**, 52.16N 7.08W
Weddell Sea, **152**, 72.00S 45.00W
Wellington, **146**, 41.17S 175.46E
Wellington Island, **38**, 49.30S 75.00W
Weser *(r.)*, **72**, 53.15N 8.34E
West Frisian Islands, **72**, 53.20N 5.00E
West Ice Shelf, **152**, 67.00S 85.00E
West Siberian Plain, **84**, 62.00N 80.00E
Western Sahara *(c.)*, **96**, 25.00N 13.30W
Westerwald *(f.)*, **72**, 50.40N 7.45E
Westport, **146**, 41.46S 171.38E
Wetar *(i.)*, **128**, 7.45S 126.00E
Wewak, **140**, 3.35S 143.35E
Wexford, **52**, 52.20N 6.28W
Whangarei, **146**, 35.43S 174.20E
Whitehorse, **16**, 60.43N 135.03W
Whitney, Mt., **22**, 36.35N 118.18W
Wicklow Mts., **52**, 53.06N 6.20W
Wight, Isle of, **52**, 50.40N 1.17W
Wilhelm, Mt., **140**, 6.00S 144.55E
Wilkes Land, **152**, 69.00S 120.00E
Windhoek, **108**, 22.34S 17.06E
Winnipeg, **16**, 49.53N 97.09W
Winnipeg, Lake, **16**, 52.00N 97.00W
Wonju, **134**, 37.24N 127.52E
Wonsan, **134**, 39.09N 127.25E
Wrangel Island, **84**, 71.00N 180.00E
Wroclaw, **78**, 51.05N 17.00E
Wuhan, **120**, 30.35N 114.19E

Xi *(r.)*, **120**, 22.23N 113.20E
Xiao Hinggan Mts., **120**, 48.40N 128.30E
Xingu *(r.)*, **38**, 1.40S 52.15W
Xi'an, **120**, 34.16N 108.54E

Yablonovyy Range, **84**, 53.20N 115.00E
Yaku *(i.)*, **134**, 30.15N 130.12E
Yakutsk, **84**, 62.10N 129.20E
Yalong *(r.)*, **120**, 26.35N 101.44E
Yalu *(r.)*, **134**, 40.10N 124.25E
Yamal Peninsula, **84**, 70.20N 70.00E
Yamoussoukro, **102**, 6.49N 5.17W
Yamuna *(r.)*, **114**, 25.25N 81.50E
Yangon (Rangoon), **128**, 16.45N 96.20E
Yaoundé, **102**, 3.51N 11.31E
Yapen *(i.)*, **128**, 1.45S 136.10E
Yaqui *(r.)*, **30**, 27.40N 110.30W
Yekaterinburg, **84**, 56.52N 60.35E
Yell *(i.)*, **52**, 60.35N 1.05W
Yellowknife, **16**, 62.27N 114.21W
Yemen *(c.)*, **90**, 15.55N 48.30E
Yenisei *(r.)*, **84**, 69.00N 86.00E
Yerevan, **84**, 40.10N 44.31E
Yichang, **120**, 30.43N 111.22E
Yokohama, **134**, 35.28N 139.28E
Yonne *(r.)*, **58**, 48.23N 2.58E
York, **52**, 53.58N 1.07W
York, Cape, **140**, 10.42S 142.31E
Yosu, **134**, 34.46N 127.44E
You *(r.)*, **120**, 23.25N 110.00E
Yu Shan *(mt.)*, **120**, 23.20N 121.03E
Yuan *(r.)*, **120**, 29.00N 112.12E
Yucatán *(pen.)*, **30**, 20.00N 89.00W
Yugoslavia *(c.)*, **78**, 43.00N 21.00E
Yukon *(r.)*, **22**, 62.35N 164.20W

Zagreb, **78**, 45.49N 15.58E
Zagros Mountains, **90**, 32.00N 51.00E
Zaire *(c.)*, **102**, 2.00S 22.00E
Zaire *(r.)*, **102**, 6.00S 12.30E
Zaisan, Lake, **84**, 48.00N 83.30E
Zákinthos *(i.)*, **68**, 37.46N 20.46E
Zambezi *(r.)*, **108**, 18.15S 35.55E
Zambia *(c.)*, **108**, 14.00S 28.00E
Zamboanga, **128**, 6.55N 122.05E
Zanzibar *(i.)*, **102**, 6.10S 39.12E
Zaragoza, **64**, 41.39N 0.54W
Zaskar Mts., **114**, 33.15N 78.00E
Zeil, Mt., **140**, 23.24S 132.23E
Zimbabwe *(c.)*, **108**, 18.55S 30.00E
Zugspitze *(mt.)*, **72**, 47.25N 10.59E
Zurich, **72**, 47.23N 8.32E

DATA PANEL SOURCES:-

The Economist, *Book of Vital World Statistics: A Complete Guide to the World in Figures*, London, Hutchinson, 1990
1991 *Britannica Book of the Year*, Encyclopedia Britannica Inc., Chicago
British Petroleum, *Statistical Review of World Energy* 1990, 1991 (London: British Petroleum)
United Nations, *Industrial Statistics Yearbooks: Commodity Production Statistics* (annually), New York: United Nations
United Nations *Demographic Yearbook 1991*
Geographical Digest 1992-1993 (George Philip with Heinemann Educational, Oxford, 1992)
World Bank's *World Development Report* (Oxford: OUP/World Bank; annual)
Economist Intelligence Unit
The Economist: *Pocket World in Figures*, 1993 Edition (London, Random Century)
United Nations *Production Yearbooks, Trade Yearbooks* and *Fisheries Yearbooks*
Statistical Abstract 1992

GLOSSARY

acid rain Rain that has become more acid by combining with waste gases discharged into the atmosphere.

Arctic The region lying north of latitude 66 32N, where for a time in summer the sun never sets and in winter it never rises.

arid dry Arid areas generally have less than 10 in. (250 mm) of rain a year.

atoll A coral reef enclosing a lagoon.

bauxite The ore that is smelted to make the metal aluminum.

biome A major global unit in ecology, with its own plants and animals, eg savanna grassland.

bituminous coal Black coal with less carbon than anthracite but more than lignite.

cash crop A crop grown for sale rather than subsistence.

cereal A food crop and member of the grass family.

colony A territory under the control of another country.

Commonwealth A loose association of countries that are former members of the British empire.

communism A social, political, and economic system based on the communal ownership of property.

coniferous forest One of cone-bearing, usually evergreen trees.

conservation The management and protection of natural resources.

constitutional monarchy A form of government with a hereditary monarch and a constitution.

consumer goods Goods bought for people's needs, rather than for manufacturing uses.

continental climate A climate with a wide daily and seasonal variation of temperature and low rainfall, usually occurring in the interior of continents.

continental drift The complex process by which the continents move their positions relative to each other on the plates of the earth's crust. Also known as plate tectonics.

coral reef An underwater ridge or mound composed mostly of dead and living coral.

deciduous Shedding leaves annually.

deforestation Cutting down and clearing of forested land.

delta A usually triangular deposit of sand and soil at the mouth of a river.

democracy A form of government in which decisions are made by the people or those elected by them.

dependency A territory subject to the laws of another country but not formally part of it.

desert An arid area with less than 10 in (250 mm) of rain a year.

desertification The creation of desert by overgrazing, soil erosion, or climate change.

dictator A ruler with absolute power.

empire The political organization of countries and territories in which one dominates the rest.

endemic species A species that is native to a specific area.

erosion The process by which exposed land is broken down into small pieces or worn away by water, wind, or ice.

evergreen Having green leaves throughout the year.

exports Goods and services sold to other countries.

fault A fracture in the Earth's crust.

federalism A form of constitutional government in which power is shared between a central, or federal, government and state or provincial governments.

ferroalloy metals Metals blended with iron in the manufacture of steel.

fjord A steep-sided inlet formed when a U-shaped valley is drowned by the sea.

fossil fuel A fuel such as oil, coal, peat, or natural gas, formed from ancient organic remains.

global warming An increase in the earth's average temperature, which some scientists believe will result from the greenhouse effect.

greenhouse effect The process in which radiation from the sun passes through the atmosphere, is reflected off the surface of the earth, and is then trapped by gases in the atmosphere. The buildup of carbon dioxide and other gases increases the effect.

Gross Domestic Product (GDP) The total value of a country's annual output of goods and services.

Gross National Product (GNP) A country's GDP plus income from abroad.

habitat The native environment in which a plant or animal lives.

hardwood The wood from trees other than conifers, which produce softwood. Hardwoods are generally stronger and more resistant to rot.

ice age A geological period during which glaciers covered large parts of the earth.

imports Goods and services bought from other countries.

indigenous people The original inhabitants of a region.

lava Molten rock from a volcano; also its solid form when cooled.

llanos Tropical grasslands in South America.

maritime climate A moist climate generally found in areas near the sea.

Mediterranean climate One with warm, wet winters and hot, dry summers.

military regime A government controlled by the armed forces.

monarchy A form of rule where there is a hereditary head of state.

monsoon Tropical wind systems that reverse direction with the seasons; also, the rain brought by these winds.

multiparty system A system of rule in which parties compete for votes in elections.

nomad A member of a group of people who migrate seasonally in search of food, water, or grazing for their animals.

official language The language used by governments, schools, courts, and other official institutions in countries where there is no single common language.

one-party system A system of rule where there is no competition at elections, and all but the government party is banned.

pampas Temperate grasslands in South America.

peat A thick layer of partly decomposed plant remains found in wetlands. High acidity, low temperatures, and low nutrient and oxygen levels prevent total decomposition.

per capita For each person.

permafrost A permanently frozen layer of soil beneath the topsoil.

plateau A large area of level, high land.

polar regions Regions extending from the poles to the lines of latitude known as the Arctic and Antarctic circles. At these high latitudes the sun does not set in midsummer.

polder Low-lying land reclaimed from the sea by the building of dikes, particularly in the Netherlands.

prairie The flat grassland in the interior of North America, used for cereal crops.

precipitation Moisture reaching the earth from the atmosphere in the form of mist, dew, rain, sleet, snow, and hail.

province An administrative division of a country.

radioactivity The radiation emitted from atomic nuclei. This is greatest when the atom is split, as in a nuclear reactor.

rain forest Forest where there is abundant rainfall all year. Tropical rain forests are rich in plant and animal species, and growth is lush and very rapid.

republic A form of government with a head of state that is elected or nominated.

rift valley A long valley formed when a block of land between two faults subsides.

Romance languages Family of languages derived from Latin.

savanna A habitat of open grassland with scattered trees in tropical and subtropical areas.

sclerophyll or scrub vegetation Hard-leaved scrub of low trees and shrubs with tough evergreen leaves, found where there is drought in summer.

sediment Material, such as gravel, sand, or silt, that has been deposited by water, ice or wind.

semiarid Having little rainfall. Semiarid areas have enough moisture to support a little more vegetation than a desert can.

softwood The wood from coniferous trees.

soil erosion The removal of the topsoil from land, mainly by the action of wind and rain.

steppe An open grassy plain with few trees or shrubs. It has low, sporadic rainfall, and wide ranges of annual temperature.

subsistence The minimum level of providing for one's needs, such as food and shelter.

subtropical zone Either of the two zones between the tropical and temperate zones. The subtropical zones have marked seasonal changes of temperature but are never very cold.

sustainable development Use of the earth's resources to improve people's lives without diminishing the ability of the earth to support life today and in the future.

taiga The coniferous, evergreen forests of subarctic lands, covering large areas of northern North America and Eurasia.

temperate zone Either of the two zones in the middle latitudes. Such zones cover areas between the warm tropics and cold polar regions.

tropics The area between the Tropic of Cancer and the Tropic of Capricorn. The lines mark latitudes farthest from the equator where the sun is still found directly overhead at midday in midsummer.

tundra Level, treeless land lying in the very cold northern parts of Europe, Asia and North America.

wetland Land having wet and spongy soil, such as a swamp, bog, or marsh.

ABBREVIATIONS

C = Celsius
F = Fahrenheit
mil. m. t. = million metric tons
N/A = data not available

INDEX